한국 인권문제

시민적 · 정치적 권리 국제규약 인권보고서 2

한국 인권문제

시민적 · 정치적 권리 국제규약 인권보고서 2

한국학술정보

머리말

일제 강점기 독립운동과 병행되었던 한국의 인권운동은 해방이 되었음에도 큰 결실을 보지 못했다. 1950년대 반공을 앞세운 이승만 정부와 한국전쟁, 역시 경제발전과 반공을 내세우다 유신 체제에 이르렀던 박정희 정권, 쿠데타로 집권한 1980년대 전두환 정권까지, 한국의 인권은 이를 보장해야 할 국가와 정부에 의해 도리어 억압받고 침해되었다. 이런 배경상 근대 한국의 인권운동은 반독재, 민주화운동과 결을 같이했고, 대체로 국외에 본부를 둔 인권 단체나 정치로부터 상대적으로 자유로운 종교 단체에 의해 주도되곤 했다. 이는 1980년 5 · 18광주민주화운동을 계기로 보다 근적인 변혁을 요구하는 형태로 조직화되었고, 그 활동 영역도 정치를 넘어 노동자, 농민, 빈민 등으로 확대되었다. 이들이 없었다면 한국은 1987년 군부 독재 종식하고 절차적 민주주의를 도입할 수 없었을 것이다. 민주화 이후에도 수많은 어려움이 있었지만, 한국의 인권운동은 점차 전문적이고 독립된 운동으로 분화되며 더 많은 이들의 참여를 이끌어냈고, 지금까지 많은 결실을 맺을 수 있었다.

본 총서는 1980년대 중반부터 1990년대 초반까지, 외교부에서 작성하여 30여 년간 유지했던 한국 인권문제와 관련한 국내외 자료를 담고 있다. 6월 항쟁이 일어나고 민주화 선언이 이뤄지는 등 한국 인권운동에 많은 변화가 있었던 시기다. 당시 인권문제와 관련한 국내외 사안들, 각종 사건에 대한 미국과 우방국, 유엔의 반응, 최초의 한국 인권보고서 제출과 아동의 권리에 관한 협약 과정, 유엔인권위원회 활동, 기타 민주화 관련 자료 등 총 18권으로 구성되었다. 전체 분량은 약 9천여 쪽에 이른다.

2024년 3월

한국학술정보(주)

| 일러두기

- 본 총서에 실린 자료는 2022년 4월과 2023년 4월에 각각 공개한 외교문서 4,827권, 76만여 쪽 가운데 일부를 발췌한 것이다.
- 각 권의 제목과 순서는 공개된 원본을 최대한 반영하였으나, 주제에 따라 일부는 적절히 변경하였다.
- 원본 자료는 A4 판형에 맞게 축소하거나 원본 비율을 유지한 채 A4 페이지 안에 삽입하였다. 또한 현재 시점에선 공개되지 않아 '공란'이란 표기만 있는 페이지 역시 그대로 실었다.
- 외교부가 공개한 문서 각 권의 첫 페이지에는 '정리 보존 문서 목록'이란 이름으로 기록물 종류, 일자, 명칭, 간단한 내용 등의 정보가 수록되어 있으며, 이를 기준으로 0001번부터 번호가 매겨져 있다. 이는 삭제하지 않고 총서에 그대로 수록하였다.
- 보고서 내용에 관한 더 자세한 정보가 필요하다면, 외교부가 온라인상에 제공하는 『대한민국 외교사료요약집』 1991년과 1992년 자료를 참조할 수 있다.

| 차례

정 리 보 존 문 서 목 록					
기록물종류	일반공문서철	등록번호	2020110103	등록일자	2020-11-20
분류번호	734.23	국가코드		보존기간	영구
명 칭	시민적.정치적 권리에 관한 국제규약(B규약) 한국 최초 인권보고서 제출 및 심의, 1991-92. 전5권				
생 산 과	국제연합2과	생산년도	1991~1992	담당그룹	
권 차 명	V.3 1992.1-6.17				
내용목차	* 제44차 인권이사회. New York,1992.3.23-4.10 - 알제리 및 니제르 보고서 심의, 한국은 연기				

0001

국제인권규약(B) 아국 최초보고서 심의

1992. 1. 7.
국제연합2과

1. 일시 및 장소

   o 92.3.24-26(3일간), 뉴욕(유엔본부)

     - 제44차 인권이사회(Human Rights Committee) 기간중(92.3.24-4.10)

     - 아국 보고서는 91.11월 유엔문서로 배포

   o 동 인권이사회 기간중 아국, 니제, 알제리의 최초보고서 및 벨지움, 콜롬비아등 3-4개국의 정기보고서 심의예정

2. 심의절차

   o 보고서 심의는 공개회의로 진행되며, 인권이사회 위원 18명(의장 : 이태리) 및 당해국 정부대표단이 참가

     - NGO 방청가능

0002

o 심의일정

1) 제1일(3.24. 오후)

- 수석대표의 제안설명(약 15분)

- 위원별 질의

. 보고서 전반을 대상으로 자유로이 질문

2) 제2일(3.25)

- 답변준비를 위해 휴회

3) 제3일(3.26)

- 수석대표 답변

- 추가질의 및 답변

- 위원별 견해표명(concluding observation)

- 수석대표 최종발언

* 통역 대동 가능

0003

3. 향후 조치사항

가. 대표단 구성

1) 고려사항

o 수석대표 역할

- 보고서 제안설명 및 최종발언, 위원들의 본질의 및 추가질의에 대한 답변을 주관하므로, 헌법등 법률지식과 인권관계 국제법 및 국내법에 대한 지식이 요구됨.

o 각국의 수석대표 임명사례

- 뉴욕 개최시

i) 검찰총장(인도, 파나마, 스리랑카)

ii) 외무부 및 국무부 국장급이상(스웨덴, 영국)

- 제네바 개최시

i) 주제네바 대사(카나다, 스페인, 모로코, 마다가스칼)

ii) 외무부, 법무부, 내무부 국장급 인사(핀란드, 우크라이나, 수단, 요르단, 이라크)

* 법무부 입장(비공식 타진)

- 부내실정상 인권과장 및 인권과 검사 1명 참석 고려중

0004

2) 대표단 구성

o 수석대표

- 인권보장과 관련된 국내법 체계 및 적용문제가 중점 심의될 것이므로, 법무부 인사가 적임

- 법무부측이 적절한 인사를 추천할수 없다면, 외무부 인사중 선정 검토

. 주유엔대사(신임대사 부임일정등 고려)

. 주유엔 차석대사(회의관례등 고려)

. 주제네바대사(회의관례 및 제네바 업무등 고려)

. 본부대사 또는 본부간부

o 사전준비등 감안, 92.2월초까지 확정 필요

나. 심의관련 준비자료 작성

o 위원들의 예상질의 및 답변자료, 수석대표 제안설명문등을 법무부와 협의, 사전준비

- 최근 재야단체의 별도 보고서(counter report) 작성 움직임도 감안

다. 인권이사회 위원 사전접촉

o 필요한 경우 3-4명의 인권이사회 위원을 사전접촉, 아국보고서에 대한 평가 및 미비점 협의

- 끝 -

0005

관리 번호	92-30

분류번호	보존기간

발 신 전 보

번 호 : WUN-0052 920108 1727 ED 종별 :

수 신 : 주 유엔 대사. ~~총영사~~

발 신 : 장 관 (연이)

제 목 : 국제인권규약(B) 아국 최초보고서 심의

1. "시민적 정치적 권리에 관한 국제인권규약" 제40조에 의거 90.7월 아국이 제출한 최초보고서에 대한 심의가 제44차 인권이사회 (Human Rights Committee) 기간중인 92.3.24-26간 유엔본부에서 개최될 예정임.

2. 상기 심의에 참가할 아국대표단 구성과 관련, 귀관 신기복 차석대사를 수석대표로, 외무부 및 법무부 담당관을 포함한 대표단 임명을 ~~추진중~~ 할 계획이니 참고바람. 끝.

(국제기구국장 문동석)

일반문서로 재분류 (1992. 6. 30.)

보안 통제	

앙 고 재	92년 1월 8일	유엔 2과	기안자 성명		과 장	심의관	국 장		차 관	장 관

외신과통제

0006

관리 번호	91 -21

외 무 부

110-760 서울 종로구 세종로 77번지 / (02) 723-8934 / (02) 723-3505

문서번호 연이 20314-35
시행일자 1992.1.8.
(경유)
수신 법무부장관
참조

취급		장 관
보존		
국 장	전결	
심의관		
과 장		
기안	김종훈	협조

제목 국제인권규약(B) 아국 최초보고서 심의

1. 국제인권규약(B) 제40조에 의거, 90.7월 제출한 아국의 최초보고서에 대한 심의가 제44차 인권이사회 기간중인 92.3.24-26간 유엔본부에서 개최될 예정입니다.

2. 상기 심의에 참가할 아국대표단에 포함될 귀부직원을 추천하여 주시기 바라며, 동 심의에 대비, 아래 자료를 당부로 송부하여 주시기 바랍니다.

- 아 래 -

가. 수석대표 연설문(Opening Statement)에 포함될 내용
- 아국보고서 주요내용 소개

나. 예상질의 및 답변자료
- 최근 주요 인권단체에서 아국 인권상황과 관련 제기한 인권보장 관련 법률 및 제도의 문제등.

일반문서로 재분류(1992.6.30.)

0007

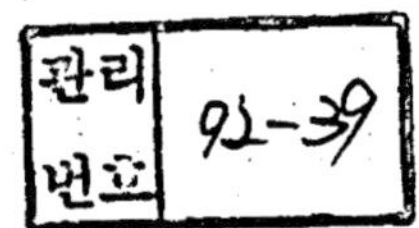

법 무 부

인권 20314- 15 503-7045 1992. 1. 15

수신 외무부장관

참조 국제기구조약국장

제목 국제인권규약(B) 아국 최초보고서 심의

1. 귀부 연이 20314-35 ('92.1.9)와 관련입니다.

2. 아국의 국제인권규약(B) 최초보고서 심의에 대비, 수석대표 연설문에 포함될 내용에 관하여는 당부 인권 2031-7472('91.6.7)자 공문에 첨부된 보고서를 참고하시기 바랍니다.

3. 아울러 위 심의 개최일자와 관련, 예상질의 답변자료 수집 등 심의참가 준비가 촉박한 실정이므로 귀부에서 이 점을 감안, 심의 개최일자를 재조정하는 문제를 검토하여 주시기 바랍니다. 끝.

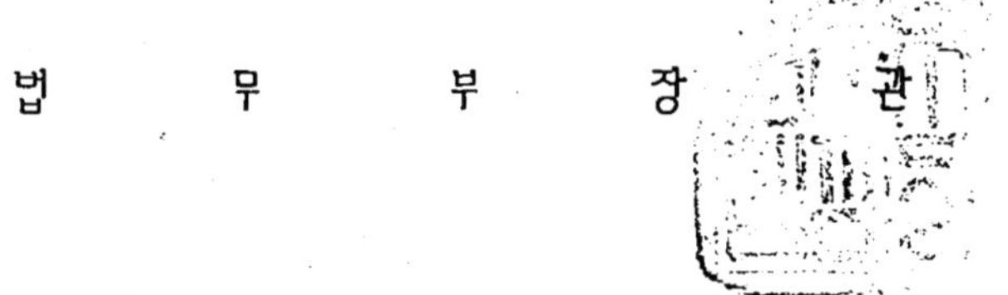

법 무 부 장 관

0008

관리번호	92-6

	분류번호	보존기간

발 신 전 보

번 호 : WGV-0075 920115 1838 BU 종별 :

수 신 : 주 제네바 대사. ~~총영사~~

발 신 : 장 관 (문동석)

제 목 : 업 연

92.3.24-3.26으로 예정된 아국 인권규약보고서의 심의를 92.7월로 연기하려 하는 것은 관계부처에서 정치일정 등 국내사정을 고려하여 연기를 요청해 옴에 따른 것이오니 참고하시기 바랍니다. 끝.

예고 : 독후파기

보안통제	

앙고재	92년 1월 15일	유엔2과	기안자 성명		과장		국장		차관	장관

외신과통제

0009

관리 번호	92-5

분류번호	보존기간

발 신 전 보

번 호 : WGV-0073 920115 1837 BU 종별 :

수 신 : 주 제네바 대사. 총영사 (사본 : 주유엔대사) WUN -0106

발 신 : 장 관 (연이)

제 목 : 아국 인권규약(B) 보고서 심의

1. 본부는 92.3.24-3.26로 예정된 인권규약(B) 아국 최초보고서 심의문제를 관계부처와 협의한바, 동 심의에 대비한 각종 준비에 보다 많은 시일이 필요하다는 관계부처 입장등 ██████을 고려, 아국 보고서 심의를 제45차 인권이사회(92.7.13-31, 제네바)로 연기하고자 함.

2. 상기 아국정부의 보고서 심의 연기요청을 인권사무국에 통보하고 결과 보고바람. 끝.

(장 관)

예고 : 92.12.31.일반

검토필 (1992. 6. 30.)	[서명]

보안 통제	[서명]

앙 고 재	92년 1월 15일	유엔2과	기안자 성명		과 장	심의관	국 장	제1차관보	차 관	장 관
			김종훈		[서명]	[서명]	[서명]	[서명]		[서명]

외신과통제

0010

2 길

관리번호	92-9

원 본

외 무 부

종 별 :

번 호 : GVW-0132 일 시 : 92 0120 1130

수 신 : 장 관(연이)사본:주유엔대사-중계필

발 신 : 주 제네바 대사

제 목 : 아국 인권규약(B) 보고서 심의

대: WGV-0073

1. 대호건 1.16 인권 사무국 관계관 TISTOUNET 를 면담, 아국의 심의 연기 희망을 일단 구두로 통보하고, 동인의 요청에 따라 이를 공한으로 1.20 정식 요청함.

2. 동인에 의하면 당관 공한 접수후 사무국이 이를 POCAR 의장에게 통보, 동의장이 44 차 회의 벽두에 심의 연기 사실을 공지하는 이외에는 아국의 연기 요청과 관련한 별도의 조치는 불요하다함. 끝

(대사 박수길-국장)

예고 92.12.31. 일반

검토필 (1992. 6. 30.)	김

국기국 차관 1차보 2차보 중계

PAGE 1

92.01.21 03:08

외신 2과 통제관 FK

0011

2

주 제 네 바 대 표 부

제네(정) 2031-93 1992. 1.21.

수신 : 장관

참조 : 국제기구국장

제목 : 44차 인권이사회

1. 92. 3.23-4.1간 뉴욕에서 개최되는 44차 인권이사회 관련 문건을 별첨 송부합니다

2. 상기 문건은 91.12 작성된 것으로서, 아국의 최초 보고서 심의 일정이 포함되어 있으며, 북한의 B 규약 2차 보고서 제출이 지연되고 있음도 언급하고 있습니다.

첨부 : CCPR/C/77 1부. 끝.

주 제 네 바 대 사

선 결			결재 (공람)		
접수일시	1992. 1. 28	번호			
처리과		06082			

0012

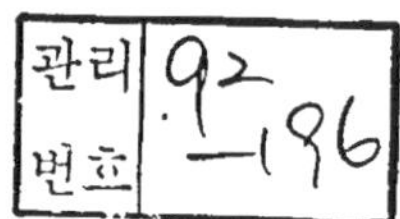
관리번호 92-196

외 무 부

110-760 서울 종로구 세종로 77번지 / (02) 723-8934 / (02) 723-3505

문서번호 연이 20314-568
시행일자 1992.3.11.
(경유)
수신 법무부장관
참조

취급		장 관
보존		
국 장	전결	
심의관		
과 장		
기안	김종훈	협조

제목 인권규약(B) 보고서 심의 대비

1. 제44차 인권이사회가 92.3.23-4.10간 뉴욕에서 개최되며, 동 회의에서는 알제리 및 니제가 제출한 최초보고서가 3.24-3.27간 심의될 예정입니다.

2. 92.7월 차기 인권이사회에서의 아국 최초보고서 심의에 대비, 상기 2개국 최초보고서 심의내용을 파악하는 것이 필요하며, 이를 위하여는 금차 회의에 귀부 직원이 참관하는 것이 바람직할 것으로 사료되오니 이를 검토하여 주시기 바랍니다. 끝.

검토필 (1992. 6. 30.)

0013

	분류번호	보존기간

발 신 전 보

번 호 : WGV-0417 920318 1523 WG 종별 : 암호송신

수 신 : 주 제네바 대사. ~~총영사~~

발 신 : 장 관 (연이)

제 목 : 제44차 인권이사회 일정

92.3.23-4.10간 뉴욕에서 개최되는 표제회의 국별보고서 심의 일정을 파악 보고바람. 끝.

(국제기구국장 김재섭)

보 안 통 제	

앙 고 재	92년 3월 18일	유엔2과	기안자 성 명		과 장	심의관	국 장		차 관	장 관

외신과통제

0014

외 무 부

110-760 서울 종로구 세종로 77번지 / (02) 723-8934 / (02) 723-3505

문서번호 연이 20314-
시행일자 1992.3.18.
(경유)
수신 건 의
참조

취급		차 관	장 관
보존			
국 장			
심의관		제1차관보 기획관리실장 총무과장 기획운영담당관	
과 장			
기안	김종훈		협조

제목 제44차 인권이사회 참가

1. 제44차 인권이사회(Human Rights Committee)가 92.3.23-4.10간 뉴욕에서 개최되어 알제리등 7개국 보고서의 심의와 선택의정서에 의거한 진정서 심의가 있을 예정입니다.

2. 우리나라 최초보고서가 동회의 제45차 회의(92.7월, 제네바)에서 심의될 예정임에 비추어, 아래와 같이 정달호 국제연합2과장이 금차 회의에 참가하여 국별 보고서 심의절차 및 내용을 파악, 아국 보고서 심의에 대비하고자 하오니 재가하여 주시기 바랍니다.

- 아 래 -

가. 참가목적

o 92.7월 제45차 회의시 예정된 아국 최초보고서 심의에 대비, 금차 회의시 최초보고서(알제리 및 니제) 심의내용 및 정부대표단 준비사항을 파악

o 인권위원과 아국 보고서 심의 관련 비공식 협의

/ 계속 /

0015

나. 출장직원 : 정달호 국제기구국 국제연합2과장

다. 출장기간 : 92.3.22-3.30. (8박 9일)

라. 소요예산 : $2,780

1) 항 공 료 : $1,504

2) 체 재 비 : $1,276

o 일식비 : ($20+$48)x9일=$612

o 숙박비 : $83x8박=$664

3) 예산항목 : 국제회의, 국외여비. 끝.

0016

관리 번호	92-2272

	분류번호	보존기간

발 신 전 보

번 호 : WUN-0639 920320 1548 WG 종별 :

수 신 : 주 유엔 대사. 총영사

발 신 : 장 관 (연이)

제 목 : 제44차 인권이사회

1. 금년 7월로 예정된 아국 인권규약(B) 최초보고서 심의에 대비, 3.23-4.10간 귀지에서 개최되는 표제회의 참석을 위해 정달호 국제연합 2과장이 3.22-3.28간 귀지 출장예정임.

2. 귀지 도착일정은 3.22(일) 09:20 KE-026편인 바, 호텔 싱글 1실 예약바람. 끝.

(국제기구국장 김재섭)

검토필 (1992.6.30.)

보안 통제	

앙 고 재	92년 3월 20일	유엔 2과	기안자 성명		과 장	심의관	국 장		차 관	장 관
			강종훈				전결			

외신과통제

0017

외 무 부

종 별 : 지 급

번 호 : GVW-0624 일 시 : 92 0320 1730

수 신 : 장 관(연이)

발 신 : 주 제네바 대사

제 목 : 44차 인권이사회일정

대: WGV-417

연: 제네(정) 2031-93

1. 표제회의 국별보고서 심의는 연호 당초 일정대로 (아국 보고서 일정만 취소된 상태에서 3.25.부터 알제리 보고서 심의) 진행된다고 함.

2. 동 회의관련 사무국 요원들은 현재 뉴욕체재중인바 연락처 참고로 아래 보고함.

O MS.HELGA KLEIN(212) 963 1234 EX.7481,7482,7488.끝

(대사 박수길-국장)

국기국

PAGE 1

92.03.21 09:23 WG

외신 1과 통제관

0018

관리 번호	92-2337

	분류번호	보존기간

발 신 전 보

번 호 : WUN-0652 920321 1419 FO 종별 : 지 급

수 신 : 주 유엔 대사. 총영사

발 신 : 장 관 (연이)

제 목 : 제44차 인권이사회

연 : WUN-0639

1. 연호, 표제회의에 참석하는 정달호 과장의 귀지 도착일정이 3.24(화) 09:20 KE-026편으로 변경되었음.

2. 표제회의 의제를 채택하는 3.23. 회의에 귀관 담당관이 참석, 아국 최초보고서 심의 연기를 확인, 보고바람. 끝.

(국제기구국장 김재섭)

검토필 (1992.6.30.)

보안 통제	

앙 고 재	92년 3월 21일	유엔 2과	기안자 성명		과 장	심의관	국 장		차 관	장 관

외신과통제

0019

관리번호	92-239

원 본

외 무 부

종 별 :

번 호 : UNW-0812 일 시 : 92 0323 1920

수 신 : 장 관(연이,법규)사본:주제네바 대사-중계필

발 신 : 주 유엔 대사

제 목 : 제 44차 인권 이사회

대:WUN-0652

제 44 차 인권이사회가 금 3.23. POCAR(이태리)의장의 사회로 유엔본부에서개최되었는바, 주요경과 아래 보고함

1. 금일 회의에서는 금번회의의 의제및 회의일정을 협의하였으며, WAKO 부의장이 사임함에 따라 후임에 EL-SHAFEI(이집트)를 선출하였음

2. 의제 5 항 각국보고서 심의관련, 의장은 아국의 차기회의시 심의희망및 니제의 심의 연기요청에 따라 이를 공지하였음(최참사관은 대호지시에 따라 개회직전, 의장및 CLINE 서기에게 상기내용을 사전 확인하였음)

3. 사무국 관계관은 1993 세계 인권회의를 베를린에 유치키로 하였던 독일정부가 이를 지난 2 월 제네바 인권위에서 철회하였다하고 현재 이태리(베니스)와 오스트리아(비엔나)가 개최의사를 표명하였다고 발언하였음

4. 주요 진행사항 추보예정임

(대사 유종하-국장)

예고:92.12.31 까지

검토필 (1992.6.30.)

국기국	장관	차관	1차보	2차보	분석관	조약국	청와대	안기부
중계								

PAGE 1

92.03.24 10:03

외신 2과 통제관 BX

0020

관리 번호	92-244

원 본

외 무 부

종 별 :

번 호 : UNW-0853 일 시 : 92 0325 2000

수 신 : 장 관(연이)

발 신 : 주 유엔 대사

제 목 : 제 44차 인권이사회

1. 3.24-25 간 표제회의 경과를 아래 보고함

가.3.24. 이사회는 인권규약(B) 제 40 조(각국보고서 제출및 심사)에 관한 실무위(의장:A. URBINA, 코스타리카)의 건의에 따라, 각국보고서 심사후 이사회의 결론적 관찰(CONCLUDING OBSERVATIONS)을 각해당국에 통보하고 동내용을 이사회의 총회 제출 연차보고서에도 포함키로 결정함

지금까지는 개별위원의 코멘트 내용만을 연차보고서에 포함 하였으나, 금년41 차 회의시 심사되는 보고서부터는 위원회 전체의 결론적 관찰을 해당국에 통보및 총회앞 보고서에 포함하게 됨 (우리나라의 보고서 심사시에도 적용)

-동 결론적 관찰의 형식은 (1)일반적 평가, (2)긍정적인 발전, (3)협약이행에 영향을 주는 요인과 애로, (4)주요관심사항 및 (5)이사회의 특정한 권고로 구성됨

나. 이사회는 금번회의중 각국보고서에 대한 중점 심의사항에 합의하였는바, 페루에 대해서는 마약 생산및 판매분야에서 특별법원의 존재여부와 토착민의상황에 대하여, 콜롬비에에 대하여는 마약거래 심리담당 판사들이 그 기능을 익명으로 수행하는지의 여부에 대해 중점심의키로 함

다. 3.25. 회의에서는 ALGERIA 최초보고서에 관한 알제리아 대표 (법무부 연구조사 국장겸 대법원 자문관)의 간략한 제출보고(6-7 분)에 이어 11 명의 위원의 논평및 질문이 있었음 (위원 11 명참석)

-위원들은 동보고서가 규약 이행에 있어서의 애로사항을 전혀 다루고 있지않는점 및 규약과 국내법과의 관계에 있어 상호 상충시의 법적용 원칙이 분명하지 않은점등을 중점적으로 지적하였으며, 최근 2 회에 걸친 비상사태 선언하에서의 정부의 행위가 규약규정과 어떻게 조화되는지 및 91.4. 보고서 제출후 최근의 국내 인권보장 상황이 여하한지에 대한 상세한 설명을 요구함 (상세사항 본부대표 귀국후 보고)

국기국 장관 차관 1차보 2차보 분석관 청와대 안기부

PAGE 1 92.03.26 10:50

외신 2과 통제관 BZ

0021

2. 상기 알제리아 대표단의 답변및 위원 보충질의는 3.27 로 예정됨

3. 정달호 유엔 2 과장은 3.24. 예정대로 도착 표제회의 참석중임

(대사 유종하-국장)

예고:92.6.30 까지

관리번호 92-253

원 본

외 무 부

종 별 :

번 호 : UNW-0890 일 시 : 92 0327 2000

수 신 : 장관(연일,연이)

발 신 : 주 유엔 대사

제 목 : 제 44차 인권이사회(3)

연:UNW-0853

1. 3.27 이사회는 알제리아 대표의 답변을 청취한 다음 위원들의 보충질문이 있었는바, 요지 아래 보고함

가. 알제리아는 연호 위원들의 질문을(1)비상조치,(2)선거과정,(3)권리와 자유,(4)인권보장제,(5)규약에 관한 정부입장등 다섯가지로 분류하여 약 1 시간반동안 답변하였음

나. 위원들은 일반적으로 알제리아 대표의 성실한 답변태도와 노력을 평가하면서도, 규약의 이행에 있어 법규정과 실행사이의 간격에 대한 설명이 부족한점(피의자 또는 피구속자가 법적 조력 절차를 대부분 모르고 있다는 사실등), 규약규정에 비추어 비상조치 선포및 정당화하는 보다 상세한 설명이 부족한점, 사법부의 독립, 언어 소수민족및 여성차별 문제, 구금자및 사형집행의 과다등을 지적하면서, 인권과 관계되는 보다 정확한 통계 자료를 요청하고, 비상조치에 관한상세하고 보다 실질적인 설명은 추가 보고서로 제출토록 요구하였음

2. 금년 7 월 아측보고서 심의에 대비, 일반답변자료 외에도 각종 인권사안에 대한 구체적인 설명자료와 상세한 통계등의 준비가 필요할 것으로 사료됨(동이사회 진행절차에 관한 상세한 내용은 ~~정[5]]진행절차에 관한 상세한 내용은~~ 정과장 귀국후 보고)

(대사 유종하-국장)

예고:92.6.30 까지

일반문서로 재분류(1992.6.30.)

국기국 장관 차관 1차보 2차보 국기국 분석관 청와대 안기부

PAGE 1 92.03.28 11:02

외신 2과 통제관 BX

0023

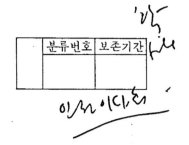

발 신 전 보

분류번호	보존기간

번 호 : WUN-0781 920406 1449 ED 종별 : 암호송신

수 신 : 주 유엔 대사. 총영사 (최종무 참사관)

발 신 : 장 관 (유엔2과 정달호)

제 목 : 업 연

1. 아측 보고서 심의 대비에 필요하니 H.R. Committee의 Summary Record 나오는대로 입수 송부바람.

2. 동 3.27. 오후회의 Press Release를 우선 FAX 송부 부탁드림.

3. 3.27. 오전회의시 Vojin Dimitrjevic(유고)는 알제리측이 비상사태 선포에 관한 설명을 간략한 추가보고서로 제출해야 한다고 하였는바, 이에 관한 이사회의 결정이 있었는지를 가능한대로 확인하여 알려주기 바람. 4.아울러 최근 NGO 위원회 보고서(방문중 Chit 가 기신청) 1부도 송부바람. 끝.

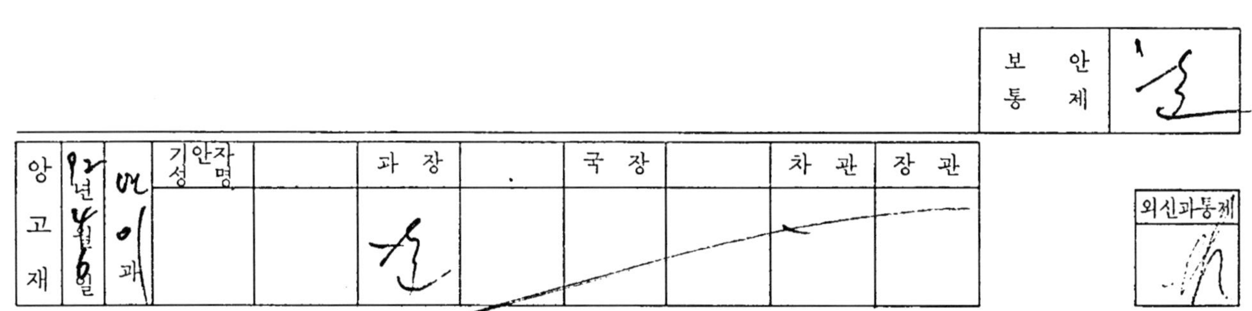

보안 통제
앙고재 92년 4월 6일
기안자 성명
과 장
국 장
차 관
장 관
외신과통제

0024

외 무 부

110-760 서울 종로구 세종로 77번지 / (02) 723-8934 / (02) 723-3505

문서번호 연이 20314-
시행일자 1992.4.6.
(경유)
수신 내부결재
참조

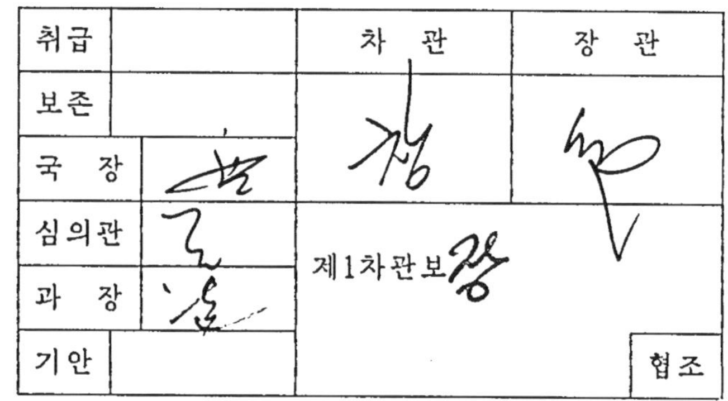

취급		차 관	장 관
보존			
국 장			
심의관		제1차관보	
과 장			
기안			협조

제목 제44차 인권이사회 참가 보고

92.3.23-4.10간 뉴욕 유엔본부에서 개최중인 제44차 인권이사회(Human Rights Committee)의 인권규약(B) 최초보고서 심의과정(대상 : 알제리아, 3.25-27)에 대한 참가결과를 별첨과 같이 보고드립니다.

첨부 : 제44차 인권이사회 참가보고서. 끝.

0025

第44차 인권이사회 참가보고서

(3.24-3.27)

1992. 4.

국 제 기 구 국

0026

1. 일반사항

가. 회의참석

o 18명의 위원중 12명 참석

- Aguillor Urbina(코스타리카), Andreas Mavrommatis(싸이프러스), Rein Myullerson(러시아), Fausto Pocar(이태리, 의장), Nisuke Ando(일본), Christine Chanet(불란서), Vojin Dimitrijevic (유고), Omran El-Shafei(이집트), Birame N'Diaye(세네갈), Waleed Sadi(요르단), Julio Vallejo(에쿠아돌), Bertil Wennergren (스웨덴), Janos Fodor(항가리)

o 알제리 대표단

- 법무부 조사국장 Noureddine Benamara(수석대표) 외 3인 (법무부 및 주유엔대표부)

o 옵서버 참석

- 10여국 대표 및 Amnesty International 등 참관
- 아국은 정달호 유엔2과장 참석(3.24-27)

나. 진행방식

o 각국 보고서 심의는 공개회의로 진행

- 언론 및 옵서버 참석 가 (국가, NGO 또는 개인)

다. 진행일정

o 제1일 오전회의시 보고서 제출국 대표의 기조발언과 위원들의 질의

o 제2일 : 답변준비기간 (단, 위원회는 회의 계속, 타국 보고서 또는 여타 의제 심의)

o 제3일 오전회의시 보고서 제출국 대표의 답변 및 보충 질의

2. 상세 진행절차

<u>제 1 일</u>

가. 보고서 제출국 대표와 보좌관은 의장단석에 착석 (의장의 오른편)

나. 의장(Fausto Pocar, 이태리)의 대표단 소개

다. 보고서 제출국 대표의 모두발언(Introductory Statement)

- Algeria의 경우 6-7분 소요

라. 위원의 논평 및 질의

- Algeria의 경우 출석위원 12인중 11인 발언, 각 5-20분간 소요 (약 2시간 소요)

<u>제 2 일</u> (보고서 제출국 답변준비)

<u>제 3 일</u>

가. 보고서 제출국 대표의 답변(약 90분 소요)

나. 위원들의 보충 질의

- Algeria의 경우 위원 9인이 발언, 약 60분 소요

다. 보고서 제출국 대표의 추가 답변

3. 주요내용

가. 모두 발언(Introductory Statement)

o 알제리의 경우 인권보장에 관한 입법의 개략적 연혁, 현 헌법의 성립 경위 및 주요 골격, 헌정체제의 개편과 인권부(Ministry of Human Rights)의 설립, 국가인권감시기구(National Human Rights Observation Body)의 설치등에 관한 설명과 함께 법과 현실간의 급격한 괴리에

2

0028

따른 위기상황의 도래(알제리는 91.12. 및 92.2. 비상사태 선포) 및 이에 대처하여 사회의 욕구와 국가 법체계의 변화를 조화시켜야 할 필요성등에 대해 설명하였음.

o 또한 신헌법 채택(89.2.) 후 인권규약(B)에 가입(89.12)하게 된 배경을 설명하고, 동 규약에 따른 최초보고서에 대해 위원들의 질의에 성실하게 답변하겠다는 의사를 표명함.

나. 논평 및 질의

o 일반적 평가

- 보고서 작성의 객관성과 성실성을 평가하고, 신헌법의 공표로 민주화 노력이 시작된 것을 환영한다고 논평함.
- 인권관계 제반협약에의 가입상황은 양호한 것으로 지적함. (선택의정서 및 규약 제41조도 수락)
- 규약의 적용이 제약되는 상황 및 제약 논리에 대한 설명이 부족한 것으로 지적되고, 특히 비상사태 선포에 관한 비판적 질문이 대부분 위원들에 의해 제기되었음.

o 구체적 내용

- 보고서는 91.6까지의 사항을 기술하고 있으나, 그 이후 현재까지의 사항도 설명되어야 함.
- 보고서는 객관적이고 포괄적으로 기술되어 있으나, 규약 시행상의 애로사항이나 인권보장에 대한 인식을 확산하기 위한 정부의 노력에 관해서는 언급이 없음.
- 규약과 국내법과의 상충시에 규약의 규정이 어떻게 이행되는지에 관한 설명이 필요함. (법원이 규약의 규정을 원용한 사례등)
- 최근 비상사태 선포로 규약의 위반사례가 관찰됨. (정당한 재판을 받을 권리 침해, 고문사례, 당국의 무기남용 등)

- 보고서가 다소 아카데믹하게 기술되어 있는 반면, 현실적인 상황에 대한 언급이 결여되어 있음. (특히 최근 비상사태 하에서의 인권 보장상황에 대한 설명 필요)
- 최근 비상사태를 선포한 정부의 행위가 규약의 어떤 규정에 근거하였는지에 대한 정당화 논리 제시 요망
- 고위 사법위원회(High Council of Judiciary) 및 헌법평의회(Constitutional Council)의 구성 및 임명방법등에 비추어 사법권의 독립이 보장되는지에 대한 설명 요망
- 경제범죄에 대해서도 사형이 적용되는 것은 사형제도의 남용이 아닌지?
- 단일민족이므로 소수집단 차별문제가 없다고 하나, Berber 어족에 대한 차별은 없는지?
- 헌법에 자유와 권리의 보장이 규정되고 있으나 이러한 권리의 제한에 관하여는 구체적 규정이 없으며, 단순히 "보장된다"라고 하는 규정이 구속력있는 효과를 갖는 것인지?
- 조약이 국내법보다 우선한다고 할수 있는바, 이슬람의 비판을 금지하는 정보법의 규정이 규약 제19조 규정을 제한하는데 대한 설명 및 일반적으로 인권분야에서 조약과 국내법과의 관계에 대한 구체적 설명 요망
- 가족법 규정은 규약과 상이한데, 이 경우 법적용 원칙 설명 요망
- 규약의 위반이 국내법상 Penal Violation이 되는지?
- 사형집행의 통계 요망
- Administrative detention procedure와 수용소내 detention 제도에 대한 설명 요망
- 언론의 자유 및 시위의 자유 제한에 대해 설명 요망
- 비상사태 선포하 민간인에 대한 군사재판시 일반재판과 다른 특별규정의 적용 여부

4

0030

- 국가에 의한 무료법률구조제도 여부
- 형법상 이슬람 모독죄 관련 규정은 종교에 의한 차별의 인정을 의미하는 것이 아닌지?
- 다당제 규정이 매우 막연한 바, 특정 정당의 해산에 관한 구체적 법률적 근거는?
- 파업권의 제한에 대한 정당화 논리는?
- 회교적 일부다처제의 인정은 남녀차별적 제도라고 보는데, 이에 대한 정당화 논리는?
- 헌법공표 이전에 채택된 조약의 효력은?
- 국적법상 부에 의한 국적승계제도는 남녀차별 금지규정에 대한 위반이 아닌지?
- 재판을 받을 권리와 관련, 재판소에의 access에 있어 내국인과 외국인간 차별은 없는지 및 내국언론인과 외국언론인에 대한 대우의 차별은 없는지?
- 표현의 자유에 대한 제한과 관련, 정확성(accuracy)이란 기준에 대한 판정자는 누구인지 및 외국의 출판물이나 비데오등의 availability는 있는지?

다. 답변형식

o 출석위원 대부분이 질문을 함으로써 질문내용에 중복 또는 공통점이 많아 답변시 위원 개인별 질문에 답변하기 보다는 일정한 주제별 및 사안별로 그룹화하여 답변하는 것이 효과적일 수 있음.
  - 알제리의 경우도 그룹화하여 답변

라. 추가보고서

o 알제리의 경우 비상사태 선포에 대하여는 그 필수불가결했던 점에 대한 설명을 추가보고서(addendum)로 제출해야 한다는 주장도 있었음.

4. 유의사항

- 아국 보고서 심의 준비 관련

가. 규약 조항별 국내 법체제에 대한 질문에 대한 답변외에도 각종 인권사안에 대한 구체적인 설명자료와 통계자료의 준비가 필요함.

o 특히 국가보안법 위반, 집회 및 시위에 관한 법률 위반, 노동조합법 위반, 장기수 문제등 인권사안에 있어 규약의 규정에 비추어 타당성을 설명할 수 있도록 대처 필요

나. 인권이사회 위원에게는 유엔 인권관련 기관에서 토의되거나 접수되는 아국 관련 인권사안은 물론 NGO나 기타 단체 또는 개별적 통신에 의한 모든 정보가 다 입수된다고 하므로, 여하한 형식으로든 과거에 제기된 사례 또는 향후 제기될 것으로 예상할수 있는 사례에 대한 질문에도 대비해야 함.

다. 답변에는 최대의 성실성을 보여야 하며, 그러기 위하여는 인권보장과 관련된 업무를 담당하거나 법률일반 및 특히 인권법에 소상한 지식을 갖춘 인사가 대표로 됨이 바람직 함. (보고서 종합 집필자도 대표단에 포함)

라. 보고서 제출시(91.7.) 이후의 특별한 진전사항에 대해서도 질문이 예상되므로 필요한 경우 아국대표의 모두발언에 최근의 인권분야 특기사항 또는 진전사항을 언급함이 바람직함.

마. 보고서 작성시 광범위한 국내의견을 수렴하였다는 표시로서 정부내 관계 부처 협의회를 구성하여 보고서 내용에 대해 부처간 협의를 거쳤다는 사실을 언급함이 바람직함.

6

0032

5. 기타사항

o 금번 이사회에서 심의되는 보고서부터는 동 보고서 심의결과를 바탕으로 이사회 명의의 결론적 관찰(concluding observation)을 작성하여, 해당국에 통보하기로 하였으며, 또한 동 내용을 총회 앞 보고서에도 포함키로 하였음.

- 지금까지는 총회 앞 보고서에만 위원 개인별 논평을 요약 게재해 왔음.

o "결론적 관찰"의 구성

(1) 일반적 평가, (2) 긍정적인 발전, (3) 규약의 이행에 영향을 주는 요인과 애로사항, (4) 주요 관심사항(major issues of concern), (5) 이사회의 구체적 권고사항 - 끝 -

UNITED
NATIONS

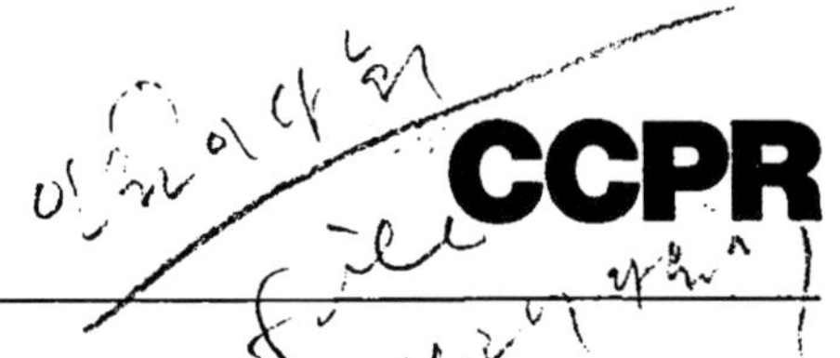

CCPR

International covenant on civil and political rights

Distr.
GENERAL

CCPR/C/62/Add.1
7 June 1991

ENGLISH
Original: FRENCH

HUMAN RIGHTS COMMITTEE

CONSIDERATION OF REPORTS SUBMITTED BY STATES PARTIES UNDER ARTICLE 40 OF THE COVENANT

Initial reports of States parties due in 1990

Addendum

ALGERIA

[15 April 1991]

CONTENTS

GE.91-16190/4169B

0034

CONTENTS (continued)

INTRODUCTION

1. The International Covenant on Civil and Political Rights was ratified by Presidential Decree No. 89-67 of 16 May 1989 after approval by the National People's Assembly (Act No. 89-08 of 25 April 1989 published in Journal Officiel No. 17 of 26 April 1989). In accordance with article 122 of the Constitution, treaties concerning the status of persons are ratified by the President of the Republic after express approval by the National People's Assembly. The Covenant entered into force for Algeria on 12 December 1989. Furthermore, Algeria has recognized the competence conferred on the Human Rights Committee by article 41 of the Covenant and the Optional Protocol thereto.

2. On submitting the initial report pursuant to article 40 of the Covenant, it is important by way of introduction to review the reforms in progress in Algeria; such a review will make it possible to grasp the scope of the changes which have taken place, and which are aimed at strengthening the democratic structures of the country, improving the operation of the national institutions and entrenching the State based on law. This State draws its strength from the affirmation of rules which lay the foundations for a multi-party system and for the separation of powers and which give a special place to citizens' participation in the conduct of public affairs and in safeguarding and promoting their rights and freedoms.

3. The reforms undertaken in Algeria in the course of the 1980s concern the country's economic, social and political life. In the economic field, a series of measures have been taken which share the objective of restoring the national productive apparatus to health so that it may master its methods of management and adjust to social, economic and technical changes. In the political field, striking changes have been ushered in by the advent of the multi-party system prescribed by the Constitution as adopted by popular referendum on 23 February 1989.

4. As stated in the preamble to the Constitution, in approving this fundamental text, "the work of their own genius, the reflection of their aspirations, the fruit of their determination and the product of profound social changes, the people intend to recognize more solemnly than ever before the primacy of law ... and to equip themselves with institutions which are based on citizens' participation in the conduct of public affairs and which translate into reality social justice, equality and freedom for each and every one ...".

5. Mr. Chadli Bendjedid, the President of the Algerian Republic, marked the anniversary of the adoption of the Constitution in these terms:

> "The anniversary of the adoption of the Constitution affords me the opportunity today to assess with you the distance covered and the tasks to be undertaken. The profound changes in society - the fruit of the economic and social progress achieved over more than two decades - have engendered in the citizen new aspirations and claims, just as they have led to imbalances and breakdowns in the functioning of society that have needed continuous attention. We were thus called upon individually and collectively to take resolute charge of the exercise of political and economic initiative dictated by this impetus for change. Borne up by the

trust and adherence of the majority in carrying the changes through, it has thus been given to me to organize the necessary consultations in order to enable the people to give practical expression to their will and their choices for their future. Today we are all entitled to feel that the rise of the fundamental freedoms embodied in the Constitution has become clearly apparent and that the new society is taking shape more and more with every day that passes. The citizens have occupied the available space in the associative field and are reducing it to order in virtue of their profound aspirations to freedom of association, of assembly and of expression, thus proving the extent and richness of the adversary discussion that devotes itself to the general progress by ensuring creative convergences."

6. The actions undertaken in order to entrench the State based on law and to consolidate the democratic institutions have been backed by various measures decided upon to translate the constitutional principles proclaimed into law and into practice and to strengthen the mechanisms for the application of democratic rules and the protection of human rights and public freedoms. These measures will be examined in relation to the comments on the articles of the Covenant. At this stage we may describe them in broad outline:

(a) The Constitution of 1989 specifies the primacy of law, political pluralism, freedom of association, the separation of the executive, legislative and judicial powers, and the principle of the independence of justice. The institutional controls have been strengthened, in particular through the establishment of the Constitutional Council responsible for monitoring compliance with the Constitution and checking the regularity of the operations of referendum, election of the President of the Republic and legislative elections. It also delivers opinions on the constitutionality of treaties, laws and regulations. The Constitutional Council was installed by the President of the Republic on 8 March 1989 and has delivered several decisions and opinions concerning the Electoral Code, the regulations for deputies and the rules of procedure of the National People's Assembly;

(b) The 1989 Constitution widens the scope of human rights and freedoms, which under the previous Constitution had been relegated to the restrictive area of law. The rights recognized by the 1976 Constitution have been reaffirmed and the procedures for their exercise strengthened and safeguarded by new constitutional provisions. "Henceforth their applicability derives directly from the Constitution and the system of supervision which guarantees the pluralism as well as the separation of powers";

(c) The procedures and jurisdictions for emergencies have been reviewed with, among other results, the abolition of the State Security Court and the referral of pending proceedings to the courts of normal jurisdiction (Act No. 89-06 of 25 April 1989);

(d) Revision of the Code of Penal Procedure so that any crime, of whatever nature, may be subject to the procedures and jurisdictions of ordinary law. Thus the economic section of the criminal court has been abolished (Act No. 90-24 of 18 August 1990 to amend and supplement Ordinance No. 66-155 of 8 June 1966 establishing the Code of Penal Procedure);

(e) Re-examination of the content of legislation in order to rid it of rules of law inherited from colonial times. In this context, the penalty of transportation was found inconsistent with our values and inhuman in character. It was consequently abolished by Act No. 89-05 of 25 April 1989, which amended article 9 and rescinded the provisions of articles 10 and 60 of Ordinance No. 66-156 of 8 June 1966 establishing the Penal Code;

(f) Amendment of the provisions of the Code of Civil Procedure concerning administrative disputes in order to streamline the appeal procedures and bring the system of justice closer to the people (Act No. 90-23 of 18 August 1990 to amend and supplement Ordinance No. 66-154 of 8 June 1966 establishing the Code of Civil Procedure);

(g) Revision of the provisions of the Code of Penal Procedure to afford better protection of the fundamental rights and freedoms of the citizen, in particular by strengthening the rights of the defence and the safeguards for the use of the procedures of police custody and pre-trial detention procedures (Act No. 90-24 of 18 August 1990 already mentioned);

(h) Revision of the judiciary regulations and promulgation of Act No. 89-21 of 12 December 1989 laying down new judiciary regulations to give full effect to the provisions of the 1989 Constitution establishing the multi-party system, the separation of powers and the independence of the judiciary, which protects society and freedoms and guarantees to each and every one the safeguarding of his fundamental rights (arts. 40, 129 and 130 of the Constitution). In this connection, the new judiciary regulations strengthen the new function of the judge. They spell out the rights and obligations that flow from it, ensure the judge's impartiality, and protect him against any form of pressure or interference that might impede the practice of his profession and the exercise of his free will. Thus the new regulations lay down the principle of irremovability of the judge, and his right to protection against all forms of pressure or interference and against threats, insults, abuse, defamation or attacks of any description whatsoever. The judge's right to organize is recognized; but, in order to guarantee his impartiality, he is forbidden to join any political association. Furthermore, if he considers himself injured in his rights, he may apply to the High Council of the Judiciary, the composition and operation of which have been revised in the light of the constitutional principles referred to above;

(i) The organization and operation of the Supreme Court have been revised in order to give the country's highest court the means of performing its function of ensuring respect for law in a State based on law and safeguarding the independence of the judiciary (Act No. 89-22 of 12 December 1989 concerning the organization and operation of the Supreme Court). In addition the Revue de la Cour suprême was founded by Executive Decree No. 90-141 of 19 May 1990 in order to make known the application of the law and to ensure unity in the decisions taken by the courts and tribunals;

(j) Promulgation of a series of Acts to organize the free exercise of the fundamental rights recognized by the Constitution (Act No. 90-07 of 3 April 1990 concerning information; Act No.90-14 of 2 June 1990 concerning the exercise of the right to organize; Act No. 89-11 of 5 July 1989 concerning political associations; recent revision (Act No. 90-31 of 4 December 1990) of the Act concerning non-political associations, streamlining the procedures for their formation, in particular by eliminating the requirement for prior approval imposed by Act No. 87-15 of 21 July 1987);

(k) Amnesty for crimes and other offences against persons and property committed with open use of force during or on the occasion of unlawful or violent assemblies, for certain localities from 1 April 1980 to 11 July 1988 and throughout the national territory from 1 to 31 October 1988 (Act No. 90-19 of 15 August 1990 declaring an amnesty and Act No. 90-20 of 15 August 1990 concerning compensation consequent upon the aforementioned Amnesty Act).

7. The process of revising the laws and regulations is continuing in order to adapt them to the new aspirations of Algerian society. A draft text revising the regulations for lawyers is at present under consideration in the National People's Assembly, which is also examining various proposed amendments to the electoral law. In addition, several sectoral and intersectoral commissions are working to recast legal texts in order to provide the legislative support which gives primacy to law and which organizes, in any democracy, the framework for plural expression and exercise of the rights solemnly proclaimed by the Constitution.

8. At the beginning of December 1990 there were 33 approved political parties and six applications pending. There were 28,500 non-political associations, including two human rights leagues, an Algerian section of Amnesty International and a National Committee against Torture.

I. GENERAL INFORMATION

A. General legal framework

9. In this first report, the Algerian Government will endeavour to describe the general legal framework that provides protection for civil and political rights in Algeria. The Constitution of 1989 states in its preamble that it "is above everybody, it is the fundamental law that guarantees individual and collective rights and freedoms, protects the rule of the people's free choice and confers legitimacy upon the exercise of the powers. It provides the means of ensuring the legal protection and supervision of the actions of the public authorities in a society in which legality and the full development of man in all its dimensions prevail".

10. It devotes an entire chapter to rights and freedoms. Here follows a brief summary of the provisions of the main articles in this chapter.

Art. 28. Citizens are equal before the law, and there shall be no discrimination on grounds of birth, race, sex, opinion or any other personal or social condition or circumstance.

Art. 30. The institutions shall seek to ensure the equality of rights and duties of all male and female citizens by eliminating the obstacles which impede the full development of the human personality and prevent the effective participation of all in political, economic, social and cultural life.

Art. 31. The fundamental freedoms and rights of man and the citizen are guaranteed. They constitute the common heritage of all Algerian men and women, which they have the duty to hand on from generation to generation in order to preserve it in its integrity and inviolability.

Art. 32. The individual or associative defence of the fundamental rights of man and of individual and collective freedoms is guaranteed.

Art. 33. The State guarantees the inviolability of the human person. Any form of physical or moral violence is prohibited.

Art. 34. Offences committed against rights and freedoms and physical or moral attacks on the integrity of the human being shall be punishable by law.

Art. 35. Freedom of conscience and freedom of opinion are inviolable.

Art. 36. The freedom of intellectual, artistic and scientific creation is guaranteed to the citizen. Copyright shall be protected by law. No publication, recording or other medium of communication or information shall be sequestrated save by order of the court.

Art. 37. The privacy and honour of the citizen is inviolable and shall be protected by law. The secrecy of private correspondence and communication in all their forms is guaranteed.

Art. 38. The State shall guarantee inviolability of the home. No search may take place save in virtue of the law and in accordance therewith. No search may be made save by written order of the competent judicial authority.

Art. 39. The freedoms of expression, association and assembly are guaranteed to the citizen.

Art. 40. The right to establish political associations is recognized. This right may not, however, be claimed for the purpose of encroaching upon fundamental freedoms, national unity, the territorial integrity or independence of the country, or the sovereignty of the people.

Art. 41. Any citizen in possession of his civil and political rights shall be entitled to choose his place of residence freely and to travel within the national territory. He is guaranteed the right to enter and leave the national territory.

Art. 42. Every person shall be presumed innocent until proved guilty by a regular court with all the safeguards required by the law.

Art. 43. No one may be found guilty except by virtue of a law duly promulgated prior to the act of which he is accused.

Art. 44. No one may be prosecuted, arrested or detained except in the cases determined by law and in accordance with the procedures prescribed thereby.

Art. 45. For the purposes of criminal investigation, police custody shall be subject to judicial supervision and may not exceed 48 hours. A person in police custody shall have the right to get into touch with his family immediately. Police custody may not be prolonged as an exceptional measure save under the conditions fixed by law. Upon the expiry of the time-limit for police custody, it shall be mandatory to carry out a medical examination of the person detained if he so requests, and he shall in all cases be informed of this option.

Art. 46. Judicial errors shall be made good by the State. The conditions and procedures for compensation shall be determined by law.

Art. 47. Every citizen who satisfies the legal conditions is entitled to vote and to stand for election.

Art. 48. Equal access to office and employment under the State is guaranteed to all citizens, subject to no conditions other than those fixed by law.

Art. 49. The ownership of private property is guaranteed. The right of inheritance is guaranteed. *Wakf* assets (religious assets) and foundations are recognized; the disposal thereof shall be protected by law.

Art. 50. The right to education is guaranteed; education shall be free of charge under the conditions fixed by law. Basic education is compulsory. The State shall organize the system of education. The State shall ensure equal access to education and to vocational training.

Art. 51. All citizens are entitled to protection of their health. The State shall provide for the prevention and control of epidemic and endemic diseases.

Art. 52. All citizens have the right to work. The right to protection and to safe and healthy working conditions shall be guaranteed by law. The right to rest is guaranteed; the law shall determine the procedures for the exercise thereof.

Art. 53. The right to organize is recognized for all citizens.

Art. 54. The right to strike is recognized and shall be exercised within the law. The law may prohibit or restrict the exercise of this right in the areas of national defence or security or for all public services or activities of vital interest to the community.

Art. 55. The family shall enjoy the protection of the State and society.

Art. 56. The living standards of citizens who are not yet able to work, can no longer work or will never be able to work shall be guaranteed.

11. The proclamation of these rights by the Constitution, which permits legal restrictions on their implementation only in rare and exceptional cases, means that their applicability derives directly from the country's fundamental law, thus strengthening the guarantees for their protection. As the constitutional provisions are at the top of the hierarchy of juridical norms, any legislative or regulatory text contrary to them would be declared unconstitutional.

12. In addition, it should be noted that the constitutional principles include: (a) the guarantee of the inviolability of the human person; (b) the prohibition of any form of violence, either physical or moral; (c) the punishment by law of offences committed against rights and freedoms and of physical or moral violations of the integrity of the human being; and (d) the guarantees which must be provided with regard to custody (judicial supervision; maximum duration of 48 hours; the right of the person held in custody to contact his family immediately; obligatory medical examination of the person held if he requests such an examination and the requirement that he must in all cases be informed of that option).

13. The Constitutional Council has the task of ensuring observance of the Constitution and takes decisions on the constitutionality of treaties, laws and regulations (arts. 153 and 155 of the Constitution). When it finds that a legislative or regulatory provision is unconstitutional, the latter ceases to have any effect from the date of the Council's decision (art. 159 of the Constitution). The effectiveness of the guarantees of the rights recognized by the Constitution is further strengthened by the system of pluralism, separation of powers and freedom of association established by the Constitution.

14. Violations of the human rights and freedoms set forth in the Constitution are sanctioned and severely punished under national legislation. The Penal Code, for example, devotes a chapter to crimes and offences against the Constitution, with one section for infringements of liberty and specific provisions concerning civil servants and officials who incur civil as well as State responsibility when they order or commit arbitrary acts or infringements either against personal liberties or the civil rights of citizens. Furthermore, torture or any other violation of the physical integrity of the individual is punishable under many provisions of the Penal Code.

15. Various basic legal texts and sectoral laws protect the rights of the individual, in particular the Code of Penal Procedure (rights to defence and supervision of penal procedures), the Civil Code (protection of persons who are legally incapable and under the age of majority; prohibition of any renunciation of a person's individual freedom; nullity of contracts where violence is employed, etc.); the code governing the penitentiary system and rehabilitation; the ordinance relating to the protection of children and young persons; the law relating to information (publications must not include illustrations, stories, information or other materials contrary to human rights; protection against defamation, etc.); the law relating to the protection and promotion of health (in particular, provisions concerning the removal of tissues or organs; experiments on human beings; the duty of physicians to report any maltreatment of children or of persons deprived of their liberty which has come to their attention in the exercise of their profession; the establishment of a national council on medical ethics, etc.).

B. Conventions to which Algeria is a party and status of Algeria's international commitments

16. Algeria is a party to a large number of international instruments which set forth a series of rights contributing to respect for the dignity and integrity of the human person. These instruments include:

African Charter on Human and Peoples' Rights of 1981;

Convention for the Suppression of the Traffic in Persons and of the Exploitation of the Prostitution of Others of 2 December 1949;

Convention on the Prevention and Punishment of the Crime of Genocide of 9 December 1948;

Convention relating to the Status of Refugees of 28 July 1951;

Convention relating to the Status of Stateless Persons of 28 September 1954;

Supplementary Convention on the Abolition of Slavery, the Slave Trade, and Institutions and Practices Similar to Slavery of 7 September 1954;

International Convention on the Elimination of All Forms of Racial Discrimination of 21 December 1965;

International Covenant on Economic, Social and Cultural Rights of 16 December 1966;

International Covenant on Civil and Political Rights of 16 December 1966;

Optional Protocol to the International Covenant on Civil and Political Rights of 16 December 1966;

Protocol relating to the Status of Refugees of 16 December 1966;

International Convention on the Suppression and Punishment of the Crime of *Apartheid* of 30 November 1973;

Convention against Torture and Other Cruel, Inhuman or Degrading Treatment or Punishment of 10 December 1984;

International Convention against *Apartheid* in Sports of 10 December 1985;

Geneva Conventions of 1949 and the Additional Protocols of 1977.

17. Under article 122 of the Constitution, treaties relating to the status of persons are ratified by the President of the Republic after their express approval by the National People's Assembly. Article 123 adds that "treaties ratified by the President of the Republic, under the conditions provided for by the Constitution, take precedence over the law". The International Covenant on Civil and Political Rights, as a treaty concerning the status of persons, was submitted for approval by the National People's Assembly and then ratified

by the President of the Republic. There is no special procedure for the integration of an international convention into the Algerian legal system. Such a convention forms an integral part of national legislation once it has been duly approved and ratified. Furthermore, by virtue of the Constitution, it acquires a higher legal status than domestic laws. Consequently, treaties which have been duly ratified rank second in the hierarchy of juridical norms, after the Constitution and before domestic laws. No contrary law may be implemented as the provisions of the convention take precedence. The provisions of a convention which has been duly ratified may be invoked directly in the courts.

18. The Constitutional Council, in its decision No. 1 DLCC/89 of 20 August 1989 on the Electoral Code, clearly reaffirmed the constitutional principle of the primacy of duly ratified treaties over domestic laws and concluded that any Algerian citizen was permitted to avail himself of the provisions of such treaties in the courts:

> "Considering that, after its ratification and following its publication, any convention forms an integral part of national law and, pursuant to article 123 of the Constitution, acquires a higher status than domestic laws, permitting any Algerian citizen to avail himself of its provisions in the courts; this is the case in particular for the United Nations Covenants of 1966, approved by Act No. 89-08 of 25 April 1989, to which Algeria acceded by Presidential Decree No. 89-67 of 16 May 1989, and for the African Charter on Human and Peoples' Rights, ratified by Decree No. 87-37 of 3 February 1987, these legal instruments solemnly prohibiting discrimination of any kind".

C. Judicial, administrative or other authorities competent to deal with matters covered by the Convention

1. The Constitutional Council

19. Matters may be brought before the Constitutional Council either by the President of the Republic or by the President of the National People's Assembly (art. 156 of the Constitution). The Council is composed of seven members, two of whom are appointed by the President of the Republic, two are elected by the National People's Assembly and two by the Supreme Court. The Constitutional Council may be called upon to declare unconstitutional any legislative or regulatory provision which is contrary to the Constitution. As we have seen, the Constitution prohibits all forms of physical or moral violence, guarantees the inviolability of the human person and devotes an entire chapter to human rights. The Constitutional Council therefore has a particularly broad field of action to monitor laws and regulations concerning human rights. Indeed, when it finds that a legislative or regulatory provision is unconstitutional, that provision ceases to have any effect from the date of the Council's decision.

20. The Constitutional Council is, furthermore, empowered to monitor certain procedures which may affect the operation of national institutions and citizens' rights. Articles 84 to 87 and 91 require the Constitutional Council to be involved and consulted whenever a state of emergency or siege or martial law is declared or whenever armistice agreements or peace treaties are signed.

0044

In the case of a constitutional amendment, the President of the Republic cannot directly promulgate the act amending the Constitution (without submitting it to a popular referendum) unless it has obtained three quarters of the votes of the members of the National People's Assembly and, in the reasoned opinion of the Constitutional Council, the draft amendment in no way violates the general principles governing Algerian society or human and citizens' rights or freedoms and in no way affects the fundamental balance of powers and institutions (art. 164 of the Constitution).

21. Since its establishment on 8 March 1989, the Constitutional Council has rendered various decisions and opinions at the request of the President of the Republic, including:

Decision No. 1 DLCC/89 of 20 August 1989 on the Electoral Code;

Decision No. 2 DLCC/89 of 30 August 1989 on the status of deputies;

Opinion No. 1 LCC/89 of 28 August 1989 on the rules of procedure of the National People's Assembly;

Decision No. 3 DRICC/89 of 18 December 1989 on the rules of procedure of the National People's Assembly;

Opinion No. 2 ALCC/89 of 9 December 1989 on the act postponing elections for the renewal of the communal people's assemblies;

Opinion No. 3 ALCC/89 of 9 December 1989 on the law postponing elections for the renewal of the wilaya people's assemblies.

2. Respect for the law

22. The judicial, administrative and other authorities are required to observe the law and Algeria's international commitments. The Constitution devotes several articles to duties, including article 57, which stipulates that no one should be ignorant of the law. Article 60 provides that all the individual's freedoms should be exercised with due regard for the rights granted to others by the Constitution, in particular the right to honour, privacy and protection of the family, young persons and children.

23. The Algerian judicial system plays a leading role in taking decisions aimed at the prevention and suppression of torture. The organization and underlying principles of the system strengthen its power of action.

3. Independence of the judiciary

24. The Constitution devotes several articles to the principle of the independence of the judiciary. Their provisions are summarized below.

Art. 129. The judiciary is independent.

Art. 130. The judiciary shall protect society and freedoms. It shall guarantee that every person's fundamental rights are safeguarded.

Art. 132. Justice shall be administered on behalf of the people.

Art. 136. All the qualified State bodies shall be required to ensure the execution of judicial decisions at any time, in any place and under any circumstances.

Art. 137. Justice shall be administered by judges. They may be assisted by people's assessors under the conditions established by the law.

Art. 138. Judges shall obey only the law.

Art. 139. Judges shall be protected against any form of pressure, interference or manipulation which could be detrimental to the performance of their duties or to their freedom of judgement.

25. The President of the Republic, in a speech in February 1990 to the National Conference of Judges, underlined the responsibility of the judiciary in the following terms:

> "Is it necessary to remind the representatives of the judiciary that you are, more than ever, the body within society which summons justice for the protection of its institutions and its freedoms? Justice today is vested with the power of overall regulation of society through the settlement of disputes to which different interests may give rise in the political, economic and social fields. There can be no doubt that the relationship between the Administration and the citizen, the free play of political and electoral competition, and the exercise of rights and freedoms which have no limit except where they impinge upon the rights and freedoms of others call for arbitration that is free from group or individual pressures and is now rendered possible by your independence.
>
> "In the field of employment, where human relations are established by means of negotiated agreements and partnership based on the free choice of the representatives, it is now the task of justice to ensure respect for the law and the resolution of individual or collective conflicts in the interests of social peace by protecting the rights of everyone.
>
> "Likewise, the organization of the economy, formed on the principles of commercialism and civil law applicable to enterprises, both public and private, calls on your exclusive competence in dealing with economic and commercial conflicts and disputes.
>
> "In other words, this enlargement of the scope of your actions and the total independence of your decisions also confer on you prime responsibility in the promotion and successful application of the new rules governing society".

26. The judicial system in Algeria is based on the principles of the separation of powers. Judicial power is independent and judges obey only the law, which is administered on behalf of the people. Act No. 89-21 of 12 December 1989 on the status of the magistrature reflects the principles set forth in the Constitution. Various articles of this Act concern the independence of judges:

Art. 7. Judges are in all circumstances required to exercise reserve guaranteeing their independence and impartiality.

Art. 8. Except where expressly stated otherwise by the law, judges are required to observe the secrecy of deliberations and shall refrain from communicating any information or details regarding court cases.

Art. 9. The duties of a judge are incompatible with the holding of any elective office at the national or local level. Judges shall be prohibited from belonging to any political association. They shall declare any affiliation to other associations or groups to the Minister of Justice so that he may, where appropriate, take the necessary measures to preserve the independence and dignity of the judiciary.

Art. 10. Judges shall be prohibited from taking any action which might halt or impede the administration of justice.

27. The Act relating to the status of the magistrature also defines the rights of judges, particularly in the following articles:

Art. 16. A judge with 10 years' effective service is irremovable and may not, without his consent, be transferred or reassigned to the procurator's office or central administration or to the administrative services of the Supreme Court.

Art. 18. Judges shall be protected against any form of pressure or interference which could be detrimental to the performance of their duties or to their freedom of judgement under article 139 of the Constitution.

Art. 19. Apart from the protection enjoyed under the provisions of the Penal Code and special laws, the State shall be required to protect judges against threats, insults, slander, libel or attacks of any kind in the performance of their duties.

Art. 21. Judges shall be granted trade union rights, subject to the provisions of articles 9 and 10 of this Act.

28. The same Act determines the composition, operation and powers of the High Council of the Judiciary entrusted with ensuring respect for the rights of judges and the proper development of their careers.

4. Equality of justice; legality of offences and individuality of penalties; presumption of innocence; non-retroactivity of the law

29. Several articles of the Constitution deal with these questions:

Art. 131. Justice is based on the principles of legality and equality. It is equal for all, accessible to all and is manifested in respect for the law.

Art. 133. Criminal penalties shall be consistent with the principles of legality and individuality.

0047

Art. 42. Every person shall be presumed innocent until proved guilty by a regular court with all the safeguards required by the law.

Art. 43. No one may be found guilty except by virtue of a law duly promulgated prior to the act of which he is accused.

Art. 44. No one may be prosecuted, arrested or detained except in the cases determined by law and in accordance with the procedures prescribed thereby.

30. The Penal Code also lays down various rules in this regard:

Art. 1. There is no offence, penalty or security measure outside the law.

Art. 2. The criminal law shall not be not retroactive, except where it is less rigorous.

Art. 3. The criminal law shall apply to all offences committed in the territory of the Republic. It shall apply also to offences committed abroad when the Algerian criminal courts have jurisdiction under the provisions of the Code of Penal Procedure.

31. The principle of non-retroactivity of the law even extends to civil cases. Article 2 of the Civil Code states that "The law provides only for the future. It has no retroactive effect".

5. The right to defence

32. Article 142 of the Constitution recognizes the right to defence, which is a safeguard in criminal matters. Any person tried in a court has the right to defend himself and to be assisted by counsel of his own choosing. Needy persons may be provided with legal assistance. In certain cases, the presence of a defence counsel to assist the accused or defendant has even been made obligatory by the legislature. The same applies to appearance in a criminal court which has full jurisdiction to try persons who have reached the age of majority and who are brought before it by a decision of the indictment division. Under article 271 of the Code of Penal Procedure, the accused shall be invited by the presiding judge to choose counsel to assist him in his defence. If the accused does not make a choice, counsel shall be appointed for him automatically. Article 292 adds, with regard to the appearance of the accused, that the presence of a defence counsel to assist him at the hearing is obligatory. Where necessary, counsel shall be appointed for him by the presiding judge. Even in the case of flagrant offences, the individual brought before the court under this procedure must be informed by the presiding judge that he has the right to request a stay of proceedings in order to prepare his defence; the notification given by the presiding judge and the defendant's reply are recorded in the judgement (art. 338 of the Code of Penal Procedure).

33. The rights of defence have been strengthened by Act No. 90-24 of 18 August 1990, which modifies and supplements the Code of Penal Procedure. This Code has in fact been revised on the basis of an examination made by a working group comprising judges, lawyers, and representatives of

0048

the two Algerian human rights leagues and the Algerian section of Amnesty International. A critical study of the Code of Penal Procedure was made, and permitted the reformulation of some of its provisions with a view to strengthening defence rights. Two paragraphs of article 51 of the Code were expanded to underline the exceptional nature of custody and the safeguards relating to it. The paragraph regarding compulsory medical examination following custody previously read: "On expiry of the time-limit for custody, a medical examination shall be made of the person detained if he requests such an examination. He shall be informed of this option". The text was amended as follows: "On expiry of the time-limit for custody, a medical examination shall be made of the person detained if he requests such an examination directly or through his counsel or his family. The examination shall be carried out by a physician of his own choosing. He shall be informed of this option".

34. With regard to searches, domiciliary visits and seizure of items of evidence, article 64 of the Code, which requires the express consent of the person in whose home the operation takes place, has been amended to take account of the problem of individuals unable to read. The new wording of this article allows a person unable to read to obtain the assistance of a third party of his choosing in order to make a written declaration of consent or refusal.

35. Defence rights have been broadened and the difficulties of access to case files have been removed. Even at the inquiry stage, counsel has the right to obtain a copy of the file. To this end, an article has been added to the Code of Penal Procedure (art. 68 *bis*). Furthermore, the defence is entitled to submit comments to the indictment division, enabling it to elucidate the actual circumstances and points of law relevant to the case, and it is now possible for the parties to attend these hearings. Lastly, the defence has been granted a right of reply to the government procurator's statement. Article 353 (3), specifying that "The defendant always has the final word", has been amended as follows: "The defendant and his counsel shall always have the final word". The same holds for article 304.

D. Remedies

36. The remedies available to anyone who alleges that his rights as set forth in the Covenant have been violated are the same as those of ordinary law. The criminal proceedings authorized by positive criminal law as applicable in Algeria should therefore be taken into account. In addition to the express provisions of the penal Code, which establishes penalties for various acts constituting infringements of human rights and freedoms as well as the integrity of the human being, it is important to recall that the provisions of the Covenant form an integral part of this law and can be directly invoked in the courts (see decision of the Constitutional Council above). Public prosecution proceedings for the determination of penalties may be initiated and carried out by the judges who are given this authority under the law. These proceedings may also be initiated by the injured party, who also has the right to initiate a criminal action for damages. This action may be brought concurrently with or separately from the prosecution proceedings. The court also hears appeals against acts by the public authorities, a principle established in articles 134 of the Constitution. Finally, appeals or applications for judicial review may be lodged against court decisions.

1. Public prosecution proceedings

37. The Code of Penal Procedure contains a number of provisions which determine the proceudres for the initiation of public prosecution proceedings:

Art. 1. Public prosecution proceedings for the enforcement of penalties shall be initiated and carried out by the judges or the public officials to whom the law has granted this authority. They may also be initiated by the injured party, under the conditions specified in the present Code.

Art. 29. The Government procurator shall carry out the proceedings on behalf of society and demand enforcement of the law. He shall be represented in every court of law.

Art. 30. The Minister of Justice may report infringements of the criminal law to the procurator-general. He may also instruct him in writing to initiate criminal proceedings or have them initiated or to make such written submissions to the competent court as he deems appropriate.

Art. 32. Any constituted authority, public official or civil servant who, in the performance of his duties, learns of a serious or ordinary offence shall be required to inform the government attorney procurator without delay and to transmit to him all the information, official reports and records relating thereto.

Art. 36. The government procurator shall receive the reports, complaints and denunciations and decide on the action to be taken thereon. He shall take all necessary measures, or cause them to be taken, for inquiry into or proceedings against infringements of the criminal law.

2. Initiation of criminal indemnity proceedings

38. Public prosecution proceedings may be initiated by the injured party, who may also initiate criminal indemnity proceedings. The Code of Civil Procedure contains the following provisions:

Art. 2. Criminal indemnity proceedings to obtain compensation for the damage caused by a serious, ordinary or minor offence may be initiated by anyone who has personally suffered the damage directly caused by the infringement. Except for the cases specified in article 6, paragraph 3, renunciation of criminal indemnity proceedings cannot halt or suspend the execution of public prosecution proceedings.

Art. 3. Criminal indemnity proceedings may be udnertaken at the same time as prosecution proceedings and in the same court. This court shall be competent to hear the case, irrespective of the natural or legal person, under civil law, responsible for the injury.

Art. 4. Criminal indemnity proceedings may also be undertaken separately from prosecution proceedings. Nevertheless, there shall be a stay of judgement in the proceedings in the civil court until a final decision has been delivered in the prosecution proceedings, where the latter have been initiated.

Art. 72. Anyone who claims that he has suffered injury as a result of an infringement may, by lodging a complaint, initiate criminal indemnity proceedings before the competent examining magistrate.

3. Remedies against actions by the public authorities

39. Act No. 90-23 of 18 August 1990 amended and added to the Code of Civil Procedure with the aim of bringing justice closer to the citizen and to simplify the procedures to be followed in appealing against acts by the public authorities and in administrative disputes. The procedures in force under the former law were in fact characterized by the centralization of annulment proceedings in the supreme court and by slowness due to the requirement that preliminary, discretionary or hierarchical appeals had to be lodged before any appeal could be made to a court. Under the new Act, appeals against acts by local authorities come under the jurisdiction of the courts of first instance and appeals may be made to the Supreme Court. The courts hear all cases of any kind to which the State, the wilaya or administrative institution is a party, in accordance with the following rules of competence.

40. The courts of Algiers, Oran, Constantine, Béchar and Ouargla are competent to hear annulment proceedings against decisions taken by wilayas, proceedings for the interpretation of a judgement and proceedings for the review of legality of the acts of these authorities.

41. Twenty-two courts which have an administrative division are competent to hear annulment proceedings against decisions taken by the presidents of the communal people's assemblies and by public institutions of an administrative nature, appeals for the interpretation of judgements and appeals for review of the legality of the acts of those authorities, as well as proceedings involving the civil liability of the State, the wilaya, the commune or a public administrative institution seeking compensation for damage.

42. The Supreme Court hears annulment proceedings against decisions taken by the central administrative authorities abuses of constituting authority, annulment proceedings against statutory or individual decisions taken by the central administrative authorities, and appeals for the interpretation of judgements or for review of the legality of acts involving any dispute which the Supreme Court is competent to decide.

43. Preliminary appeals (discretionary and hierarchical remedies) have been abolished and replaced by the requirement that the judge should try to reconcile the parties on the occasions of appeals to the courts. Such appeals are maintained only for disputes referred to the Supreme Court.

E. Other measures taken to ensure the application of the provisions of the Covenant

44. As is apparent from the introduction and the information provided in part I of this report, Algeria has ratified the Covenant and accepted all the supervisory mechanisms established therein, and has systematically revised the existing laws in order to give full effect to the constitutional principles which have been solemnly established. The process of reform is going ahead, with the active participation of all the sectors which constitute civilian

society, organized into political groupings or non-political associations which enjoy complete freedom of expression and assembly. Human rights are openly discussed in Algeria and are included in most programmes of the political parties. Throughout the past year, some of these parties have held seminars on subjects such as the rights of the child, torture, Islam and human rights, etc. Several Algerian associations are actively working in complete freedom to safeguard human rights.

II. INFORMATION CONCERNING THE ARTICLES OF THE COVENANT

Article 1: The right of peoples to self-determination and to dispose of their natural wealth and resources

45. Algeria reiterates its unwavering support for the right of peoples to self-determination, their right to dispose of their natural wealth and resources and their right to choose freely their political system and their pattern of economic, social and cultural development. In no circumstances should a people be deprived of its own means of subsistence or of its inalienable right to self-determination and to dispose of its natural wealth and resources. Algeria endorses the provisions of article 47 of the Covenant, which reads: "Nothing in the present Covenant shall be interpreted as impairing the inherent right of all peoples to enjoy and utilize fully and freely their natural wealth and resources". Algeria considers furthermore that the maintenance of certain territories in the state of dependence referred to in article 1, paragraph 3, of the Covenant is contrary to the purposes and principles of the United Nations Charter and the Declaration on the Granting of Independence to Colonial Countries and Peoples (General Assembly resolution 1514 (XV) of 14 December 1960).

46. Algeria's attachment to the ideals and principles of the United Nations derives from its deep-seated values and the tradition of solidarity and justice of the Algerian people who, throughout their long history, have unfailingly given evidence of their openness to other cultures and civilizations and their abhorrence and rejection of all forms of domination. The tribulations endured during the colonial period and during the national liberation war strengthened the already established conviction of the Algerian people that they should lend their full support to peoples struggling for their emancipation and to recover their fundamental rights, among which the right of self-determination is fundamental.

47. Algeria's solidarity with the peoples fighting against colonialism, apartheid, zionism and any other forms of occupation, domination or racial discrimination was asserted well before independence and even while the Algerian people were waging their own struggle for national liberation. For example, reference may be made to the declaration of 24 March 1960 issued by the Ministry of Foreign Affairs of the Provisional Government of the Republic of Algeria after the Sharpeville massacres: "The recent massacres of the unarmed population of Sharpeville have caused deep distress among the fighting people of Algeria. On behalf of the Algerian Government, we wish to reassert our indignation at this barbaric act which is a denial of the humanitarian principles of human rights. However, this abominable repression which is being imposed on the South African people bloodily confirms that the colonialism which is being inflicted on South Africa is that of one kind only

and that the complete liberation of Africa is a single and indivisible cause. The ideal of freedom, independence and unity which inspires the people of Africa is one and the same. Only effective and positive action by the peoples and Governments of Africa, supported by all freedom-loving nations can put an end to barbarity and remove the yoke of colonialism".

48. Algeria is working steadily and unceasingly to eliminate colonialism and its vestiges and all forms of racial discrimination and exploitation of a country's wealth and resources, to bring about the total dismantling of apartheid, and to restore the inalienable rights of the peoples who are victims of these practices. Algeria's support for the legitimate struggle of peoples is voiced at all levels - bilateral, multilateral, regional or universal. Algeria has made the cause of the Palestinian people and the completion of the liberation of the African continent one of the main objectives of its foreign policy and, in accordance with the Charter of the OAU and the African Charter on Human Rights and Peoples' Rights, has pledged to continue working actively for the total eradication of apartheid. Algeria's front-line struggle against colonialism and its after-effects, racism, apartheid and all the other ways in which the right of self-determination is denied continues in the form of aid to the peoples who are fighting, to their legitimate representatives and to their national liberation movements. The adoption in Algiers in 1976 of the International Charter for the Right of Peoples (the Algiers Charter) has stamped the name of Algeria's capital on the principle of the right of peoples to self-determination and their right to dispose of their national wealth and resources.

49. In the area of domestic legislation, one of the first acts of independent Algeria was to make all the laws predating independence temporarily subject to the following mandatory conditions: "All laws and provisions which impair the internal and external sovereignty of the Algerian State, are inspired by colonialism or are discriminatory, and all laws and provisions which impair the normal exercise of democratic freedoms are hereby declared null and void" (art. 2 of Act No. 62-57 of 31 December 1962).

50. Since then, several enactments have been added to Algerian law. Thus, Ordinance No. 73-21 of 5 July 1973 repealed, with effect from 5 July 1975, all non-Algerian laws which had had to be temporarily extended at independence. The laws currently in force are based upon the fundamental principle of the right of peoples to self-determination and to dispose of their natural wealth and resources.

51. Only recently, this principle was reaffirmed by the 1989 Constitution which underlines, in its Preamble, that "the history of the Algerian people is a long series of battles which have made Algeria forever a country of freedom and dignity", and that:

> "its faith in the collective choices has enabled the Algerian people to achieve decisive victories, marked by the recovery of national wealth and the construction of a State designed exclusively to serve the people, exercising its powers in full independence and free from any external pressure. Having always fought for freedom and democracy, the people intend, through this Constitution, to establish institutions that are based on the participation of citizens in the conduct of public affairs

> and make social justice, equality and the liberty of each and every one a reality ... . Strong in its deeply-rooted spiritual values and its traditions of solidarity and justice, the people are confident of their ability to work fully for the cultural, social and economic progress of the world now and in the future".

The Constitution further states Algeria "is honoured by the influence of its revolution of 1 November and the respect which the country has gained and preserved because of its commitment to all the just causes of the world".

52. Article 6 of the Constitution states that the people are the source of all power and that national sovereignty belongs to the people; article 8 proclaims that the people shall establish institutions whose objective is to safeguard and consolidate national independence, protect the fundamental freedoms of the citizen, and promote the social and cultural development of the Nation and the national economy. Article 9 states that the institutions forbid, *inter alia*, "the establishment of relations of exploitation and bonds of dependency". Article 24 provides that "The National People's Army has a permanent mission to safeguard national independence and to defend national sovereignty". Article 25 states that "Algeria pledges to refrain from resorting to war to violate the legitimate sovereignty or liberty of other peoples", and that "it will endeavour to settle international disputes by peaceful means". Article 26 stipulates that "Algeria declares its solidarity with all peoples fighting for political and economic liberation, for the right of self-determination and against all racial discrimination". Article 27 declares that "Algeria will work to reinforce international cooperation and to develop friendly relations between States on the basis of equality, mutual interest and non-interference in internal affairs. It subscribes to the principles and objectives of the Charter of the United Nations".

Article 2, paragraph 1: Guarantee of the rights recognized in the Covenant

53. Under article 2, paragraph 1, each State party undertakes to respect and to ensure to all individuals within its territory and subject to its jurisdiction the rights recognized in the Covenant without discrimination of any kind. As stated earlier, one of the first measures taken by Algeria on attaining independence was to eliminate from national legislation all laws or regulations inherited from its colonial past which were considered racist and discriminatory. The country subsequently passed a new set of laws which cover all areas of political, economic, social and cultural life and are in full compliance with the fundamental principle of non-discrimination and respect for human rights. Respect and guarantees for human rights are written into the Algerian Constitution, an entire chapter of which is devoted to these rights. Article 28 stipulates that "Citizens are equal before the law, and there shall be no discrimination on grounds of birth, race, sex, opinion or any other personal or social condition or circumstance". Article 64 provides that "Any alien lawfully present in the national territory shall enjoy the protection of the law for the purposes of his person and his property".

Article 2, paragraph 2: Obligation to incorporate and implement the provisions of the Covenant in domestic legislation

54. Apart from the fact that most of the rights set forth in the Covenant have already been embodied in the Constitution and are incorporated in the national legislation in force, it should be recalled that, under the terms of the Constitution itself, international conventions ratified by Algeria take precedence over the law. The Constitutional Council, by its decision No. 1 of 20 August 1989, deemed that "after ratification and upon publication, every convention shall be incorporated into national law and, pursuant to article 123 of the Constitution, shall acquire a higher authority than that of the laws, and that any Algerian citizen may cite them in the courts. One such example is the case of the United Nations Covenants of 1966, which were adopted by Act No. 89-08 of 25 April 1989 and to which Algeria acceded by Presidential Decree No. 89-67 of 16 May 1989".

Article 2, paragraph 3: Remedies

55. The reader's attention is drawn to the first part of this report entitled "General information", where we dealt with the independence of the judiciary (paras. 24-28) and remedies, in particular public prosecution proceedings, criminal indemnity proceedings, discretionary proceedings and appeals against actions by the public authorities (paras. 36-43).

56. Public prosecution proceedings may be initiated by the government procurator or by the party injured by an infringement who, by lodging a complaint, can initiate proceedings before the competent examining magistrate. Furthermore, when an infringement has been reported to them, the officers of the criminal investigation department, on the instructions of the government procurator or *ex officio*, undertake preliminary inquiries.

57. Anyone who claims to have had his rights violated is entitled to lodge a complaint with the competent courts. The authorities responsible for receiving the complaints are the government procurator and his assistants. The officers of the criminal investigation department are required to inform the government procurator immediately of any offences reported to them. The victims are entitled to lodge a complaint either directly with the government procurator and his assistants or by initiating prosecution proceedings in the competent courts. They are also entitled, by lodging a complaint, to initiate proceedings before the competent examining magistrate. If a plaintiff or his witnesses are in danger, the government procurator and his assistants are required to provide protection for them.

58. Anyone whose rights have been violated may not only institute prosecution proceedings, but may also bring charges. "Criminal indemnity action, in compensation for the damage caused by a serious, ordinary or minor offence, is the right of all those who have personally suffered damage as a result of the infringement" (art. 2 of the Code of Penal Procedure). The criminal indemnity proceedings may be brought at the same time as the prosecution proceedings and before the same court. This court shall be competent, regardless of the natural or legal person under civil law responsible for the damage. Criminal indemnity proceedings are admissible for all types of damages, whether material, corporal or moral, which derive from the act in respect of which

prosecution proceedings have been initiated (art. 3 of the Code of Penal Procedure). The criminal indemnity proceedings may also be brought separately from the prosecution proceedings. The Civil Code provides that anyone who suffers an illegal infringement of rights as a person may demand the cessation of, and compensation for, the damage resulting therefrom (art. 7). A remedy shall be available to the victim even if the violation of a right or freedom was allegedly committed by persons acting in the performance of their official duties.

59. There are thus many legal provisions that prohibit a series of acts of commission or omission or negligence by civil servants or any other public officials which may violate the rights of the individual. A number of non-exhaustive examples taken from the Penal Code may be mentioned:

(a) An entire section is devoted to infringements of freedom. Article 107, for example, stipulates: "When an official has ordered or committed an arbitrary act or an act which infringes either the personal freedom or the civil rights of one or more citizens, he shall be liable to a penalty of long-term rigorous imprisonment for five to ten years". Article 108 reads: "The offences provided for in article 107 render their perpetrator, as well as the State, personally liable, unless action is taken by the latter against the aforesaid perpetrator". Articles 107 to 111 establish penalties for:

(i) Refusal to comply with an application intended to confirm illegal and arbitrary detention (5 to 10 years' imprisonment);

(ii) Reception of a prisoner without the prescribed detention order, or refusal to produce the prisoner or his records to the authorities empowered to visit him (6 months' to 2 years' imprisonment and fine);

(iii) Refusal by any officer of the criminal investigation department to allow the medical examination of a person under police custody (1 to 3 months' imprisonment and/or fine); and

(iv) Torture or ordering torture in order to obtain a confession (6 months' to 3 years' imprisonment).

(b) Another section establishes penalties for the abuse of authority against individuals and the abuse of authority against the State (arts. 135 and 140 of the Penal Code). Thus "Any official of the administrative or judicial branches, any police officer, or any commander or officer of the police or armed forces who, when acting in that capacity, enters the home of a citizen against the latter's will, save in those cases provided for by the law and without the formalities prescribed therein, shall be liable to imprisonment for 2 months to 1 year and a fine of 500 to 3,000 Algerian dinars without prejudice to the application of article 107" (art. 135).

(c) Article 143 provides for heavier penalties for certain serious and ordinary offences committed by civil servants or public officials. It reads: "Except in those cases where the law specifically provides for penalties for serious or ordinary offences committed by civil servants or public officials, if they are involved in other serious or ordinary offences which it is their responsibility to prevent and punish they shall be liable to the following penalties:

- For an ordinary offence, the penalty shall be doubled;

- For a serious offence, the sentences shall be as follows:

  (1) Long-term rigorous imprisonment for 10 to 20 years, if the penalty imposed on any other person guilty of the offence is long-term rigorous imprisonment for 5 to 10 years;

  (2) Life imprisonment if the penalty imposed on any other person guilty of the offence is long-term rigorous imprisonment for 10 to 20 years.

Apart from the cases just listed, the usual penalty shall be applied without increase".

Article 3: Equal rights of men and women

60. Equality of rights for men and women is established as a constitutional principle. Article 28 of the Constitution provides that "Citizens are equal before the law, and there shall be no discrimination on grounds of birth, race, sex, opinion or any other personal or social condition or circumstance". Article 30 adds: "The institutions shall seek to ensure the equality of rights and duties of all male and female citizens by eliminating the obstacles which impede the full development of the human personality and prevent the effective participation of all in political, economic, social and cultural life". Article 31 reads: "The fundamental freedoms and rights of man and the citizen are guaranteed. They constitute the common heritage of all Algerian men and women".

61. National legislation makes no distinction between men and women, who enjoy full equality of rights and duties. Furthermore, Algerian women enjoy specific rights which are expressly guaranteed or protected by the laws in force, such as the Family Code (Act No. 84-11 of 9 June 1984), which governs relations between members of the family. Algerian women have the right to acquire, administer, enjoy, dispose of or inherit goods acquired during marriage, and may dispose of them in the same way as men. Married women enjoy the rights and obligations in respect of ownership, administration and disposal of their personal property during marriage and on its dissolution. There is no universal or other community of property regime in Algeria. The goods owned by the woman at the time of her marriage, and any gifts, bequests or inheritance received by her before or after the marriage continue to be her exclusive property. She alone administers the proceeds of her work or occupation, and the husband may intervene to administer the proceeds of his wife's work only if the latter expressly authorizes him to do so. The law stresses the need for mandatory maintenance of the wife and even establishes penalties, including imprisonment, in the event of infringement of this obligation (art. 36 of the Family Code). Orders issued by the courts with respect to maintenance are enforceable, appeals notwithstanding, and without bond.

62. Algerian women have the same rights as men under civil law. They have the same legal capacity as men and freely exercise this capacity. Article 45 of the Civil Code stipulates that "No one may renounce his capacity or modify its conditions". Like men, Algerian women are included on jury lists drawn up during the last quarter of each year for the following year (art. 264 of the Code of Penal Procedure). They may therefore sit on a criminal court as sworn jurors.

63. Algerian women may vote and stand for election under the same conditions as those prescribed for men and are entitled to participate in the conduct of public affairs, sit in parliament and in departmental or local assemblies, hold positions in the civil service and be appointed to senior positions in government. They take an active part in the political, economic, social and cultural life of the country.

64. Algerian women may also enter all categories of educational establishments, including universities and vocational and technical institutions on the same basis as men. The curricula and examinations set are the same for all. Women have the same opportunities as men for obtaining scholarships. Adult women have equal access to literacy programmes.

65. There is no provision in the Algerian Penal Code or Civil Code which discriminates between men and women. Furthermore, in the interest of society in general and women in particular, Algerian legislation, in particular Ordinance No. 66/156 of 8 June 1966, which establishes the Penal Code, tries to combat the phenomenon of prostitution by severely punishing the incitement of minors to vice, soliciting and incitement to prostitution (arts. 342 to 349 of the Penal Code).

Article 4: States of emergency

66. In the event of exceptional public danger threatening the existence of the nation, the Algerian Constitution provides for a series of measures in article 86 (state of emergency and state of siege) and article 87 (state of exception). A state of emergency or state of exception is decreed, for a specific period, in the event of compelling necessity, by the President of the Republic after consultation with the Head of Government and the President of the Constitutional Council, in accordance with article 86 of the Constitution: "In the event of compelling necessity, the High Council of Security being assembled and having consulted the President of the National People's Assembly, the Head of Government and the President of the Constitutional Council, the President of the Republic shall decree a state of emergency or a state of siege for a specified period, and shall take all necessary measures for the re-establishment of the situation. The duration of the state of emergency or the state of siege may not be extended without the approval of the National People's Assembly".

67. A state of emergency is decreed, if the country is threatened by imminent peril, by the President of the Republic after consultation with the Constitutional Council and the consent of the High Council of Security and the Council of Ministers. The National People's Assembly meets as a matter of right. The High Council of Security is a body that was established on the basis of article 162 of the Constitution and is responsible for advising the

0058

President of the Republic on all questions relating to national security. Article 87 of the Constitution regarding the state of emergency reads as follows: "Whenever the country is threatened by imminent peril to its institutions, its independence or its territorial integrity, the President of the Republic shall decree a state of emergency. This measure shall be taken in consultation with the Constitutional Council and with the consent of the High Council of Security and the Council of Ministers. The state of emergency empowers the President of the Republic to take the exceptional measures required in order to safeguard the independence of the Nation and the institutions of the Republic. The National People's Assembly shall meet as a matter of right. The state of emergency shall be terminated in the same manner and in accordance with the same procedures as stipulated above for its proclamation."

68. The constitutional provisions concerning the states of emergency, siege and exception are in complete conformity with the provisions of article 4. In a situation of a state of emergency or siege, which must be decreed in the manner prescribed, the President of the Republic takes the necessary measures for the re-establishment of the situation and may not extend the state of emergency or siege without the approval of Parliament. In a situation of exception which can be decreed, in the manner prescribed, only in the event of imminent peril threatening the institutions, independence and territorial integrity of the country, the President of the Republic takes the exceptional measures required in order to safeguard the Nation and the institutions of the Republic.

69. The power which the Algerian Constitution confers upon the President of the Republic to "take all necessary measures for the re-establishment of the situation" and the "exceptional measures required in order to safeguard the independence of the Nation and the institutions of the Republic" cannot be limited by a restrictive interpretation of the terms "to the extent strictly required by the exigencies of the situation". Algeria recognizes that these measures must not be incompatible with the other international obligations which it has undertaken, must not be discriminatory and must not derogate from the fundamental rights of the human being referred to in article 4, paragraph 2 (right to life; prohibition of torture, slavery, servitude, imprisonment merely on the ground of inability to fulfil a contractual obligation; non-retroactivity of criminal law; right to legal personality; freedom of thought, conscience and religion).

70. Since ratifying the Covenant, Algeria has not decreed a state of siege, emergency or exception. It considers itself bound by the provisions of article 4, paragraph 3, of the Covenant, which requires that States parties shall notify the Secretary-General of the United Nations of any exceptional measures they have been called upon to take.

<u>Article 5</u>

71. The 1989 Constitution broadens the scope and exercise of human rights and freedoms. Their applicability derives directly from the Constitution, which subjects their exercise to legal restriction only in very few cases. The first part of this report showed that the Constitution devotes an entire chapter to rights and freedoms, which are set out in some 30 articles.

In Algeria, the rights recognized by the Covenant enjoy the status of constitutional principles, from which no derogation is possible by treaty, law or regulation, under penalty of unconstitutionality. We have also stressed that the Constitutional Council ensures that laws comply with the Constitution: when the Council considers a legislative provision or regulation to be unconstitutional, it ceases to have effect from the day of the Council's decision. Similarly, if it considers a treaty, agreement or convention to be unconstitutional, it may not be ratified.

72. From the above, it is clear that an international convention or law may neither allow derogation from the basic principles enshrined in the Constitution nor restrict the exercise of the rights and freedoms defined therein. Moreover, national legislation is required to comply with the international obligations entered into by Algeria, all the more so since treaties ratified by Algeria form an integral part of domestic law and take precedence over the law.

73. Algeria has unreservedly subscribed to the provisions of article 5, paragraph 2, under which there must be no restriction upon, or derogation from, any of the fundamental rights recognized in Algeria pursuant to laws, conventions, regulations or custom on the pretext that the Covenant does not recognize such rights or that it recognizes them to a lesser extent.

74. As regards the obligation for the State, groups or persons to refrain from any activity or act aimed at the destruction of the rights and freedoms recognized in the Covenant, it is important to note that the Algerian Constitution adopts a similar principle by stipulating as follows: (i) The institutions shall seek to ensure the equality of rights and duties of all male and female citizens (art. 30); (ii) The right to establish political associations is recognized. However, this right may not be invoked in order to violate fundamental freedoms (art. 40); (iii) Every citizen shall loyally fulfil his obligations towards the national community (art. 59); (iv) All personal freedoms shall be exercised with due respect for the rights to which others are entitled under the Constitution (art. 60).

75. The Penal Code punishes acts that infringe the rights and freedoms of others (serious and ordinary offences against the public interest and against the Constitution, including electoral offences, infringements of liberty, abuse of authority against individuals and against the public interest, insulting behaviour and violence against officials, usurpation and improper use of office, serious and ordinary offences against individuals, including capital offences, torture and other intentional violence, infringements of personal freedom and of inviolability of the home, abduction; damage to the honour and reputation of persons and violation of secrecy; exposure and neglect of children or legally incompetent persons; serious and ordinary offences designed to prevent identification of children, kidnapping and failure to speak for minors; immoral acts; inciting minors to vice, and prostitution, etc.).

76. Various other provisions of sectoral laws establish the duty to respect the rights of others. The following examples, which are not exhaustive, may be cited:

(a) The Political Associations Act (No. 89-11 of 5 July 1989) stipulates that any association must by its aims contribute to consolidation of the sovereignty of the people and of respect for their freedom of choice, to safeguarding the republican character of the State and the fundamental freedoms of citizens, to respect for the democratic system, etc.

(b) The Information Act makes it mandatory for journalists strictly to observe professional ethics. They are required in particular to respect the constitutional rights and personal freedoms of citizens and to refrain from justifying, either directly or indirectly, racism, intolerance or violence.

(c) The Public Meetings and Demonstrations Act stipulates that public meetings are free. Those responsible for the meeting are, however, required to ensure that it takes place in an orderly fashion and in compliance with the law, and that the constitutional rights of citizens are respected.

Article 6: Right to life; capital punishment

77. The right to life, which is the basis of all human rights, is enshrined in articles 33 and 34 of the Constitution. Although the death penalty is indeed the maximum sentence laid down by article 5 of the Algerian Penal Code, it should be noted that it is only exceptionally carried out in Algeria, and that it is intended to have a deterrent effect. Cases in which it has been carried out have involved crimes of violence committed under aggravating circumstances, and in particular crimes against children.

78. Amnesty is a prerogative under the law, as specified in article 115, paragraph 7, of the Constitution:

> "The National People's Assembly shall legislate in the areas assigned to it by the Constitution: general rules of criminal law and criminal procedure and, in particular, the determination of serious and ordinary offences, the application of the corresponding penalties of any kind, amnesty and extradition".

79. Furthermore, the President of the Republic has the right to grant a pardon and to reduce or commute a sentence (art. 74, para. 8, of the Constitution). The right of pardon has frequently been exercised by the President for the benefit of convicted persons who have applied for it. Decrees granting pardon are also issued by the President on the occasion of major national events.

80. As far as criminal liability is concerned under article 50 of the Penal Code the death sentence is not imposed on minors aged between 13 and 18: "If a minor is liable to the death penalty or life imprisonment, he shall be sentenced to 10 to 20 years' imprisonment". Pursuant to article 49 of the Code, "a minor aged under 13 may be subjected only to protective measures or re-education measures".

81. In Algiera, the death sentence is not carried out on pregnant women. Article 16 of the Prison Organization Code provides for the deferment of penal sentences imposed, in particular, on "pregnant women or the mothers of children aged under 24 months". Article 197 of the same Code stipulates that "The

death penalty may only be carried out after an appeal for pardon has been rejected. The death penalty may not be carried out in the case of a pregnant woman or a woman nursing a child aged under 24 months, or a seriously ill convicted prisoner or one who has become insane. Executions may not be carried out on national or religious holidays, on a Friday or during the period of Ramadan".

82. Decree No. 72-38 of 10 February 1972 determines the manner in which the death sentence is carried out. The person under sentence of death must be informed of the rejection of his application for pardon at the time of his execution, which shall not be public. Any person sentenced to death is entitled to the support of a minister of his religion and to the presence of a doctor. A record of the execution of the death penalty is drawn up on the spot by the court clerk and signed by the magistrates attending the execution.

83. The death penalty may be carried out only by virtue of a final judgement handed down by a criminal court with jurisdiction over acts classified as serious offences, and over ordinary and minor offences associated with them, for which a final committal order has been issued by the indictment division. Application for judicial review may be made against the orders of the indictment division and the judgements of the criminal court.

84. Within the Ministry of Justice, a commission is responsible for revising the Penal Code. It has begun consideration of the question of the death penalty. It would appear from the Committee's consultations that opinion is in favour of the abolition of the death penalty for economic offences. One of the first results of its work has been the abolition of the economic section of the criminal court (Act No. 90-24 of 28 August 1990 amending the Code of Penal Procedure).

85. Algeria is a party to the Convention on the Prevention and Punishment of the Crime of Genocide, which it ratified on 31 October 1963, and subscribes to the provisions of article 6, paragraph 3, of the Covenant, under which nothing in the article authorizes any State party to derogate in any way from any obligation assumed under the provisions of that Convention.

<u>Article 7: Prohibition of torture</u>

86. In Algeria, the prohibition of torture is a constitutional principle, and various legal and other measures have been adopted fully to enforce this prohibition in law and in practice. Furthermore, Algeria is a party to numerous international instruments, including the African Charter on Human Rights and Peoples' Rights, the 1966 Covenants, the International Convention on the Elimination of All Forms of Racial Discrimination, the Geneva Conventions of 1949 - which contain specific provisions against torture and ill-treatment, and the International Convention against Torture and Other Cruel, Inhuman or Degrading Treatment or Punishment. Algeria has made no reservations to the latter Convention and has recognized in full the competence of the Committee against Torture. It submitted its initial report in February 1991.

87. All laws and regulations derive their inspiration from this principle of the total prohibition of torture and respect for the dignity and physical and moral integrity of the human personality. Acts of torture are criminal offences. No legal provision authorizes a State official to order or carry out acts of torture or other forms of violence or ill-treatment. Furthermore, the Penal Code and various sectoral laws such as the Prison Organization and Rehabilitation Code punish and/or prohibit abuses of authority as well as violations of human freedom of dignity (see below, comments on arts. 15 and 16). The objective of current legislation is to forestall and prevent any act of torture. It has recently been amended (see relevant observations in the first part of this report) so as to increase measures for the protection of human rights.

88. The Penal Code punishes acts of torture and other forms of violence and ill-treatment. Articles 254 to 280 of the Code provide for the punishment of murder and other capital offences and intentional acts of violence; acts of torture constitute a capital offence that carries the death penalty. Article 261 establishes the death penalty for anyone guilty of homicide, while article 262 stipulates that "Any offender, regardless of the nature of the charge against him, who uses torture or commits acts of cruelty in the perpetration of his offence shall be punished as for first-degree murder". Article 255 classifies as first-degree murder any homicide committed with premeditation or in an ambush. Article 257 defines an ambush as "waiting for a person for a long or short period in one or more places for the purpose of either killing him or assaulting him".

89. A series of articles of the Penal Code relate to intentional violence, which is punished by appropriate penalties. Article 264 relating to injury, striking and wounding, or other violence or assault causing illness or more than 15 days' incapacity for work calls for a sentence of from two to five months' imprisonment and a fine. The period of imprisonment may be increased to five years if the violence has involved mutilation, blindness or other infirmity; in the case of accidental homicide, the offender is liable to a prison sentence of 10 to 20 years. Article 265 further increases the penalties in cases of premeditation or ambush. Unintentional violence carries lighter penalties.

90. The Penal Code contains specific provisions punishing persons guilty of violence against minors and of wilfully depriving minors of food or care in such a way as to jeopardize their health (arts. 269 to 272). The penalties are imprisonment for 3 to 20 years, depending on the consequences of the violence or deprivation. The penalty is life imprisonment if the result has been unintentional homicide that is nevertheless attributable to a habitual practice. "If the striking, wounding, violence, assault or deprivation was committed with intent to cause death, the offender shall be punished as for murder or attempted murder" (art. 271).

91. Article 274 prescribes a sentence of life imprisonment for anyone guilty of castration. If death has resulted therefrom, the offender is punishable by death. The Penal Code also establishes penalties for the administration of substances that are harmful to health (arts. 275 and 276) and for threats (arts. 284 *et seq.*). A section of the Code is devoted to infringements of personal freedom, the inviolability of the home and abduction. Various

articles concern kidnapping and sequestration (arts. 291 and 292). If the victim of the kidnapping, arrest, detention or sequestration has been physically tortured, the offender is liable to the death sentence (art. 293).

92. The Penal Code also prescribes punishment for damage to a person's honour or reputation (damage to honour, injurious behaviour, defamation, etc.), as well as for exposure and neglect of children or legally incompetent persons, kidnapping and failure to speak for minors, abandonment of the family and immoral acts. Thus, rape is punishable by 5 to 10 years' imprisonment. This penalty may be increased to 10 to 20 years if the rape has been committed against a girl aged under 16. If the rapist is a relative of the victim or a person with authority over her, this constitutes a further aggravating circumstance.

93. Medical ethics are governed by Act No. 90-17 of 31 July 1990, which amends and supplements the Health Protection and Promotion Act (No. 85-05 of 16 February 1985). Pursuant to article 168/1, the National Ethical Council of Health Sciences is "responsible for providing guidance and issuing views and recommendations on the removal of tissues or organs, transplants and experiments involving organs, as well as any other therapeutic methods required by the development of medical techniques and scientific research, while ensuring respect for the life of human beings and the protection of their physical integrity and dignity ...". Article 168/2 stipulates that "Experiments on human beings for the purposes of scientific research shall comply with the moral and scientific principles governing the exercise of medicine. It shall require the free and informed consent of the subject or, failing that, of his legal representative. Such consent shall be required at all times".

Article 8: Prohibition of slavery, servitude and forced or compulsory labour

94. Slavery, servitude and forced or compulsory labour are alien to Algerian society. As soon as Algeria became independent, all laws that might constitute a violation of human rights were repealed. National labour law was developed in accordance with the relevant international standards, with the welfare of workers as its objective.

95. Algeria is a party to the international conventions prohibiting slavery, servitude, forced or compulsory labour or other similar practices, and in particular the following: the 1949 Convention for the Suppression of the Traffic in Persons and of the Exploitation of the Prostitution of Others; the 1926 Geneva Convention; the Supplementary Convention on the Abolition of Slavery, the Slave Trade, and Institutions and Practices Similar to Slavery; the 1921 Convention for the Suppression of the Trade in Women and Children; the 1933 Convention for the Suppression of the Trade in Adult Women, as amended in 1947; the International Convention for the Suppression of the White Slave Trade; the International Convention on the Elimination of All Forms of Racial Discrimination; the International Convention on the Suppression and Punishment of the Crime of Apartheid; and the International Convention against Apartheid in Sports.

96. Algeria is a party to a number of International Labour Organisation conventions, including the following: Convention No. 29 on Forced Labour (1930); Convention No. 87 on Freedom of Association and Protection of the Right to Organize (1948); Convention No. 98 on the Right to Organize and Collective Bargaining (1949); Convention No. 100 on Equal Remuneration (1951); Convention No. 105 on the Abolition of Forced Labour (1957); and Convention No. 111 on Discrimination in respect of Employment and Occupation (1958).

97. In addition to these conventions, which now form an integral part of Algerian substantive law, a number of legal measures have been adopted in order to ensure respect for human rights and freedoms, in accordance with these international standards which are henceforth complied with in Algeria. The Constitution contains a number of articles prohibiting the exploitation of human beings and underscoring the purpose of institutions to promote their fulfilment (arts. 8, para. 4, 28, 30 to 32, 34, etc.). The Algerian Penal Code, in particular articles 291 to 295, devotes special attention to the punishment of any act intended to jeopardize the personal liberty of citizens. Articles 321 and 326 to 330 are more particularly designed to protect minors.

98. As far as the suppression of the trade in human beings and the exploitation of prostitution are concerned, Algerian legislation contains a set of measures designed to eradicate such practices by focusing on their causes and consequences. Algerian criminal law focuses in particular on the suppression of the trade in human beings and the exploitation of prostitution; it contains specific articles to punish the incitement of minors to vice and soliciting. Article 96 of the Algerian Civil Code stipulates that "The contract shall be null and void if its purpose is contrary to public order and morals", while article 97 provides that "The contract shall be null and void if it entails unjustified obligations or obligations contrary to public order or morals". Article 46 reads: "No one may renounce his personal freedom".

99. Rehabilitation measures for the victims of prostitution by the Ministries of Justice and Health, which have established several specialized departments to assist the following groups: young women convicted of prostitution, if the judge decides to place them in an institution; potential victims of sexual deviance who seek help; young women placed in institutions to remove them from the consequences of prostitution or sexual deviation; young women who, after investigation, prove to have been, or are liable to be, victims of sexual deviance. These institutions provide social, health, psychological and educational care for the internees, while ensuring their vocational rehabilitation so as to enable them to resume normal life in society.

Article 9: Liberty and security of person

Article 9, paragraph 1

100. Individuals are entitled to liberty and security of person, and no one in Algeria may be arbitrarily arrested or detained. Persons may be arrested or detained only in the manner, on grounds and under the conditions laid down by law. Persons who fail to comply with these requirements are liable to criminal prosecution, even if they commit the violations of the law in the performance

0065

of their duties. Article 44 of the Constitution stipulates that "No one may be prosecuted, arrested or detained except in the cases determined by law and in accordance with the procedures prescribed thereby". And, moreover, the Constitution directly governs the regime of police custody and subjects it to judicial control. Under article 45 of the Constitution, a person held in police custody is entitled immeditely to contact his family and to be examined by a doctor of his choice. The Constitution furthermore stresses that detention in police custody is exceptional in character and may not be extended otherwise than as prescribed by law. The recent reform of the Code of Penal Procedure has made it possible to reinforce the safeguards surrounding detention in police custody (see below).

101. A whole section of the Penal Code is devoted to violations of personal freedom, the inviolability of the home, abduction, kidnapping and sequestration. Article 291 establishes penalities for kidnapping, arbitrary detention or sequestration in the following terms:

> "Any person who kidnaps, arrests, detains or sequesters another person without an order from the established authorities, except in those cases authorized or ordered by law, shall be sentenced to rigorous imprisonment for 5 to 10 years. The same penalty shall apply to any person who allows a place to be used in order to detain or sequester the other person. If the detention or sequestration has continued for more than a month, the penalty shall be 10 to 20 years' imprisonment."

It should be noted that the wording of this article in no way makes it possible to justify such acts by an order received, as the conditions laid down are cumulative: individuals may not be arrested without an order from the established authorities or in circumtances other than those allowed by law.

> "If the arrest or kidnapping has been carried out by a person or persons wearing an official uniform or insignia or items that appear to be official under the terms of article 346, or using a false identity or a false order from the authorities, the penalty shall be life imprisonment. The same penalty shall apply if the arrest or kidnapping has been carried out using motor transport or if the victim has been threatened with death" (art. 292).

> "If the victim of the kidnapping, arrest, detention or sequestration has been physically tortured, the offenders shall be liable to the death penalty" (art. 293).

> "Any person who, through the use of violence, threats of fraud, kidnaps another person or causes another person to be kidnapped, regardless of that person's age, shall be sentenced to from 10 to 20 years' rigorous imprisonment. If the victim has been physically tortured, the offender shall be liable to the death penalty. If the purpose of the kidnapping was to obtain payment of a ransom, the offender shall also be liable to the death penalty" (art. 293 bis).

The Penal Code also establishes penalties for violations of freedom committed by persons in the performance of their duties (see above, comments on art. 2, in particular para. 59).

101 *bis*. The Prison Organization and Rehabilitation Code (Ordinance No. 72-2 of 10 February 1972) stipulates: "Sentences in criminal proceedings may be executed only when the judgement has become final" (art. 8); "For a custodial penalty to be enforced, a copy of the judgement or decision shall be drawn up in order that the sentenced prisoner may be admitted to prison" (art. 11); "Every penal establishment shall keep a prison register" (art. 13); and "No official responsible for the re-education and social rehabilitation of prisoners may, under penalty of prosecution for arbitrary detention, detain a person without a proper detention order or a definitive sentence, previously recorded in the prison register referred to in the preceding article" (art. 14).

102. Article 110 of the Penal Code establishes penalties for arbitrary detention in the following terms:

> "Any rehabilitation official in a prison establishment or in premises in which detainees are held who has accepted a prisoner without a lawful committal order, or has refused, without such refusal being justified by a prohibition order from the examining magistrate, to present the prisoner to the authorities or to persons authorized to visit him, or has refused to present his records to the said authorized person is guilty of arbitrary detention and is liable to six months' to two years' imprisonment and a fine of 500 to 1,000 dinars."

Article 9, paragraph 2

103. The procedural rules relating to arrest are set out in articles 109 to 122 of the Code of Penal Procedure, which deal with judicial warrants and their execution:

> "The examining magistrate may, as appropriate, issue an arrest warrant, a detention warrant or an arrest and detention warrant.
>
> "Every mandate shall specify the nature of the charge and the relevant articles of the law. It shall specify the identity of the accused; it shall be dated and signed by the issuing magistrate and shall bear his stamp. Warrants issued by him shall be countersigned by the government procurator and transmitted by him" (art. 109).
>
> "The arrest warrant is the order from the judge to the police immediately to bring the accused before him. The warrant is served and enforced by an officer of the criminal investigation department or by an ordinary police officer, who shall serve the warrant on the accused and provide him with a copy thereof. The government procurator may issue an arrest warrant" (art. 110).

Article 9, paragraph 3

104. Any person arrested or detained for a criminal offence must be brought before the examining magistrate as quickly as possible and must be immediately questioned. It should be mentioned that the Code of Penal Procedure was amended by Act No. 90/24 of 18 August 1990 in order to provide accused persons with greater guarantees. Thus the former article 112 of the Code read:

0067

"The accused, having been brought before the examining magistrate pursuant to an arrest warrant, shall be immediately questioned. If it is impossible to carry out this examination immediately, he shall be transferred to a prison establishment, in which he may not be detained more than 48 hours. When this period has expired, and if he has still not been examined, he shall be automatically brought by the chief of the prison establisment before the government procurator, who shall require the magistrate responsible for the examination or, in his absence, any other magistrate immediately to carry out the examination, failing which the accused shall be released."

This article has been amended to read:

"The accused, having been brought before the examining magistrate pursuant to an arrest warrant, shall be immediately questioned, in the presence of his counsel. If it is impossible to carry out this examination immediately, he shall be brought before the government procurator, who shall require the magistrate responsible for the examination or, in his absence, any other magistrate immediately to carry out the examination, failing which the accused shall be released."

105. If, for the purposes of the inquiry, the police officer has to detain a person, he "shall immediately inform the government procurator, and the period of detention may not exceed 48 hours. He shall, moreover, be required to provide the detained person with every means to contact his family immediately and directly and receive visits" (Code of Penal Procedure, art. 51, para. 1, as amended). "If there is sufficient serious and consistent evidence on which to charge a person, he shall bring that person before the government procurator and may not keep him in custody for more than 48 hours" (ibid., art. 51, para. 2). "On expiry of the period of custody, the detainee shall undergo a compulsory medical examination, either at his own request or at the request of his counsel or family. The examination shall be carried out by a doctor of his choice. He shall be informed of this right" (ibid., art. 51, para. 4, as amended). Breach of the provisions concerning the duration of police custody shall render the police officer concerned liable to the penalties for arbitrary detention (ibid., art. 51, para. 5). As we have already seen, the above-mentioned guarantees have been made constitutional principles (Constitution, art. 45).

106. In the case of serious offences, the pre-trial proceedings are compulsory (Code of Penal Procedure, art. 66). Pursuant to the law, the examining magistrate carries out all the investigatory acts he deems necessary in order to ascertain the truth. The accused is summoned for questioning and, if he fails to appear, an arrest warrant is issued by the examining magistrate. On the occasion of the first appearance of the accused, the magistrate verifies his identity, and informs him specifically of each of the acts with which he is charged and of his right to remain silent. He also informs him of his right to chose a counsel and, if he fails to do so, the magistrate appoints a counsel *ex officio*, if the accused so requests (ibid., art. 100). "The accused may communicate freely with his counsel from the moment he is detained. The examining magistrate has the right to prohibit communication for a period of 10 days. In no circumstances may this prohibition apply to the counsel of the accused" (ibid., art. 102, as amended).

0068

107. The execution of judicial warrants is protected by guarantees as established in articles 109 to 122 of the Code of Penal Procedure. Accordingly,

> "The accused, having been brought before the examining magistrate pursuant to an arrest warrant, shall be immediately questioned, in the presence of his counsel. If it is impossible to carry out this examination immediately, he shall be brought before the government procurator, who shall require the magistrate responsible for the examination or in his absence, any other magistrate immediately to carry out the examination, failing which the accused shall be released" (ibid., art. 112, as amended).

Any accused person arrested pursuant to an arrest warrant who is held for more than 48 hours in a local prison without having been examined shall be deemed to be arbitrarily detained. Any magistrate or official who has ordered or knowingly tolerated such detention shall be liable to the penalties established by the provisions relating to arbitrary detention (ibid., art. 113). The examining magistrate may issue a detention warrant only after the accused has been questioned and if the offence carries a correctional penalty of imprisonment or other more serious penalty (ibid., art. 118). The suspect is examined within 48 hours of his being placed in detention. Failing this, and on expiry of this period, the provisions of articles 112 and 113 apply (ibid., art. 121).

108. Pre-trial detention is an exceptional measure. Article 123, as amended, of the Code of Penal Procedure clearly establishes this principle and adds:

> "However, if the obligations relating to judicial control are inadequate, pre-trial detention may be ordered or maintained in the following circumstances:
>
> (1) If it is the only means of preserving the proof or material evidence or of preventing pressure from being exerted on witnesses or victims, or of preventing collusion between the suspects and their accessories which might hamper the discovery of the truth;
>
> (2) If it is necessary to protect the suspect, to put an end to the offence or to prevent its repetition;
>
> (3) If the suspect wilfully fails to comply with his obligations arising from the judicial control ordered."

Pre-trial detention may not exceed 20 days in the case of an ordinary offence (Code of Penal Procedure, art. 124) and 4 months in other cases (art. 125). It may be extended only once, by a substantiated order from the examining magistrate, if the maximum penalty laid down by the law is more than three years' imprisonment, and twice in the case of a serious offence. Neither extension may exceed four months (art. 125).

109. Flagrante delicto is governed by articles 59, 338 and 339 of the Code of Penal Procedure. It cannot apply to press and political offences, as stated in article 59, which adds:

"In cases involving *flagrante delicto* and if the offender cannot provide satisfactory guarantees as regards representation where the offence carries a prison sentence, and if the examining magistrate has not yet been seized, the government procurator shall issue a detention warrant against the offender after having questioned him about his identity and about the acts of which he is suspected. He shall immediately seize the court in accordance with *flagrante delicto* procedure. The case shall be heard within eight days of issue of the detention warrant."

Article 338 stipulates as follows:

"A person brought before the court under *flagrante delicto* procedure shall be informed by the presiding judge that he is entitled to request a period in which to prepare his defence; a record of his having been so informed and of his reply shall be entered in the judgement. If the accused makes use of this right, the court shall grant him a period of at least three days."

If the case is not ready to be heard, the court orders it to be deferred to a subsequent hearing for further information to be gathered and, if appropriate, grants the accused pre-trial release, with or without security (art. 339).

110. Judicial control may be ordered by the examining magistrate if the accused is liable to a penalty of ordinary imprisonment or a more serious penalty. The magistrate decides the control measures to which the accused may be subjected, the measures being restricted to those set out in the amended article 125 *bis* of the Code of Penal Procedure. The magistrate may, if he has reasonable grounds, add or modify one of the obligations set out in this article.

111. In every case, whenever pre-trial release is not automatic, it may be ordered *ex officio* by the examining magistrate, after consultation with the government procurator. The accused is required to undertake to attend all the procedural acts and to keep the examining magistrate informed of his whereabouts. The government procurator may also apply for it at any time. The examining magistrate is required to take a decision within 48 hours of the date of the application, failing which the accused is immediately released (Code of Penal Procedure, art. 126).

Article 9, paragraph 4

112. Any person deprived of his liberty is entitled to apply for a remedy to a court, which must decide without delay on the lawfulness of the person's detention and order his release if the detention is unlawful. Arbitrary detention and infringements of rights and freedoms are punished by the Penal Code (see above). Any victim of such violations of the law may bring a criminal indemnity action for the injury suffered and/or initiate prosecution proceedings for the enforcement of the penalties laid down by the Penal Code. Moreover, throughout his period of detention and at every stage of the proceedings against him, remedies are available to a victim whereby he may safeguard or restore his rights.

113. It is appropriate to recall the provisions of the Code of Penal Procedure described above under which police officers are required to allow a person held in police custody to undergo a medical examination at his own request, or at the request of his counsel or family, and in any case to inform him of his right to make such a request and to be examined by a doctor of his choice. Every police officer is also required to draw up a record of statement as prescribed by law, which shall be signed by the person concerned or indicate his refusal to sign. The statement must in particular indicate the date and time on which the person held in custody was either released or brought before the competent magistrate (art. 52). All records or reports have probative value only if they are correct as to form and if their author has acted in the performance of his duties and has reported on a matter within his competence which he has personally seen, heard or observed. The victim may also invoke nullity of the information. Articles 157 and 161 of the Code of Penal Procedure deal with this question. Thus the requirements concerning interrogation of the accused and hearing of any claim for indemnification must be observed under pain of nullity of both the act itself and the subsequent proceedings. There is also nullity if the rights of the defence or of any party in the case have been violated. A party may always refrain from invoking nullity that has been declared in his own interest. Such a waiver must be explicit.

114. The indictment division closely monitors pre-trial detention. Thus the president of the division may require any necessary explanations from the examining magistrate regarding pre-trial detention; he may visit any prison establishment within the court's competence to ascertain the conditions in which an accused person is detained. If the detention appears unlawful, he makes the necessary observations to the examining magistrate. He may seize the indictment division in order that it may decide whether to keep an accused person in detention (Code of Penal Procedure, arts. 204 and 205). The indictment division also monitors the activities of police officers. It may be seized, either by the procurator-general or by its president, of any reported lapses by officers in the performance of their duties. It may take action of its own motion, on examination of the proceedings submitted to it (ibid., arts. 206 and 207). It orders an inquiry and may, without prejudice to any disciplinary or penal sanctions, address comments to the police officer or decide to suspend or dismiss him (ibid., arts. 208 to 211).

115. Any accused person may apply for the lifting of judicial control and pre-trial release. Judicial control may be lifted by the magistrate ex officio, on the application of the government procurator or at the request of the accused, subject to approval by the government procurator. The examining magistrate must take a decision on the accused's application within 15 days, failing which the accused or the government procurator may directly seize the indictment division, which must decide within 30 days of being seized (Code of Penal Procedure, art. 125, para. 2, as amended). Pre-trial release may be ordered ex officio by the magistrate or be applied for by the government procurator; a request may be made by the accused or his counsel to the examining magistrate at any stage in the proceedings (ibid., arts. 126 and 127). In the latter case, the examining magistrate must take a decision, by a specially substantiated order, within 10 days following the date of the communication to the government procurator. If the examining magistrate fails to take a decision within this time-limit, the accused may directly seize the indictment division with his application, and the division

is required to take a decision on the basis of the written and substantiated submissions of the government procurator within 30 days of the application, failing which the accused is automatically granted pre-trial release, unless verification has been ordered in connection with his application. The government procurator also has the right to seize the indictment division under the same conditions. A further application by the accused or by his counsel for pre-trial release may only be made one month after his previous application has been turned down (ibid., art. 127).

116. If a trial court is seized, it is responsible for taking a decision on pre-trial release. When the court takes a decision relating to an application for such release, an appeal must be made within 24 hours of its decision. The accused is kept in detention until a decision has been made on the appeal by the government procurator's office, and in all cases until expiry of the deadline for the appeal, unless the procurator agrees to immediate release. Prior to transfer to the criminal court and during the period between that court's sessions, this power is exercised by the indictment division. In the case of an application for judicial review and until the supreme court has passed judgement, a decision relating to the application for pre-trial release is taken by the court which last dealt with the merits of the case. If the review application has been made against a decision of the criminal court, a decision on detention is made, within 45 days, by the division of the Supreme Court dealing with the application, failing which the accused is automatically granted pre-trial release, unless verification has been ordered relating to his application. Should the court declare itself incompetent, and in general in all cases in which no court has been seized, the indictment division deals with applications for pre-trial release (Code of Penal Procedure, art. 128).

Article 9, paragraph 5

117. Article 46 of the Constitution stipulates that "Judicial error shall create an entitlement to compensation from the State. The conditions and procedures for compensation shall be determined by law." In addition to the provision for compensation in civil and criminal matters, available to any person who considers that he has been injured, Act No. 86-05 of 4 March 1986, which amended and supplemented the ordinance of 8 June 1966 laying down the Code of Penal Procedure, establishes the possibility for any convicted person whose innocence is established by the Supreme Court to obtain, either himself or through his rightful claimants, damages for the moral and material injury caused by the conviction.

118. The provisions of this Act, which have been incorporated in the Code of Penal Procedure, are as follows:

> "Any accused person who has been acquitted or discharged may request the court by which he was tried to publish the decision in the manner chosen by him" (art. 125, para. 4).
>
> "The decision by the Supreme Court establishing a convicted person's innocence entitles him or his rightful claimants to damages for the moral and material injury caused by his conviction. The application for compensation made by the accused or by his rightful claimants shall be admissible at any stage in the review procedure" (art. 531 *bis*).

0072

"Damages awarded to the victim of a judicial error or to his rightful claimants, the costs of publishing the court's decision and court expenses shall be borne by the State, unless the latter lodges an appeal against the claimant, informant or person whose false testimony led to the conviction.

"If the applicant so requests, the review decision establishing the innocence of the convicted person shall be publicized within the jurisdiction of the court that handed down the conviction, in the commune where the offence was committed, in the commune in which the applicant for review resides and in that in which the victim of the error last resided if he is deceased.

"Similarly, the decision shall also be published in the press in three newspapers chosen by the court that handed down the decision" (art. 531 bis, para. 1).

Article 10: Humane conditions of detention

119. The rules that apply to the treatment of detainees are laid down in: Ordinance No. 72-2 of 10 February 1972 establishing the Prison Organization and Rehabilitation Code; Ordinance No. 72-3 relating to the protection of children and young persons; Decree No. 72-35 of 10 February 1972 establishing a coordinating committee for the promotion of prisoners' rehabilitation and work; Decree No. 72-36 of 10 February 1972 relating to the observation and orientation of prisoners.

120. Furthermore, the Code of Penal Procedure strictly governs pre-trial investigation procedures, search operations, interrogation and inquiry methods, as well as police custody and pre-trial arrangements, and provides safeguards, having regard to the recognized right of the defence (see above, observations on the review of the Code of Penal Procedure, one object of which was to strengthen the right to defence and the safeguards that must be provided in the case of police custody and pre-trial detention). It should be added that article 52 of the Code of Penal Procedure makes it compulsory for all officers of the judicial police "to enter on the record of the statement made by any person held in custody, the length of the questioning they underwent, the rest periods separating the interrogations, and the date and time when the person was either released or brought before the competent judge. This entry must be accompanied, in the margin, by the signature of the person concerned or an indication of his refusal to sign. It must indicate the grounds for the custody. A similar entry must also be made in a special register, numbered and initialled by the government procurator, which must be kept for this purpose in all police or gendarmerie stations where persons may be held in custody".

121. The preamble to the Prison Organization and Rehabilitation Code reasserts Algeria's attachment to respect for individual freedoms and to the principle of the legality of penalties, the upholding and enforcement of which is vested in the judiciary; it also states that, in determining the regulations applicable to the treatment of detainees, it follows the recommendations of the United Nations. In article 1 the Code emphasizes the objective of enforcement of criminal sanctions as a means of defending society but also of

contributing to the re-education of offenders and helping them to readjust in order to return to their place in their family, at work and in society. In article 2, it stipulates that prisoners shall be deprived of the exercise of their rights only in so far as is necessary to achieve the objective of the sentences imposed and in accordance with the law. These provisions ensure the protection of detainees, who are a particularly vulnerable category of persons, against torture and all similar acts and practices or acts of an inhuman, cruel or degrading nature. Other provisions of the Code provide even greater protection, as illustrated below:

(a) Prison organization is based on the principle of the individualization of sentences and of treatment. Accordingly, one national and two regional observation and orientation centres have been established. Prisoners are sent to and classified within prisons on the basis of their penal status, the seriousness of the offence, their age, their personality and the extent to which they have reformed. After their stay in the centre, prisoners are sent either to a closed prison, or to another institution within the progressive system (outside work site; restricted freedom; open prison). The closed prisons include two types of specialized centres, one for women and the other for minors;

(b) The implementation of criminal sanctions may be postponed in certain cases, in particular in the case of a serious illness incompatible with a prison sentence, a death in the family, if the prisoner has to take an important examination or, in the case of the imprisonment of both spouses, if their absence would cause irreparable harm to minor children, if a woman is pregnant or the mother of a child less than two years of age, etc. (Code, art. 16);

(c) In closed regimes, the duration of solitary confinement may not exceed one tenth of the length of the sentence, or three years in the case of persons sentenced to life imprisonment (Code, arts. 35 and 36). Dangerous prisoners may be kept in isolation only by a decision of the visiting magistrate, who shall determine the duration of this measure (Code, art. 37);

(d) The Code devotes a whole section (arts. 41 to 71) to the conditions of detainees and to their rights and duties, providing, in particular, as follows: the right to hygiene and to hygienic buildings and places of detention; the right to free medical assistance; the right to healthy and adequate food; the right to visits (neither a prohibition on communicating nor sanctions of any kind may suppress or restrict the detainee's right freely to communicate with his counsel); his right to correspondence, etc.;

(e) The Code focuses on measures for the rehabilitation and education of detainees: organization of literacy courses, general instruction, vocational training and the possibility of taking higher education courses by correspondence. Diplomas obtained must never mention the fact that the holder is a prisoner. Subject to provisions relating to order or security within prisons, labour legislation on the hours of work, hygiene and security extends to detainees in employment. Furthermore, the working hours and conditions of prison labour used on outside work sites are subject to the legislation applicable to free workers. Specific measures apply to the rehabilitation of minors, who are, moreover, held in specialized centres.

122. It should be added that the Prison Organization and Rehabilitation Code forbids, "under pain of punishment, personnel from the Department of Re-education and Social Rehabilitation of Prisoners and any persons coming into contact with prisoners from taking direct or indirect action vis-à-vis the prisoners in order to influence their defence or choice of counsel" (art. 53). The same Code accords prisoners the right, "in the event of infringement of their rights, to lodge a complaint with the governor. The latter shall examine the complaint, ascertain the accuracy of the allegations made and take appropriate action on it. If the alleged acts constitute a serious or ordinary offence, the governor shall immediately report them to the government procurator in the court within whose jurisdiction his establishment is situated and to the visiting magistrate. Where a prisoner finds that no action has been taken on his application, he shall be authorized to inform the visiting magistrate directly. Prisoners shall also have the right to lodge complaints and submit grievances to the officials and magistrates responsible for making periodic inspections of prisons. The interview shall be held without staff members being present" (art. 63). In practice, representatives of human rights associations (Algerian Human Rights Leagues, national section of Amnesty International, national Anti-Torture Committee) have also been allowed to participate in inspections. The Code further stipulates that prison personnel "may not use force against prisoners except in self-defence, in the event of an attempted escape or violent resistance, or in response to a refusal to carry out orders. If they do resort to force, they may do so only to the extent strictly necessary" (art. 71). The Code adds that prison administration officials and staff "who, through negligence, carelessness or non-observance of regulations, jeopardize the health of prisoners or prison order or security shall be liable to not less than two years' imprisonment" (art. 204).

123. Among the preventive measures which the authorities are endeavouring to promote, attention should be drawn to the importance attached to: conditions of detention in prisons (improvement of conditions, emphasis on the re-education, rehabilitation and social reintegration of prisoners); controls (increase in number of visits to places of detention by authorized magistrates; authorization of prison visits by human rights associations); and the training of prison and police personnel.

Article 11

124. Algeria has no legislative provisions which impose custodial sentences simply because a person is unable to fulfil a contractual obligation, provided that the non-fulfilment was in good faith and not tainted with fraud or fraudulent acts constituting an offence punishable under the Penal Code. Article 1 of this Code states: "There can be no offence or punishment or security measure except as provided by law". In criminal cases, "The execution of sentences to fines, restitution, compensation and costs may be pursued by means of enforcement by committal" (Code of Penal Procedure (CPP), art. 599). Article 100 of this Code stipulates: "However, enforcement by committal may not be ordered or effected, in particular, in the case of a political offence, in respect of an offender aged under 18 years or over 65 years, or a person in debt to his spouse, ascendants, descendants, brothers, sisters, uncle, aunt, nephew of niece or a person related to the same degree". Article 601 states: "Enforcement by committal may not be

0075

effected simultaneously against husband and wife, even for the recovery of sums relating to different convictions". Article 103 reads: "The execution of enforcement by committal shall be suspended for convicted prisoners who give evidence of their insolvency to the government procurator by producing either a certificate of indigence issued by the president of the Communal People's Assembly of their place of residence or a certificate of non-taxation issued by the tax collector of that place". In addition, the arrest of the person liable to enforcement by committal may not be effected until a payment order has remained unpaid for more than 10 days and until an application for imprisonment has been made by the prosecuting party" (art. 604).

125. In civil matters, the Code of Civil Procedure (Ordinance No. 66-154 of 8 June 1966) establishes, in articles 407 to 412, the conditions and procedures for execution of judicial decisions by means of enforcement by committal. Article 407 stipulates that "in cases involving commerce or loans, the execution of orders, judgements or decrees issued as res judicata and carrying a sentence of payment of a principal sum greater than 500 dinars may be pursued through enforcement by committal. However, such enforcement may not be effected until the means of execution provided for in this Code have been exhausted". Furthermore, only persons who prove effective domicile in Algeria may avail themselves of this procedure (art. 408). The plaintiff is required to apply to the presiding judge of the court of the place of execution (art. 410) within three years following the date on which the decision acquired the force of res judicata (art. 409). The judge may not rule on the application until it has been ascertained that the legal formalities relating to the other means of execution have been complied with (art. 410) and "may grant a debtor who is the victim of misfortune and has acted in good faith a time-limit within which to redeem his debt, except with regard to bills of exchange". This time-limit may be up to one year (art. 411). In addition, the above-mentioned provisions of the Code of Penal Procedure which are not incompatible with this provision are applicable.

126. From the foregoing, it should be noted that recourse to enforcement by committal is confined within limits such that in no circumstances may a person be imprisoned solely because he is unable to fulfil a contractual obligation. It may be imposed only on a person who has been lawfully convicted by a judicial decision that has acquired the force of res judicata, once all other means of execution have been exhausted. Suspension of such enforcement is accorded, even in criminal cases, to persons who prove their insolvency. In civil cases, apart from indigence, good faith may constitute a ground for a judge's decision to grant a debtor a time-limit within which to redeem his debt.

Article 12: Liberty of movement and residence; right to leave any country, including one's own; right to enter one's own country

127. Article 41 of the Algerian Constitution provides that "Any citizen in possession of his civil and political rights shall be entitled to choose his place of residence freely and to travel within the national territory. He is guaranteed the right to enter and leave the national territory". Positive Algerian law does not impose limitations on the right of citizens to travel freely throughout the national territory, or on their right freely to choose their place of residence and to leave and enter their country. The

0076

formalities for leaving the national territory comprise only the normal Customs and frontier police controls and possession of a travel document in proper form (valid passport).

128. In criminal cases, offences may carry, in addition to the principal penalties, complementary penalties, including restricted residence or local expulsion. Retricted residence is defined by article 11 of the Penal Code as consisting of "the obligation imposed on a convicted prisoner to remain in a territorial district specified in the verdict. The duration of [restricted residence] may not be greater than five years. The residence obligation takes effect as from the date of expiry of the principal penalty or release of the convicted prisoner. The conviction is notified to the Ministry of the Interior, which may issue temporary authorizations for travel within the national territory". In accordance with article 12 of the Penal Code, local expulsion consists in "forbidding a convicted prisoner to visit certain places. Its duration may not be greater than 5 years in the case of an ordinary offence or 10 years in the case of a serious offence, except where otherwise provided for by law". A local expulsion order must be notified to the prisoner.

129. The Algerian Government, anxious to guarantee the physical and moral security and dignity of its nationals abroad, has concluded with various Governments a number of agreements aimed at regulating the movement, employment and residence of Algerians abroad, on a mutually acceptable basis which ensures their protection and dignity. In no circumstances may an Algerian be arbitrarily deprived of the right to enter his own country.

Article 13: Aliens

130. Article 64 of the Constitution stipulates that "Any alien lawfully present in the national territory shall enjoy the protection of the law for the purposes of his person and his property". Article 65 provides that "No one may be extradited except on the basis of and pursuant to legislation on Extradition". Article 66 emphasizes that in no circumstances may a political refugee who has been lawfully accorded the right of asylum be handed over or extradited. An alien lawfully resident in Algeria may be expelled only in the legal circumstances provided for and with due respect for the rules established by the various international agreements and instruments to which Algeria has acceded. It will be recalled that Algeria is a party to several international conventions on refugees and stateless persons, including the Convention relating to the Status of Refugees, the Convention relating to the Status of Stateless Persons and the OAU Convention Governing the Specific Aspects of Refugee Problems in Africa.

131. Article 5 of the Civil Code stipulates that "The police and security laws are binding on all persons resident within the national territory". The conditions of travel and residence of aliens are governed by Ordinance No. 66-211 of 21 July 1966 relating to the situation of aliens in Algeria, as supplemented by Ordinance No. 67-190 of 27 September 1967 and Ordinance No. 75-80 of 15 December 1975 relating to the enforcement of judicial decisions on local expulsion and restricted residence. These provisions are of a general nature and, as such, are valid for all aliens who have lawfully entered Algeria, without need for recourse to an agreement. In fact, Algeria

0077

has concluded some 30 bilateral mutual judicial assistance agreements, with, *inter alios*, France, Tunisia, Egypt, Mauritania, Belgium, Bulgaria, Poland, Hungary, Romania, Czechoslovakia, Syria, USSR, Yugoslavia, Mali, United Arab Emirates, Niger, Libya, Turkey and Cuba.

132. An alien may be deported only pursuant to a decision taken in conformity with the above-mentioned Ordinance No. 66-211, article 20 of which stipulates that "the expulsion of an alien from the national territory shall be pronounced by an order of the Ministry of the Interior". Deportation may be effected if his presence in Algeria constitutes a threat to public order, if he has been the subject of a judicial decision which has become final and carries a penalty of imprisonment for a serious or ordinary offence, or if he has been refused a residence permit or has had such a permit withdrawn and has not left the national territory within 15 days following the date of notification of that action, has not had that period extended and cannot prove that his delay is attributable to *force majeure*. The deportation order must be notified to the person concerned: an alien who proves that he is unable to leave the national territory may, until such time as he is in a position to comply with the order, be compelled, by decree of the Ministry of the Interior, to reside in a place assigned to him (arts. 12, 20, 21 and 22 of the above-mentioned Ordinance).

133. Article 13 of the same Ordinance establishes the principle that "an alien may reside and travel freely within Algerian territory", subject to the obligation to produce on request by agents of the authorities the evidence or documents authorizing him to reside in Algeria, and to report his domicile or any change of domicile to the police station or *mairie* of his place of residence (arts. 14 and 15).

Article 14: Equality before the courts and right to justice

Article 14, paragraph 1

134. The principle of the equality of all before Algerian courts is established by the Constitution, article 28 of which provides that "Citizens are equal before the law, and there shall be no discrimination on grounds of birth, race, sex, opinion or any other personal or social condition or circumstance". Article 131 stipulates that "Justice is based on the principles of legality and equality. It is equal for all, accessible to all and is manifested in respect for the law". Article 135 provides that "Judicial decisions shall be substantitated and pronounced at a public hearing". Article 138 states that "Judges shall obey only the law" and article 142 recognizes the right of defence, which is guaranteed in criminal cases. The right of access to, and to defend one's case before, a competent, independent and impartial tribunal is provided for in Algerian legislation, in particular in articles 1 to 10 and 72 to 78 of the Code of Penal Procedure and articles 1 to 11 of the Code of Civil Procedure.

135. The question of the public nature of trials is governed by various provisions of the Code of Penal Procedure. Thus, article 285 stipulates that the proceedings of a criminal court shall be public unless such a trial would jeopardize public order or morals. In such a case, the court makes an appropriate declaration in a judgement rendered at a public hearing.

However, the presiding judge may forbid minors to attend the hearing. If _in camera_ proceedings have been ordered, only the judgement on the merits may be pronounced at a public hearing. Judicial decisions must be substantiated and pronounced at a public hearing. Article 355 of the Code of Penal Procedure provides that "Any judgement shall be rendered at a public hearing, either at the hearing when the proceedings take place or at a subsequent date. In the latter case, the presiding judge shall inform the parties present of the day when judgement is to be pronounced. On that occasion, the presiding judge shall, again, note the presence or absence of the parties". When, by derogation from the principles of the public nature of the proceedings, the judge has ordered proceedings to be held _in camera_, the judgement must in any event be pronounced at a public hearing and must, under pain of nullity, indicate that _in camera_ proceedings have been lifted for the purposes of the pronouncement of the judgement.

136. In civil cases, article 31 of the Code of Civil Procedure stipulates that hearings shall be public and that the judge shall keep order in court; article 38 provides that judgements shall be rendered at a public hearing, shall be substantiated and shall specifically indicate that they have been rendered at a public hearing.

137. Criminal cases involving minors are governed by specific rules for juvenile delinquency contained in book III of the Code of Penal Procedure (arts. 439 to 494). Under articles 447 and 450, every court comprises a juvenile section composed of the juvenile magistrate, the presiding judge and two co-magistrates. Article 461 stipulates that proceedings shall be held _in camera_, once the parties have been heard. The decision is also rendered _in camera_ (art. 463) and every case is tried separately in the absence of all the other defendants (art. 468). The juvenile section reaches a decision after having heard the minor, the witnesses, the parents, the tutor or guardian, the government procurator and the defence counsel. It may, if the minor's interest so requires, dispense the minor from attending the hearing (art. 467). Furthermore, "The publication of the record of juvenile court proceedings in books or the press, on radio or film, or through any other medium is prohibited. The publication by the same means of any text or illustration concerning the identity or personality of juvenile offenders is also prohibited" (art. 477), under pain of criminal sanction. The judgement may be published but the minor's name may not be indicated, even by initials.

Article 14, paragraph 2

138. The principle that any person charged with a criminal offence shall be presumed innocent until proved guilty according to law is set forth in the Constitution, article 42 of which states: "Every person shall be presumed innocent until proved guilty by a regular court and with all the safeguards required by the law". These safeguards are spelt out in the Code of Penal Procedure.

Article 14, paragraph 3

139. Reference should be made to the introductory part of the report relating to the independence of the judiciary, the right of defence and judicial remedies. It should be emphasized that the minimum guarantees enunciated in article 14, paragraph 3, are all established in the Code of Penal Procedure.

0079

140. Any person charged with a criminal offence has the right, in full equality, to be informed promptly and in detail in a language which he understands of the nature and cause of the charge against him. Reference should also be made to the observations on police custody, the conduct of examinations, the drafting of records of statements, the execution of judicial warrants and the guarantees which must accompany them. It should further be pointed out that, in accordance with article 109 of the Code of Penal Procedure, any judicial warrant (arrest warrant, detention warrant or combined arrest and detention warrant) must state the nature of the charge and the applicable legal provisions. Once the examination stage has been completed (this is mandatory in criminal cases), the examining magistrate issues, as appropriate, a dismissal order or orders the case to be referred to the court, transmitting the dossier with his committal order to the government procurator, who is required to forward it without delay to the registry of the trial court and summon the defendant for an early hearing before the court seized, complying with the time-limit for summonses (CPP, arts. 162 to 165). If the defendant is being held in pre-trial detention, the case must be heard within one month (new paragraph of art. 165 introduced by Act. No. 90/24 of 18 August 1990). The language used is Arabic, the official language of the country. A person charged with a criminal offence may, throughout the proceedings, be assisted by a third person apart from his counsel, in particular if he cannot read or write. By way of illustration, reference should be made to article 64 of the Code, which stipulates that "Searches, domiciliary visits and seizures of items of evidence may not be effected without the express consent of the person in whose home the operation is conducted. The consent shall be given by means of a handwritten statement by the person concerned or, if he is unable to write, he may avail himself of the assistance of a third person of his choice".

141. A person who is the subject of prosecution is entitled to have adequate time and facilities for the preparation of his defence and to communicate with counsel of his own choosing (see above, observations on the right of defence, in particular paras. 32 and 33 of this report). Every person has the right to be tried without undue delay (see above, police custody regime, maximum period of pre-trial detention, examination stage and obligation on the government procurator, in response to an order committing the case to a court, to summon the defendant for an early hearing, with due observance of the time-limit for summonses, the said time-limit not to exceed one month in the case of pre-trial detention). In addition, article 279 states that "Any case which is ready for trial shall be referred to the court at its following session".

142. Any person charged with a criminal offence has the right to be tried in his presence and to defend himself in person or through legal assistance of his own choosing, to be informed, if he does not have legal assistance, of this right, and to have legal assistance assigned to him, in any case where the interests of justice so require, and without payment by him in any such case if he does not have sufficient means. Article 142 of the Constitution stipulates that "The right of defence is recognized. In criminal matters, it is guaranteed". This guarantee covers all stages of the proceedings, as from the first appearance of the defendant. At the examination stage, the magistrate notifies the defendant that he is free not to make any statement, informs him of his right to choose a counsel and, if no such choice is made, appoints a counsel _ex officio_ if the defendant so requests (CPP, art. 100).

If incommunicado detention is ordered by the judge, the ban on contact may in no circumstances apply to the defendant's counsel (art. 102). Article 272 of the Code stipulates that, during the preparatory stage of sessions of a criminal court, and after an order by the indictment division committing the accused for trial by the court, the accused must be able to communicate freely with his counsel, who may have access to all evidence in the dossier, which must be made available to counsel not less than five days before the trial. During the trial stage proper, the presence of the accused and his defence counsel is mandatory. Article 292 stipulates that "The presence of a defence counsel to assist the accused at the hearing is mandatory. If necessary, a defence counsel shall be appointed _ex officio_ by the presiding judge". Article 293 provides that the accused shall appear in court free of any bond and accompanied only by his guards. Once the introductory proceedings have been completed, the claimant for criminal indemnification or his counsel is heard. The government procurator makes his submissions, and the counsel and the accused make their pleas. Both the claimant and the government procurator are permitted to reply, but the accused and his counsel always have the final word (art. 304).

143. Any person prosecuted for a criminal offence has the right to examine or have examined, the witnesses against him and to obtain the attendance and examination of witnesses on his behalf under the same conditions as witnesses against him. This right is recognized even during the pre-trial stage. The examining magistrate summons before him any person whose evidence he considers relevant; this person is required to comply with the summons and give evidence. However, persons concerning whom there are serious and consistent presumptions of guilt may not be heard as witnesses - in order to avoid jeopardizing the rights of defence. The hearing of witnesses before examining magistrates is governed by articles 89 to 99 of the Code of Penal Procedure. Articles 220 to 234 of this Code establish the conditions and procedures for hearing witnesses before trial courts (joint provisions). In addition, articles 273 and 274 establish the obligation on the government procurator and the claimant for criminal indemnification, on the one hand, and the accused, on the other, to notify the opposing party at least three days before the start of the trial of the persons they wish to summon as witnesses. Article 233 provides that the presiding judge, after each statement, shall ask the witness such questions as he deems necessary and, where appropriate, those which he is requested to ask by the parties; the government procurator may put questions directly to the witnesses. Article 288 stipulates that the accused or his counsel may put questions to the witnesses through the presiding judge. A claimant for criminal indemnification or his counsel may put questions in the same manner. The government procurator may examine witnesses directly. The examination of prosecution witnesses and defence witnesses is conducted in the same conditions. The summoning of witnesses may be required or ordered if necessary by the police.

144. Any person charged with a criminal offence has the right to the free assistance of an interpreter if he cannot understand or speak the language used in court. Various articles of the Code of Penal Procedure contain provisions pursuant to this right, which is also recognized and accorded to deaf mutes (CPP, arts. 91, 92, 94, 95, 108, 165 and 298) at all stages of the proceedings. Thus, article 91 provides that "The examining magistrate may call an interpreter, who may not be his registrar or a witness. If he is not

0081

sworn, the interpreter shall take the oath in the following terms: 'I hereby swear and promise to interpret faithfully the words spoken by persons expressing themselves in different languages or dialects'." Article 92 stipulates that, if a witness is deaf or dumb, the questions and answers shall be given in writing. If the witness is illiterate, the examining magistrate is required to appoint ex officio an interpreter capable of talking with him. The court record must mention the surname, first name, age, occupation, domicile and oath of the interpreter, who has to sign it. Article 108 adds that the records of statements and confrontation must be prepared in the form provided for in articles 94 and 95, and, if an interpreter is used, the provisions of articles 91 and 92 are applicable. Articles 94 and 95 stipulate that every page of the records must also be signed by the interpreter if he has been concerned, and that he must endorse any erasures or references. Article 298 makes the presiding judge of the criminal court responsible for ensuring that an interpreter is present and available if needed.

145. A person is entitled not to be compelled to testify against himself or to confess guilt. Article 89 of the Code of Penal Procedure provides that any person summoned as a witness is required to testify, but at the same time specifies: "However, a person mentioned by name in a complaint accompanied by the bringing of criminal indemnification proceedings may refuse to testify. The examining magistrate shall warn him to that effect after informing him of the complaint. Reference to this matter shall be made in the record. In the event of a refusal to testify, the examining magistrate may hear him only as a defendant".

146. In Algerian law, since a confession is a statement by means of which a person acknowledges as true an action which is liable to have unfavourable legal consequences for him, he must be aware that his statement is liable to constitute evidence against him. For this reason, when it is established before the court that a statement has been made under duress, this statement may not be used as evidence in the course of any proceedings either against the person in question or against any other person. Article 213 of the Code of Penal Procedure stipulates: "Confession, like any element of proof, shall be left to the complete discretion of the judge". Article 215 goes as far as to state: "Except as otherwise provided for by law, the records and reports recording serious and ordinary offences shall be valid only as simple items of information". The question whether a statement constitutes a confession is resolved by the court. An Algerian judge may base his decision only on evidence adduced in the course of the trial and discussed before him in adversary proceedings (CPP, art. 212, second paragraph).

Article 14, paragraph 4

147. The procedure applicable to minors is governed by the specific provisions of book III of the Code of Penal Procedure (rules on juvenile delinquents, arts. 442 to 494). Their objective is to protect children and they make allowance for the desirability of re-educating them. Article 442 sets the age of majority in criminal proceedings at 18 years. Article 444 states the principle that "In the case of a serious or ordinary offence, a child aged under 18 years may be subjected only to one or more of the precautionary or re-education measures listed below:

(a) Restoration to his parents, legal guardian or person worthy of trust;

(b) Non-custodial supervision;

(c) Placement in an authorized institution or public or private education or vocational training establishment;

(d) Placement in an authorized medical or medical-pedagogical establishment;

(e) Placement by the public service responsible for assistance; or

(f) Placement in a boarding school suitable for juvenile delinquents of school age."

A minor aged over 13 may, however, also be placed in a public supervised-education or corrective-education institution. In all cases the above measures must be ordered for a specified time, which may not extend beyond the date upon which the minor reaches the age of 21.

148. Every court has a juvenile section comprising a juvenile magistrate, who is its president, and two advisers. This section has jurisdiction over offences committed by minors and is governed by the specific rules of procedure established in book III of the Code. Cases are heard and decisions rendered _in camera_ and the minor may be excused from appearing in person if his interests so require. Sentences handed down by the juvenile section are subject to appeal in the juvenile division attached to each higher court. The right to defence is guaranteed, as is the right to initiate criminal indemnification action against the minor in the person of his legal representative. Non-custodial supervision is subject to specific arrangements depending on the age of the delinquent. Precautionary and protective measures ordered by virtue of article 444 may be modified or reviewed at any time by the juvenile magistrate.

149. Articles 493 and 494 define measures to protect child victims of offences. A child aged under 16 who is the victim of an offence committed by his parents, tutor or guardian is placed by court order with an individual or in an establishment, or entrusted to the public service responsible for assistance. The government procurator's office may also, when an offender is convicted of an offence against a minor, bring the matter before the juvenile section, which will order any necessary protective measures.

Article 14, paragraph 5

150. Any person found guilty of an offence is entitled to have the judgement and conviction reviewed by a higher court in accordance with the Code of Penal Procedure, which maintains the principle of dual-instance jurisdiction. An appeal for judicial review may be lodged against verdicts of the criminal courts.

151. Article 416 specifies the kinds of decision which are subject to appeal: judgements handed down in connection with ordinary offences; judgements handed down in connection with minor offences when accompanied by a sentence of

imprisonment or a fine exceeding 100 dinars, or when the sentence incurred exceeds five days' imprisonment. An appeal may be lodged by the accused; the person or persons liable at civil law; the government procurator; the procurator-general; the public authorities when they are exercising the public right of action; and the parties to any criminal indemnity action. When civil damages have been awarded, appeal may be lodged by the accused and the person or persons liable at civil law. Appeal may be lodged by the parties to a criminal indemnity action in respect of civil interests only (art. 417).

152. Article 495 states: "The following may be challenged by lodging an appeal for judicial review before the Supreme Court, which may refer them to the criminal court:

(a) Decisions of the *chambre d'accusation* other than decisions on pre-trial detention and referral to the criminal courts;

(b) Judgements handed down by the courts without right of appeal or after a separate ruling as to competence."

In criminal cases, article 313 also states that "after delivering the judgement, the president of the court shall notify the convicted person that he has eight clear days to lodge an appeal for judicial review". An appeal for judicial review may be lodged by the government procurator, the convicted offender, the person or persons liable at civil law or the parties to any criminal indemnity action.

Article 14, paragraph 6

153. "Judicial errors shall be made good by the State", says the Constitution in article 46. The victim of a judicial error is entitled to redress and appropriate remedies are available for this purpose. The Code of Penal Procedure states that any person convicted of a serious or ordinary offence is entitled to seek rehabilitation, which expunges for the future the effects of a *fair* conviction and the concomitant losses of rights. Such rehabilitation is automatic under the conditions laid down in articles 677 and 678, or can be granted by decision of the *chambre d'accusation* or the Supreme Court according to circumstances and the procedures laid down in articles 679 to 693 of the Code.

154. Article 530 of the Code provides for appeal in the interests of the law. On instructions from the Minister of Justice, the procurator-general may denounce before the Supreme Court judicial acts, judgements or decisions at variance with the law against which no party has appealed. Those acts, verdicts and decisions may be set aside. This has no effect on civil damages but will benefit any person convicted under the provisions concerned.

155. Lastly, the Code deals with applications for review in articles 531, 531 *bis* and 531 *bis* (1), the latter two having been incorporated into the Code by Act No. 86/05, passed by the Assembly on 4 March 1986, to allow any convicted person later found innocent by the Supreme Court or his rightful claimants to seek damages for the moral and physical injury caused by the conviction. It should be stressed that an application for redress may be

0084

submitted at any stage of the proceedings (for the text of the aforementioned Act, see para. 118 of this report). Article 531, on applications for review, reads as follows:

> "Applications for review may be lodged only against judgements and decisions having the force of _res judicata_, convicting a person or persons of a serious or ordinary offence.
>
> They must be supported by:
>
> (1) The production, after conviction for homicide, of evidence giving reason to believe that the supposed victim of the homicide is still alive;
>
> (2) The conviction for false witness against the convicted person of a witness whose testimony helped to secure his conviction;
>
> (3) The conviction for the same offence of another individual when the two convictions are mutually inconsistent; or
>
> (4) The discovery of a new fact or the presentation of evidence, of which the court was unaware when it convicted him, making it appear probable that the convicted person is innocent.
>
> In the first three instances, the Supreme Court shall be seized directly of the matter by the Minister of Justice or by the convicted person or, where he is unable to do so, by his legal representative or, if the condemned person has died or his whereabouts are unknown, by his spouse, descendants or ascendants.
>
> In the fourth instance the Supreme Court may only be seized of the matter by the procurator general of the court, acting at the request of the Minister of Justice.
>
> In reviewing a case, the Court shall rule on the substance, the reporting judge furnishing it with all necessary material, by rogatory commission where necessary.
>
> _If an application is accepted, the Court shall quash without appeal the convictions it finds unjustified_" (this last paragraph was added by Act No. 86/05).

Article 14, paragraph 7

156. No one may be prosecuted or punished for a breach of the law of which he has already been acquitted or convicted in final judgement, in accordance with the Penal Code and Code of Penal Procedure. The Constitution upholds the principle that no one can be prosecuted, arrested or detained except as determined by law (art. 44), and that criminal penalties must be consistent with the principles of legality and individuality (art. 133).

0085

157. The Code of Civil Procedure specifies in article 6 that "prosecution for execution of sentence lapses upon the death of the accused, expiry of the statutory period of limitations, amnesty, repeal of the penal law or setting aside of the res judicata". The Code of Penal Procedure states in article 175 that: "An accused person in respect of whom the examining magistrate has issued an order dismissing a case may not be investigated again for the same matter unless new charges arise"; it also defines what may constitute new charges. Reopening an investigation is a matter for the government procurator's office. When the chambre d'accusation decides that the acts in question do not constitute an offence or that there are not sufficient charges against the accused, or if the perpetrator is unknown, it dismisses the case. Any suspects in pre-trial detention are set free, unless they are also being detained for other reasons (art. 195).

158. With regard to the criminal courts, article 311 of the Code states that: "If the accused is absolved or acquitted he shall immediately be set free unless detained for another reason ... No person legally acquitted may be rearrested or charged again in connection with the same matter, even if differently described".

159. The principle laid down in article 14, paragraph 7, of the Covenant also benefits foreigners. Article 589 of the Code of Penal Procedure stipulates that: "No prosecution for a serious or ordinary offence committed in Algeria may be conducted against a foreigner who provides proof that he has been definitively tried abroad for that offence and, if convicted, that his sentence has been served or is unenforceable or that he has been pardoned". The Code also establishes conditions relating to statutory limitations on penalties in articles 612 to 617.

Article 15: Non-retroactivity of penal legislation

160. The non-retroactivity of penal legislation is a constitutional principle. Under Algerian law, no petty, minor, ordinary or serious offence can be prosecuted except as determined by law, or punished with penalties not laid down by law before it was committed. A person may be found guilty only by virtue of a law duly promulgated before the act with which he is charged took place (art. 43 of the Constitution). Furthermore, new legislation does not affect rights acquired under the previous legislation, or revive any right which has actually disappeared under the previous legislation. Article 1 of the Penal Code states that "In the absence of law there can be no breach of the law, nor any penalties or security measures". Article 2 says that "Penal legislation shall not be retroactive except where it is less rigorous", allowing the offender to benefit from lighter penalties under the new law.

Article 16: Right to legal personality

161. The right to recognition of one's legal personality in all circumstances is recognized and protected by the Algerian Constitution, specifically articles 30, 33, 34 and 37. The Algerian Civil Code contains a number of provisions recognizing legal personality. The Civil Registry Act lays down the procedure for entering information in the civil registers kept in each commune. Besides registers of births and deaths and related declarations such as marriage and divorce, it governs the taking and changing of a name.

0086

Article 25 of the Civil Code states that personality begins upon the birth of a living child and ends at death; paragraph 2 of the article adds that the child enjoys civil rights from conception provided it is born alive. Birth and death are established by the civil registers. In the absence of such evidence or if the information they contain is imprecise, proof may be furnished by any other means in the forms provided for in the Civil Registry Act (art. 26 of the Civil Code). Article 28 states that everyone must have a surname and one or more given names; article 40, that "any adult person in possession of his mental faculties and not subject to a disqualification is fully able to exercise his civil rights. Civil majority is attained at the age of 19 years". The Civil Code also stipulates that no one can renounce his capacity or change the conditions under which it is exercised (art. 45); that no one can renounce his personal freedom (art. 46); that anyone subjected to unlawful encroachment upon the rights inherent in his personality may seek the cessation of such encroachment and redress for any injury resulting therefrom (art. 47); and that anyone whose right to the use of a surname is unjustly impugned or whose name has been improperly borne by another may require those responsible to cease and desist and seek redress for the injury (art. 48). Cases of incapacity and the conditions under which people may be stripped of certain rights are strictly governed by law.

162. The Penal Code makes it a punishable offence to hinder the identification of an infant, rendering the culprit liable to up to 10 years' imprisonment (art. 321), or to usurp or improperly assume titles and names (arts. 243 to 250). Article 247 deals with the improper attribution of a patronymic name other than one's own; article 248, with the use of false names or false identities; article 249, with usurpation of the name of a third party. Article 250 states that in all the cases provided for in articles 243 to 249, the Court hearing the case may, at the expense of the guilty party, order the decision to be announced in the newspapers or publicly displayed and corrections to be made to the authentic deeds or civil registration documents in which the title has been improperly entered or altered.

163. It should also be mentioned that Decree No. 88-131 of 4 July 1988 deals with relations between the administration and the public. It imposes on "institutions, public authorities, public bodies and their employees the duty to protect the liberties and rights acknowledged by the Constitution and legislation in force" (art. 2). Article 3 emphasizes that "the Administration is required to respect the human person and uphold human dignity. Its relations with the public shall in all circumstances be marked by civility and endued with courtesy". Article 5 states that "any abuse of authority shall be subject to reparation in accordance with current legislation, without prejudice to any penal, civil and disciplinary sanctions to which the party responsible may be liable". Public servants must perform their duties in accordance with current legislation; they may not on any pretext refuse to perform a service or issue an administrative document to which the person administered is normally entitled, refuse to provide information, cause unwarranted delay in the issuance of administrative acts and documents, or demand acts or documents not required by the legislation or regulations in force (art. 30). Besides discretionary remedies, the person administered may use all legal avenues to contest decisions by the administration, including action to seek redress for any injury suffered (art. 39).

Article 17: Protection against arbitrary or illegal interference

164. This right is protected under article 37 of the Algerian Constitution: "The privacy and honour of the citizen are inviolable and shall be protected by law. The secrecy of private correspondence and communication in all their forms is guaranteed". The Penal Code devotes an entire section to damage to honour or reputation and breach of secrecy (defamation, art. 296; insult, arts. 297, 298, 298 bis and 299, including insults against one or more persons belonging to a specific ethnic or philosophical group or religion; slander, art. 300; breach of professional secrecy, arts. 301 and 302).

165. Breaches of medical confidentiality are punishable under article 301 of the Penal Code. Medical confidentiality is also safeguarded by various provisions of the Health Protection and Promotion Act (No. 85/05), as amended by Act No. 90-17 of 31 July 1990. The amendments to the Act strengthened the safeguards for medical confidentiality. The new article 206 (1) reads as follows: "Respect for the dignity of the patient and protection of his personality are guaranteed by the professional confidentiality to which all doctors, surgeons, dentists and pharmacists are bound". The obligation to maintain professional confidentiality is general and absolute in the absence of permission from the patient or a legal waiver, in accordance with article 206 (2). The patient, however, is free to discuss anything to do with his health. Article 206 (3) requires practitioners to report ill-treatment of minors and persons in detention; article 206 (4) deals with the limits and conditions to which practitioners summoned before the courts or providing expert evidence are subject. A practitioner is absolved of professional confidentiality only "vis à vis the Court in connection with the specific subject of its inquiry ... He may reveal only those matters which are strictly relevant to the questions put to him, and must remain silent about anything he may have learnt during the performance of his duties, or be guilty of a breach of professional confidentiality". Article 206 (5) stipulates that a practitioner "summoned to give evidence shall not disclose matters covered by professional confidentiality unless the patient authorizes him to do so". Article 207 (2) makes it incumbent on a practitioner "entrusted with carrying out a check or inspection to notify the persons he proposes to examine of the capacity in which he is acting".

166. The secrecy and inviolability of correspondence are guaranteed by article 37, paragraph 2, of the Constitution: "The secrecy of private correspondence and communication in all their forms is guaranteed". Furthermore, article 137 of the Penal Code stipulates that: "Any public servant or representative of the State, employee or official of the postal service who opens, diverts or destroys letters in the mails or abets such opening, diversion or destruction is liable to imprisonment for three months to five years and a fine of 500 to 1,000 dinars. The same penalty shall apply to any employee or official of the telegraph service who diverts or destroys a telegram or divulges the contents thereof. The offender shall furthermore be barred from any public office or employment for 5 to 10 years".

167. The home is inviolable. Under article 38 of the Constitution, "The State shall guarantee inviolability of the home. No search may take place save in virtue of the law and in accordance therewith. No search may be made save by written order of the competent judicial authority". Searches and inquiries

are conducted subject to the procedures and conditions laid down in the Code of Penal Procedure (arts. 44 to 50, 64 and 65). Thus searches, domiciliary visits and seizures of evidence may not take place without the express consent of the person in whose home they occur given in a written statement by the hand of the person concerned who, if he cannot write, may obtain the assistance of a third person of his choice (art. 64, amended, of the Code of Penal Procedure). Searches may be conducted only upon written authorization of the government procurator or examining magistrate (art. 45). Some of these safeguards have the effect of avoiding evidence improperly obtained (art. 48). Article 122 states that "An officer may not enter a citizen's home in execution of an arrest warrant before 5 a.m. or after 8 p.m." The Penal Code provides, in article 135, that: "Any administrative or judicial official, any police officer or any commander or member of the security forces who, acting in that capacity, enters a citizen's home against that citizen's wish, except as provided and subject to the formalities prescribed by law, is liable to imprisonment for two months to one year and a fine of 500 to 3,000 dinars, without prejudice to the application of article 107". Article 107 makes arbitrary or freedom-infringing acts committed or ordered by a public servant punishable by 5 to 10 years' rigorous imprisonment.

168. Decree No. 88/131 on relations between the Administration and the public makes it the duty of institutions, public authorities and public bodies and their employees to protect the rights of citizens, respect the human person and uphold human dignity, etc. (see above). Furthermore, it strictly regulates the procedure by which an individual may be summoned to appear before the authorities (arts. 15 to 20), emphasizing the exceptional nature of such a summons, which may not be made outside working hours or at night.

169. The Information Act (No. 90-07 of 3 April 1990) states that the right to information may be exercised freely with due regard for the dignity of the individual (art. 3), and that information must not infringe a citizen's constitutional rights or liberties (art. 36). It governs the rights of correction and reply, and provides that "Any person mentioned in a report containing erroneous information or malicious assertions apt to cause moral or material injury" may exercise his right to reply and/or initiate proceedings against the editor of the organ and the journalist, who are jointly responsible (art. 45).

Article 18: Freedom of thought, conscience and religion

170. Freedom of thought, conscience and religion is guaranteed by Algerian law. Although Islam is the State religion (art. 2 of the Constitution), the Constitution establishes, in article 35, that freedom of conscience and freedom of opinion are inviolable. The freedom of worship and religion of communities of other faiths living in Algeria is thus respected and protected by the Ministry of Religious Affairs. The archdiocese of Algiers covers several dioceses, including Algiers (seven churches), Laghouat (one church), Oran (four churches) and Constantine (two churches). The Jewish consistory is based in Algiers and there are two synagogues, one in Blida, the other in Algiers.

0089

171. The Penal Code (art. 298 bis) makes insulting one or more persons belonging to a specific ethnic or philosophical group or religion a punishable offence. The Information Act provides, in article 77, that anyone who, in writing or by sounds, images, drawings or any other direct or indirect means, offends against Islam and the other celestial religions is liable to criminal penalties (six months' to three years' imprisonment and/or a fine).

Article 19: Freedom of opinion, expression and information

172. Freedom of opinion is inviolable by virtue of article 35 of the Constitution, which states that "Freedom of conscience and freedom of opinion are inviolable". Article 36 of the Constitution guarantees to citizens freedom of intellectual, artistic and scientific creation. Copyright is also guaranteed. Freedom of expression is guaranteed by article 39 of the Constitution, which provides that the freedoms of expression, association and assembly are guaranteed to the citizen.

173. Information is governed by Act No. 90-07 of 3 April 1990, which amended the Information Code contained in Act No. 82-01 of 6 February 1982 in order to give full effect to the constitutional provisions concerning matters such as the multi-party system, the effective participation of everyone in political, economic, social and cultural life, and freedom of conscience, opinion, intellectual, artistic and scientific creation, expression, association and assembly. The new Act stipulates that the right to information shall be exercised freely, having due respect for the dignity of the human person, through any form of mass communication, including writing, radio, sound systems and television; newspapers, periodicals and information organs may belong to both the public sector and to political associations and natural or legal persons in Algerian law (arts. 3 and 11).

174. The right to information is defined by article 2 as follows:

> "The right to information shall consist of the citizen's right to be informed fully and objectively of facts and opinions of interest to society at the national and international levels, and of the right to participate in information through the exercise of the fundamental freedoms of thought, opinion and expression in accordance with articles 35, 36, 39 and 40 of the Constitution".

This definition of information covers both facets of the right to information: the right to inform and the right to be informed. By making them indissoluble, the legislature has enlarged the scope of this fundamental freedom. The right is secured as provided for in article 4 by the newspapers, periodicals and information organs of the public sector and by the newspapers, periodicals and organs belonging to, or created by, political associations. It is exercised by means of any form of mass communication, including writing, radio, sound systems and television.

175. The limits on the exercise of this right are those laid down, in particular, by articles 3 and 40 of the Act. Article 3 stipulates that the right to information shall be exercised freely with due respect for the dignity of the human person and the requirements of foreign policy and

national defence. Article 40 states that "In the exercise of his profession, a professional journalist shall ensure full respect for professional and general ethics. In particular, he shall:

Respect the constitutional rights and individual freedoms of citizens;

Make every effort to provide full and objective information;

Rectify any information that proves to be inaccurate;

Comment on facts and events honestly and objectively;

Refrain from any direct or indirect advocacy of racism, intolerance and violence;

Refrain from plagiarism, slander, defamation and acting as an informer;

Refrain from using the moral prestige attaching to his profession for personal or material purposes.

A journalist has the right to refuse to accept any editorial directive originating from any source other than the management of the publication for which he works".

The Act also regulates the right of reply and the right to rectification (see above).

176. The publication of any periodical is free and is subject, for the purposes of registration and verification of accuracy, only to an advance declaration made 30 days before the appearance of the first number (art. 14). National or foreign periodicals and specialized publications must not contain any illustration, report, information or insertion contrary to human rights or advocate racism; in addition, they must not contain any advertisement or announcement likely to promote violence or crime (art. 26). Institutions, agencies or approved associations responsible for the promotion of human rights and the protection of children may exercise the rights recognized to parties bringing criminal indemnity actions (art. 27). The journalist is protected in the exercise of his profession. If a professional journalist is the victim of violence or aggression, attempted corruption and intimidation or blatant pressure in the performance of his duties, the employer must refer the matter to the competent court and become a party to a criminal indemnity action. The right of access to sources of information is recognized for professional journalists (art. 35). It does not, however, authorize a journalist to divulge information likely to violate the constitutional rights and freedoms of the citizen (art. 36). Thus a person who directly or indirectly advocates, through any medium, acts categorized as serious or ordinary offences is liable to one to five years' imprisonment and a fine (art. 96). Since the entry into force of the new Information Act, the national press has been enriched by a large number of daily and periodical publications, some of which have chosen to be independent while others reflect the views of particular political groups.

Article 20: The prohibition of propaganda for war and of advocacy of hatred

177. Pursuant to article 25 of the Constitution, "Algeria shall refrain from resorting to war for the purpose of violating the legitimate sovereignty and freedom of other peoples. It shall endeavour to settle international disputes by peaceful means". The oath sworn by the President of the Republic (art. 73 of the Constitution) imposes on him an express obligation, *inter alia*, to do everything he can to achieve the great ideals of justice, freedom and peace in the world.

178. Algeria does not tolerate any propaganda for war; the advocacy of national, racial or religious hatred is prohibited and punished. As has already been seen, injurious behaviour and defamation are punishable under the Penal Code, which imposes penalties for any defamation against a person or an ethnic, philosophical or religious group when it is designed to stir up hatred among citizens or inhabitants (art. 298, para. 2). In the case of the provisions contained in the Information Act, reference should be made to the comments on article 19. It should also be pointed out that the Associations Act and the Political Associations Act prohibit associations from engaging in activities likely to violate human rights or to promote intolerance, racism and incitement to violence. Thus article 3, paragraph 8, of the Political Associations Act (No. 89-11 of 5 July 1989) stipulates that associations must, in their programmes and activities, proscribe intolerance, fanaticism, racism and incitement and/or recourse to violence in any of its forms. Article 5 states that no association may put forward, as the basis for its establishment and activities, the pursuit of objectives involving sectarian and regionalist practices, feudalism or nepotism.

Article 21: Right of peaceful assembly

179. The right of peaceful assembly is recognized in Algeria pursuant to article 39 of the Constitution, which reads "The freedoms of expression, association and assembly are guaranteed to the citizen". The arrangements for its exercise are set forth in articles 2 to 20 of the Public Meetings and Demonstrations Act (No. 89-28 of 31 December 1989). The text of the Act indicates that Algerian legislation has established a flexible procedure for the exercise of this right, for which the only requirement is that notice must be given in advance (three days for a meeting, five days for a demonstration). Article 3 of the Act establishes the principle that public meetings shall be free. The restrictions imposed by legislation are set forth in the same Act and relate to measures to promote security and maintain order and measures necessary to secure respect for the law and for the constitutional rights of citizens and the preservation of morality.

Article 22: Freedom of association

180. Everyone has the right to associate freely with others, including the right to form and join trade unions for the protection of his interests. Article 53 of the Constitution recognizes trade union rights for all citizens; article 39 guarantees freedom of association. Furthermore, article 40 states that the right to establish political associations is recognized. This right may not, however, be claimed for the purpose of encroaching upon fundamental freedoms, national unity, the territorial integrity or independence of the

country, or the sovereignty of the people. The founding of associations used to be subject to the conditions set forth in Ordinance No. 71-79 of 3 December 1971 and to prior approval by the Ministry of the Interior, but on 21 July 1987 this Ordinance was replaced by Act No. 87-15, supplemented by implementing decree No. 88-16 of 2 February 1988. The latter texts laid down the framework for exercising freedom of association by providing greater flexibility in the conditions and arrangements for the founding of associations. For example, the prior approval procedure was abolished for purely local associations; it was however, retained for any association having or intending to have nationwide influence and for any association whose objectives or aspirations fell within a field of activity that could be undertaken by a public service. Although approval was granted very liberally, practice showed that such a procedure could give rise to delays and ponderous formalities incompatible with the full exercise of the right to freedom of association affirmed by the Constitution. So a new Associations Act (No. 90-31 of 4 December 1990) was approved by the National People's Assembly; it takes care of that aspect of the problem and consequently abolishes the prior approval required under the old legislation.

181. From now on the arrangements for constituting, organizing and operating associations are regulated and determined by Act No. 90-31, the main provisions of which are as follows:

(a) An association is defined as an agreement governed by the laws currently in force whereby natural or legal persons join together on a contractual basis for a non-profit-making purpose. To this end they pool, for a specified or unspecified period, their knowledge and resources in order to promote activities of a professional, social, scientific, religious, educational, cultural, sporting or other nature. The purpose of the association and the name to be given to it must be accurately stated (art. 2).

(b) Any person of full age may found, administer or direct an association if he is of Algerian nationality, if he is in possession of his civil and civic rights, and if he has not been engaged in conduct contrary to the interests of the national liberation struggle (art. 4).

(c) Any association founded in pursuit of an objective contrary to the nation's institutions, to public order, to morality or to current legislation and regulations or whose founding members do not fulfil the conditions set forth in article 4 shall be of no legal effect (art. 5).

(d) Associations are to be constituted freely (art. 6) and are considered to be duly constituted after a notice of constitution has been filed by the founder members with the <u>wali</u> (prefect) of the <u>wilaya</u> (prefecture) where the association has its head office in the case of local associations, and with the Minister of the Interior in the case of national associations, and after a certificate of registration has been issued within a maximum period of 60 days and the formalities concerning publicity have been completed in at least one daily newspaper having a nationwide circulation (arts. 7 and 10). Prior approval is therefore abolished. Furthermore, if the competent authority considers the constitution of an association to be illegal, it must, no later than eight days before the expiry of the 60 days required for the issue of a certificate of registration, refer the matter to the administrative division of the court having territorial jurisdiction, which must decide the case within 30 days following the date of referral (art. 8). The association is thereby protected against the danger of an arbitrary refusal to issue the certificate of registration, in so far as, if the matter is not referred to the court, under article 8 the association will be considered as being duly constituted upon expiry of the 60-day period.

(e) Associations are endowed with legal status and civil capacity and may, inter alia, go to law, enter into contracts, acquire property for the conduct of their activities, and receive donations and legacies; they may publish and circulate bulletins, magazines and other information papers in keeping with their purpose; national associations may also join international associations after obtaining the agreement of the Minister of the Interior (arts. 16, 19, 91 and 126).

(f) All natural and legal persons are forbidden to interfere in the functioning of an association (art. 15). An association must, for its part, regularly provide the appropriate public authority with information relating to changes in its statutes, its governing bodies, its membership and the sources of its funds (arts. 17 and 18).

(g) Except in cases of voluntary dissolution, an association may be suspended or dissolved only through the courts at the request of the public authority or on a complaint lodged by a third party (arts. 32 to 38).

(h) Special arrangements are made for foreign associations (arts. 39 to 44). A foreign association is deemed to be any association which has its headquarters abroad or is managed wholly or partly by foreigners (art. 39). The establishment of such an association is still subject to prior approval by the Minister of the Interior (art. 40). Only persons duly entitled to be in the country may found or join a foreign association (art. 41). Approval may be suspended or withdrawn by the Minister of the Interior if the association's activities deviate from what is laid down in its statutes or are prejudicial to the Nation's institutions, its integrity or values, public order or morality (art. 42).

182. In Algeria, there are more than 28,500 local and national associations. Their activities cover all sectors of economic, social, cultural, religious, scientific, technical and professional life. In addition to the large number of professional associations, associations are mainly to be found in the following areas: health protection; maladjusted children; handicapped persons; nature; the environment; archaeological sites; the promotion of sports and leisure activities; music; drama; the cinema; the promotion of charity, particularly for the benefit of abandoned children; the promotion of the national language and other languages; and the defence of women's rights, children's rights and human rights in general.

183. Political associations are governed by Act No. 89-11 of 5 July 1989, promulgated in order to give effect to article 40 of the Constitution, which provided for a multi-party system. The main provisions of the Act are as follows:

0094

Art. 2. The purpose of a political association, under the provisions of article 40 of the Constitution, is to serve as a rallying-point for Algerian citizens who, grouped around a political programme for a non-profit-making purpose, work together with a view to participating in political life by democratic and peaceful means.

Art. 3. Any political association shall, through its objectives, help to:

- Safeguard and strengthen the Nation's independence, territorial integrity and unity;

- Strengthen the sovereignty of the people and respect for its freely made choices;

- Protect the republican form of government and the fundamental freedoms of the citizen;

- Respect democratic organization;

- Protect the national economy against any form of embezzlement, misappropriation, monopolization or illegal confiscation.

In addition, the association shall, in its programme and activities, proscribe intolerance, fanaticism, racism and incitement and/or recourse to violence in all its forms.

Art. 5. No political association may put forward, as the basis for its establishment and activities, objectives involving:

- Sectarian and regionalist practices, feudalism and nepotism;

- The establishment of relationships of exploitation and dependency;

- Behaviour contrary to Islamic morals and the values of the Revolution of 1 November 1954.

In this context a political association may also not put forward, as the basis for its establishment or activities, exclusively confessional, linguistic or regionalist, considerations, membership of a particular sex or race, or a specific professional status.

Art. 6. Political associations shall be established and operate in strict compliance with the Constitution and the laws in force. In this connection, political associations are not allowed to engage in any violation of security or public order or of the rights and freedoms of others. They are not allowed to use any of their assets for the establishment of military or paramilitary organizations.

Art. 9. Membership shall be open to any Algerian having reached voting age, except for members of the Constitutional Council, judges, members of the armed forces and officers of the security services.

Art. 10. A political association shall be organized on the basis of democratic principles.

For an association to be established, notice of its constitution shall be given by depositing an application and the statutes with the Minister of the Interior, who, after checking that they are in order, shall arrange for the publication, in the Journal Officiel, of the acknowledgement of receipt of the application, mentioning specifically the name and address of the association. This publication shall be made within two months following the deposit of the documents, failing which the Minister of the Interior shall refer the matter to the administrative division of the Court of Algiers, which shall decide the case within the month following referral. Applications for the suspension and/or dissolution of an association shall also be examined by the same division. The Court's decision shall be appealable before the Supreme Court.

Arts. 20 to 29. The acknowledgement of receipt published in the Journal Official confers legal status and capacity upon the association, which may acquire, possess and administer any assets necessary for its activity, receive gifts, legacies and membership dues, and produce one or more publications (arts. 20 to 24). The association may benefit from State aid. Gifts and legacies may be received only from identified individuals and may not represent more than 20 per cent of the income accruing from members' dues. The association may also derive income from its activities and from non-commercial investments (arts. 25 to 29). State aid shall be allocated in proportion to the number of deputies representing the political group concerned (art. 29).

184. The right to form and join trade unions is guaranteed by the Constitution. The arrangements for the exercise of trade union rights are set forth in Act No. 90/14 of 2 June 1990. Algeria is a party to the ILO Convention of 1948. The above-mentioned Act sets forth the arrangements for exercising trade union and trade association rights applicable to all wage-earners and employers. The main provisions of the Act are as follows:

Art. 2. Wage-earners and employers in the same occupations, branches or sectors of activity have the right to form trade unions and trade associations for the purpose of defending their material and moral interests.

Art. 3. For this purpose wage-earners and employers have the right to found trade unions and trade associations or to join, freely and voluntarily, existing trade unions and trade associations on the sole condition that they comply with current legislation and with the statutes of the organizations concerned.

Arts. 7 to 10. A trade union or trade association shall be constituted following a constituent general meeting attended by its founder members (art. 7) and shall be declared duly constituted after a notice of constitution has been filed with the wali (prefect) or the Minister of Labour, after a certificate of registration has been issued, and after the necessary formalities concerning publicity, have been completed (arts. 8 to 10). The organization shall be endowed with legal status and capacity, with the attributes attaching thereto. It may publish and circulate bulletins and other information papers.

0096

Arts. 27 to 33. Suspension and dissolution (other than voluntary) may be pronounced by judicial means only, on the application of the public authority or any other interested party.

Trade union organizations shall be entitled to join international trade union organizations, both continental and regional, that pursue the same or similar aims.

Arts. 46 to 57. The Act also provides for facilities and protective measures for trade union delegates and members (granting of time during working hours for performing their duties; facilities for holding meetings; protection of workers against any discrimination on grounds of their trade union activities; prohibition of threats or pressure; prohibition of dismissal, transfer or disciplinary sanctions against trade union delegates, etc.).

Article 23: Family rights

185. "The family shall enjoy the protection of the State and society" (Constitution, art. 55). Article 2 of the Family Code (Act No. 84-11 of 9 June 1984 establishing the Family Code) defines the family as the basic unit of society: it is composed of persons united by the bonds of marriage and of kinship." Article 3 of the Code, by delimiting the basis of its mode of life, gives the family an active role in society: "The family's mode of life shall be based on union, solidarity, understanding, proper education and morals and the elimination of social evils".

186. The right to marry and to raise a family is guaranteed to men and women of marriageable age. The Family Code stipulates in article 4 that, "Marriage is a contract concluded between a man and a woman in legal form. Among its purposes is to found a family based on affection, kindness and mutual help, to provide moral protection for the spouses and to preserve family ties". To protect girls against marriage before puberty, the Code stipulates in article 7, paragraph 1, that marriageable age is considered to be 21 years for men and 18 years for women. Paragraph 2 of the article stipulates that a judge may, however, grant an exemption from the age requirement on grounds of interest or in case of need.

The free and full consent of the future spouses is one of the constituent elements of marriage. The Family Code stipulates that a marriage shall be declared null and void if one of its constituent elements is invalidated (art. 32). Article 9 stipulates that marriage is contracted through the consent of the future spouses, the presence of the matrimonial guardian and of two witnesses, as well as the award of a dowry. In addition, article 10 reads:

> "Consent shall derive from the request of one of the two parties and the explicit acceptance of the other signifying legal marriage. The request and consent of disabled persons shall be valid when expressed in any written or gestural form signifying marriage in language or custom".

The marraige ceremony is concluded before a notary or legally empowered official, subject to the provisions of article 9 of this Act (art. 18). The provisions of the Civil Status Code are applicable to the procedure for registering the act of marriage. In order to protect Algerian women the entering of the marriage in the civil registry is obligatory. To this end, article 72 of the Civil Status Code stipulates: "When the marriage takes place before the registrar, he shall immediately record it in his register. He shall then provide the couple with a family record book certifying that the marriage has taken place ...".

Also in the woman's interest, article 119 of the Code provides that, "in the event of divorce, a second family record book may be provided for the spouse not in possession of the first book, at his or her request". The second book contains copies of all the certificates and information contained in the other book.

187. The equality of the rights and responsibilities of the spouses as regards the marriage, during the marriage and at its dissolution is ensured by the provisions of the Family Code. Algerian women are entitled, on the same basis as men, to choose their spouse and to enter into marriage only with their free and full consent, an essential condition for the marriage to be valid (Family Code, art. 9). The consent must be explicit and unequivocal and cannot be given for a future time or conditionally upon the occurrence or non-occurrence of a future or uncertain event. It must be expressed publicly and in person (art. 10). The Civil Code also states in article 46 that "No one may renounce his personal freedom." The Family Code defines, in chapter 4, "the rights and obligations of the spouses"; in particular, it stipulates that the obligations of the spouses are the following:

"(a) To protect marital ties and the duties of life together;

(b) To contribute jointly to the protection of the interests of the family and the children and to the children's proper upbringing;

(c) To protect the ties of kinship and good relations with parents and close relatives" (art. 36).

A husband is obliged to:

"(a) Support his wife to the best of his ability, except where it has been established that she has left the marital home;

(b) Act with perfect fairness towards his wives if he has more than one wife" (art. 37).

The Code grants women "the right to dispose of their goods with complete freedom" (art. 38). Like the husband, a wife may request a divorce before the court (Family Code, art. 53). The Code provides in particular for divorce by mutual consent. The wife automatically receives custody of minor children (Family Code, art. 64) unless the higher interests of the child require that she be deprived of this right.

0098

Article 24: The child

Article 24, paragraph 1

188. Paragraph 1 of this article stipulates that every child shall have, without any discrimination, the right to such measures of protection as are required by his status as a minor, on the part of his family, society and the State. The protection of children is dealt with first of all by a number of provisions of the Constitution, which guarantees the protection of citizens in general. Thus, article 23 provides that the State is responsible for the security of every citizen, whose protection abroad it must ensure. Similarly, article 33 stipulates that the State guarantees the inviolability of the human person and that any form of physical or moral violence is prohibited. This provision is complemented by article 34, according to which offences committed against rights and freedoms and physical or moral attacks on the integrity of the human being shall be punishable by law.

189. Children are mentioned explicitly in the Constitution in article 60, which stipulates that all the freedoms of every individual shall be exercised with respect for the rights guaranteed to others by the Constitution, especially with respect for the right to honour, privacy and protection of the family, young people and children. Protection of the family, the basic unit for the natural development of the child, is also mentioned in article 55 of the Constitution, which stipulates that "The family shall enjoy the protection of the State and society." Article 62 states, "The law sanctions the duty of the parents in the education and protection of their children." In addition, the child's right to education and instruction is laid down in article 50, which guarantees education and lays down the principle of free education. Also in accordance with article 50, basic education is compulsory, and the State is required, in organizing the system of education to ensure equal access to education and vocational training. In health matters, the Constitution provides, in article 51, that "All citizens are entitled to protection of their health. The State shall provide for the prevention and control of epidemic and endemic diseases." In social matters, the living conditions of citizens who cannot yet, can no longer or will never be able to work are guaranteed under article 56, which is implicitly aimed in the first place at children.

190. In matters of health, upbringing, instruction, labour and social welfare, several laws have been enacted with the aim of implementing and exercising the rights laid down in the Constitution. Besides the Protection of Children and Young Persons Act, which reaffirms the rights of the child enshrined in the Constitution and organizes the exercise of those rights, the protection of children is also dealt with in other laws, such as the Health Protection and Promotion Act (No. 85-05 of 16 February 1985), the Labour Act, which sets the minimum working age at 17 and Ordinance No. 68-82 of 16 April 1968 establishing national service, which sets the call-up age at 19. Among the various texts organizing education, the Basic Education Act stipulates that education is free and compulsory for the 6 to 15 age group. Vocational training enables children over 15 years of age whose school performance does not permit them to go on to secondary education to have a minimum of two years' free training to teach them a skill.

191. The Information Act (No. 90-07 of 3 April 1990) contains a series of provisions providing for the protection of children. Under the Act, children may not receive information that endangers their physical or moral integrity, offenders being liable to a fine and imprisonment. Article 24 of the Act stipulates that the editor of a children's publication must have the assistance of an advisory educational body. Article 26 provides that no publication may contain material contrary to human rights or apt to foster violence and delinquency. Article 27 enables any institution concerned with human rights and the protection of children to initiate criminal indemnity proceedings. Article 37 stipulates that a journalist cannot invoke professional secrecy before the judicial authority when the information in question relates to children or young persons, out of concern for the protection of the child. Finally, article 91 provides for imprisonment and a fine for anyone who, with intent to do harm, publishes or disseminates, by any means whatsoever, any text or illustration concerning the identity or personality of minor children.

192. The Penal Code, which attaches great importance to the protection of children, establishes severe penalties for offences committed against children and sets criminal responsibility at 18 years. Severe penalties are laid down in article 320 against anyone who forces or tries to force one or both parents to sign a document agreeing to give up a child about to be born, and against any person who is in possession of, uses or attempts to use such a document. The penalties for giving up a child for purposes of gain are equally severe for the principals and for any other person taking part in the commission of the offence, by acting or attempting to act as intermediary in order to obtain the child. Article 342, which protects children against vice and prostitution, stipulates that anyone who incites, promotes or facilitates vice or corruption involving persons under 19 years of age shall be liable to 5 to 10 years' imprisonment and a fine of 500 to 25,000 dinars. Article 344 increases the penalties laid down in article 343 when the offence of aiding, abetting or protecting the prostitution of others is committed with respect to persons under 19 years of age. The Penal Code is even more severe when minors are involved, since it establishes the same penalties for attempts to commit these offences as it does for the actual offences.

193. The Family Code (Act No. 84-11 of 9 June 1984) deals with the protection of children. The various provisions concerning custody, the duty to provide for children's needs, legal representation, guardianship, the legal compendium (the Kafala) and inheritance are aimed at protecting and safeguarding children's interests. It should also be mentioned that young offenders enjoy special procedures and specific measures aimed at rehabilitation and social reintegration (see comments on arts. 10 and 14 above).

Article 24, paragraph 2

194. Article 24, paragraph 2, stipulates that every child shall be registered immediately after birth and shall have a name. Regarding registration after birth, Ordinance No. 70-20 of 19 February 1970 relating to civil status stipulates, in article 61, that "Births shall be declared within five days to the registrar in the place of birth, offenders being subject to the penalties laid down in article 442, paragraph 3, of the Penal Code." Article 60 lists the persons required to make this declaration and specifies that the birth

0100

certificate shall be drawn up immediatley. Foundlings must also be declared immediately. Thus article 66 obliges anyone who has found a newborn child so to declare to the registrar in the place in which the child was found.

195. As for naming the child, article 63 states that, in addition to the date, time and place of birth and sex of the child, the birth certificate must state the child's given names. The child automatically takes his father's patronymic when the father is known. If no father or mother is in evidence, the person declaring the child shall choose its given names (art. 64). For foundlings or newborn children whose parents are not known, the registrar himself shall give the child his or her given names, and the last given name shall serve as patronymic (art. 64).

Article 24, paragraph 3

196. Paragraph 3 stipulates that all children have the right to acquire a nationality. Article 29 of the Constitution states that Algerian nationality is defined by law. The conditions for acquiring, keeping, losing and deprivation of nationality are defined by law. The conditions are defined by the Nationality Code (Ordinance No. 70-86 of 15 December 1970), which states in article 1 that, in addition to the law, international treaties and agreements that have been ratified and published shall set the requirements for enjoyment of Algerian nationality. Under the Constitution, such agreements take precedence over internal laws.

197. With regard to children in particular, article 6 of the Nationality Code stipulates:

> "The following are of Algerian nationality by filiation:
>
> (1) A child born of an Algerian father;
>
> (2) A child born of an Algerian mother and an unknown father;
>
> (3) A child born of an Algerian mother and a stateless father."

Article 7 stipulates:

> "The following are of Algerian nationality by virtue of having been born in Algeria:
>
> (1) A child born in Algeria of unknown parents; a newborn child found in Algeria is presumed to have been born in Algeria until evidence is found to the contrary;
>
> (2) A child born in Algeria of an Algerian mother and an alien father who was himself born in Algeria, unless the child rejects Algerian nationality within the year preceding his coming of age."

And article 17 stipulates that the minor children of persons who acquire Algerian nationality become Algerian at the same time as their parents. The unmarried minor children of an Algerian who has resettled in Algeria, when they actually reside with that person, automatically acquire or reacquire

0101

Algerian nationality. Finally, under the naturalization process the minor children of a naturalized foreigner may acquire Algerian nationality. However, the children have the option of renouncing Algerian nationality between the ages of 18 and 21.

Article 25: Right to take part in the conduct of public affairs, to vote and to be elected; right to access to public service in one's country

198. Article 6 of the Constitution affirms: "The people are the source of all power. National sovereignty belongs to the people." Article 7 states: "Constituent power belongs to the people. The people exercise their sovereignty through the institutions which they establish. The people exercise sovereignty by means of referendums and through their elected representatives. The President of the Republic may have direct recourse to the expression of the will of the people." Article 10 says: "The people shall choose their representatives freely. The representation of the people has no limits other than those set by the Constitution and electoral law." Article 11 adds: "The State derives its legitimacy and its raison d'être from the will of the people." Article 14 recognizes that: "The State is founded on the principles of democratic organization and social justice. The elected assembly constitutes the framework within which the will of the people is expressed and control of the actions of the public authorities is exercised."

199. The right to take part in the conduct of public affairs is guaranteed by the multi-party system and the organization of the powers established by the Constitution. With regard to the multi-party system, see above, part I of the report and the comments on article 22, in particular, the paragraphs relating to political associations. The organization of powers is subject to the principle of the separation of the executive, legislative and judicial powers. The judiciary is independent (see above, part I of the report).

200. With regard to the executive branch, the President of the Republic and Head of State is elected by universal, direct and secret suffrage. He is elected by an absolute majority of the votes cast. The other procedures relating to the presidential election are established by law (see below, decision of the Constitutional Council, which declared unconstitutional a provision of the Electoral Code establishing an additional condition for eligibility introducing discrimination which ran counter to the Constitution and the 1966 Covenants ratified by Algeria). The President of the Republic is elected for a term of five years and may be re-elected. He appoints the Head of Government. The latter selects the members of his Government and presents them to the President of the Republic for appointment. The Head of Government submits his programme for approval by the National People's Assembly, which initiates a general debate for that purpose. In the event of his programme not being approved, the Head of Government submits the resignation of his Government to the President of the Republic.

201. Legislative power is exercised by a single assembly (the National People's Assembly), which has sovereign power to draft and enact legislation and exercise control over the actions of the Government. Members of the Assembly are elected by universal, direct and secret suffrage for a period of five years. The procedures relating to the election of deputies are established by law (see below).

0102

202. The Constitution provides that every citizen fulfilling the legal conditions has the right to vote and to be elected. The conditions are established by Act No. 89-13 of 7 August 1989 relating to the Electoral Code. This Act amends the previous electoral law in order to take account of the multi-party system. It should be mentioned that the new Act adopted by the Assembly has been the subject of referral, by the President of the Republic, to the Constitutional Council, which gave a decision on the constitutionality of articles 61, 62, 82, 84 to 86, 91, 108, 110 and 111 (decision No. 1 DLCC/89 of 20 August 1989 relating to the Electoral Code). The Council declared articles 86, 91, 108, 110 and 111 to be unconstitutional. It appended to its decision new texts for articles 86, 91, 108 and 110. The provisions of article 111 ceased to have effect from the date of the Council's decision, in conformity with article 159 of the Constitution.

203. The Electoral Code, as reformulated by the Constitutional Council, strengthens the right recognized by the Constitution to vote and to be elected, while establishing the general regulations governing elections. It also defines the conditions for conducting them, infractions of the Code and penalties. The general provisions of the Code are the following:

(a) Voting is universal and direct and by secret ballot (art. 2).

(b) All Algerian men and women aged 18 or over on the date of the poll who are in possession of their civil and political rights and who do not suffer from any legal disability under the legislation in force are eligible to vote (art. 3). The following may not be included in the electoral register: persons sentenced for a serious or ordinary offence to a term of imprisonment without possibility of remission, together with suspension of the right to vote, as provided for under articles 8 and 14 of the Penal Code; persons whose conduct during the National Liberation Revolution was contrary to the interests of the country; undischarged bankrupts; prisoners; and persons subject to legal disability (art. 5).

(c) The Act lays down the procedures for drawing up and revising the electoral registers (arts. 6 to 22). Such registers are drawn up and revised in each commune by a government commission which includes a public officer with judicial authority. All electors may examine the register of concern to them and enter claims with regard to entries or deletions. The chairman of the Communal Assembly (the mayor) is required to issue an elector's card to every citizen entered on the electoral register.

(d) Voting is personal and by secret ballot (art. 28). The Act sets forth voting procedures in articles 23 to 60. Every polling station is equipped with one or more polling booths. The vote of every elector is certified by his signature.

(e) The votes are counted in public, immediately after the polls are closed. The operation is conducted by tellers. The results are recorded in a report, to which are attached ballot papers whose validity the tellers consider doubtful or which have been challenged by electors. These papers are kept until the period allowed for appeal has expired.

0103

204. The Electoral Code establishes regulations concerning the election of local bodies (communes and wilaya) in articles 61 to 83. Such bodies are elected for five years on one ballot by proportional representation on party lists, with a premium to the majority. All electors aged 25 years or over at the date of the poll are eligible to stand as candidates. The names of those standing are declared on a list fulfilling the legal regulations, which is lodged at the wilaya level. The list must be authorized by one or more political associations; alternatively, the candidate may support his candidature by the signatures of at least 10 per cent of the electorate in his constituency.

205. The Code also provides for the election of members of the National Assembly, which is elected on one ballot by proportional representation on party lists, with a premium to the majority. Candidates must be at least 30 years of age and of Algerian nationality (art. 86). The Constitutional Council considered that the conditions initially established by the Act (Algerian national by birth of the candidate and of his/her spouse) were unconstitutional and contrary to the international human rights conventions ratified by Algeria, including the 1966 Covenants and the African Charter on Human Rights and Peoples' Rights. The Constitutional Council considered that "it is for the electors to form a judgement on the fitness of each candidate to assume public office" and declared that the requirement as to the nationality at birth of candidates in legislative elections was not in conformity with the Constitution. It further considered that the requirement of Algerian nationality by birth for the spouse was not in conformity with the Constitution in that it was a requirement both extrinsic to the candidate and of a discriminatory nature.

206. The Code contains the provisions relating to the election of the President of the Republic and to referendums (arts. 104 to 122). Rules for presidential elections comprise voting for one person on two ballots, to achieve an absolute majority of the votes cast. Candidates must lodge a request to stand with the Constitutional Council. This organ has decided that such a request should not be accompanied by a certificate showing the Algerian nationality by birth of the spouse, as required by article 108, paragraph 3, which has been declared unconstitutional. The Council considered that this requirement "cannot be regarded as comprising a procedure of the presidential election and constitutes in fact a supplementary condition of eligibility; furthermore, it introduces discrimination contrary to the provisions of the Constitution and to the 1966 Human Rights Covenants" ratified by Algeria. The Constitutional Council further declared unconstitutional the provision of article 110 which makes it obligatory for the candidate to be expressly approved or put forward by one or more political associations. The Council considered that "the obligation for a candidate for the office of President of the Republic to produce an authorization, as defined in article 110, in practice eliminates candidates from outside political associations; that constitutes an obstacle to exercise of a right enshrined in article 47 of the Constitution".

207. The Constitutional Council likewise handed down a decision on articles 111 and 91 of the Electoral Code. Article 111 exempted the President of the Republic in office from the conditions set out in article 110. Article 91, paragraph 3, dispensed an outoing deputy not included on a party list from the

obligation of supporting his candidature with the signatures of 10 per cent of the electorate in his constituency or 500 electors. The Council considered that "the fundamental principle of the sovereignty of the people and the normal functioning of the democratic system require that those holding an electoral mandate must without exception surrender it on its expiry to the electorate; it is for the latter to judge the way in which it has been performed. Under the terms of article 47, which recognizes the right of all citizens to be elected, and of article 28 of the Constitution, which establishes the equality of all before the law, candidates in all elections must equally fulfil the same obligations and enjoy the same rights; such exemptions may well be regarded as a breach of the principle of equality of treatment of candidates". Consequently, the Council declared article 111 and article 91, paragraph 3, of the Electoral Code to be at variance with the Constitution.

208. The Code also establishes the procedures for organizing the electoral campaign (arts. 123 to 132) and contains provisions relating to financial matters. Electoral campaigns are funded by means of contributions from the parties, the income of the candidate and possible assistance from the State provided on an equitable basis.

209. Finally, the Code sets out the penal provisions applicable in cases of breaches of the Act (falsification of electoral registers; fraudulent declarations; altering of ballot papers; carrying weapons in the polling station; improper removal of ballot papers; disrupting polling operations; insulting behaviour and violence towards polling station officials; improper removal of the ballot box, punishable by 5 to 10 years' imprisonment and 10 to 20 years' if accompanied by violence; intimidation of electors, etc.).

210. Article 48 of the Constitution stipulates that "Equal access to office and employment under the State is guaranteed to all citizens, subject to no conditions other than those fixed by law". Access to State service is not based on any discrimination. It is open to all citizens who meet the criteria of proficiency, integrity and commitment (Act No. 78-12 of 5 August 1978 relating to the general statute of workers). Decree No. 85-59 of 23 March 1985, relating to the standard qualifications for workers in public institutions and offices, regulates conditions of access and promotion, which ensure equality of opportunity to all Algerian citizens. Article 31 relating to recruitment provides:

"No one may be recruited for a public institution or office:

1. Unless he is of Algerian nationality;

2. Unless he is in possession of his political rights and is of good character;

3. Unless he can provide proof of possessing the qualifications required by the post;

0105

4. Unless he satisfies the conditions in respect of age and physical fitness required for carrying out the duties in question;

5. Unless he can produce proof of having complied with national service requirements.

Specific regulations shall, as necessary, establish conditions regarding seniority in the acquisition of Algerian nationality for access to certain branches of the civil service."

Article 26: Equality before the law and right without discrimination to the protection of the law

211. The principle that all persons are equal before the law and are entitled without discrimination to the equal protection of the law is clearly set out in the Constitution, article 28 of which states: "Citizens are equal before the law, and there shall be no discrimination on grounds of birth, race, sex, opinion or any other personal or social condition or circumstance." Various other constitutional provisions, in particular articles 30 to 32, 34 to 37, 39, 40, 47, 48, 50 to 53, 57, 60, 61, 65, 129 to 131, 133, 138 and 141 contribute to the same objective of ensuring and guaranteeing the rights of the individual, in accordance with the basic principle of non-discrimination and the equality of all before the law.

212. Since its independence, Algeria has abrogated all discriminatory legislative measures and regulations and developed legislation intended to look after the interests, aspirations and values of the Algerian people which, throughout its long history, has given proof of its tolerance, its openness to other cultures and civilizations, and its complete abhorrence of any form of racism, injustice, domination and discrimination. Algeria is a party to the International Convention on the Elimination of All Forms of Racial Discrimination and has made the declaration under article 14 whereby it recognizes the competence of CERD to receive and consider complaints of violations of the rights enunciated in the Convention.

213. National legislation, in which are incorporated the numerous international conventions to which Algeria is a party, is based on this fundamental principle of non-discrimination. Furthermore, all laws contain a series of measures aimed at translating this principle into practical reality. The comments on the preceding articles of the Covenant given an insight into national legislation on the subject. It should be added that sectoral legislation on health, labour, education, etc. also contributes to the implementation of the basic rights of the individual, without any discrimination. Thus, by way of illustration, it may be mentioned that Act No. 78/12 of 5 April 1978 relating to the general statutes of workers stipulates that "The rights of the worker are guaranteed by law. Workers are equal in rights and duties. They shall receive the same remuneration and benefits for the same work based on equality of qualifications and productivity". The Act adds that "Disabled persons who cannot be employed under normal working conditions shall have suitable employment or, if need be, sheltered workshops and the right to specialized training." In addition to the right to education being guaranteed, education is compulsory, free and

accessible to everyone under conditions of equality. Act No. 76/35 of 16 April 1976 relating to the organization of education and training stresses that the Algerian educational system must:

"(a) Inculcate in young people the principles of justice and equality among citizens and peoples, and inspire them to combat any form of discrimination;

"(b) Provide an education which promotes understanding and cooperation among peoples for universal peace and agreement among nations;

"(c) Develop education in accordance with human rights and fundamental freedoms."

214. Even the laws relating to freedom of association, opinion, expression and assembly contain provisions whereby all practices liable to harm human rights are prohibited (see above). It should be added that the law relating to the exercise of trade union rights "prohibits trade union organizations from introducing into their statutes or practising any discrimination between members liable to infringe their fundamental freedoms" (art. 22).

215. It should also be stated that the Constitutional Council sees to it that the principle of non-discrimination enshrined in the Constitution is scrupulously respected. In addition to decision No. 1 (mentioned in comment on art. 25), the Constitutional Council, by its decision No. 2 DLCC/89 of 30 August 1989, declared article 8 of the Status of Deputy Act (No. 14 of 8 August 1989) to be at variance with article 28 of the Constitution. Article 8 of that Act dealt with the compatibility of the duties of a teacher in higher education and a doctor in the public sector with the mandate of deputy. The Constitutional Council considered that "the law, which is the expression of the general will, cannot create inequitable situations between citizens; the lifting of incompatibility for certain holders of public office, as envisaged in article 8, creates a discriminatory situation with respect to the holders of identical offices coming under other legal dispensations".

<u>Article 27</u>: <u>Rights of ethnic, religious or linguistic minorities</u>

216. The Algerian people are characterized by homogeneity. Islam is one of the components in the national character, which was forged in a cultural crucible with many inflows. All attempts at colonialism, at denying the existence of the Algerian nation, ran up against the resistance of the Algerian people. As early as under Massinissa, the founder of the first Numidian State, and of Jugurtha, who initiated resistance to Roman imperialism, the national character began to be forged and the idea of an Algerian nation strengthened. Both were to assert themselves through the historical development of Algeria over more than 2,000 years. From the seventh century onwards, Islam was a decisive factor. The States which succeeded one another on Algerian soil from the Middle Ages, from the Rostoumides to Emir Abdelkader, from the Zirides-Hamadites dynasty to that of the Abdelwadites-Zyanides, set their seal on the historic heritage of the central Maghreb, in the form of its Muslim values and its marked distinctiveness as a Nation, which thus continued and enriched the traditions

0107

from the distant past. The different periods of Algerian history constituted a melting-pot of ethnic mixtures, enriching contributions to the creativity of the national genius, which resulted in the distinctive Algerian character.

217. Confronted with repeated attacks from Europe from the sixteenth century onwards, and in spite of a policy of foreign settlement conducted after the French colonial invasion of 1830, the Algerian character remained unchanged. The survival of Algeria was the result of ceaseless struggles and long resistance to oppression, which culminated in the reconquest of national sovereignty and national identity. The divisive efforts of the colonizer had the opposite effect of strengthening the unity of the Algerian people, which today, its liberty and identity regained, is pursuing the work of economic, social and cultural development in a modern State where the law is supreme.

218. The opening article of the Constitution states: "Algeria is a Democratic People's Republic; it is one and indivisible." Articles 2 and 3 stipulate that Islam is the religion of the State and that Arabic is the national and official language. Article 28 provides that Algerian citizens are equal before the law and that there shall be no discrimination on grounds of birth, race, sex, opinion or any other personal or social condition or circumstance. Article 30 states: "The institutions shall seek to ensure the equality of rights and duties of all male and female citizens by eliminating the obstacles which impede the full development of the human personality and prevent the effective participation of all in political economic, social and cultural life." The Constitution also establishes freedom of conscience, opinion, intellectual and scientific creativity, expression, association and assembly, as well as the other fundamental freedoms and human rights.

219. The affirmation in the Constitution that Islam is the religion of the State and Arabic the national and official language is the outcome of attempts to depersonalize and divide the Algerian people, who by referendum made a point of reaffirming and inserting in the Constitution the basic features of their character, thus stressing the homogeneity of their human and cultural make-up. Accordingly, in Algeria, censuses are never conducted on the basis of ethnic, religious or linguistic criteria. However, that affirmation should not be interpreted as a narrow, restrictive view of the Algerian character, which is also rich in its age-old traditions.

220. In addition to Arab and Islamic culture, Algeria also recognizes its Berber culture and its kinship with Africa and the Mediterranean. Berber is widely spoken in various regions of Algeria and used as a means of expression in many cultural and artistic events both within and outside the country and on the second channel of the national radio, which broadcasts in Berber, from 6 a.m. till midnight, artistic, educational and cultural programmes and news bulletins. Berber culture and language are increasingly fostered as constituent elements of the national cultural heritage. For this reason, a Department of Berber Culture and Language has been set up within Tizi-Ouzou University. In addition to teaching the language, the Department has undertaken a series of studies and research and organized various symposia on Berber culture. Recently, it offered a third course-level to students wishing to specialize in this field.

221. The various elements of the national cultural heritage are fostered in order to encourage the development of pluralistic cultural expression. This has led to the abolition of the Ministry of Culture so as to relieve culture of the weight of bureaucracy and ensure that it is taken in hand by its real promoters, including the very many cultural associations set up as part of the development of group movements since the adoption of the 1989 Constitution, as well as the various cultural institutions already existing at the national, regional and local levels. At the national level, in addition to the specialized cultural institutions, the former Ministry of Culture has been replaced by a National Council for Culture, whose mission is defined in Executive Decree No. 90-250 of 18 August 1990. In conjunction with the various cultural institutions, the Council has the task of promoting and developing culture by granting material and financial support to encourage the activities of those institutions and of cultural associations.

222. Freedom of religion and worship is covered by several articles of the Constitution. In addition to articles 28 and 30, article 35 states that freedom of conscience and opinion is inviolable. Article 37 provides that privacy and honour are inviolable and protected by law. Article 39 guarantees the freedoms of expression, association and assembly. These provisions translate into law the fact that tolerance has always prevailed in Algerian society, which has permitted the cohabitation of the three great monotheistic religions. The Christian and Jewish communities, made up primarily of Europeans, have continued since independence to enjoy freedom of religion. Their respective places of worship are protected by the Ministry for Religious Affairs (see above, comments on art. 18).

CONCLUSION

223. The present report provides a summary of the juridical framework and its main provisions relating to the protection and promotion of the rights set forth in the International Covenant on Civil and Political Rights, in the overall context of the reforms being carried out in Algeria. Those aspects of the reforms relating to the field covered by the Covenant are briefly surveyed in the first part of this report. The economic, social and cultural reforms which constitute an integral part of the reform process being undertaken by Algeria will be set out in the initial report to be submitted pursuant to the relevant provisions of the International Covenant on Economic, Social and Cultural Rights, which Algeria has likewise ratified. It should also be mentioned that the members of the Human Rights Committee will be able to find further information in the comments on article 7 in the initial report submitted by Algeria in February 1991 to the Committee against Torture.

224. It should further be noted that Algeria, in addition to revising its domestic legislation, has put in hand a series of practical measures aimed at giving effect to the basic principles enshrined in the Constitution and the international undertakings to which Algeria has subscribed. Encouragement of the development of associations forms part of that aim. Algeria is also aware of the important role played by information and training in the field of human rights. In Algeria, everyone is taught, from their earliest age, the principle of the equality of all human beings, tolerance, respect for others, abhorrence of racial prejudice, love and understanding among peoples. To this end courses of civic, moral and religious education are given in all educational establishments.

0109

225. The obligation to respect human rights is one of the constitutional principles which, as such, underlie the curricula for general education and specialized training. In the universities of Algiers and Oran, particularly in the faculties of law and jurisprudence, courses are given on human rights, the rights of refugees and humanitarian law, at degree and postgraduate levels. A number of research topics have been devoted to human rights and chosen by students as subjects for Master's theses. In addition, a number of schools and institutes organize specialized training courses for judges, central and local government officials, and personnel in the police, gendarmerie, prison administration, security services and armed forces. The content and scope of these principles are also reflected in the basic training programmes for the other occupations which may be relevant to the exercise of the basic rights of the individual - or doctors and journalists, for example.

226. A number of symposia and workshops were organized during 1990. For example, a training course was organized, with the Office of the United Nations High Commissioner for Refugees, for the officials of various ministries on the subject of refugees (applicable rules for determining the status of refugees and respect for their rights). The Ministry of Justice organized several seminars. One, devoted to litigation and administrative law, was for judges in the administrative divisions, who studied ways to implement the reforms introduced by the Code of Civil Procedure in that field, with a view to streamlining recourse procedures relating to administrative litigation. Another seminar was for presiding judges, procurators and examining magistrates of courts in the Central Region, who met experts and specialists in immunology, ballistics, graphology, food chemistry, forensic medicine and criminal science, with the main purpose of studying the applications of criminal science and forensic medicine in judicial proceedings in order to enhance performance and standards in the administration of justice. Further regional and national seminars in the programme of action of the Ministry of Justice are aimed at improving judicial action by enabling a judge to learn about developments in the various sciences involved in the application of the law. Seminars are also envisaged, in the context of continuing training, _inter alia_, on the subjects of custody, judicial review, information and its judicial application.

227. The national print, audiovisual and sound media regularly and widely reflect, from many standpoints, the numerous discussions, seminars, conferences and exhibitions held in Algeria on the subject of human rights. It should be noted that the forty-second anniversary of the Universal Declaration of Human Rights provided an opportunity for several political parties and associations to organize lectures, discussions and seminars on human rights. For example, the Algerian Amnesty International Association gave a lecture on "Amnesty and human rights". The National Committee against Torture organized a number of lectures and discussions on the subject of torture, including a round table by radio. The Algerian League for Human Rights organized a press conference in Algiers to which the national and international press were invited, as well as lectures, discussions and exhibitions on human rights in various towns. Several other cultural associations organized discussions on the subject of economic, social and cultural rights.

228. The Algerian League for Human Rights organized, in collaboration with the Arab Institute for Human Rights and the National Algerian Lawyers' Organization, a Maghrebi training seminar on human rights at Sidi-Fredj (Algiers) from 8 to 11 December; it was attended by representatives of many other Maghrebi human rights associations. On the occasion of that seminar Mr. Benflis, the Algerian Minister of Justice, delivered the following message:

> "Mankind, deeply devoted to freedom, justice, progress and peace, has made undeniable strides in the field of human rights. And yet, 42 years after the proclamation of the Universal Declaration of Human Rights, it is still a burning issue in our country and everywhere in the world.
>
> The vastness of the sphere of action for plural, individual and collective freedoms and for the fundamental political, economic, social and cultural rights of citizens is to some extent the reason for this.
>
> The constant progress, and at times the intensive exercise, of human rights may perhaps reflect a certain concern to convert these precarious rights into inalienable rights, given the frequently justified fear for their fragile nature.
>
> By means of measures at the national and international levels, and through the action of numerous institutions, and international, continental, regional and non-governmental organizations and associations, human rights and freedoms are becoming increasingly accepted in our world, which is resolved to drive back the forces of tyranny and oppression until all islands of hope have been invested with the rule of law.
>
> In our spirit of fraternity, human rights apply to all human beings, men, women and children, who are equal in dignity and rights. To exercise these rights requires not only the enjoyment of the various types of freedom, but also the complete eradication of the horrendous spectre of torture, all forms of servitude, persecution, arbitrary action or interference, and cruel, inhuman or degrading treatment.
>
> Human rights constitute the major element in our country's political, economic, social and cultural development. The Constitution of 23 February 1989 expressly enshrined the arrival of the body of plural, individual and collective freedoms and fundamental rights of citizens, as well as the promotion of the rule of law, *inter alia*, through the establishment of an independent judiciary.
>
> Protection of the person, his honour, property, privacy and freedom of conscience, opinion, creativity, expression, association, assembly, movement and information, the right to vote, the right to litigate, the right of defence, trade union rights, the right to strike and the rights to education, work, health protection, rest and recourse before competent courts against acts in violation of the fundamental rights and freedoms of citizens as recognized by the Constitution and the law are not only enshrined, but are implemented in the firm belief in the justice of causes involving the freedom, dignity and worth of the human personality.

This struggle to establish human rights is difficult, long and no doubt endless. It requires that enlightened minds should occupy all spheres of expression and action by swelling to the utmost the ranks of committed combatants in the cause of bringing human rights to the point from which there is no turning back. It calls upon all persons to take charge of their destiny in freedom and human grandeur. In this sensitive domain, the heritage of all mankind which entails active solidarity and involvement with all human rights causes throughout the world - in suffering Palestine, in Africa and everywhere else, no reservation, no monopoly should be allowed to dissipate the exercise of human rights, which must be the prerogative of the entire world without exception. The priceless achievements brought about by advances in human rights must be unswervingly upheld for the sake of the constant promotion of a free society."

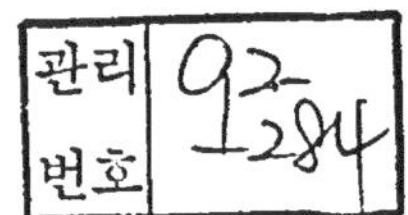

외 무 부

110-760 서울 종로구 세종로 77번지 / (02) 723-8934 / (02) 723-3505

문서번호 연이 20314-066
시행일자 1992.4.8.
(경유)
수신 법무부장관
참조 법무실장

취급		장 관
보존		
국 장	전결	
심의관		
과 장		
기안	함상욱	협조

제목 제44차 인권이사회 참가 결과

1. 3.23-4.10. 뉴욕 유엔본부에서 개최중인 제44차 인권이사회 회의의 인권규약("B") 최초보고서 심의과정(3.25-27, 알제리) 참가결과를 별첨과 같이 통보하오니, 제45차 인권이사회 회의(7.13-31, 제네바) 아국 최초보고서 심의 준비에 참고하시기 바랍니다.

2. 아울러, 유엔 인권사무국(UN Center for Human Rights)과 UNITAR가 공동발간한 "Manual on Human Rights Reporting"을 별첨 송부합니다.

첨부 : 1. 제44차 인권이사회 참가보고서
2. Manual on Human Rights Reporting. 끝.

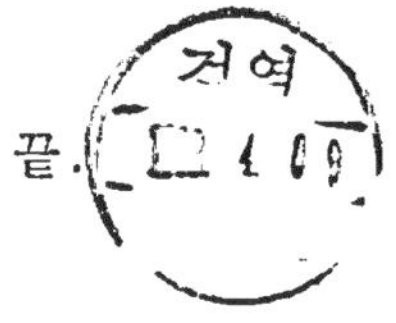

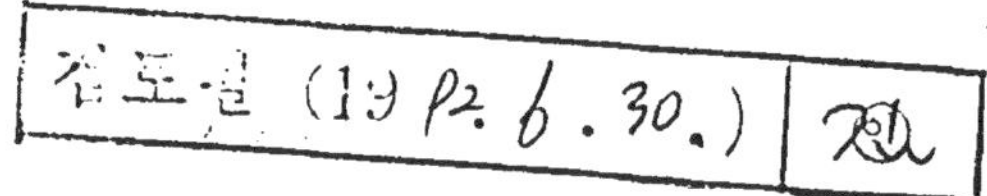

0113

제44차 인권이사회 참가보고서

(3.24-3.27)

1992. 4.

국 제 기 구 국

0114

1. 일반사항

가. 회의참석

o 18명의 위원중 12명 참석

- Aguillor Urbina(코스타리카), Andreas Mavrommatis(싸이프러스), Rein Myullerson(러시아), Fausto Pocar(이태리, 의장), Nisuke Ando(일본), Christine Chanet(불란서), Vojin Dimitrijevic (유고), Omran El-Shafei(이집트), Birame N'Diaye(세네갈), Waleed Sadi(요르단), Julio Vallejo(에쿠아돌), Bertil Wennergren (스웨덴), Janos Fodor(항가리)

o 알제리 대표단

- 법무부 조사국장 Noureddine Benamara(수석대표) 외 3인 (법무부 및 주유엔대표부)

o 옵서버 참석

- 10여국 대표 및 Amnesty International 등 참관

나. 진행방식

o 각국 보고서 심의는 공개회의로 진행

- 언론 및 옵서버 참석 가 (국가, NGO 또는 개인)

다. 진행일정

o 제1일 오전회의시 보고서 제출국 대표의 기조발언과 위원들의 질의

o 제2일 : 답변준비기간 (단, 위원회는 회의 계속, 타국 보고서 또는 여타 의제 심의)

o 제3일 오전회의시 보고서 제출국 대표의 답변 및 보충 질의

2. 상세 진행절차

제 1 일

가. 보고서 제출국 대표와 보좌관은 의장단석에 착석 (의장의 오른편)

나. 의장(Fausto Pocar, 이태리)의 대표단 소개

다. 보고서 제출국 대표의 모두발언(Introductory Statement)

- Algeria의 경우 6-7분 소요

라. 위원의 논평 및 질의

- Algeria의 경우 출석위원 12인중 11인 발언, 각 5-20분간 소요 (약 2시간 소요)

제 2 일 (보고서 제출국 답변준비)

제 3 일

가. 보고서 제출국 대표의 답변(약 90분 소요)

나. 위원들의 보충 질의

- Algeria의 경우 위원 9인이 발언, 약 60분 소요

다. 보고서 제출국 대표의 추가 답변

3. 주요내용

가. 모두 발언(Introductory Statement)

o 알제리의 경우 인권보장에 관한 입법의 개략적 연혁, 현 헌법의 성립 경위 및 주요 골격, 헌정체제의 개편과 인권부(Ministry of Human Rights)의 설립, 국가인권감시기구(National Human Rights Observation Body)의 설치등에 관한 설명과 함께 법과 현실간의 급격한 괴리에

2

0116

따른 위기상황의 도래(알제리는 91.12. 및 92.2. 비상사태 선포) 및 이에 대처하여 사회의 욕구와 국가 법체계의 변화를 조화시켜야 할 필요성등에 대해 설명하였음.

o 또한 신헌법 채택(89.2.) 후 인권규약(B)에 가입(89.12)하게 된 배경을 설명하고, 동 규약에 따른 최초보고서에 대해 위원들의 질의에 성실하게 답변하겠다는 의사를 표명함.

나. 논평 및 질의

o 일반적 평가

- 보고서 작성의 객관성과 성실성을 평가하고, 신헌법의 공표로 민주화 노력이 시작된 것을 환영한다고 논평함.
- 인권관계 제반협약에의 가입상황은 양호한 것으로 지적함. (선택의정서 및 규약 제41조도 수락)
- 규약의 적용이 제약되는 상황 및 제약 논리에 대한 설명이 부족한 것으로 지적되고, 특히 비상사태 선포에 관한 비판적 질문이 대부분 위원들에 의해 제기되었음.

o 구체적 내용

- 보고서는 91.6까지의 사항을 기술하고 있으나, 그 이후 현재까지의 사항도 설명되어야 함.
- 보고서는 객관적이고 포괄적으로 기술되어 있으나, 규약 시행상의 애로사항이나 인권보장에 대한 인식을 확산하기 위한 정부의 노력에 관해서는 언급이 없음.
- 규약과 국내법과의 상충시에 규약의 규정이 어떻게 이행되는지에 관한 설명이 필요함. (법원이 규약의 규정을 원용한 사례등)
- 최근 비상사태 선포로 규약의 위반사례가 관찰됨. (정당한 재판을 받을 권리 침해, 고문사례, 당국의 무기남용 등)

- 보고서가 다소 아카데믹하게 기술되어 있는 반면, 현실적인 상황에 대한 언급이 결여되어 있음. (특히 최근 비상사태 하에서의 인권 보장상황에 대한 설명 필요)
- 최근 비상사태를 선포한 정부의 행위가 규약의 어떤 규정에 근거 하였는지에 대한 정당화 논리 제시 요망
- 고위 사법위원회(High Council of Judiciary) 및 헌법평의회 (Constitutional Council)의 구성 및 임명방법등에 비추어 사법권의 독립이 보장되는지에 대한 설명 요망
- 경제범죄에 대해서도 사형이 적용되는 것은 사형제도의 남용이 아닌지?
- 단일민족이므로 소수집단 차별문제가 없다고 하나, Berber 어족에 대한 차별은 없는지?
- 헌법에 자유와 권리의 보장이 규정되고 있으나 이러한 권리의 제한에 관하여는 구체적 규정이 없으며, 단순히 "보장된다"라고 하는 규정이 구속력있는 효과를 갖는 것인지?
- 조약이 국내법보다 우선한다고 할수 있는바, 이슬람의 비판을 금지하는 정보법의 규정이 규약 제19조 규정을 제한하는데 대한 설명 및 일반적으로 인권분야에서 조약과 국내법과의 관계에 대한 구체적 설명 요망
- 가족법 규정은 규약과 상이한데, 이 경우 법적용 원칙 설명 요망
- 규약의 위반이 국내법상 Penal Violation이 되는지?
- 사형집행의 통계 요망
- Administrative detention procedure와 수용소내 detention 제도에 대한 설명 요망
- 언론의 자유 및 시위의 자유 제한에 대해 설명 요망
- 비상사태 선포하 민간인에 대한 군사재판시 일반재판과 다른 특별 규정의 적용 여부

- 국가에 의한 무료법률구조제도 여부
- 형법상 이슬람 모독죄 관련 규정은 종교에 의한 차별의 인정을 의미하는 것이 아닌지?
- 다당제 규정이 매우 막연한 바, 특정 정당의 해산에 관한 구체적 법률적 근거는?
- 파업권의 제한에 대한 정당화 논리는?
- 회교적 일부다처제의 인정은 남녀차별적 제도라고 보는데, 이에 대한 정당화 논리는?
- 헌법공표 이전에 채택된 조약의 효력은?
- 국적법상 부에 의한 국적승계제도는 남녀차별 금지규정에 대한 위반이 아닌지?
- 재판을 받을 권리와 관련, 재판소에의 access에 있어 내국인과 외국인간 차별은 없는지 및 내국언론인과 외국언론인에 대한 대우의 차별은 없는지?
- 표현의 자유에 대한 제한과 관련, 정확성(accuracy)이란 기준에 대한 판정자는 누구인지 및 외국의 출판물이나 비데오등의 availability는 있는지?

다. 답변형식

o 출석위원 대부분이 질문을 함으로써 질문내용에 중복 또는 공통점이 많아 답변시 위원 개인별 질문에 답변하기 보다는 일정한 주제별 및 사안별로 그룹화하여 답변하는 것이 효과적일 수 있음.
  - 알제리의 경우도 그룹화하여 답변

라. 추가보고서

o 알제리의 경우 비상사태 선포에 대하여는 그 필수불가결했던 점에 대한 설명을 추가보고서(addendum)로 제출해야 한다는 주장도 있었으나, 차기 보고서에서 다루기로 함.

4. 유의사항

- 아국 보고서 심의 준비 관련

가. 규약 조항별 국내 법체제에 대한 질문에 대한 답변외에도 각종 인권사안에 대한 구체적인 설명자료와 통계자료의 준비가 필요함.

- 특히 국가보안법 위반, 집회 및 시위에 관한 법률 위반, 노동조합법 위반, 장기수 문제등 인권사안에 있어 규약의 규정에 비추어 타당성을 설명할 수 있도록 대처 필요

나. 인권이사회 위원에게는 유엔 인권관련 기관에서 토의되거나 접수되는 아국 관련 인권사안은 물론 NGO나 기타 단체 또는 개별적 통신에 의한 모든 정보가 다 입수된다고 하므로, 여하한 형식으로든 과거에 제기된 사례 또는 향후 제기될 것으로 예상할수 있는 사례에 대한 질문에도 대비해야 함.

- 단, 사실관계 질의는 동 규약의 아국에 대한 발효일(90.7.10) 이후 부터 해당

다. 답변에는 최대의 성실성을 보여야 하며, 그러기 위하여는 인권보장과 관련된 업무를 담당하거나 법률일반 및 특히 인권법에 소상한 지식을 갖춘 인사가 대표로 됨이 바람직 함. (보고서 종합 집필자도 대표단에 포함)

라. 보고서 제출시(91.7.) 이후의 특별한 진전사항에 대해서도 질문이 예상되므로 필요한 경우 아국대표의 모두발언에 최근의 인권분야 특기사항 또는 진전사항을 언급함이 바람직함.

마. 보고서 작성시 광범위한 국내의견을 수렴하였다는 표시로서 정부내 관계부처 협의회를 구성하여 보고서 내용에 대해 부처간 협의를 거쳤다는 사실을 언급함이 바람직함.

6

0120

5. 기타사항

o 금번 이사회에서 심의되는 보고서부터는 동 보고서 심의결과를 바탕으로 이사회 명의의 결론적 관찰(concluding observation)을 작성하여, 해당국에 통보하기로 하였으며, 또한 동 내용을 총회 앞 보고서에도 포함키로 하였음.

- 지금까지는 총회 앞 보고서에만 위원 개인별 논평을 요약 게재해 왔음.

o "결론적 관찰"의 구성

(1) 일반적 평가, (2) 긍정적인 발전, (3) 규약의 이행에 영향을 주는 요인과 애로사항, (4) 주요 관심사항(major issues of concern), (5) 이사회의 구체적 권고사항

- 끝 -

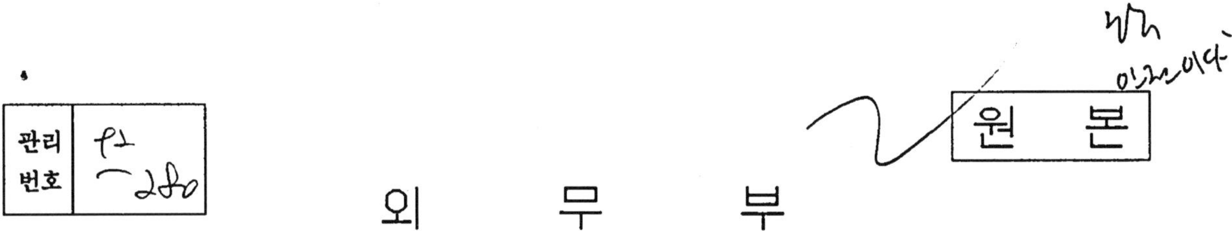

관리번호	92-280

원 본

외 무 부

종 별 :

번 호 : UNW-1028 일 시 : 92 0407 1930

수 신 : 장 관(유엔 2과 정달호과장님)

발 신 : 주 유엔(최종무)

제 목 : 인권관계조사

1.LIST OF ISSUES 문제

본건은 최초보고서 심의시에는 해당되지 않으며 최초보고서 심의절차는 1. 구두질의 (1 SESSION),2. 답변준비시간 부여(1-2 일정도),3. 답변,4. 총평의 순이됨

2.REVIEW 대상기간

최초보고서의 경우, 동국에 대한 협약 효력발생 시점이 기산점이 됨.(아국은 90.7.10 이후) 헌법등이 동시점 이전에 제정된것은 질의의 대상이 될수도 있으나 사실관계 (FACT)는 동 시점이후의 사항만 취급하게됨. (그이전에는 동국을 구속할 법적의무가 없음)

3. 알제리아 추가보고서

알제리아측에게 추가 보고서를 공식 요청하지 않았으며 금번회기에 요청하지 않을것임. 알제리아 관계관도 자국관계는 모두 종료된것으로 이해하고 있었음. 비상사태 선포관계는 차기보고서에서 다루게 될것임

4. 3.27 오후 회의 PR 별첨 송부함

5.RULES OF PROCEDURE, NGO 보고서 PR 은 금파편 송부예정임

6.UNCED 로 바빠서 회신 늦었음을 양지바라며 건승빔

예고:92.12.31 까지

첨부:UNW(F)-0363

검토필 (1992. 6. 30.)	

국기국

PAGE 1

92.04.08 09:25

외신 2과 통제관 BZ

0122

United Nations

(별첨) Press Release UNW(万)-0363 20401

Department of Public Information • News Coverage Service • New York

Human Rights Committee
Forty-fourth Session
1129th Meeting (PM)

HR/CT/178
27 March 1992

HUMAN RIGHTS COMMITTEE CONCLUDES EXAMINATION OF ALGERIA'S REPORT

To Take Up Peru's Second Report on 31 March

The head of the Algerian delegation told the Human Rights Committee this afternoon that his Government was anxious to restore the democratic process as soon as possible.

In a final statement to the Committee, following the presentation of Algeria's initial report under the International Covenant on Civil and Political Rights, Noureddine Benamara said the imposition of a state of emergency had been unavoidable. Since the adoption of the new Constitution, the transition to democracy had been too hasty and Government action had been necessary to respond to a substantial threat to that democratic process.

Responding to specific questions, he indicated that the freeing of a number of prisoners in the near future would improve the medical situation in the detention centres. He also further detailed his Government's plans to ensure equality of the sexes and the availability of legal aid.

The Committee will meet again at 10 a.m. on Tuesday, 31 March, to take up the second periodic report of Peru.

* *** *

363-1-1

관리 번호	92-293

원 본

외 무 부

종 별 :

번 호 : UNW-1069 일 시 : 92 0410 1830

수 신 : 장 관(연이)

발 신 : 주 유엔 대사

제 목 : 인권이사회 44차 회의

1. 표제회의가 금 4.10 오전 폐회되었는바, 동이사회는 7.13-31 간 제네바에서 개최 예정인 차기회의에서 아국및 부룬디의 최초보고서, 벨라루스 및 몽골리아의 3 차 보고서를 심의키로 결정하였음

2. 또한 동 이사회는, 금차 회의시 페루의 2 차보고서 심의와 관련, 최근 동국의 비상사태 선포에 따른 인권문제에 관하여 동국이 추가보고토록 할것을 결정하였으며, 차기회의 직전에 개최되는 WG(청원및 규약 40 조)의 구성을 합의하였음.

(대사 유종하-국장)

예고:92.12.31 까지

검토필 (1992. 6 .30.)	

국기국 차관 1차보 외정실 분석관 청와대 안기부

PAGE 1

92.04.11 08:21

외신 2과 통제관 BX

0124

관리번호	92-311

외 무 부

110-760 서울 종로구 세종로 77번지 / (02) 723-8934 / (02) 723-3505

문서번호 연이 20314- 1010
시행일자 1992.4.22.

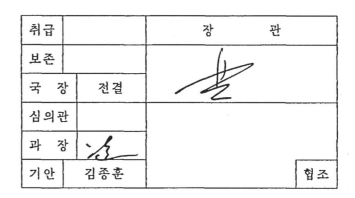

수신 법무부장관
참조 법무실장

취급		장 관
보존		
국 장	전결	
심의관		
과 장		
기안	김종훈	협조

제목 아국 인권규약(B) 최초 보고서 심의

1. 연이 20314-866(92.4.8)과 관련입니다.

2. 92.7.13-7.31간 제네바에서 개최예정인 제45차 인권이사회에서의 아국 인권규약(B) 최초 보고서 심의와 관련, 아국 대표단 구성을 추진중인바, 동 수석대표는 인권이사회의 관례에 비추어 국내 법무행정 업무를 담당하고, 국내법 전반 특히 인권관련 법규 및 제도에 정통한 고위인사를 임명하는 것이 필요할 것으로 판단됩니다.

3. 따라서 아국 대표단 수석대표를 귀부 ~~실·국장급~~ 고위 인사로 임명하는 것이 좋을 것으로 사료되는바, 이에 대한 귀부 의견을 알려 주시기 바랍니다.

4. 수석대표는 필요한 경우 통역을 대동할수 있음을 참고하시기 바랍니다. 끝.

0125

민간단체 인권보고서 첫선

정부작성내용 비판…신체자유 미흡평가

민변·한교협 공동발간…설명회 갖기로

한국정부가 90년 국제인권규약에 가입한 뒤 규약규정에 따라 91년 7월 국제연합 인권이사회에 제출한 인권보고서를 반박하는 재야인권단체의 반대보고서가 작성됐다.

민주사회를 위한 변호사모임(민변)과 한국기독교교회협의회 인권위원회는 28일 △국가보안법 △신체의 자유 △사상과 양심의 자유 등 23개 항목에서 정부가 낸 인권보고서의 내용을 비판하는 한글 1백50여쪽, 영문 1백50여쪽에 이르는 방대한 분량의 반대보고서 작성을 마쳤다. 이번 반대보고서는 우리사회의 법체계 전반에 걸친 인권실태를 국제사회에 알리는 최초 민간보고서라는 점에서 큰 관심을 끌고 있다.

반대보고서는 정부보고서에 대해 "많은 부분에서 규약의 조항과 관련된 남한의 법조문을 열거하는 데 그치고 있을 뿐"이라며 "실제의 인권보장 상황을 보여주는 사실들이 언급되어있지 않으며 인권에 영향을 주는 법원의 판례나 정부의 조처 등을 설명하지 않고 있다"고 평가했다.

반대보고서는 이에 따라 "결론적으로 정부보고서는 규약이 보장하는 인권이 침해되는 상황에 관해 설명하지 않음으로써 한국의 인권상황에 대해 양호한 것으로 오해를 일으킬 수 있도록 만들어져 있다"고 비판했다.

반대보고서는 한국에서 규약의 이행에 영향을 끼치는 가장 중요한 요소와 장애를 한반도의 분단이라고 규정한 뒤 "국가안보를 명분으로 인권을 침해하는 억압적인 법률들이 만들어졌고 정부에 대한 비판적인 말과 행동이 북한을 이롭게 한다는 이유로 모두 처벌의 대상이 돼왔다"고 평가했다. 반대보고서는 국가보안법과 관련해 "남한에서 '실질적 의미의 헌법'이라고 말해도 지나치지 않은데도 정부보고서는 설명이 너무 부족하고 이 법에 의한 인권의 침해상황을 전혀 설명하지 않고 있다"고 반박했다.

반대보고서는 이에 따라 △간첩죄 및 목적수행죄 △잠입·탈출죄 △찬양·고무·동조·이적단체구성·이적표현물 제작죄 △회합·통신죄 등 국가보안법 조항에 대한 자의적 해석·적용이 끼친 인권침해 실태를 문익환목사·임수경씨 방북사건, 서울사회과학연구소사건 등을 예로 들어 설명하고 있다. 신체의 자유와 관련해 반대보고서는 헌법과 형사소송법, 경찰관 직무집행법 등의 규정에도 불구하고 △권리실현에 장애를 주는 특별법의 존재 △정부당국자나 수사담당자들의 관행화된 불법구속·구금 등이 규약이 규정한 신체의 자유와 안전을 보장하기에 미흡하다고 평가했다.

반대보고서는 특히 △국가안전기획부, 경찰청 대공분실 등 수사기관에서의 고문 및 가혹행위 △국가안전기획부, 기무사 등 특별수사기관의 인신 구속 △불공정한 장기 구속과 구속적부심 제도 등이 신체의 자유를 침해하고 있다고 실례를 들어 지적했다.

한편 민변과 인권위원회는 다음달초 유엔인권이사회에 반대보고서를 보내는 한편 정부보고서를 평가하는 7월초의 유엔인권이사회 회의에 인권대표단을 파견할 방침이다. 이와 함께 다음달 안으로 두 보고서의 차이점을 소개하는 설명회도 열 예정이다.

0126

報 告 畢

長官報告事項

1992. 4. 28.
國 際 機 構 局
國際聯合2課(19)

題 目 : 第44次 人權理事會 勸告

第44次 人權理事會(92.3.23-4.10)는 알제리等 5개국 報告書를 審議하고 同 國家들의 人權狀況에 대한 評價 및 勸告와 次期會議 計劃을 採擇한 바, 同 內容을 아래 報告드립니다.

1. 理事會 勸告內容

- o 알제리 (最初 報告書) : 民主化 中斷 및 女性差別 措置 是正
- o 페루 (2차 報告書) : 最近 事態와 관련, 追加 報告書 提出 要請
- o 콜롬비아 (3차 報告書) : 最近의 人權狀況 進展을 評價, 政府의 持續的 努力 强調
- o 벨지움 (2차 報告書) : 外國人에 대한 差別事例에 憂慮 表明
- o 유고 (3차 報告書) : 聯邦軍의 人權侵害 是正 및 小數民族 人權保障 促求

2. 我國 關聯事項

- o 次期會議(92.7.13-31, 제네바)에서 韓國, 부룬디, 벨라루스, 몽골, 아프가니스탄 報告書 및 페루 追加 報告書 審議 豫定

3. 關聯 對策

- o 我國 報告書 審議와 관련, 法務部 人士를 首席代表로 하는 일반적 傾向과 人權問題 主務部署가 法務部인 점을 考慮, 우선 法務部 高位人士를 首席代表로 任命하는 問題를 法務部와 協議中 (法務部 人士가 어려울 경우 駐제네바 大使를 任命)
- o 報告書 審議관련 準備事項을 92.5월중 法務部와 實務協議 豫定

92.5.4
7.3.22
122 일

4. 言論對策

- o 해당 없음. 끝.

0127

報 告 畢

長官報告事項

1992. 4. 28.
國 際 機 構 局
國際聯合2課(19)

題 目 : 第44次 人權理事會 勸告

第44次 人權理事會(92.3.23-4.10)는 알제리等 5개국 報告書를 審議하고 同 國家들의 人權狀況에 대한 評價 및 勸告와 次期會議 計劃을 採擇한 바, 同 內容을 아래 報告드립니다.

1. 理事會 勸告內容

o 알제리 (最初 報告書) : 民主化 中斷 및 女性差別 措置 是正

o 페루 (2차 報告書) : 最近 事態와 관련, 追加 報告書 提出 要請

o 콜롬비아 (3차 報告書) : 最近의 人權狀況 進展을 評價, 政府의 持續的 努力 强調

o 벨지움 (2차 報告書) : 外國人에 대한 差別事例에 憂慮 表明

o 유고 (3차 報告書) : 聯邦軍의 人權侵害 是正 및 小數民族 人權保障 促求

2. 我國 關聯事項

o 次期會議(92.7.13-31, 제네바)에서 韓國, 부룬디, 벨라루스, 몽골, 아프가니스탄 報告書 및 페루 追加 報告書 審議 豫定

3. 關聯 對策

o 我國 報告書 審議와 관련, 法務部 高位人士를 ~~代表團~~ 首席代表로 任命하는 問題를 法務部와 協議中

o ~~92. 5월중~~ 報告書 審議관련 準備事項을 法務部와 協議 豫定

4. 言論對策

o 해당 없음. 끝.

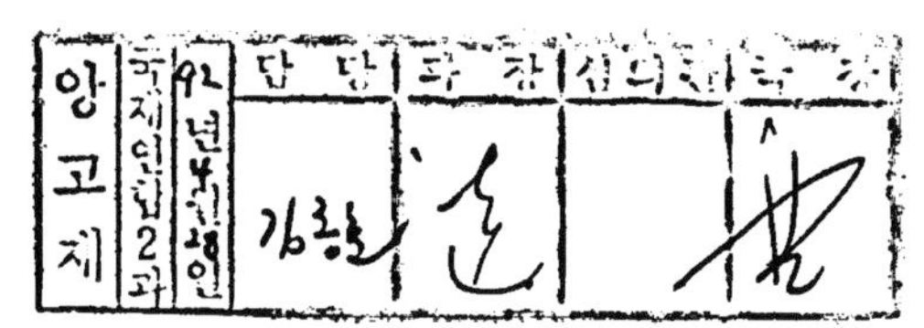

0128

Press Release

Department of Public Information • News Coverage Service • New York

Round-up of Session

HR/CT/195
13 April 1992

FORTY-FOURTH SESSION OF HUMAN RIGHTS COMMITTEE

NEW YORK, 23 MARCH - 10 APRIL

Comments on Reports of Algeria, Belgium, Colombia, Yugoslavia,
Clarifies Rights of Detained Juveniles, Standards for Torture Cases

The suspension of the democratic process in Algeria, institutionalized violence in Peru and the impunity of the military and drug traffickers in Colombia were among the concerns stressed by members of the Human Rights Committee during that body's forty-fourth session, which concluded Friday, 10 April, at Headquarters.

The Committee, which examined periodic reports by five countries on their compliance with the International Covenant on Civil and Political Rights, also expressed its concern about discrimination against immigrants in Belgium. Regarding Yugoslavia, it focused on human rights violations by the Army, which the Federal Government no longer controlled, as well as inter-ethnic conflicts and the treatment of minorities.

In other action during its three-week meeting, which began on 23 March, the Committee decided to request Peru to report back to it on recent events affecting human rights.

The Committee, which monitors implementation of the Covenant by its 104 State parties, is composed of 18 experts who serve in their invididual capacities.

The Committee decided that at its next session, which is to be held in Geneva from 13 to 31 July, it will consider the following reports: the third periodic report of Belarus; the third periodic report of Mongolia; the second periodic report of Afghanistan; the first periodic report of the Republic of Korea; and the first periodic report of Burundi. It will also resume consideration of Peru's second periodic report. In addition, it decided to accept Germany's request to submit its fourth periodic report as scheduled in August 1993.

(more)

0129

During the course of the session, the Committee adopted revised general comments on two articles of the Covenant. The general comment on article 10 -- which deals with the treatment of prisoners -- elaborates on States parties' obligations towards accused juvenile persons and juvenile offenders, including the supervision of places of detention and the training of supervisory personnel. The need to segregate accused persons from convicts, and accused juveniles and juvenile offenders from adults, is clarified in the text.

In its discussion of the revised general comment on article 7, on torture and degrading treatment, the Committee focused on language concerning detention and amnesty for acts of torture.

General comments are intended to clarify and interpret provisions of the Covenant in order to assist States parties in preparing their reports.

In addition, the Committee studied confidential communications from nine individuals claiming to be the victims of violations of any of the rights set forth in that treaty. The Committee last met in November 1991.

The Committee agreed on the membership and mandates of two working groups scheduled to meet prior to its next session. The Working Group on Communications will comprise: Birame Ndiaye, expert from Senegal; Janos Fodor, expert from Hungary; Andreas V. Mavrommatis, expert from Cyprus; Waleed Sadi, expert from Jordan; and Julio Prado Vallejo, expert from Ecuador. The Working Group on article 40 of the Covenant, dealing with reports by Governments, will comprise: Francisco Jose Aguilar Urbina, expert from Costa Rica; Nisuke Ando, expert from Japan; Vojin Dimitrijevic, expert from Yugoslavia; and Fausto Pocar, expert from Italy.

For the first time, the Committee adopted comments on the periodic reports considered during the session. These concerned Algeria, Colombia, Belgium and Yugoslavia, since consideration of the report of Peru will be continued at the Committee's next session.

The comments highlight the positive aspects of recent actions to implement the Covenant, as well as factors and difficulties impeding its application. They also describe the Committee's principal subjects of concern and specific actions to be taken by the State party to ensure that its citizens enjoy the rights and freedoms guaranteed by the Covenant.

Algeria

The Committee's discussion of Algeria's initial report had centred on the political situation in that country since the cancellation of elections last January, with experts questioning the fact that an Islamic political movement was considered a threat to a democracy in which Islam was the State religion. Several members felt that the ruling party had abused the democratic process in order to stay in power. They wondered how the Government reconciled its statement of equality of the sexes with Algeria's patriarchal culture and traditional Muslim social norms, such as dowries and polygamy.

(more)

0130

In its comment on the report, the Committee regrets that the report includes little information concerning the actual application of human rights standards and that it makes no reference to the states of emergency. It expresses concern about the suspension of the democratic process, the high number of arrests and the excessive use of firearms by members of the police. It expresses doubts about respect for due process, especially before military tribunals, about the numerous cases of torture and ill-treatment and about restrictions on freedom of opinion and expression and press freedom.

The Committee also regrets the many cases of discrimination against women and considers that measures to assist minorities, especially the Berbers, are insufficient. It reminds the State party that the Covenant does not permit derogation from certain rights even in times of emergency.

Responding to the issues raised by the Committee, the representative of the Government of Algeria had said it was anxious to restore the democratic process as soon as possible, but that imposition of a state of emergency had been unavoidable. Since the adoption of the new Constitution, the transition to democracy had been too hasty and Government action had been necessary to respond to a substantial threat to that democratic process. The representative also stated that restrictions on political associations whose values were contrary to those of Islam, and the fact that Algeria had a State religion, were not incompatible with the Covenant.

Peru

In their discussion of the second periodic report of Peru, Committee members had focused on the "institutionalization of violence" in that country, and the related gap between theory and practice in respecting human rights there. While acknowledging the difficulties faced by the Government in implementing the Covenant as a result of terrorist and drug trafficking activities, the Committee was concerned by the thousands of cases of disappearances, rape, torture, killings and other forms of violence, and with what it called the "extensive" derogations from the rights enshrined in the Covenant.

The Committee was also concerned about how the successive states of emergency affected the human rights situation; about exoneration of the military from responsibility for acts committed under orders; and about the courts' inability to enforce their jurisdiction over emergency zones. The independence of the judiciary, and the extent to which provisions of the Covenant on non-discrimination, equality of the sexes and minority rights were respected, were also stressed.

In its replies to the Committee, the Government of Peru had said that while it was not denying mistakes could be and were being made, it was faced with an unconventional enemy -- the Sendero Luminoso (the Shining Path). The so-called "terrorism from above" must be placed in the context of "terrorism from below". The "imminent danger of war" was sufficient reason for imposing a state of siege.

(more)

0131

The Government had admitted that terrorist violence was no excuse for excesses by the security forces in defending the people and institutions. While there had been some "unfortunate" situations, a new judicial system had emerged to prevent their recurrence.

Following the debate, the Committee had asked Peru to provide supplementary information which would be reviewed at the next session.

Colombia

The Committee, in its debate on the third periodic report of Colombia, had praised that country for many of its efforts but had urged it to put an end to impunity, which the Government itself admitted was still Colombia's main problem. The absence of investigations of sometimes grave crimes, the failure of the judicial system to function with real effect and the inability of the civilian Government to take appropriate action to end the situation had all been discussed by the Committee.

In its comments, the Committee notes with satisfaction the constitutional reform in Colombia and other reforms important for the strengthening of human rights, particularly the establishment in 1987 of the Office of the Presidential Adviser for the Defence, Protection and Promotion of Human Rights and the establishment of a National Human Rights Unit in the Directorate General of Criminal Investigation.

It further notes that not all obstacles to the full application of the Covenant have been removed, and expresses concern about the unacceptable rate of homicides, disappearances and torture. Of special concern are the murders of sectors of the population in so-called "clean-up" operations, the phenomenon of impunity for police and military personnel, the use of military courts to try civilians and the persistence of paramilitary groups. Likewise, the Committee is concerned that the principle of equal pay for men and women has not yet been fully applied, and feels that the country's child labour situation violates the Covenant.

The Committee recommends that the State party intensify its action against all violence resulting in human rights violations, eliminate impunity, limit the competence of the military courts and disband all military groups.

The Government, elaborating on the "substantial changes" that had taken place in Colombia over the past two years, had said that the reforms had been accompanied by relatively endemic and grave violence on the part of guerrilla groups, paramilitary "self-defence" groups and drug traffickers. Although that violence continued, reports of torture, disappearances and mass murders had declined considerably; the Government was following up on complaints of violations, was dealing with acts of violence against families and children, negotiating with guerrilla groups and investigating cases of murder or torture involving the police and military.

(more)

0132

Belgium

The existence of discrimination on the basis of nationality had been stressed by the Committee in its discussion of the second periodic report of Belgium, whose representative had explained that foreigners could be excluded from residing in certain Belgian communes because a concentration of them could promote racist reactions. According to the relevant decree, certain categories could be excluded if a population increase would jeopardize the public interest.

In its comment, the Committee expresses concern about the difference between civil rights enjoyed by citizens and those enjoyed by aliens, which may lead to discrimination. Other areas of concern include the adequacy of monitoring pre-trial detention, the impartiality of the authorities who examine those arrested, the inadequacy of information on freedom of expression and arrangements as to freedom of assembly in open air.

Among the Committee's recommendations are that the State party more adequately reflect provisions of the Covenant which are not reflected in the European Convention on Human Rights, and that it further improve the effectiveness of the protection granted to minority rights at the communal level. The State party should also reconsider its reservations to provisions of the Covenant in order to withdraw as many as possible.

Yugoslavia

The right to self-determination of the peoples of Yugoslavia, and human rights violations being carried out by the Federal army in the name of restoring constitutional authority, headed the list of the Committee's preoccupations with regard to the present crisis in that country.

The Government had asserted that it recognized the rights to self-determination and secession, but only according to constitutional law. It felt that Yugoslavia's own right to self-determination -- which included respect for territorial integrity and non-interference in internal affairs -- had not been respected by some members of the international community. Experts pointed out, however, that it was only when the Government had used force that the European Economic Community had begun to recognize the secessionist republics.

The Government said there was no doubt as to its responsibility for the acts of violence, regardless of which individuals or institutions had committed them. It none the less insisted that since the Federation was in a state of disintegration, it could not bear the sole blame for the destruction of towns and villages or for summary executions and other atrocities. It did, however, promise to investigate all such cases.

The Committee, in its comments on the third periodic report of Yugoslavia, states that the current crisis does not permit the State party to supervise implementation of the Covenant throughout the territory, but welcomes Yugoslavia's creation of a committee for investigation of genocide

(more)

and violations of humanitarian law. The Committee further emphasizes the urgency of a continuing implementation of the Covenant in the breakaway republics.

The Committee regrets that the right to secession recognized in the Federal Constitution has not been implemented in domestic law, which would have enabled the peaceful settlement of the crisis. It equally regrets that within the framework of the state of emergency in Kosovo, excessive measures have been taken that limit the rights and freedoms guaranteed by the Covenant.

The Committee's deepest concern is reserved for the atrocities committed during the inter-ethnic conflicts; it particularly deplores the numerous cases of summary or arbitrary executions, forced or involuntary disappearances, torture, rape and pillage committed by members of the Federal Army or paramilitary groups. It also deplores the extremely low number of investigations into those violations, the failure to punish the guilty and the impunity enjoyed by the perpetrators.

The Committee is additionally concerned with the deteriorating situation of ethnic, religious and linguistic minorities, particularly those of Albanian and Hungarian origin. It recommends that the Government take all necessary action to bring an end to the violations, by restoring control over the Army, disbanding the paramilitary groups, punishing the guilty and preventing the recurrence of such acts.

Background on Covenant

The Covenant was adopted by the General Assembly and opened for signature in 1966, together with the International Covenant on Economic, Social and Cultural Rights, both of which entered into force in 1976.

The Covenant begins by stating that all peoples have the right of self-determination. It guarantees to everyone the right to life, liberty and security of person. It prohibits torture, cruel or degrading treatment or punishment, and the arbitrary deprivation of life. Anyone arrested has the right to be informed of the reasons for the arrest, and anyone arrested or detained on a criminal charge shall be brought promptly before a judge or other legally authorized person.

The Covenant also provides for freedom of movement and places limitations upon the expulsion of aliens from the territory of a State party. In addition, the right to freedom of thought, conscience, religion and expression are recognized, and the Covenant provides for the prohibition of war propaganda and advocacy of national, racial or religious hatred.

The following 104 States have ratified or acceded to the Covenant: Afghanistan, Albania, Algeria, Angola, Argentina, Australia, Austria, Barbados, Belarus, Belgium, Benin, Bolivia, Brazil, Bulgaria, Burundi, Cameroon, Canada, Central African Republic, Chile, Colombia, Congo, Costa Rica, Côte d'Ivoire, Cyprus, Czechoslovakia, Democratic People's Republic of Korea, Denmark, Dominican Republic, Ecuador, Egypt, El Salvador, Equatorial

(more)

0134

Guinea, Estonia, Finland, France, Gabon, Gambia, Germany, Grenada, Guinea, Guyana, Haiti, Hungary, Iceland, India, Iran, Iraq, Ireland, Israel, Italy, Jamaica, Japan, Jordan, Kenya, Lebanon, Libya, Lithuania, Luxembourg, Madagascar, Mali, Malta, Mauritius, Mexico, Mongolia, Morocco, Nepal, Netherlands, New Zealand, Nicaragua, Niger, Norway, Panama, Peru, Philippines, Poland, Portugal, Republic of Korea, Romania, Russian Federation, Rwanda, Saint Vincent and the Grenadines, San Marino, Senegal, Somalia, Spain, Sri Lanka, Sudan, Suriname, Sweden, Syria, Togo, Trinidad and Tobago, Tunisia, Ukraine, United Kingdom, United Republic of Tanzania, Uruguay, Venezuela, Viet Nam, Yemen, Yugoslavia, Zaire, Zambia and Zimbabwe.

First Optional Protocol

The first Optional Protocol to the Covenant provides for the confidential consideration of communications from individuals who claim to be victims of a violation of any of the rights proclaimed in the Covenant. No communication can be received by the Committee if it concerns a State party to the Covenant that is not also a party to the first Optional Protocol.

The following 63 States are parties to the first Optional Protocol: Algeria, Angola, Argentina, Australia, Austria, Barbados, Benin, Bolivia, Cameroon, Canada, Central African Republic, Colombia, Congo, Costa Rica, Côte d'Ivoire, Czechoslovakia, Denmark, Dominican Republic, Ecuador, Equatorial Guinea, Estonia, Finland, France, Gambia, Hungary, Iceland, Ireland, Italy, Jamaica, Libya, Lithuania, Luxembourg, Madagascar, Malta, Mauritius, Mongolia, Nepal, Netherlands, New Zealand, Nicaragua, Niger, Norway, Panama, Peru, Philippines, Poland, Portugal, Republic of Korea, Russian Federation, Saint Vincent and the Grenadines, San Marino, Senegal, Somalia, Spain, Suriname, Sweden, Togo, Trinidad and Tobago, Ukraine, Uruguay, Venezuela, Zaire and Zambia.

The Committee is also mandated under Article 41 of the Covenant to consider communications from a State party alleging violations of the Covenant's provisions by another State party. This procedure can be applied when both States have made declarations recognizing the Committee's competence to consider such communications. So far, the following 33 States have done so: Algeria, Argentina, Austria, Belgium, Canada, Chile, Congo, Czechoslovakia, Denmark, Ecuador, Finland, Gambia, Germany, Hungary, Iceland, Ireland, Italy, Luxembourg, Malta, Netherlands, New Zealand, Norway, Peru, Philippines, Poland, Republic of Korea, Senegal, Russian Federation, Spain, Sri Lanka, Sweden, United Kingdom and Zimbabwe.

Second Optional Protocol

The second Optional Protocol, aiming at the abolition of the death penalty, entered into force on 11 July 1991. Nine States have ratified or acceded to it as of 1 August 1991: Australia, Finland, Iceland, Netherlands, New Zealand, Portugal, Romania, Spain and Sweden.

(more)

0135

Committee Officers, Membership

The Committee's members are elected by the States parties to the Covenant for a term of four years. According to article 28 of the Covenant, "they shall be persons of high moral character and recognized competence in the field of human rights". The Chairman of the Committee is Fausto Pocar, expert from Italy. Its Vice-Chairmen are Francisco Jose Aguilar Urbina, expert from Costa Rica; Vojin Dimitrijevic, expert from Yugoslavia; and Omran El Shafei, expert from Egypt. The Rapporteur is Nisuke Ando, expert from Japan.

The other members are: Christine Chanet, expert from France; Janos Fodor, expert from Hungary; Kurt Herndl, expert from Austria; Rosalyn Higgins, expert from the United Kingdom; Rajsoomer Lallah, expert from Mauritius; Andreas V. Mavrommatis, expert from Cyprus; Rein A. Müllerson, expert from the Russian Federation; Birame Ndiaye, expert from Senegal; Julio Prado Vallejo, expert from Ecuador; Waleed Sadi, expert from Jordan; Alejandro Serrano Caldera, expert from Nicaragua; Amos Wako, expert from Kenya; and Bertil Wennergren, expert from Sweden.

* *** *

0136

4

법무부 인권과

1992. . .

아래 문건을 수신자에게 전달하여 주시기 바랍니다.

제 목 : ____________

수 신 : 외무부 국제연합과

(수신처 FAX NO: 723-3505)

발 신 : 법무부 인권과

표지포함 총 ___매

0137

정 보 보 고

(법무부 인권과, 1992.4.29)

제목 : 인권관련기사 진상보고

1. 관련기사 요지 (한겨레신문 4.29자 14면)

   o KNCC인권위.민변 공동으로, 정부가 '91.7. 유엔에 제출한 인권 보고서에 대해 반대보고서를 작성, 5월초 유엔인권이사회에 제출예정

   o 위 반대보고서는 정부의 보고서가 "추상적인 법률의 나열"에만 그치고 있다고 주장하면서
   - 국가보안법에 의한 인권침해상황
   - 불법구속, 구금 등 신체의 자유 침해상황

   등 23개 항목으로 구성

   * 동아일보(4.29자 22면)도 유사한 내용으로 보도

2. 확인결과

   o KNCC인권위원회 및 민변측은 문제의 보고서 원고작성을 마무리 하고 있는 단계이며, 책자로 발간되는 시기는 5월 중순경으로 예상됨

   o 상기 보고서는 당부에서 기히 예견하고 있었던 사항으로, 보고서 내용을 조속입수, 분석할 것임

첨부 : 관련기사 사본 1부.

0138

RECEIVED FROM 1992.04.29 16:59 P. 2

*동아일보 '92.4.29 22면

"政府人權보고서는 잘못"

KNCC·民辯「반대보고서」UN 제출키로

한국 기독교 교회협의회(KNCC) 인권위원회와 민주화사회를 위한 변호사모임(민변)은 28일 정부가 지난해7월 유엔인권이사회에 제출한 인권보고서의 내용을 반박하는 반대보고서를 작성, 영문번역작업을 마치는대로 유엔인권위에 제출키로했다.

민변등이 작성한 반대보고서는 △국가보안법 △신체의 자유 △사상과 양심의 자유등 23개 항목으로 구성돼있으며 16절지 1백50페이지 분량이다.

이 반대보고서는 정부측의 보고서에 대해 대부분 부분에서 국제인권규약과 관련된 법조문을 열거하는데 그치고있다며 「특히 실제의 인권상황을 알수있는 법원의 판례나 정부의 조치등에 관한 언급이 없다」고 지적했다.

반대보고서는 또 국제인권규약이 한국에서 이행되는데 가장 큰 장애요인은 「한반도의 분단」이라면서 이는 정부가 국가안보를 이유로 인권을 탄압하는 억압적 법률을 만들었기 때문이라고 주장했다.

반대보고서는 이와함께 △국가안전기획부 경찰대공분실에 의한 고문및 가혹행위 △안기부 기무사등의 인신구속 △불공정한 장기구금등의 실례를 들어 신체의 자유가 침해되고 있다고 지적했다.

KNCC인권위와 민변은 이 반대보고서를 제출한후 오는7월초 유엔인권위원회에 대표단도 파견할 예정이다.

0139

RECEIVED FROM 1992.04.29 17:00 P. 3

민간단체 인권보고서 첫선

정부작성내용 비판…신체자유 미흡평가

민변·한교협 공동발간…설명회 갖기로

한국정부가 90년 국제인권규약에 가입한 뒤 규약규정에 따라 91년 7월 국제연합 인권이사회에 제출한 인권보고서를 반박하는 재야인권단체의 반대보고서가 작성됐다.

민주사회를 위한 변호사모임(민변)과 한국기독교교회협의회 인권위원회는 28일 △국가보안법 △신체의 자유 △사상과 양심의 자유 등 23개 항목에서 정부가 낸 인권보고서의 내용을 비판하는 한글 1백50여쪽, 영문 1백50여쪽에 이르는 방대한 분량의 반대보고서 작성을 마쳤다. 이번 반대보고서는 우리사회의 법체계 전반에 걸친 인권실태를 국제사회에 알리는 최초 민간보고서라는 점에서 큰 관심을 끌고 있다.

반대보고서는 정부보고서에 대해 "많은 부분에서 규약의 조항과 관련된 남한의 법조문을 열거하는 데 그치고 있을 뿐"이라며 "실제의 인권보장 상황을 보여주는 사실들이 언급되어있지 않으며 인권에 영향을 주는 법원의 판례나 정부의 조처 등을 설명하지 않고 있다"고 평가했다.

반대보고서는 이에 따라 "결론적으로 정부보고서는 규약이 보장하는 인권이 침해되는 상황에 관해 설명하지 않음으로써 한국의 인권상황에 대해 양호한 것으로 오해를 일으킬 수 있도록 만들어져 있다"고 비판했다.

반대보고서는 한국에서 규약의 이행에 영향을 끼치는 가장 중요한 요소와 장애를 한반도의 분단이라고 규정한 뒤 "국가안보를 명분으로 인권을 침해하는 억압적인 법률들이 만들어졌고 정부에 대한 비판적인 말과 행동이 북한을 이롭게 한다는 이유로 모두 처벌의 대상이 돼왔다"고 평가했다. 반대보고서는 국가보안법과 관련해 "남한에서 '실질적 의미의 헌법'이라고 말해도 지나치지 않은데도 정부보고서는 설명이 너무 부족하고 이 법에 의한 인권의 침해상황을 전혀 설명하지 않고 있다"고 반박했다.

반대보고서는 이에 따라 △간첩죄 및 목적수행죄 △잠입·탈출죄 △찬양·고무·동조·이적단체 구성·이적표현물 제작죄 △회합·통신죄 등 국가보안법 조항에 대한 자의적 해석·적용이 끼친 인권침해 실태를 문익환목사·임수경씨 방북사건, 서울사회과학연구소사건 등을 예로 들어 설명하고 있다. 신체의 자유와 관련해 반대보고서는 헌법과 형사소송법, 경찰관 직무집행법 등의 규정에도 불구하고 △권리실현에 장애를 주는 특별법의 존재 △정부당국자나 수사담당자들의 관행화된 불법구속·구금 등이 규약이 규정한 신체의 자유와 안전을 보장하기에 미흡하다고 평가했다.

반대보고서는 특히 △국가안전기획부, 경찰청 대공분실 등 수사기관에서의 고문 및 가혹행위 △국가안전기획부, 기무사 등 특별수사기관의 인신 구속 △불공정한 장기 구속과 구속적부심 제도 등이 신체의 자유를 침해하고 있다고 실례를 들어 지적했다.

한편 민변과 인권위원회는 다음달초 유엔인권이사회에 반대보고서를 보내는 한편 정부보고서를 평가하는 7월초의 유엔인권이사회 회의에 인권대표단을 파견할 방침이다. 이와 함께 다음달 안으로 두 보고서의 차이점을 소개하는 설명회도 열 예정이다.

* 한겨레신문 '92.4.29 4면

0140

주 국 련 대 표 부

주국련 2031252- 493　　　　　　　　1992. 4. 30.

수신 : 장 관

참조 : 국제기구국장

제목 : 인권이사회 토의요록

1. 금 4.30까지 발간된 제44차 인권이사회 토의요록을 별첨 송부합니다.

2. 여타분은 추송예정이며 주제네바 대표부에는 별도 송부하였음을 참고로 첨언합니다.

첨부 : CCPR/c/sr. 1121-41 (단, 25, 26, 30, 31, 32, 35, 36, 38, 39, 40 제외) 끝.

주 국 련 대 사

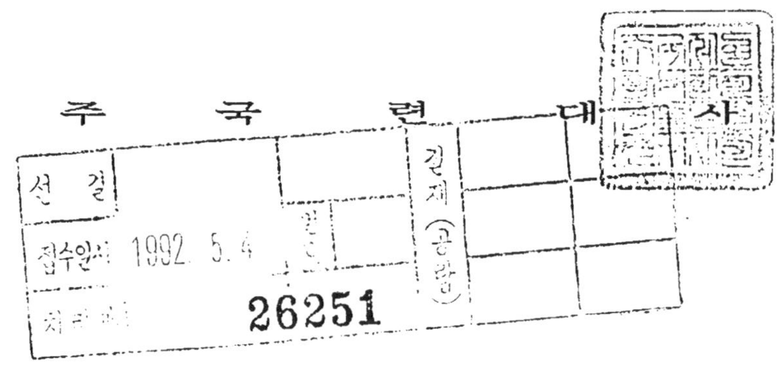

0141

요 보 안

國際人權規約(B規約) 政府報告書에 대한

유엔 審議會 對備計劃

1992. 5.

0142

- 목 차 -

0143

I. 審議會 槪要 및 現 準備狀況

1. 유엔 審議會 槪要

o 심의위원의 구성

- 총 18인의 인권분야 전문가로 구성
- 의장1인, 부의장3인, 간사(Rapporteur)1인
- 임기4년 (의장단 임기는 2년), 규약가입국 회의에서 선출

o 심의절차 (UN Manual P 120 이하)

(제1일 7.13)
- 수석대표 모두 발언 (30분 이내)
- 위원(18인) 각자 질문 (2시간)

(제2일 7.14) - 답변준비로 휴회

(제3일 7.15)
- 질문에 대한 답변 (2시간)
- 위원 각자의 논평(observation)발언 (1시간)
- 위원회 명의의 Comment발표로 종료

※ 특이한 경우 다음 회기로 속행, 계속 심의하거나 추가보고서 제출요구 결의를 하는 경우도 있음

1

0144

2. 現 準備狀況

o 심의대비 계획수립 ('92.1 - 2)

- 타부처 추가자료 요청 ('92.1.9)
- 관련부처 실무책임자회의 개최 ('92.1.29, 청와대 정조주관)

o 보유자료 정리 및 검토 ('92.3 - 5)

- B규약 27개 조문별 기존 답변관련자료 화일작성
- 각 조문별 예상질문사항 검토 및 답변정리
- 관련 9개부처 실무위원회 개최 ('92.2.13 인권과 주관)
- 추가자료의 성실한 작성, 제출요청

o B규약 심의관련 정보 및 자료 입수.분석

- 제44차 인권이사회 참가보고서 ('92.3.24-27) 입수 (외무부)
- 심의대비 Manual(편람) 입수.분석
- 일본 등 타국 심의시 관련자료의 취합.분석
- KNCC·민변 반박보고서 입수

0145

Ⅱ. 問題點 및 留意事項

1. KNCC·民辯 反駁報告書 問題

o 총 28개 항목 122쪽에 걸쳐 국가보안법, 집시법, 노동관련법규, 재소자 처우 문제, 수사과정상의 고문.가혹행위문제, 규약의 국내적 적용문제 등 정부보고서의 전 항목을 반박

o 심도있고 구체적인 설명과 통계자료 제시 → 국제무대에서의 호소력 고양효과에 치중

※ 반박보고서 요약 (별첨)

2. 國際人權團體의 普遍化된 視角問題

o 정부의 방어논리보다 재야(특히 종교단체)의 공격논리에 쉽게 공감하여 온 종래의 체질고수

o 분단의 특수성, 북의 대남적화야욕에 대한 현실적 감각 결여

o 국가보안법은 표현의 자유에 관한 국제적 인권기준에 위배된다는 인식 일반화

o 미전향 장기수에 대한 이해 부족

→ 대응자료는 이러한 외국인의 시각을 고려하여 작성(비교우위의 논리는 설득력 없음)

3

0146

3. 留意事項

o KNCC·민변 반박보고서에 대하여 허구성, 편향적 시각 등을 밝힐 수 있는 철저한 대응자료 준비 시급

- 종래의 보수적, 방어적, 단순논리적, 비교우위적 접근에서 더 나아가 국제적 감각에 맞는 대응자료 준비
- 6.15까지는 작성완료 (책자발간 등 별도 활용문제 추후검토)
- 상기 반박보고서에 대한 보수성향단체명의 비판성명 등 정책적 문제는 관계부처 협의후 결정

o 관계부처와 긴밀한 협의

- 답변내용중 사전에 관계부처간 협의하여 준비할 사항
- 답변방법 등 외교기술적 문제 협의

o 정확하고 설득력있는 영문답변 준비

- 주요 답변내용은 사전에 영문화 작업하여 전문가 (해외공보관) 검토요청

0147

Ⅲ. 向後 準備計劃 및 建議事項

1. 準備하여야 할 對應資料

o 수석대표의 모두발언

o 보고서 제출이후 변경.추가된 사항

- 관계법률, 시행령·시행규칙의 제.개정된 내용
- 헌법재판소 결정, 대법원 판례변경 등 추가사항
- 각종 통계자료의 update

o KNCC·민변의 반박보고서에 대한 대응자료

- 국가보안법, 정치범·양심수(장기수), 각종 고문사례, 노동관련 공안사범 등 23개 항목
- 구체적이고 설득력있는 대응논리

o B규약 27개 조문별 답변자료

- B규약 보고서 27개조문 관련 답변자료
- Manual의 분석 및 대응

o 중요 답변내용의 영문 번역문

o 최근 국내외 인권단체, 언론기관 등의 집중거론사항 대응자료

- AI, Asia Watch, Robert Kennedy Center, 국내 야권 및 재야단체 등의 집중 거론사항 관련자료

o 6공화국의 인권개선 실적관련 홍보자료

→국제감각에 맞고 설득력있는 대응자료 준비 필수적

2. 關係部處 協助事項

o 심의관련 각종 추가자료의 신속.성실한 제출

- '91.7.이후 변경. 추가된 사항 관련자료

- 근래 국내외적으로 쟁점이 된 소관업무 관련자료

- 인권향상 및 실적관련 홍보자료

- 각종 최신통계들의 보완

o 중요답변 항목들에 대한 내용 검증

- 관계부처 심사위원회 운용

. B규약 보고서 작성시 편성된 "실무책임자회의(청와대 정책조사보좌관 주관, 9개부처 국장)" 가동

. 심의대책회의, 중간평가회의 개최

0149

. 정책적.외교적 차원에서의 답변내용 재검토 (국가보안법 적용사례, 북한인권상황 언급범위 등)

→ 노동부, 안기부 등 주요 유관부서는 대표단에 참여하도록 요청

3. 當部內 協助事項 (建議事項)

o 자료협조

- '91.7. B규약 보고서 제출후 변경, 추가된 사항 작성

- KNCC·민변 반박보고서 대응자료 작성 (대검 공안부)

※ 준비기간이 촉박하며 국제무대에서 설득력있는 대응논리를 준비하여야 하므로, 대검 공안연구관들이 분석, 준비함이 적절

- 중요답변 영문번역문 작성(인권과 책임하에 법무부내 미국유학 검사 수시활용)

o 인원협조

- 가칭 '심의대비기획단' 구성, 가동

. 인권과장 책임하에 3개 준비반 편성.운용 - 총괄, 영문화 작업반 (검사 김웅기), B규약 보고서 관련반 (검사 정기용), 반박보고서 관련반 (공안검사)

. 공안검사 1인 지정, 반박보고서 등 공안관련사항 답변자료 준비 전담 (6월부터 인권과 파견, 대표단에 합류)

※ 전담할 공안검사는 반박자료 작성을 주도함과 동시에 공안관련사항 답변자료 총괄 (대검 공안연구관 중 1인이 적절)

7

0150

4. 細部作業 進行計劃

o 가칭 '심의대비기획단' 조직 및 업무분장

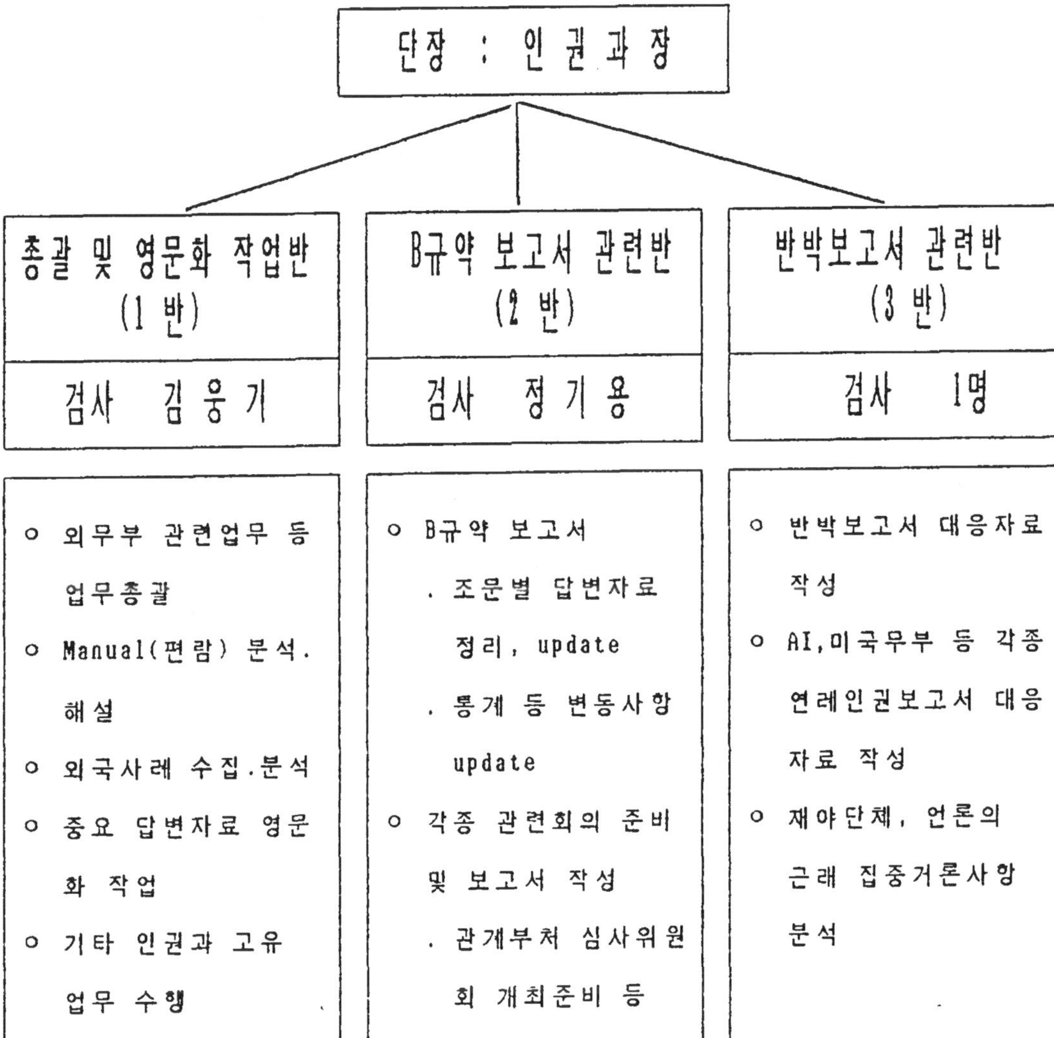

0151

o 대응 답변자료 작성지침 (기발문제)

- 답변자료 분류방법

. 1차분류 - B규약 보고서 조문별 분류

. 2차분류 - 쟁점별 분류

. 3차분류 - 국회질의 응답식

※ (예) B규약 제10조 - 재소자 관련 - 미결수용자의 처우문제

- 피구금자처우최저기준규칙의 국내법 적용문제

(1차분류) (2차분류) (3차분류)

- 별도 주요쟁점(ISSUE)별 분류

. 국가보안법 관련문제

. 정치범·양심수 문제

. 최근 남북한 관계변화문제 <

. 장기 좌익수용자문제

. 노동관련 법규문제 (복수노조, 제3자 개입 등)

9

0152

o 날짜별 추진계획

날짜 / 구분	5 월 3주 18-23	5 월 4주 25-30	6 월 1주 1 - 6	6 월 2주 8 - 13	6 월 3주 15-20	6 월 4주 22-27	7 월 1주 29 - 4	7 월 2주 6 - 11
1 반	.Manual(편람)분석,해설 (5월 3주 ~ 4주)							
	. 중요 답변자료 영문화 (6월 1주 ~ 7월 2주)							
	. 외국자료 수집· 분석 (5월 3주 ~ 7월 2주)							
2 반	.관계부처회의 .보고서 작성 (6월 1주)							
	.관계부처회의 .보고서 작성 (6월 4주 ~ 7월 1주)							
	.B규약 보고서 관련자료 update, 통계 등 변동사항 취합.대응자료 작성 (5월 3주 ~ 7월 1주)							
3 반	. 반박인권보고서 대응자료 작성 (5월 4주 ~ 7월 1주)							
	.AI,미국무부 등 각종 연례인권보고서 분석,대응자료 작성 (5월 3주 ~ 7월 1주)							

o 심의회 참가계획

- 참가요원

수석대표:

. 인권과장, 검사 정기용 및 지정될 검사 1명

- 참가일정

. 심의회 개최(7.13) 1주일전 출국하여 외무부 대표단과 현지에서 합류

. Fax 등 상시 연락체제 유지

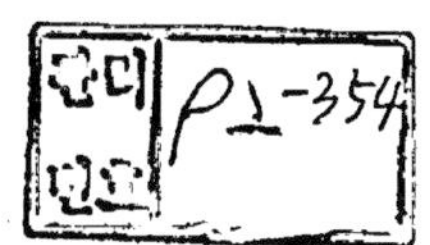

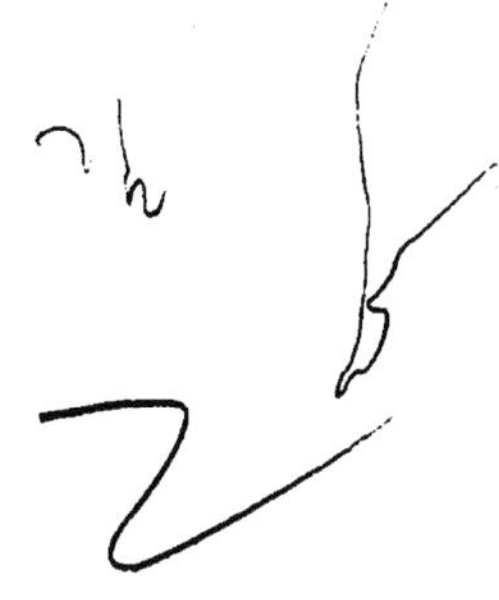

법 무 부

427-760 경기도 과천시 중앙동 1번지 / 전화 (02)503-7045 / 팩시 (02)503-7046

문서번호 인권 20314-175

시행일자 1992. 5.8

수신 외무부장관

참조 국제기구조약국장

선결			지시		
접수	일자 시간	92. 5.12	결재		
	번호	1821			
처리과			공람		
담당자					

제목 아국 인권규약(B) 최초보고서 심의

1. 연이 20314-1010 ('92.4.22)과 관련입니다.

2. 제45차 인권이사회에서의 아국 인권규약(B) 최초보고서 심의와 관련, 당부에서는 인권관련업무를 총괄하고 있는 당부 인권과장과 관계검사를 아국대표단에 파견할 것을 검토중이므로 이를 알려드립니다. 끝.

법 무 부 장 관

0154

주 국 련 대 표 부

주국련2031252- 519 1992. 5 . 8.

수신 장관

참조 국제기구국장

제목 인권이사회 토의요록

연 : 주국련2031252-493(92.4.30)

표제 토의요록 추가분을 별첨 송부하오며 금일까지 발간되지 아니한 아래 토의요록은 추송 예정입니다.

- 아 래 -

CCPR/C/SR, 26, 30, 31, 32(4부)

첨 부 : CCPR/C/SR, 25, 35, 36, 38, 39, 40, 42, 43, 44, 45, 46, 47, 48

끝.

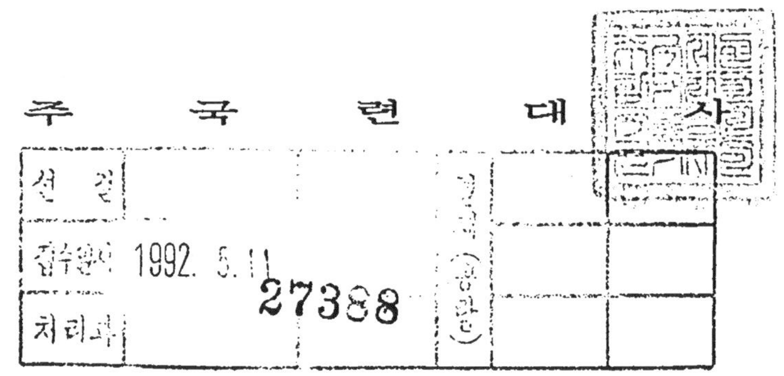

주 국 련 대 사

선 결					
접수일시	1992. 5. 11				
처리과	27388				

0155

관리번호	92-345

	분류번호	보존기간

발 신 전 보

번 호 : WGV-0738 920512 1143 WG 종별 :

수 신 : 주 제네바 대사. 총영사

발 신 : 장 관 (연이)

제 목 : 인권보고서 심의

대 : GVW-2387

1. 금 5.11. 법무부가 알려온 바에 의하면 KNCC 인권위와 민변은 "반대 보고서"(영문)를 공동으로 작성, 지난 주말 DHL편으로 제네바 소재 인권사무국에 송부하였다고 함.

2. 상기 관련, ~~인권사무국 담당관 접촉, 상기~~ 사무국의 동 자료 접수여부 및 처리방안에 대하여 가능한대로 파악 보고바람. 끝.

(국제기구국장 김재섭)

검토필 (1992.6.30.)

보안통제	

앙고재	92년 5월 11일	유엔2과	기안자 성명		과 장	심의관	국 장		차 관	장 관

외신과통제

0156

"政府「유엔人權보고서」왜곡"

KNCC·民辯주장

가혹행위 수사관數 축소

在所者 인권침해 은폐보고

한국기독교교회협의회(KNCC)인권위원회와 민주화사회를 위한 변호사모임(민변)은 정부가 지난해7월 유엔인권이사회에 제출한 인권보고서의 상당부분이 국내인권상황을 왜곡하고있다고 주장하는「비교인권보고서」를 최근 작성했다。

KNCC인권위는 이「비교보고서」를 영문으로 번역, 기왕에 작성된「반박보고서」와 함께 유엔인권위에 제출키로 했다。

KNCC인권위와 민변은 이 보고서에서『정부는 지난86년부터 5년간 고문협의로 기소된 경찰등 수사담당공무원이 모두 29명이라고 밝혔으나 법무부가 국회에 제출한 자료에 따르면 고문 또는 가혹행위로 고소 고발된 공무원이 지난89년9월부터 1년동안에만도 1백15명(53건)에 이르고있다』며『정부측이 고문행위자에 대한 최종처리결과만을 유엔에 보고, 결과적으로 국내수사기관의 고문상황을 축소은폐하고있다』고 주장했다。

KNCC등은 또『정부가 재야단체의 평화적 집회를 뚜렷한 이유없이 불허하고 경찰을 동원, 원천봉쇄하고 있으면서도 유엔에 제출한 정부측 인권보고서에는 집회를 신고만으로 허용하고 있는 것처럼 왜곡하고 있다』고 지적했다。

재소자 인권문제와 관련 해서도 재야 단체들은 정부의 보고서와는 달리△재소자의 1인당 허용면적이 0.5~1.1평방m에 불과하며△대부분의 재소자 감호시설에 영양사나 조리사가 없는 실정이고△재소자가 징벌을 받을 경우 이에대한 구제조치가 전혀없어 재소자의 인권침해가 자주 일어나고 있다고 주장했다。

이밖에 재야단체들은 국가보안법의 일부조항이 개정된 이후에도 검찰이나 법원의 국가보안법 적용은 개정이전과 다를바 없으며 국가보안법 관련 구속자의 수도 계속 증가하고 있다고 반박했다。

비교인권보고서는 정부측보고서의 23개항목중△신체의 자유△평화적 집회의 자유△국가보안법 △재소자의 인권등 9개항목의 내용이 특히 왜곡 또는 축소가 많았다고 분석했다。

동아일보 (23면) 92.5.11.

0157

<국내 인권상황 비교>

주요항목	정 부 보 고 서	비 교 보 고 서
고문금지와 신체의 자유	—경찰관등 공무원의 고문혐의 기소 86년 : 9명 87년 : 9명 88년 : 4명 89년 : 5명 90년 : 2명(5년간 29명)	—89년 9월~90년10월 고문가혹행위 고소고발공무원 53건 115명 —형식적 이유만으로 구속기간연장 —구속적부심、보석허가에 의한 석방률 저조
평화적 집회의 권리	—申告制채택 —질서유지인 있을때 가두시위 허용	—사실상의 허가제 —집회주체에 따라 원천봉쇄 빈번 —진압방법 과격
국가보안법	—법개정이후 인권침해 해소 —북한을 제외한 사회주의국가와의 교류허용	—개정이후법해석과적용에변화없음 —국보법구속자 꾸준히 증가 —일반형법보다 인권침해요소 여전
재소자 인권	—1일 3,150Kcal영양공급 —1인당감방허용면적 충분	—대부분 수용시설 영양사 없음 —1인당 0.5~1.1평방m 비좁음
사상과 양심의 자유	—보장 —단 국가보안법상 일부불허	—국보법불고지죄는양심의자유침해 —국보법 재소자 전향서 미작성시 일체의 혜택 배제
알 권 리	—보장	—정보공개법 미제정 —정부보유정보 공개미흡

人權논란 국제사회 飛火

KNCC「비교보고서」파장

한국기독교교회협의회(KNCC)인권위원회와 민주화사회를 위한 변호사모임(민변)이 지난해7월 유엔인권이사회에 제출된 정부측인권보고서내용을 반박하는 자체비교보고서를 작성,유엔인권이사회에 제출키로함에 따라 국내인권상황에 대한 논란이 국제무대로 비화될 조짐이다.

당초 KNCC인권위등은 정부측 신고서에 대한 반박보고서만을 제출할 계획이었으나 국내 인권상황을 보다 부각시키기위해서는 항목별 비교분석이 효과적이라고 판단, 이비교보고서를 작성했다.

KNCC등은 이 보고서를 통해 정부측이 의도적으로 생략 또는 누락시킨 인권실태를조목조목 비교, 유엔에 보고함으로써 우리정부가 국제인권규약을 더욱성실히 이행토록 촉구하는 계기로 삼기로 했다.

KNCC인권위등은 특히 비교보고서에 정부측의 국회국정감사자료, 판례등 객관적인 비교자료를 제시,『정부측이 국내인권상황의 상당부분을 은폐 축소하려한다』고 주장했다.

"고문 집회자유 대표적 왜곡" 지적

이번 보고서에서 KNCC등은 정부측 인권보고서가 국내의 고문및 가혹행위상황과 집회결사의자유등의 부문에서 대표적으로 실제상황을 왜곡하고있다고 지적했다.

이같은 인권단체의 보고서가 유엔등 국제사회에서「근거있다」고 인정될 경우 국내인권상황은「법적으로는 틀을 갖추었지만 실질적인 인권은 보장되지않는 상황」으로 비쳐질수밖에없다.

결국 국제사회 일각에서 제기한 것처럼 한국이「인권후진국」으로 남느냐, 이를 탈피하느냐는 것은 인권단체의 보고서를 유엔인권이사회가 어떻게 받아들이느냐에 달려있는셈이다. 〈崔壽默〉

동아일보 (22면) 92. 5. 11.

0158

人權보고서 왜곡 사실인가

지난 强權정치 시대에서 적지 않게 말썽을 빚었던 人權문제가 최근 다시 거론되어 주목을 끌고있다。民主化시대를 여는 제6공화국이 출범한지도 벌써 5년째를 맞고 있고 국제인권규약에 가입한지도 3년이 되었는데도 아직까지 인권문제시비가 그치지않고 있다는것은 부끄러운 일이다。이번에 나타난 시비는 인권후진국의 불명예를 씻기위해 90년에 가입한 국제인권규약에 따라 유엔에 처음 제출한 정부의 보고서에서 비롯되고 있어 자칫하면 국제적으로 망신을 당하지나 않을까 우려된다。즉 작년 7월 유엔인권위원회에 제출한 인권보고서의 상당부분이 실제상황을 축소 왜곡하고 있다고 한국기독교 교회협의회와 민주사회를위한 변호사모임에서 주장하고 나온것이다。

그 보고서는 작년 법무 내부 노동 보사등 11개 관련부처가 분야별로 작성 종합한것으로 총3백12개 항목에 걸쳐 시민적 정치적 권리보장과 관련한 일반적 법률체계와 사법적 행정적 조치들이 포함되어 있다。바로 이 보고서에 대해 두단체는 특히 신체의자유、평화적 집회의 자유、국가보안법、재소자의 인권등의 항목에서 축소 왜곡이 많았다고 반박하는 비교보고서를 발표한것이다。예를 들면 정부보고서는 지난 86년부터 5년간 고문협의로 기소된 경찰등 수사담당공무원은 모두 29명이라고 밝히고 있으나 법무부가 국회에 제출한 자료는 고문 가혹행위로 고소 고발된 공무원이 지난89년9월부터 1년동안만해도 53건에 1백15명이라는 것이다。

이들 단체는 여러 항목별로 비교한 그들의 보고서를 발표하는데 그치지 않고 이를 유엔인권위원회에 제출할 예정이어서 국제적논란을 불러일으킬 가능성도 없지않다。만일 유엔인권위원회가 이 비교보고서를 접수한뒤 일리가 있다고 판단해서 실제조사에 나설수도 있을 것이다。

금년초 발표된 미국 국무부 人權보고서는 한국의 인권상황에 대해『아직도 권위주의적인 잔재가 남아있다』고 언급하면서『야당정치인 과격학생 노조운동가들에 대한 정보수집이 계속되고 있으며 민감한 정치사건에 대해 사법부가 행정부의 영향력아래 있다』고 꼬집은바 있다。

두단체가 지적한것처럼 정부보고서가 실제의 국내인권상황을 축소 왜곡한게 사실이라면 체약국으로서 지켜야할 국제적 신의에 흠집을 내는 실수를 범한 것이다。정부보고서와 비교보고서는 인권침해의 기준이나 시각이 다를수 있기때문에 다소간 차이는 날수있다。그렇더라도 정부는 사실을 속시원하게 해명해야 할것이다。그리고 교회협의회나 변호사 모임측도 그런 반박보고서를 국제기구에 제출하기에 앞서 먼저 정부측에대해 사실규명을 촉구하는 것이 순서일 것이다。그들이 목적하는 바도 인권보호이지 나라망신이 아닐것이기 때문이다。

한국일보 〈2면〉 92.5.12.

경향신문 (92.5.12)

″정부 人權보고서 조작

KNCC등 주장 고문警官數 축소″

한국기독교 교회협의회(KNCC)인권위원회와민주사회를 위한 변호사모임(민변)은 11일 정부가 지난해 7월 유엔인권이사회에 제출한 인권보고서에서 국내 인권상황을 상당부분 왜곡해 보고했다며 「비교인권보고서」를 작성、영문으로 옮긴뒤「반박보고서」와 함께 유엔에 제출키로 했다。

KNCC등은 이 보고서에서『정부는 지난86년부터 5년간 고문협의로 기소된 수사담당공무원이 모두 29명이라고 밝혔으나 법무부가 국회에 제출한 자료에는 고문 또는 가혹행위로 고소·고발된 공무원은 지난89년9월부터 1년동안에만도 53건에걸쳐 1백15명으로 나와있다』고 밝혔다。

이 단체들은 또『정부가 재야단체의 각종 집회를 뚜렷한 이유없이 불허하고 원천봉쇄 했으면서도 유엔에는 집회를 신고만으로 허용하고 있는 것처럼 왜곡하고 있다』고 지적하고 ▲재소자의 인권 ▲국가보안법을 통한 인권유린 부분에 대해서도 왜곡보고했다고 주장했다。

0159

배부처	비 부 부	대검	청와대	기 타 기 관
	정치비김기고 무원법장 실국실차 관관장장관	공안부장		계안외공법 기무보게 조부부처치

정 보 보 고

1. 제 목 2. 출 처

인권관련 언론보도 진상 및 대책보고 인 권 과

(1992. 5. 12)

3. 내 용

1. 정부가 작년 7월 유엔에 제출한 국제인권규약(B규약) 보고서 에 대하여 이를 반박하는 내용의 이른바 "비교보고서"를 KNCC 인권위원회와 민주화를위한변호사모임이 작성, 유엔에 제출키로 했다는 취지의 국내 언론보도가 있어 그 내용과 분석 및 대응 여부를 검토하여 첨부와 같이 보고드림

2. 첨 부

o 인권관련 언론보도 진상 및 반박 1부.

0160

RECEIVED FROM 1992.05.12 11:36 P.2

인권관련 언론보도 진상 및 반박

1. 관련 보도내용

o 동아일보(5.11자 22,23면), 경향신문(5.12자 23면),
한국일보 사설(5.12자 2면)

o 보도요지

- KNCC인권위원회와 민주사회를위한변호사모임(민변)은 정부가 작년 7월 유엔에 제출한 국제인권규약(B규약) 보고서의 상당 부분이 국내 인권상황을 왜곡하고 있다고 주장하는 「비교보고서」를 최근 작성

- 상기 「비교보고서」는 정부보고서가 '86년부터 5년간 고문혐의로 기소된 수사담당공무원이 29명이라고 밝혔으나, 실제는 '89. 9부터 1년동안에만도 115명이 고소.고발되었음을 지적하면서,

0161

1

정부측이 의도적으로 고문행위자에 대한 처리결과만을 유엔에 제출, 국내 수사기관의 고문상황을 은폐하고 있다고 주장

- 또한 동 보고서는 정부가 재야단체의 평화적 집회를 이유없이 불허 또는 원천봉쇄하고 있으며, 재소자 1인당 점용면적이 0.5 내지 1평방미터에 불과한 점 등 재소자 인권침해가 자주 일어나고 있다고 하면서 정부가 평화적 집회의 자유, 국가보안법, 재소자 인권 등 9개항목에서 국내 인권상황을 왜곡 또는 축소하였다고 주장

2. 진상 및 반박

가. 진상 및 반박

o 가혹행위 수사담당공무원 숫자 축소부분

- 정부작성의 보고서는 고소.고발 등에 따라 수사담당공무원을 고문혐의로 수사한 뒤 그 혐의가 인정되어 기소한 숫자를

0162

밝힌 것으로 범죄혐의가 입증된 피의자에 대한 통계만을 발표하는 것은 정부의 공식문서인 이상 너무 당연한 것임.

(고소.고발된 공무원 중에는 허무인 또는 성명불상자, 고소인이 허무인이거나 소재불명인 경우, 무고성 고소.고발, 재야단체가 정치적 의도에서 집단적으로 수십명의 공무원을 고소.고발하는 경우 등이 포함되어 있으며, 이들 통계를 아무런 검증없이 무책임하게 발표할 수는 없음)

- 언론보도에 의하면 상기 『비교보고서』는 수사이전에 고소.고발된 공무원의 총 숫자를 제시하면서 마치 이들 전원이 고문행위자인양 기술한 것으로 보이는 바, 만일 보도내용이 사실이라면 동 『비교보고서』의 발표는 아무런 혐의가 없는 대부분의 피고소(발)인에 에 대한 또다른 인권침해인 동시에 국민을 오도하는 불순한 목적이 개입된 것으로 생각하지 않을 수 없음

3

0163

o 재소자 인권부분

- 재소자 1인당 적용면적은 1평당 2명(1인당 1.65평방미터) 정도이며, 일본 등 타국도 같은 수준임에도 상기 『비교보고서』는 이를 0.5-1.1평방미터로 주장하여 왜곡

- 보도내용대로 거실이 최소 0.5평방미터라고 한다면 방의 한쪽 길이가 사람의 신장을 1.7미터로 할 경우 방의 다른쪽은 불과 0.3미터밖에 되지 못함. 이러한 크기(1.7미터X0.3미터)의 거실은 우리나라 교정시설에 없으며, 1인당 0.5내지 1.1평방미터로 비좁다는 것은 0.5평 내지 1.1평의 착오로 사료됨.

- 정부보고서에서는 이 부분을 구체적으로 언급치 아니하고 있음

o 평화적 집회 자유의 제한부분

- 정부는 집회및시위에관한법률에 따라 합법적인 모든 집회와 시위를 신고만으로 가능하도록 적극 보장하여 왔으며, 다만 집단적인 폭행·협박·손괴·방화 등으로 공공의 안녕질서에

0164

4

직접적인 위협을 가할 것이 명백한 집회·시위 등에 대해서 만 제한적으로 최소한의 범위내에서 금지해 왔음

- 보도내용에 따르면, 위 『비교보고서』는 구체적인 사례의 언급을 회피한 채 정부가 "뚜렷한 이유없이" 재야단체의 모든 집회를 불허 또는 원천봉쇄한다고 오도하고 있음

o 기타부분

- 국가보안법 등 기타부분은 KNCC나 민변측이 종래의 주장을 그대로 비교보고서에 인용한 것으로 그 내용이 진부하며, 별도의 분석대상 없음

나. 확인결과

o 언론보도내용이 상식적으로도 수긍할 수 없는 사항이 포함된 점 등이 주목되며, 과연 문제의 『비교보고서』가 보도내용대로 되어 있는지는 확인되지 아니함

0165

5

o 민변측은 오늘 현재까지 「비교보고서」에 관한 어떠한 내용의 공식적 발표도 한 바 없다고 함. 상기 보도는 공식자료가 아닌 다른 자료 등에 의한 추측보도로 사료됨

다. 대응방안

o 왜곡기사에 대하여는 관계언론사에 그 진위를 분명히 설명하여 항의하고, 정부의 공식논평은 일단 유보한뒤 추후 상황전개를 보아 재검토함이 상당

※ 참고사항

- 문제의 「비교보고서」는 일부 사적인 재야단체가 작성한 것으로 유엔에서도 이를 정식문서로 접수하지 아니하고, 단지 참고자료로 취급 (이들 재야단체 대표자들은 유엔 심의회에 방청만 할 뿐 발언을 하지 못함)

- 국제인권규약보고서의 경우 그 심의회에 즈음하여 해당국의 재야단체들이 반박보고서 등을 유엔에 제출하는 것은 타국의 경우에도 흔히 있는 관례임

0166

6

김 명 식

1. 인적사항

. 생년월일 : '45. 10. 3생

. 직 업 : 아라리연구원장, 전민련 국제협력국장

2. 범죄사실 요지 (국가보안법 위반)

1987.9부터 1990.7까지 사이에 제주 4.3폭동이 미제국주의의 식민지보부터 남한지역을 해방시키는 반미구국투쟁 운동이자 남한지역에서 조선민주주의 인민공화국을 수립하기 위한 투쟁이라고 주장하고, 지금 현실은 4.3 당시와 마찬가지로 분단고착세력 (미군, 친미파)에 의하여 포위되어 있고, 미국에 의해 지배 침략당하고 있는 실정이므로 우리들의 강토에서 외세 (미국)와 친미세력을 깨끗이 몰아낸 일만이 우리들에게 남겨져 있다는 등을 내용으로 하는 제주민중항쟁 I,II, 제주 4.3 민족민중해방투쟁의 배경과 그 원인, 제주민중항쟁의 현대적 의의 등 이적표현물을 제작하여 북한이 대남적화혁명을 위해 행하고 있는 선전, 선동에 동조한 것임

3. 처리상황

. '90. 7.12 구속

. '90.11.23 서울형사지법, 징역1년6월 선고
감은남 피고인 항소

. '91. 4.24 2심법원, 항소기각

. '91. 9.24 대전교도소에서 출소 (감형 3월29일)

* 당초 형기종료예정일은 '92.1.22 이었음

0167

長官報告事項

報 告 畢

1992. 5. 12.
國 際 機 構 局
國際聯合2課(23)

題 目 : ~~國際人權規約~~ 我國 ~~最初~~인권報告書 審議 關聯 動向

> 92.7월로 豫定된 國際人權規約 我國 最初報告書 審議와 관련,
> KNCC 人權委等 在野團體의 最近 動向을 아래와 같이 報告드립니다.

1. KNCC 人權委 및 民辯의 動向

o 아국 最初報告書에 대한 "反駁 報告書"(영문)를 92.5월초 유엔 人權事務局에 送付 (5.11. 법무부 제보)

o 최근 "反駁 報告書"와 별도로 "比較 人權報告書"를 作成, 人權事務局에 提出 計劃 (5.11자 동아일보, 5.12자 한국일보, 경향신문 보도)

- 아국 報告書中 身體의 自由, 集會의 自由, 國家保安法, 在所者 人權等과 관련한 縮小, 歪曲이 있었다고 主張

2. 對應措置

o 人權事務局의 "反駁 報告書" 接受 與否 및 處理~~方案을~~절차를 把握토록 5.12. 주제네바 大使에 指示

- 人權委員들에게 일반 郵便物로서 傳達될 것으로 豫想

o 法務部는 "比較 人權報告書" 關聯 報道에 대하여 該當 言論社에 事實 說明과 함께 抗議할 豫定이며, 政府 公式論評은 일단 留保한다는 立場

3. 言論對策

o 해당 없음. 끝.

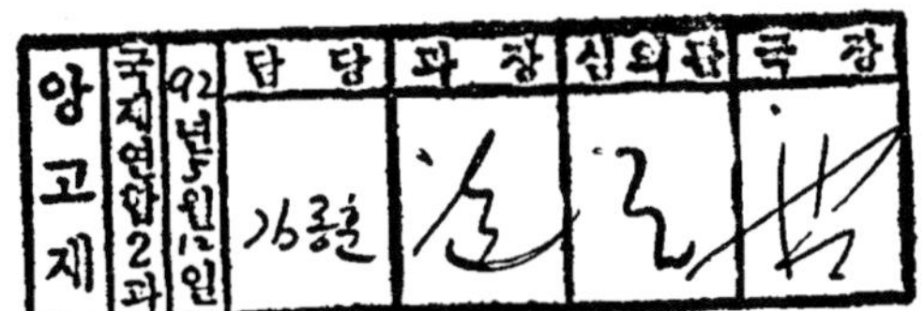

0168

報 告 畢
(서명)

1992. 5. 12.
國 際 機 構 局
國際聯合2課(23)

長 官 報 告 事 項

題 目 : 我國 人權報告書 審議 關聯 動向

92.7월로 豫定된 國際人權規約 我國 最初報告書 審議와 관련, KNCC 人權委等 在野團體의 最近 動向을 아래와 같이 報告드립니다.

1. KNCC 人權委 및 民辯의 動向

o 아국 最初報告書에 대한 "反駁 報告書"(영문)를 92.5월초 유엔 人權事務局에 送付 (5.11. 법무부 제보)

o 최근 "反駁 報告書"와 별도로 "比較 人權報告書"를 作成, 人權事務局에 提出 計劃 (5.11자 동아일보, 5.12자 한국일보, 경향신문 보도)

- 아국 報告書中 身體의 自由, 集會의 自由, 國家保安法, 在所者 人權等과 관련한 縮小, 歪曲이 있었다고 主張

2. 對應措置

o 人權事務局의 "反駁 報告書" 接受 與否 및 處理節次를 把握토록 5.12. 주제네바 大使에 指示

- 人權委員들에게 일반 郵便物로서 傳達될 것으로 豫想

o 法務部는 "比較 人權報告書" 關聯 報道에 대하여 該當 言論社에 事實 說明과 함께 抗議할 豫定이며, 政府 公式論評은 일단 留保한다는 立場

3. 言論對策

o 해당 없음. 끝.

0169

KNCC 人權보고서 상당부분 사실과 달라

법무부 주장

법무부는 13일 KNCC인권위원회와 민주사회를 위한 변호사모임(민변)이 정부측의 국제인권규약보고서내용을 반박해 최근 작성한 「비교보고서」 내용의 상당부분이 근거가 없거나 사실과 다르다고 주장했다.

법무부는 민변등이 비교보고서를 통해 정부가 지난86년부터 5년간 고문혐의로 기소된 수사담당공무원의 숫자를 29명이라고 밝혔으나 실제 89년부터 1년동안 고소고발된 사람이 1백15명임을 지적,「이는 정부측이 의도적으로 국내의 고문상황을 은폐축소한것」이라고 주장한것과 관련,『정부작성 보고서가 혐의의 입증도 없이 고소고발자를 모두 고문행위자로 규정할수 없는 것은 너무 당연한 일』이라고 반박했다.

동아일보 (14면) 92.5.13.

0170

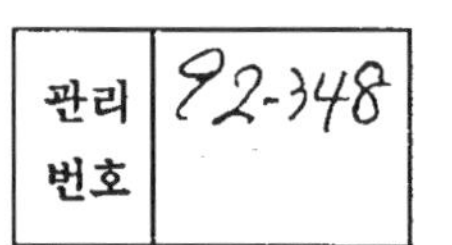

원 본

외 무 부

종 별 :

번 호 : GVW-0977　　　　　　　일 시 : 92 0512 1830

수 신 : 장관(연이)

발 신 : 주 제네바 대사

제 목 : 아국 인권보고서 심의

1. 표제관련 KLEIN 인권사무국 담당관이 금 5.12 당관에 비공식으로 알려온아국보고서 심의 일정은 아래와 같으며 사무국측이 이를 추후 공식 서면 통보할 예정이라함.

7.13(월) 15:00 아측의 보고서 개요 설명 및 질문

7.15(수) 15:00 질문에 대한 답변 및 평가

2. 동 담당관은 다만 답변 및 평가시 시간이 부족한 경우 익 7.16(목) 오전까지 연장될 가능성도 전혀 배제할 수는 없다하며, 한편 심의후 약 2 페이지 정도의 이사회 종합 평가서(COMMENT OF THE COMMITTEE AS A WHOLE)가 나올 예정인바 이는 금년 3 월부터 새로이 도입된 제도라함.

3. 이와관련 동담당관은 인권위원들에게 사전 배포할 아국 헌법 영문본 25 부를 요청하여 왔는바, 파편 송부 바람. 끝

(대사 박수길-국장)

예고:92.12.31. 까지

검토필 (1992.6.30.)

국기국　차관　1차보　분석관

PAGE 1　　　　　　　　　　92.05.13　05:17

외신 2과　통제관 EC

0171

외 무 부

110-760 서울 종로구 세종로 77번지 / (02) 723-8934 / (02) 723-3505

문서번호 연이 20314-117
시행일자 1992.5.14.
16320

수신 주제네바 대사
참조

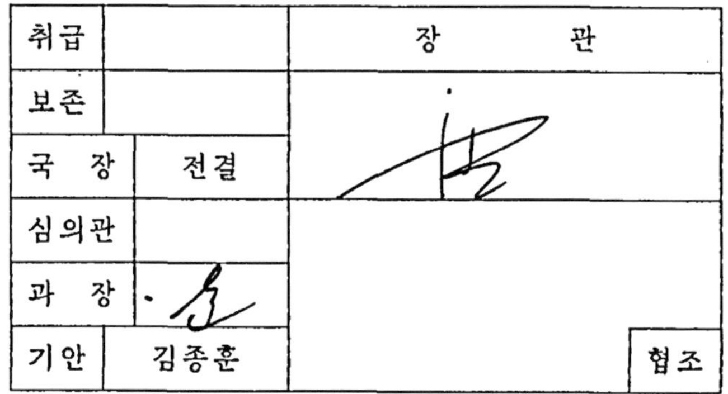

취급		장 관
보존		
국 장	전결	
심의관		
과 장		
기안	김종훈	협조

제목 인권보고서 심의 관련 자료송부

대 : GVW-0977

대호 인권보고서 심의와 관련, 아국 헌법 영문본 25부를 별첨 송부합니다.

첨부 : 헌법 영문본 25부. 끝.

검열 관제관

0172

인권규약 보고서 심의 대책

1992.5.15.
국제연합2과

1. 경 위

o 아국이 90.7월 가입한 시민적.정치적 권리에 관한 국제규약(B규약)에 의거, 아국 최초 보고서를 91.7월 제출

o 동 보고서는 제네바에서 개최되는 제45차 인권이사회에서 92.7.13-15간 심의될 예정

* 보고서 작성 경위

- "인권 옹호정책 협의회"에서 보고서 작성 관련 기본정책 결정
  . 구성 : 사정수석, 행정수석, 정책조사 보좌관, 외교안보 보좌관, 국무총리 행조실장, 법무, 내무, 외무, 공보처 차관, 안기부 특보
- 법무부, 내무부, 노동부, 보건사회부 등 11개 관련부처가 상기 기본 정책에 따라 담당 분야별로 세부내용을 작성, 이를 법무부가 종합하고, 외무부가 영문으로 번역

2. 절 차

o 7.13.오전 수석대표의 제안설명(10-15분) 및 위원(18인)의 논평 및 질의 (2-3시간)

o 7.15.오전 수석대표 1차 답변 및 위원 보충질의와 보충답변
- 1차 답변은 사전 작성, 보충답변은 즉석 시행

* 필요시 통역 대동 가능

o 심의종료 후 인권이사회 명의의 종합 평가 및 권고 채택, 해당국 송부 및 총회 보고

3. 대 책

가. 대표단 구성

o 답변 준비를 위해 대표단, 특히 수석대표의 조기 결정 필요
  - 5월말 이전이 바람직

o 수석대표는 아래 사항을 고려, 법무부 고위인사로 임명하는 것이 타당
  - 인권이사회는 "해당국가의 인권상황에 대하여 인권위원들의 질문 및 평가에 대하여 답변할수 있으며, 인권현황을 설명할수 있는 지위와 경험이 있는 대표로 임명할 것"을 요청하고 있음.
  - 인권보장과 관련된 국내법 체제 및 운용과 관련된 제반사항이 중점 심의될 것이므로 실질적으로 법사행정을 담당하는 부처의 책임있는 인사가 직접 참가, 답변하는 것이 상당함. (심의의 목적도 해당국의 인권보장 향상에 있음.)
  - 최초 보고서 심의 대응에 있어 성실한 자세를 보이는 것이 중요하며, 이를 위하여는 인권보장 관련업무를 관장하고 법률 일반에 상세한 지식을 갖춘 인사를 대표로 내세우는 것이 요망됨.
  - 대부분 국가의 경우 최초보고서 심의에 법무부 고위인사가 수석 대표로 참가 (2차 보고서 부터는 꼭 법무부 인사가 아니라도 무방)
  - 금번 아국 최초보고서 심의 관련 재야단체의 반대 보고서 제출 (5월 중순 인권사무국 접수 확인), 심의과정 참여(방청), 국내 보도, 정치적 민감성 등 감안 요

나. 심의관련 준비

o 법무부에서 제안 설명서 및 답변자료 준비중

2

0174

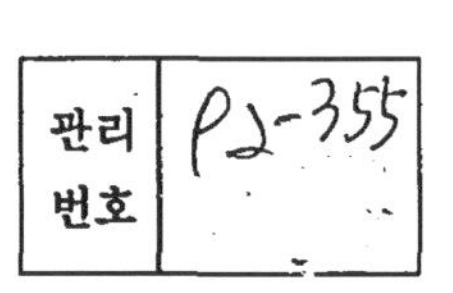

2 원 본

외 무 부

가..

종 별 :

번 호 : GVW-0995 일 시 : 92 0514 1900

수 신 : 장관(연이)

발 신 : 주 제네바 대사

제 목 : 인권보고서 심의

대: WGV-0738

연: GVW-0977

대호 관련 당관 문봉주 참사관이 인권 사무국 KLEIN 협약 담당관을 접촉 파악한 내용 아래 보고함.(이하 KLEIN 담당관 발언 요지)

1. 반대보고서

0 대호 KNCC 와 민변이 송부한 반대 보고서(COUNTER REPORT) 는 수일전 사무국에 접수되었음.

0 동 반대 보고서는 공식 문서화 되지 않으며 사무국은 이를 인권이사회 위원들에게 단순히 전달하는 외에 다른 조치를 취하지 않음.

0 과거 여타국가의 인권 보고서 심의시에도 국내 단체 또는 국제 NGO 로부터 유사한 자료가 사무국을 통하거나 또는 직접 인권 이사회 위원들에게 전달되는 사례가 많이 있었음.

0 인권보고서 심의는 정부가 제출한 보고서를 심의하는 것이나, 개별 위원들이 심의에 참고코자 비공식 경로를 통해 자료나 정보를 입수하는 것은 흔히 있는 일인바, 민간단체들이 송부하는 소위 반대 보고서는 위원들의 참고자료로서 활용될 뿐임.

2. 심의 관련 사항

가. INTRODUCTORY REMARKS

0 보고서가 제출된후 이사회 심의시까지 기간동안의 (우리의 경우 보고서 제출시기인 작년 7 월이후 금년 7 월까지 약 1 년간) DEVELOPMENT 에 관해 반드시 SUPPLEMENTARY REPORT 는 약 15 분 정도로 하는 것이 관례이며, 기제출된 보고서 내용의 요약 반복 설명에 치중하는 것 보다는 제출후 현재까지의 새로운 진전 상황 설명에 중점을 두는 것이 보다 효과적일 것으로 봄.

국기국 차관 1차보 분석관

92.05.15 06:01
외신 2과 통제관 FM

0175

나. 심의절차 및 예상 소요 시간

0 연호 일정 관련, 여타국 심의사례에 비추어 7.13(월) SESSION 은 아국 대표의 INTRODUCTORY REMARKS 와 위원들의 질문에 약 3 시간 정도로 7.15(수) SESSION 은 특별한 사정이 없는한 답변에 약 2 시간, 개별위원들의 COMMENT 및 SUMMING-UP 에 약 1 시간 정도를 예상하면 될것으로 봄.

0 아울러 이사회의 종합 평가서는 이사회 회기가 끝날 무렵에 이사회에 제출될 것인바 대개 심의시 위원들의 개별 평가를 요약 종합한 내용이 될것임.

다. 기타 사항

0 금번 회기중 INITIAL REPORT 심의 대상국은 아국과 브룬디 2 개국임.

0 INTRODUCTORY REMARKS 는 가능한 심의 개시전에 문안을 사무국에 제출해주기 요망함.

3. 아국 보고서 심의와 관련 충분한 사전 준비를 위해 아국 대표단을 가능한 조속히 확정하는 것이 바람직할 것으로 사료됨. 끝

(대사 박수길-국장)

예고 92.12.31. 까지

검토필 (1992.6.30.)

PAGE 2

0176

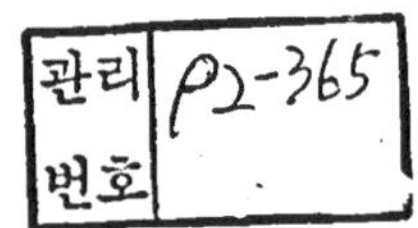

외 무 부

110-760 서울 종로구 세종로 77번지 / (02) 723-8934 / (02) 723-3505

문서번호 연이 20314-1288
시행일자 1992.5.16

수신 법무부장관

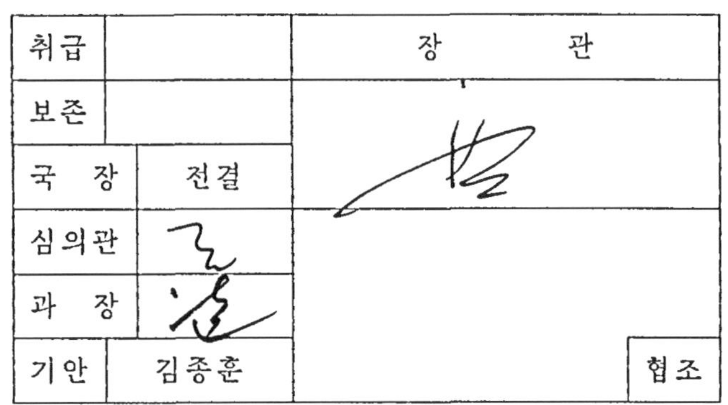

취급		장 관
보존		
국 장	전결	
심의관		
과 장		
기안	김종훈	협조

제목 국제 인권규약(B) 아국 최초보고서 심의

1. 아국이 90.7월 제출한 국제 인권규약(B) 최초 보고서에 대한 심의가 제45차 인권이사회 기간중인 92.7.13-7.15간 제네바에서 개최될 예정입니다.

2. 인권 사무국측이 비공식적으로 알려온 바에 의하면 상기 심의 상세일정은 아래와 같습니다.

   o 7.13(월) 오후
   - 수석대표 연설(15분)
   - 인권위원 질문(3시간)

   o 7.15(수) 오후
   - 아국 대표단 답변(2시간)
   - 인권위원들의 논평 및 종합평가(1시간)

   o 필요한 경우 7.16(목) 오전에 회의 속개

/ 계속 /

0177

3. 금번 심의에 대비, 아래 자료를 사전에 준비하여 주시기 바랍니다.

- 아 래 -

가. 수석대표 연설문(Introductory Remarks) 안

- 아국 보고서 주요내용 소개
- 90.7월 보고서 제출후 현재까지의 인권보장 관련 새로운 진전 상황 (형법 개정 추진등 포함)

나. 예상질의 및 답변자료

- ~~최근 국내외 인권단체가 아국 인권상황과 관련하여 제기한 인권 관련 법률 및 제도 운용상의 문제 등~~. 끝.

검열
통제관

검토필 (1992.6.30.)

0178

관리 번호 92-292

	분류번호	보존기간

발 신 전 보

번 호 : WGV-0772 920518 1926 BU 종별 :

수 신 : 주 제네바 대사. ~~(박수길 대사님)~~

발 신 : 장 관 (~~국제기구국장~~ 김재섭 배)

제 목 : 업 연

1. 그간 법무부와 인권이사회 수석대표 문제를 협의해 보았습니다만, 법무부측이 맡기 어렵다는 입장이므로, 장관님께도 의논드렸던 바, 이번이 첫번째 우리 인권보고서 심의이므로 법적인 대응뿐 아니라 정치적인 감각이 요구되니 결국 대사님께서 수고해 주시는게 좋겠다는 말씀입니다.

2. 대사님의 별도 의견이 있으시면 하시하여 주시기 바라며, 대표단 조기 구성 및 모든 실무적 준비는 최대한 빠른 시간내 조치하도록 하겠습니다. 끝.

예고 : 독후 파기

보안 통제	

앙고재	92년 5월 18일	기안자 성명		과 장	심의관	국 장		차 관	장 관

외신과통제

0179

2 원 본

외 무 부

종 별 :

번 호 : GVW-1027 일 시 : 92 0519 1200

수 신 : 장관(연이)

발 신 : 주제네바대사

제 목 : 인권보고서 심의

연: GVW-0977, 0995

1. 유엔 인권 사무국은 아국의 인권 보고서 심의 일정을 별첨 서한(FAX) 을 통해 공식 통보하여왔음.

2. 일정은 연호 보고한바와 같으며, 동 서한 원본은 본부로 직송되었음.

첨부: 서한 (FAX)(GVW(F)-326)

(대사 박수길-국장)

국기국

PAGE 1 92.05.19 20:34 BU

외신 1과 통제관 ✓

0180

주 제 네 바 대 표 부

번 호 : GVF(F) - 326 년월일 : 2051P 시간 : 1200

수 신 : 장 관 (연이)

발 신 : 주 제네바대사

제 목 : GVW-1027

보 안	
통 제	

총 2 매(표지포함)

외신과	
통 제	

326-2-1

0181

1992-05-19 11:39 KOREAN MISSION GENEVA 2 022 791 0525 P.07

OFFICE DES NATIONS UNIES A GENÈVE

CENTRE POUR LES DROITS DE L'HOMME

UNITED NATIONS OFFICE AT GENEVA

CENTRE FOR HUMAN RIGHTS

Télefax: (022) 733 98 79
Télégrammes: UNATIONS, GENÈVE
Télex: 412 962 UNO CH
Téléphone: 734 60 11 731 02 11

COPIE - COPY

Palais des Nations
CH-1211 GENÈVE 10

RÉF. N°: G/SO 221/922 (3)
(à rappeler dans la réponse)

The Secretary-General of the United Nations presents his compliments to the Minister for Foreign Affairs of the Republic of Korea and has the honour to refer to the initial report of His Excellency's Government, submitted in accordance with article 40, paragraph 1 (a) of the International Covenant on Civil and Political Rights for transmission to the Human Rights Committee.

At its forty-fourth session, the Committee decided to consider the initial report of the Republic of Korea at its forty-fifth session, which will be held at the United Nations Office at Geneva from 13 to 31 July 1992. Under the timetable for consideration of reports of States parties at the forty-fifth session of the Committee, the initial report of the Republic of Korea (contained in document CCPR/C/68/Add.1) is scheduled for consideration on Monday (afternoon) and Wednesday (afternoon), 13 and 15 July 1992.

In this connection, the Secretary-General wishes to indicate that members of the Committee need to have before them, well in advance of the consideration of States reports, copies of the Constitution and other relevant legal documents.

Furthermore, the Committee considers it important that the representatives of the States parties present at the meetings of the Committee when their reports are examined have such status and experience as will permit them to respond to questions asked and comments made by members of the Committee and to give up-to-date information on the situation of human rights in the country concerned.

The Secretary-General would appreciate being informed, as soon as possible, of the name(s) and title(s) of the representative(s) whom the Government of the Republic of Korea wishes to designate for the above-mentioned purpose.

14 May 1992

0182

326-2-2

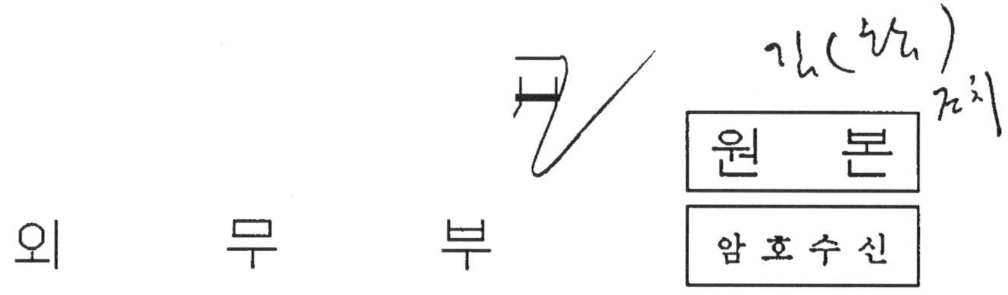

외 무 부

종 별 :

번 호 : EQW-0220 일 시 : 92 0519 1540

수 신 : 장관(연이,미남)

발 신 : 주 에쿠아돌 대사

제 목 : 인권 및 남북대화 자료 요청

대: 국연 2031 - 28013(91. 3. 5)

1. 금 5. 19 전직외상(1967-68)이며, 중앙대학의 국제법 교수(1955-현재) 및 유엔 인권위 위원인 JULIO PRADO VALLEJO 가 본직을 방문, 동인은 금년 7. 6 - 31 간 제네바에서 개최 예정인 유엔 인권회의에 참석 예정이라고 하면서 금번회의에서는 아국 및 페루를 포함한 아시아 및 중남미 3 -4 개국의 인권이 논의될 것이라 함

2. 상기인은 인권회의 참석전 아국의 인권 및 남북대화에 관해 알고 싶다고하면서 이에 관한 자료를 요청함. 동인은 친한적인 입장에서 자료 요청을 한 바 가능하면 영문 또는 서반아어로 된 자료를 송부 바람

3. 상기 자료 송부가 늦을 경우, 인권에 관해서는 대호 영문본을 제공 예정인 바, 의견 회시 바람. 끝

(대사 정해융 - 국장)

국기국 미주국

PAGE 1

92.05.20 08:09

외신 2과 통제관 BX

0183

관리 번호	92-377

	분류번호	보존기간

발 신 전 보

번 호 : WEQ-0122 920521 2128 FO 종별 :

수 신 : 주 에쿠아돌 대사. 총영사

발 신 : 장 관 (연이)

제 목 : 인권 및 남북대화 자료

대 : EQW-0220

연 : 국연 2031-28013

1. 대호 Julio Prado Vallejo 교수는 인권 이사회 (Human Rights Committee) 위원으로서, 동인이 참석 예정인 92.7. 제네바 개최 제44차 인권 이사회 에서는 아국이 제출한 인권규약(B) 최초 보고서에 대한 심의가 있을 예정임.

2. 따라서 동인에 대하여 연호 영문본을 제공할 필요는 없으며, 금주 정파편 송부하는 아국 인권 및 남북대화 관련 영문자료를 ~~전달~~ 활용 바람. 끝.

(국제기구국장 김재섭)

검토필 (1992. 6. 30.)	인

보안 통제	(서명)

앙 고 재	92년 5월 21일	유엔 2과	기안자 성명		과 장	심의관	국 장		차 관	장 관
			김종훈		(서명)	(서명)	전결			(서명)

외신과통제

0184

외 무 부

110-760 서울 종로구 세종로 77번지 / (02) 723-8934 / (02) 723-3505

문서번호 연이 20314-130
시행일자 1992.5.22.

21186

수신 주에쿠아돌 대사
참조

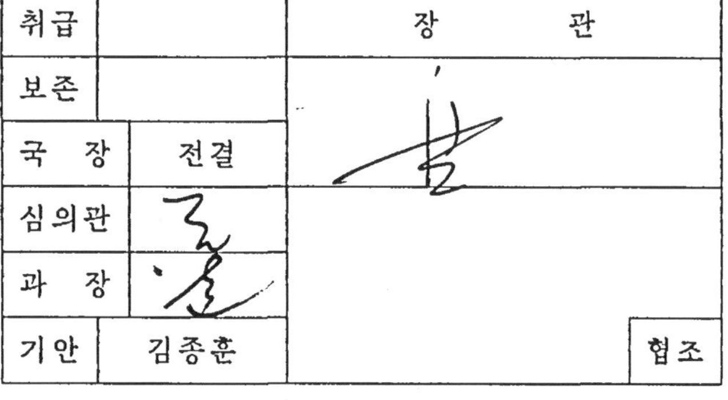

취급		장 관
보존		
국 장	전결	
심의관		
과 장		
기안	김종훈	협조

제목 인권 및 남북대화 관련자료 송부

연 : WEQ-0122

대 : EQW-0220

연호, 표제 관련자료를 별첨 송부합니다.

첨부 : 1. Human Rights in Korea 1부.

2. 남북대화 관련자료 1부. 끝.

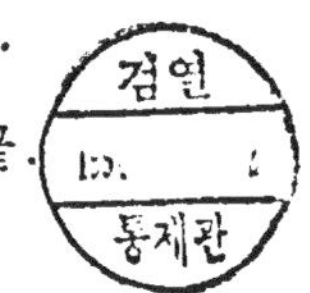

0185

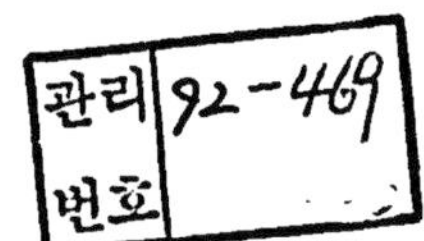

외 무 부

110-760 서울 종로구 세종로 77번지 / (02) 723-8934 / (02) 723-3505

문서번호 연이 20314- 1346
시행일자 1992.5.23.

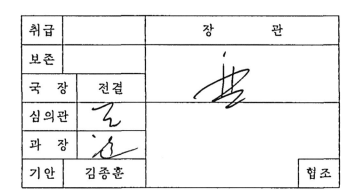

취급		장 관
보존		
국 장	전결	
심의관		
과 장		
기안	김종훈	협조

수신 주제네바 대사
참조

제목 인권규약 보고서 심의 대비자료

1. 제45차 인권이사회에서의 아국 인권규약 보고서 심의에 대비, 아래 자료를 송부하오니 귀업무에 활용하시기 바랍니다.

- 아 래 -

가. "반대보고서" 및 동 요약

나. AI의 아국 관련 보고서

- "South Korea : Prisoners Held for National Security Offences"
- "South Korea : Arrests of Political Prisoners During 1991"

다. 케네디 인권센타의 아국 관련 보고서

- "Broken Promises, Unfulfilled Dreams"

라. 알제리 최초보고서 심의 관련 인권이사회 회의요록 (CCPR/C/SR 1125, 1128)

마. 관계 법령

- 국가보안법(국.영문)
- 형사소송법(국.영문)

/ 계속 / 0186

- 집회 및 시위에 관한 법률(국.영문)

- 사회보호법(국.영문)

- 보안관찰법(국문)

- 보호관찰법(국문)

- 노동조합법(국.영문)

- 근로기준법(국.영문)

바. 제44차 인권이사회 결과보고(본부작성)

2. 인권위원들의 보고서 검토를 위하여 사전에 인권사무국에 제출할 법령자료의 내용에 대하여 귀관 의견을 보고하여 주시기 바랍니다.

첨부 : 상기 자료 각 1부. 끝.

검토필 (1992. 6. 30.)

0187

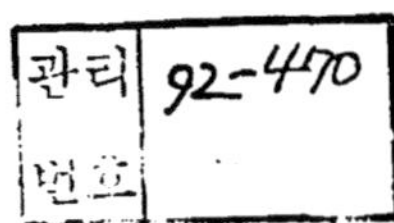

외 무 부

110-760 서울 종로구 세종로 77번지 / (02) 723-8934 / (02) 723-3505

문서번호 연이 20314- 141
시행일자 1992.5.30.

수신 주제네바 대사
참조

취급		장 관
보존		
국 장	전결	
심의관		
과 장		
기안	김종훈	협조

제목 인권보고서 심의 관련자료 송부

연 : 연이 20314-117

1. 연호, 인권보고서 심의와 관련, 국가보안법 개정에 관한 영문자료를 추가로 별첨 송부하오니 참고하시기 바랍니다.

2. 심의 대비자료는 현재 법무부와 협의, 작성중인 바, 가급적 6월초 귀관에 송부 예정임을 알려 드립니다.

첨부 : 상기자료 1부. 끝.

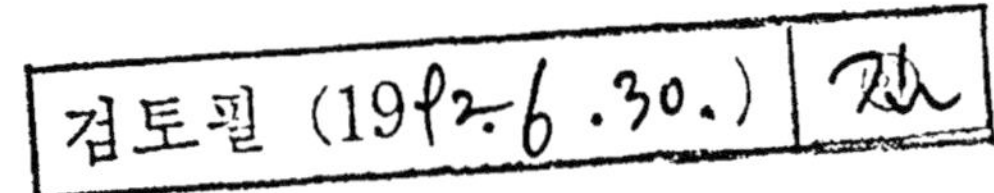

0188

92- 6-25 ;PM 2:35 ; ;# 1

법무부 인권국

1991. . .

아래 문건을 수신자에게 전달하여 주시기 바랍니다.

제 목 :

수 신 : 외무부 유엔과 김 [illegible] 사무관님

(수신처 FAX NO: 723-3505)

발 신 : 법무부 인권국

표지포함 총 ___ 매

0189

RECEIVED FROM 1992.06.25 14:36 P. 1

김종훈 서기관님

o 법률 목록

- 민법, 헌법, 형법, 형사소송법, 헌법재판소법, 법률구조법
  행형법, 국가보안법(개정법 영문화 안됨-개정법률 설명자료 첨부)
  집시및시위에관한법률, 노동관련법률(7월초에 노동부에서
  발간예정)

0190

Highlights of Amendments to the National Security Law

As Passed by the National Assembly on May 10, 1991

0191

RECEIVED FROM 1992.05.30 10:45 P. 2

The amendments are designed to eliminate overly stringent aspects of the past National Security Law and to ensure that it provides for only minimal restrictions needed to defend freedom and democracy against external and internal subversion and sabotage. To that end, 14 of the 25 articles of the law have been rewritten to abolish 20 punitive clauses, which pertain, among other things, to meeting or communicating with or contacting foreign Communists or Communist organizations, misprision of clandestine travel to or from the territory controlled by an antistate organization and various forms of preparations and conspiracies to undermine national security.

A new paragraph (Paragraph 2, Article 1) has been created. It provides that in interpreting and implementing the National Security Law, only minimum necessary legal steps shall be taken to achieve its intrinsic purposes of preserving national security and survival and protecting freedom of the people and that there shall be no extended interpretation of the law. This provision is intended to prevent any abuse of the law, and thus end past controversies over its enforcement.

1

0192

RECEIVED FROM 1992.05.30 0:6

Special care has been taken to make sure that human rights abuses will not be perpetrated under the law. In particular the amended statute much more narrowly defines an "antistate organization" as a group equipped with a "command and control system" so that there will be no room for arbitrary applications of the "antistate organization" clause.

In the past, the law prescribed unconditional punishment for the giving or receiving of money or goods to or from an antistate organization or its member (Para. 2, Article 5) ; clandestine travel to or from the territory controlled by an antistate organization (Article 6) ; the praising, encouraging or siding with an antistate organization or its members (Article 7) ; and meeting or communicating with or contacting a member of an antistate organization (Article 8). The just-revised National Security Law, however, punishes such acts only when they are committed "with the knowledge that this will imperil national survival and security or the basic free and democratic order." This revision is in keeping with the April 2, 1990 ruling of the Constitution Court that the National Security Law is "constitutional with certain reservations." The narrowing of the scope of punishment will end human rights controversies in connection with the enforcement of the law.

Furthermore, the just-passed amendments have deleted the vague phrase, "otherwise gives aid and comfort to an antistate organization" from Article 7, which is intended to punish anyone who "praises, encourages and sides with" an enemy. This has eliminated a lattitude for arbitrary enforcement of that article.

The revised National Security Law is aimed at actively promoting and guaranteeing peaceful inter-Korean exchanges with a view to advancing the goal of national reconciliation leading to unification. This is the revised statute punishes such acts as the giving or receiving of money or goods to or from an antistate organization or its member, clandestine travel to or from the territory controlled by an antistate organization, the praising, encouraging or siding with an antistate organization or its member only when such acts endanger national security and survival. In that way, all legal obstacles to genuine peaceful inter-Korean exchanges have been eliminated.

In addition, the revised law exempts from punishment the above-mentioned acts in regard to foreign Communist organizations and their members with the aim of providing institutional guarantees for active exchanges and cooperation with all former or present Communist countries, except North Korea, in the political, economic, social and all other fields.

The amended National Security Law has other revised provisions also designed to reflect the people's desire for full democratization to the maximum possible extent with a view to helping build a truly free and democratic nation advancing into the 21st century.

In the provisions against espionage (Items 2 and 3, Para. 1, Article 4), the revised law much more narrowly and clearly defines "state secrets" as "knowledge access to which is limited to authorized persons only in order to prevent serious disadvantages to national security" that will stem from its leakage or disclosure and other specific types of information. This will promote freedom of information to the maximum extent.

Whereas Article 14 of the old National Security Law provided that anyone sentenced to imprisonment for a definite term for treason should mandatorily be subjected to post-imprisonment suspension of civil rights, the amended version provides that such suspension of rights may be waived in consideration of extenuating circumstances. This change aims to more effectively protect the civil rights of citizens.

Article 10, which punishes misprision, has been amended to limit its application only to failures to report acts (including espionage) committed to serve the purposes of an antistate organization by its member or any other person following its instructions. To elaborate, the amended version of Article 10 does not punish failures to report the giving or receiving of money or goods, clandestine travel, praising, encouraging or siding with the enemy, and meeting or communicating with the enemy, as defined earlier. In other words, misprision is now punishable only when unreported acts imperil national survival. The scope of misprision has thus been minimized.

Furthermore, the revised version requires a lightening or waiver of punishment for misprision when such an offense is committed by a relative of the person found guilty of treason. The old law provided that such leniency might be granted at the discretion of the judge. This revision is designed to protect freedom of conscience and thought to the maximum extent.

It should be noted that the governing Democratic Liberal Party accepted most of the demands raised by the opposition in the course of negotiations with it over amendments to the National Security Law. The DLP thus revised its draft bill to extensively reflect the spirit of the ruling by the Constitution Court regarding the constitutionality of the old law.
In particular, unauthorized travel to or from enemy territory has been excluded from the list of offenses to which misprision is applicable. Furthermore, the DLP withdrew a proposed clause for permitting an additional extension of the pretrial detention of suspects charged with grave violations of the National Security Law.

In sum, the just-passed amendments represent the maximun relaxation of the law permissible under the prevailing security situation of the nation.

'92- 6- 1 ;PM 4:40 ; ;# 1

법 무 부 인 권 과

1992. . .

아래 문건을 수신자에게 전달하여 주시기 바랍니다.

제 목 : 정보보고

수 신 : 외무부 유엔2과장님

(수신처 FAX NO: 723-3505)

발 신 : 법무부 인권과

표지포함 총 ___ 매

0198

1992.06.01 16:41 P. 1

정 보 보 고

법무부 인권과
1992. 6. 1

제목 : 인권관련 동향 및 대응조치 보고

※ [1992.5.12. 인권관련 언론보도 진상 및 대책보고] 정보보고와 관련임

1. 관련 동향

o 민변측은 6.2(화) 08:30경 종로구 연지동 기독교회관 6층에서 국제인권규약(B규약)에 따라 정부가 유엔에 제출한 최초보고서를 탄핵하는 반박보고서를 작성, 유엔에 송부한 배경을 홍보하는 기자회견을 가질 예정이며, 그 내용이 언론보도될 것으로 예상됨

2. 대응조치

o 각 언론사에 상기 『반박보고서』및 기자회견 내용을 언론에 보도하는 것이 부적절 함을 설명함과 동시에, 굳이 언론이 보도할 경우를 대비하여 정부의 반론을 작성, 같은 비중으로 보도되도록 요청하였음

o 문제의 『반박보고서』는 기히 입수, 주요쟁점을 대검 공안부, 검찰국, 교정국, 안기부 등 각 소관부서별로 심층 정밀분석, 유엔 심의대비 답변자료 작성중임

첨부 : 1. 자료 1, 2.
　　　2. 보도자료 .

0199

[자료 1]

민변 기자회견의 보도에 관한 의견

6.2(화) 08:30, 종로구 연지동 기독교회관 6층에서 민변측은 국제인권규약(B규약)에 따라 정부가 유엔에 제출한 최초보고서를 탄핵하는 반박보고서를 작성, 유엔에 송부한 배경을 홍보하는 기자회견을 가질 예정이며, 그 내용이 언론보도 될 것으로 예상되므로, 차제에 우리의 의견을 드리고자 함

1. 이번 민변기자회견은 민변측이 기히 수회에 걸쳐 홍보하여 보도되었던 진부한 내용을 재차 홍보하는 것 뿐임

   - 민변 반박보고서에 관하여는 기히 보도된 바 있으며, 그때마다 당부의 반박이 함께 보도되었음

0200

※ 보도사례

- 동아일보 : 4.29자 22면
  5.11자 22. 23면
  5.13자 14면
- 한국일보 : 5.12자 2면 사설
- 경향신문 : 5.12자 23면
- 한겨레신문 : 4.29자 14면

- 민변은 1년전부터 반박보고서를 준비하는 과정에서 별도 홍보전략을 수립, 수시 언론에 홍보 → 이번도 상기 홍보전략의 일환

- 문제의 반박보고서는 기히 5월 초순경 유엔에 발송, 유엔으로부터 접수통지 수령하였으므로 상황 종료되었음 → 홍보시기 부적절, 홍보를 위한 홍보

0201

2. 유엔에서 정부보고서를 검토하기 전에 미리 국내에서 논쟁함은 바람직하지 아니함

- 정부보고서는 유엔 인권이사회에서 조만간 검토예정, 검토결과 공표

- 민변 등 국내인권단체에서 정부보고서를 비판하는 문건을 유엔에 송부하였으므로 그로써 족함 → 별도로 국내에서 이 문제에 대하여 왈가왈부하고, 그 내용을 언론이 보도함은 적절치 아니함
  (이러한 논쟁은 유엔의 검토결과를 기다려 그 이후의 시점에서 거론할 성질의 것임)

- 국내언론에서 이 문제에 관하여 사전에 민감한 반응을 보일 경우 우리나라의 이미지가 유엔에 왜곡되어 투영될 우려 있음

0202

3. 민변 기자회견 내용이 굳이 보도된다면 형평과 객관성 유지의 원칙상 상대방인 정부의 반론도 반드시 같은 비중으로 함께 보도되어야 함

- 상기 반박보고서는 일방적이고 극단적인 시각에서 국내 과격운동권의 주장을 그대로 원용하여 우리나라 인권상황을 의도적으로 왜곡평가 → 그럼에도 마치 위 보고서가 국민 전체의 의사인양 과대포장

- 원래 민변은 극소수의 과격·소장변호사들이 주도하는 사적인 단체로 공식기구인 변협에서도 인정치 아니함. 이들에 대하여 정부차원에서 대응함은 부적절 → 그러나, 언론에서 이들 주장을 보도할 경우 우리나라의 인권상황이 악의적으로 왜곡 전파될 우려가 있으므로 상기 보고서의 허구성, 편향성을 지적하여 반박하지 않을 수 없음

※ 정부의 반론은 [자료 2] 첨부

0203

[자료 2]

한국기독교교회협의회("KNCC")인권위원회·민주사회를 위한변호사모임("민변")의 반박보고서 및 민변 기자회견내용에 대한 반론

법 무 부

0204

6

본 반론은 기히 유엔에 제출된 정부의 국제인권규약(B규약) 보고서에 대하여 KNCC인권위원회·민변 공동명의로 작성된 이른바 『반박보고서』 및 민변이 1992.6.2자로 개최한 기자 회견내용에 대한 것임

1. 왜 정부반론을 제기하는가

o 주지하는 바와 같이 정부는 작년 7.31. 국제인권규약 제40조에 따라 시민적·정치적 권리에 관한 우리나라의 법령, 제도, 관행 등에 관하여 규약이 정하는 지침 및 타국보고서들을 참조하여 자세하고 성실한 보고서를 작성, 유엔에 제출한 바 있으며, 조만간 유엔측과 위 보고서를 검토할 기회를 갖고 아울러 한반도 전체의 인권신장을 위한 건설적이고 진지한 토론을 할 예정으로 있음

o 정부보고서에 대하여는 누구든지 비판할 자유가 있음
그러나 그 비판은 객관적이고 형평성을 유지하여야 하는 것임

0205

1

o 최근 KNCC 인권위원회와 민변이 정부보고서를 반박하는 내용의 반박보고서를 작성, 유엔에 제출한 것은 다원화된 민주사회에서 당연히 보장되는 권리이며 또한 의미있는 일로 평가함

o 그러나 문제의 반박보고서가 객관성과 형평성을 잃고 극단적인 시각에서 진상을 왜곡하여 작성된 것이라면 동 보고서가 건전한 비판을 제공한다는 본래의 소임에서 벗어나 부정확하고 불필요한 오해를 유발한다는 점을 지적하지 않을 수 없는 것임

o 분명히 할 것은 민변은 극소수의 과격.소장변호사들이 주도하는 사적모임으로 공식기구인 대한변협에서 인정하지 아니하고 있는 단체이며, 위 보고서는 민변에 소속된 수명의 변호사가 각자의 주관에 따라 집필한 것에 지나지 아니하므로, 이러한 보고서에 대하여 정부차원에서 반론을 제기할 가치는 별무함.

o 그러나, 객관성.합리성이 결여된 논리전개와 편향된 정보의 자의적 인용으로 우리의 인권상황을 악의적으로 왜곡 기술하고, 그 내용을 언론에 홍보하므로써 국민을 오도할 소지가 없지 아니하므로 정부로서는 그 진상을 명백히 할 필요를 느끼는 것임

2

0206

2. 소위 『반박보고서』의 허구성

자세한 내용은 앞으로 유엔에서 거론될 것이므로 몇가지만 예시함

o 보고서는 우리나라의 안보상황과 정부의 법집행에 대하여 일방적, 편향적 시각을 견지하는 일부 재야운동권의 진부한 논리를 그대로 수용

(예시 :

. 한국전쟁후 40여년이 지난 지금은 공산주의의 위협이 완전히 사라졌다

. 한국에는 전투경찰대가 상설적으로 활동하고 있으며, 그 한도 내에서 한국은 사실상 항구적인 계엄상태에 놓여 있다

. 국가보안법이 인권에 관한 실질적 의미의 헌법이며, 국가보안법에 의하여 처벌을 받은 사람과 그 가족은 정상적으로 사회생활을 꾸려나가는 것조차 불가능하다. 등)

o 객관적이며 구체적인 근거제시도 없이 대다수의 법관 등 법조인, 언론인 등을 부정과 권력의 앞잡이로, 헌법재판소, 대법원, 국회 등 헌법기관을 정치권력과 부의 시녀로 매도

(예시 :

. 과거에 독재세력에 아부했던 법관들이 1988년 이후에도 그대로 남아 오로지 독재세력을 유지, 강화하는 행동을 반복하고 있어 사법부가 독립과 공정성을 지키지 못하며, 법원은 검찰에 종속되어 있는 것으로 일반적으로 인식되고 있다

. 헌법재판소의 권한은 인권을 탄압한다고 비판받아 온 핵심적인 반민주적 법률에 손상을 가하지 않는 범위 이내로 명백하게 제한되어 있다

. 기자단은 출입처로부터 '촌지'를 받고 출입처의 필요에 따라 정보를 왜곡하여 국민의 알 권리를 침해한다, 등)

0208

4

o 법집행 과정에서 발생하는 돌발적.개별적인 사건 - 예컨대 고문, 가혹행위 등 - 을 국가권력에 의한 체계적.조직적인 인권탄압으로 일반화

(예시 :

. 한국에는 형사피의자와 피고인을 사실상 유죄로 추정하는 법률과 관행이 존재한다

. 법집행 과정에서는 고문과 그밖의 비인도적인 대우가 흔히 자행되고 구속수사, 구속재판이 관행으로 되어 있는 실정이다. 등)

o 법원판결내용중 일부만을 발췌, 왜곡 해석

(예시 :

. 대법원은 수사관이 형사소송법 제244조제2항에 위반하여 피의자 신문조서를 피의자에게 열람하게 하거나 읽어주지 않은 경우에도 그 피의자 신문조서의 증거능력이 인정된다고 판시했다. (1988.5.10, 87도 2716) 고 기술하고 있으나, 동 판결은 형사소송법 제244조제2항에 위반한 경우에도 동법 제312조 소정의

요건 - 피의자 신문조서 등은 공판준비 또는 공판기일에서 원 진술자의 진술에 의하여 그 성립의 진정함이 인정된 때에는 증거로 할 수 있다는 규정 - 을 갖추게 되면 그것을 증거로 할 수 있다고 엄격하게 판시하고 있음에도 판결내용중 이 부분을 의도적으로 누락하여 왜곡 해석하고 있음)

o 각종 자료를 조작 또는 자의적으로 인용

(예시 :

. 교도소 수감자 1인당 점유면적이 0.5-1.1 평방미터라고 주장하나, 실은 0.5-1.1평으로 의도적으로 면적단위 조작

. 전체 형사사건중 구속기소율은 7% 전후로 현저히 낮음에도 이에 관한 통계를 자의적으로 인용, 기소된 사건중의 구속기소율을 제시하여 마치 대부분 형사범이 구속 기소되는 것으로 왜곡

. 보석허가에 대한 검찰의 즉시항고가 법률상 이유없이 남용되고 있다고 주장하나, 보석허가에 대한 즉시항고율은 0.33% 전후로 극히 낮음)

0210

6

3. 결 론

o 시국 인권문제는 이제 국제사회에서도 진부한 문제이며 오히려 북한 인권이 촛점임

o 상기 단체들은 우리 사회의 극히 일부분을 구성하는 재야운동권의 허구적 주장에만 의존하여 단편적, 독단적인 논리로 보고서를 작성하였음에도, 마치 위 보고서가 우리국민 대다수의 의사인 것으로 과대 포장하여 유엔에 제출함으로써 정부의 실정법 위반자에 대한 엄정한 법집행을 인권침해인양 호도하고, 우리의 인권상황에 대한 국제사회의 인식을 오도할 수 있는 소지를 제공하였다는 점에서 그 저의가 의심스러울 뿐 아니라 그간 정부가 꾸준히 추진해 온 민주화에 역기능을 초래하는 크나큰 오류를 범하고 있는 것임

o 정부는 위 『반박보고서』에 나타난 극히 편향적인 시각에 대하여 깊은 유감을 표명하는 바이며, 이들의 인권문제에 대한 접근자세가 바로 잡혀지기를 촉구하는 바임

0211

[보도자료]

한국기독교교회협의회("KNCC")인권위원회 · 민주사회를 위한변호사모임("민변")의 반박보고서 및 민변 기자회견 내용에 대한 반론

1992. 6. 2

0212

o 본 반론은 기히 유엔에 제출된 정부의 국제인권규약(B규약) 보고서에 대하여 KNCC인권위원회·민변 공동명의로 작성된 이른바 『반박보고서』 및 민변이 1992.6.2자로 개최한 기자회견 내용에 대한 것임

o 우선 위 반박보고서는 대한변협 등 공식기구가 아닌 임의단체인 민주사회를위한변호사모임 소속 변호사 수명이 각자의 주관에 따라 집필한 것에 지나지 아니하므로, 이러한 보고서에 대하여 정부차원에서 반론을 제기할 가치는 별무함.
그러나, 객관성.합리성이 결여된 논리전개와 편향된 정보의 자의적 인용으로 우리의 인권상황을 악의적으로 왜곡 기술하고, 그 내용을 언론에 홍보하므로써 국민을 오도할 소지가 없지 아니하므로 정부로서는 그 진상을 명백히 할 필요를 느끼는 것임

o 위 반박보고서의 허구성을 몇가지 예시함

- 우리나라의 안보상황과 정부의 법집행에 대하여 일방적, 편향적 시각을 견지하는 일부 재야운동권의 진부한 논리를 그대로 수용

0213

/5

(예시 :

. 한국전쟁후 40여년이 지난 지금은 공산주의의 위협이 완전히 없어졌다

. 한국에는 전투경찰대가 상설적으로 활동하고 있으며, 그 한도 내에서 사실상 항구적인 계엄상태에 놓여 있다. 등)

- 객관적이며 구체적인 근거제시도 없이 대다수의 법관 등 법조인, 언론인 등을 부정과 권력의 앞잡이로 매도

(예시:

. 법원은 검찰에 종속되어 있다

. 기자단은 출입처로부터 '촌지'를 받고 출입처의 필요에 따라 정보를 왜곡하여 국민의 알 권리를 침해한다. 등)

- 의도적으로 각종 자료를 조작 또는 자의적으로 인용하여 인권실상에 관한 오해를 유발

(예시:

. 교도소 수감자 1인당 점유면적이 0.5-1.1 평방미터라고 주장하나 실은 0.5-1.1평으로 의도적으로 면적단위 조작

0214

16

. 전체 형사사건중 구속기소율은 7% 전후로 현저히 낮음에도 이에 관한 통계를 자의적으로 인용, 기소된 사건중의 구속기소율을 제시하여 마치 대부분 형사범이 구속 기소되는 듯 왜곡

o 결국 상기 단체들은 우리 사회의 극히 일부분을 구성하는 재야운동권의 허구적 주장에만 의존하여 단편적, 독단적인 논리로 보고서를 작성하였음에도, 마치 위 보고서가 우리 국민 대다수의 의사인 것으로 과대 포장하여 유엔에 제출함으로써 정부의 실정법 위반자에 대한 엄정한 법집행을 인권침해인양 호도하고, 우리의 인권상황에 대한 국제사회의 인식을 오도할 수 있는 소지를 제공하였다는 점에서 그 저의가 의심스러울 뿐 아니라 그간 정부가 꾸준히 추진해 온 민주화에 역기능을 초래하는 크나큰 오류를 범하고 있는 것임

o 정부는 위 『반박보고서』에 나타난 극히 편향적인 시각에 대하여 깊은 유감을 표명하는 바이며, 이들의 인권문제에 대한 접근자세가 바로 잡혀지기를 촉구하는 바임

0215

92- 6- 1 PM 4:55

관리번호	

원 본

외 무 부

2
(局長께 보고 完)

종 별 :

번 호 : GVW-1099 일 시 : 92 0601 1200

수 신 : 장관(김재섭 국기국장)

발 신 : 주 제네바 대사(친전)

제 목 : 업연

대: WGV-0772

1. 대호 인권이사회 수석대표 문제는 본부 의견대로 할 용의가 있으나, 가능한한 법무부로 하여금 맡(604)도록 하는 것이 좋겠다는 생각임.

2. 동 시기에 TPRM 도 있어 부담을 분산하는데도 도움이 될것으로 생각함. 끝

(박수길)

예고 독후 파기

국기국

PAGE 1

92.06.02 04:37
외신 2과 통제관 FM

0216

정부 인권보고서 반박

民辯-KNCC

민주사회를 위한 변호사 모임(민변)과 한국기독교교회협의회(KNCC)는 정부가 유엔에 제출한 인권보고서를 반박하는 보고서를 공개했다.

조선일보 92. 6. 3.

0217

92- 6- 3 ;AM11:31 ;

법 무 부 인 권 국

1992.

아래 문건을 수신자에게 전달하여 주시기 바랍니다.

제 목 : 정보보고

수 신 : 외무부 유엔 2과장님

(수신처 FAX NO: 723-3505)

발 신 : 법무부 인권과

표지포함 총 ___ 매

0218

RECEIVED FROM 1992.06.03 11:32

정 보 보 고

법무부 인권과
1992. 6. 3

제목 : 인권관련 동향보고 (제2보)

o 인권관련 동향 및 대응조치 보고(6.1)의 후속보고임

o 민변측(회장 홍성우, 총무 김창국)은 예정대로 6.2. 08:30, 기독교회관 6층에서 기자회견을 개최하여 정부보고서에 대한 반박보고서를 유엔에 제출한 배경을 설명하고, 유엔심의회에 자체대표단을 파견, 반박보고서를 심의위원들에게 홍보함과 아울러 아국 보고서에 대한 유엔 심의회 방청기를 발간할 계획임을 밝혔음

o 상기 기자회견 내용에 대하여는 조선일보, 기독교방송에서 매우 미약하게 보도하였을 뿐 거의 대부분의 언론사에서는 보도하지 아니하였음

o 민변 기자회견 내용에 대한 별도의 대응조치는 불요하며, 그외 특이사항 없음

0219

법 무 부

2 길 검토

427-760 경기도 과천시 중앙동 1번지 / (전화) 503-7045 / (전송) 503-7046

문서번호 인권 20314-172

시행일자 1992. 6. 3

수신 외무부장관

참조 국제연합2과장

선결			지시	
접수	일자 시간	92. 6. 4	결재		
	번호	20068			
처리과			공람		
담당자					

제목 국제인권규약(B규약) 최초보고서 심의대비관련 자료요청

1. 정부는 '91.7.31자로 "시민적 및 정치적 권리에 관한 국제규약 (B규약) 최초보고서"를 UN에 제출한 바 있습니다.

2. 이에따라 위 최초보고서에 대한 UN 인권이사회의 심의가 7월 개최예정인바, 동 심의는 대한민국의 전반적 인권상황을 국제사회에 알릴 수 있는 기회로, 이에 철저히 대비코자 하오니 별첨 질문사항에 대한 상세한 답변자료를 작성, '92.6.10까지 송부하여 주시기 바랍니다.

3. 답변자료 내용은 국제적인 시각에서 우리의 입장을 설득력있게 표현할 수 있도록 작성(전문용어는 영문 표기)하시고, 아울러 별첨 질문사항 이외에도 귀부소관 업무중 B규약상의 기본적인권과 관련되는 내용에 대한 답변자료도 작성하여 주시기 바랍니다.

* 참고사항 :작성방법은 서술식으로 A4용지 2-3장 이내 (단 관련내용이 많을 경우 예외)

첨부 : 질문사항 1부. 끝.

법 무 부 장 관

0220

외 무 부

[제1조] 대외인권정책 - 민족자결권

o 중동문제에 대한 정부입장

- 팔레스타인문제, 각종 지원내역 등

o 쿠르드족 등 이라크 난민 문제에 대한 정부입장

o 남아프리카 아파타이트정책에 대한 정부입장

o 대한민국의 민족자결주의 원칙에 관한 기본원칙

o 주요 인권관련조약 가입.미가입 현황 및 향후계획

o 고문방지협약 가입문제

- 유엔 고문피해자 구호기금 포함 ('88-'91까지)

0221

관리번호	92-425

	분류번호	보존기간

발 신 전 보

번 호 : WGV-0853 920603 1701 WH 종별 :

수 신 : 주 제네바 대사. 총영사 (친전)

발 신 : 장 관 (국기국 김재섭 배상)

제 목 : 업 연

대 : GVW-1099

1. 제번하옵고, 법무부측이 수석대표를 맡도록 여러 방면으로 설득해 보았으나 결국 법무부로서는 맡을 만한 형편이 안된다고 하며, 청와대(비서실)쪽에서도 보고서심의 및 수석대표 문제에 관심을 가지고 있어, 장관님께서는, 대사님의 의견에 대해 현지 사정도 이해되나 우리 보고서 심의가 잘 처리되는 것이 중요하다는 점에서 대사님께서 맡는 것이 좋겠다는 결정을 하셨읍니다.

2. 준비사항은 법무부에서 철저히 하고 있고, 저희들 나름대로도 충분한 연구를 하고 있읍니다. (준비문제와 관련 청와대에서 관계부처 국장급 회의도 있을 예정입니다.) 준비관계로 대사님의 특별한 지침이 있으시면, 하시 바랍니다. 끝.

(예고 : 독후파기)

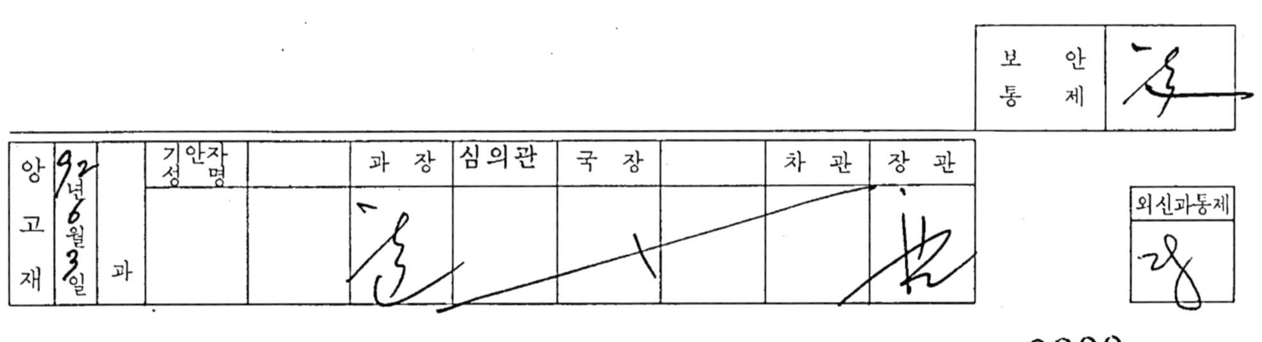

보안통제	

앙고재	92년 6월 3일	과	기안자 성명		과 장	심의관	국 장		차 관	장 관

외신과통제

0222

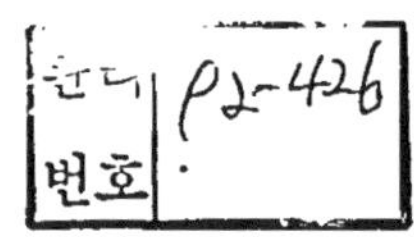

외 무 부

110-760 서울 종로구 세종로 77번지 / (02) 723-8934 / (02) 723-3505

문서번호 연이 20314-

시행일자 1992.6.3.

수신 조약국장

참조

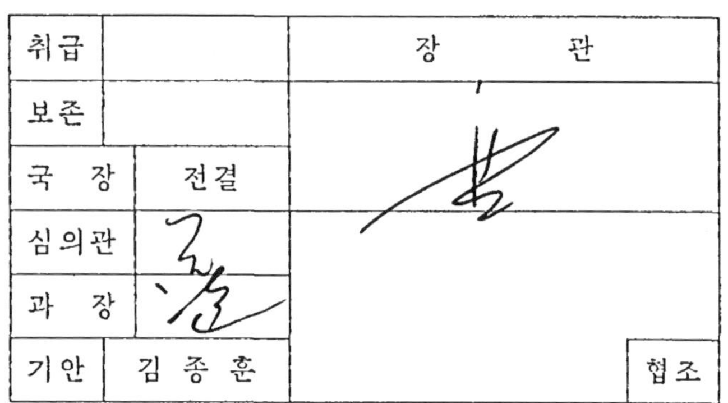

취급		장 관
보존		
국 장	전결	
심의관		
과 장		
기안	김 종 훈	협조

제목 국제인권규약(B) 유보문제

1. 90.4.10. 아국이 국제인권규약(B) 비준서 기탁시 행한 유보에 대하여 영국(91. 5.14.) 및 체코(91.6.7.)는 별첨과 같이 각각이의 또는 유보 입장을 표명한 바 있습니다.

2. 상기 양 국가의 입장표명에 대하여 우리정부가 대응 조치를 취하여야 하는지 여부를 검토하여 주시기 바라며, 또한 인권이사회 등에서 동 문제가 제기될 경우에 대비하여 우리 입장을 설명할 수 있는 발언 요지를 당국에 통보하여 주시기 바랍니다.

첨부 : 상기 자료 1부. 끝.

검토필 (1992. 6. 30.)

0223

ST/LEG/SER.E/10

MULTILATERAL TREATIES DEPOSITED WITH THE SECRETARY-GENERAL

Status as at 31 December 1991

all cases, since if the latter form were used doubt might arise concerning whether the text of the Covenant allows for the interpretation put upon it. By using the reservation form the Kingdom of the Netherlands wishes to ensure in all cases that the relevant obligations arising out of the Covenant will not apply to the Kingdom, or will apply only in the way indicated.

NEW ZEALAND

Reservations

"The Government of New Zealand reserves the right not to apply article 10(2)(b) or article 10(3) in circumstances where the shortage of suitable facilities makes the mixing of juveniles and adults unavoidable; and further reserves the right not to apply article 10(3) where the interests of other juveniles in an establishment require the removal of a particular juvenile offender or where mixing is considered to be of benefit to the persons concerned.

"The Government of New Zealand reserves the right not to apply article 14(6) to the extent that it is not satisfied by the existing system for *ex gratia* payments to persons who suffer as a result of a miscarriage of justice.

"The Government of New Zealand having legislated in the areas of the advocacy of national and racial hatred and the exciting of hostility or ill will against any group of persons, and having regard to the right of freedom of speech, reserves the right not to introduce further legislation with regard to article 20.

"The Government of New Zealand reserves the right not to apply article 22 as it relates to trade unions to the extent that existing legislative measures, enacted to ensure effective trade union representation and encourage orderly industrial relations, may not be fully compatible with that article."

NORWAY[12]

Subject to reservations to article 10, paragraph 2 (b) and paragraph 3 "with regard to the obligation to keep accused juvenile persons and juvenile offenders segregated from adults" and to article 14, paragraphs 5 and 7 and to article 20, paragraph 1.

REPUBLIC OF KOREA[13]

Reservations:

The Government of the Republic of Korea [declares] that the provisions of paragraphs 5 and 7 of article 14, article 22 [. . .] of the Covenant shall be so applied as to be in conformity with the provisions of the local laws including the Constitution of the Republic of Korea.

ROMANIA

Upon signature:

The Government of the Socialist Republic of Romania declares that the provisions of article 48, paragraph 1, of the International Covenant on Civil and Political Rights are at variance with the principle that all States have the right to become parties to multilateral treaties governing matters of general interest.

Upon ratification:

(a) The State Council of the Socialist Republic of Romania considers that the provisions of article 48(1) of the International Covenant on Civil and Political Rights are inconsistent with the principle that multilateral international treaties whose purposes concern the international community as a whole must be open to universal participation.

(b) The State Council of the Socialist Republic of Romania considers that the maintenance in a state of dependence of certain territories referred to in article 1 (3) of the International Covenant on Civil and Political Rights is inconsistent with the Charter of the United Nations and the instruments adopted by the Organization on the granting of independence to colonial countries and peoples, including the Declaration on Principles of International Law concerning Friendly Relations and Co-operation among States in accordance with the Charter of the United Nations, adopted unanimously by the United Nations General Assembly in its resolution 2625 (XXV) of 1970, which solemnly proclaims the duty of States to promote the realization of the principle of equal rights and self-determination of peoples in order to bring a speedy end to colonialism.

SWEDEN

Sweden reserves the right not to apply the provisions of article 10, paragraph 3, with regard to the obligation to segregate juvenile offenders from adults, the provisions of article 14, paragraph 7, and the provisions of article 20, paragraph 1, of the Covenant.

SYRIAN ARAB REPUBLIC

[See chapter IV.3.]

TRINIDAD AND TOBAGO[14]

(i) The Government of the Republic of Trinidad and Tobago reserves the right not to apply in full the provision of paragraph 2 of article 4 of the Covenant since section 7(3) of its Constitution enables Parliament to enact legislation even though it is inconsistent with sections (4) and (5) of the said Constitution;

(ii) Where at any time there is a lack of suitable prison facilities, the Government of the Republic of Trinidad and Tobago reserves the right not to apply article 10(2)(b) and 10(3) so far as those provisions require juveniles who are detained to be accommodated separately from adults;

(iii) The Government of the Republic of Trinidad and Tobago reserves the right not to apply paragraph 2 of article 12 in view of the statutory provisions requiring persons intending to travel abroad to furnish tax clearance certificates;

(iv) The Government of the Republic of Trinidad and Tobago reserves the right not to apply paragraph 5 of article 14 in view of the fact that section 43 of its Supreme Court of Judicature Act No. 12 of 1962 does not confer on a person convicted on indictment an unqualified right of appeal and that in particular cases, appeal to the Court of Appeal can only be done with the leave of the Court of Appeal itself or of the Privy Council;

(v) While the Government of the Republic of Trinidad and Tobago accepts the principle of compensation for wrongful imprisonment, it is not possible at this time to

Consequently, and without prejudice to its firm belief that Congolese law is in complete conformity with the provisions of article 11 of the Covenant, [the Belgian Government] fears that the reservation made by the Congo may, by reason of its very principle, constitute a precedent which might have considerable effects at the international level.

[The Belgian Government] therefore hopes that this reservation will be withdrawn and, as a precautionary measure, wishes to raise an objection to that reservation.

CZECHOSLOVAKIA

7 June 1991

"The Government of the Czech and Slovak Federal Republic considers the reservations entered by the Government of the Republic of Korea to the provisions of paragraphs 5 and 7 of article 14 and article 22 of the International Covenant on Civil and Political Rights as incompatible with the object and purpose of the Covenant. In the opinion of the Czechoslovak Government these reservations are in contradiction to the generally recognized principle of international law according to which a state cannot invoke the provisions of its own internal law as justification for its failure to perform a treaty.

"Therefore, the Czech and Slovak Federal Republic does not recognize these reservations as valid. Nevertheless the present declaration will not be deemed to be an obstacle to the entry into force of the Covenant between the Czech and Slovak Federal Republic and the Republic of Korea."

FRANCE

1.The Government of the Republic takes objection to the reservation entered by the Government of the Republic of India to article 1 of the International Covenant on Civil and Political Rights, as this reservation attaches conditions not provided for by the Charter of the United Nations to the exercise of the right of self-determination. The present declaration will not be deemed to be an obstacle to the entry into force of the Covenant between the French Republic and the Republic of India.

GERMANY[3]

[See under "Objections" in chapter IV.3.]

21 April 1982

"The Government of the Federal Republic of Germany objects to the [reservation (i) by the Government of Trinidad and Tobago]. In the opinion of the Government of the Federal Republic of Germany it follows from the text and the history of the Covenant that the said reservation is incompatible with the object and purpose of the Covenant."

28 May 1991

[The Federal Republic of Germany] interpretes the declaration to mean that the Republic of Korea does not intend to restrict its obligations under article 22 by referring to its domestic legal system.

NETHERLANDS

12 June 1980

"In the opinion of the Government of the Kingdom of the Netherlands it follows from the text and the history of the Covenant that [reservation (i) by the Government of Trinidad and Tobago] is incompatible with the object and purpose of the Covenant. The Government of the Kingdom of the Netherlands therefore considers the reservation unacceptable and formally raises an objection to it."

12 January 1981

[See under "Objections" in chapter IV.3.]

17 September 1981

"I. Reservation by Australia regarding articles 2 and 50

The reservation that article 2, paragraphs 2 and 3, and article 50 shall be given effect consistently with and subject to the provisions in article 2, paragraph 2, is acceptable to the Kingdom on the understanding that it will in no way impair Australia's basic obligation under international law, as laid down in article 2, paragraph 1, to respect and to ensure to all individuals within its territory and subject to its jurisdiction the rights recognized in the International Covenant on Civil and Political Rights.

II. Reservation by Australia regarding article 10

The Kingdom is not able to evaluate the implications of the first part of the reservation regarding article 10 on its merits, since Australia has given no further explanation on the laws and lawful arrangements, as referred to in the text of the reservation. In expectation of further clarification by Australia, the Kingdom for the present reserves the right to raise objection to the reservation at a later stage.

III. Reservation by Australia regarding 'Convicted Persons'

The Kingdom finds it difficult, for the same reasons as mentioned in its commentary on the reservation regarding article 10, to accept the declaration by Australia that it reserves the right not to seek amendment of laws now in force in Australia relating to the rights of persons who have been convicted of serious criminal offences. The Kingdom expresses the hope it will be possible to gain a more detailed insight in the laws now in force in Australia, in order to facilitate a definitive opinion on the extent of this reservation."

6 November 1984

[Same objection as the one made by Belgium]

18 March 1991

With regard to interpretative declaration made by Algeria:

[See under "Objections" in chapter IV.3]

10 June 1991

"In the opinion of the Government of the Kingdom of the Netherlands it follows from the text and the history of the International

Covenant on Civil and Political Rights that the reservations with respect to articles 14, paragraphs 5 and 7 and 22 of the Covenant made by the Government of the Republic of Korea are incompatible with the object and purpose of the Covenant. The Government of the Kingdom of the Netherlands therefore considers the reservation unacceptable and formally raises objection to it. This objection is not an obstacle to the entry into force of this Covenant between the Kingdom of the Netherlands and the Republic of Korea."

PORTUGAL

26 October 1990

[See under "Objections" in chapter IV.3]

UNITED KINGDOM OF GREAT BRITAIN AND NORTHERN IRELAND

24 May 1991

"The Government of the United Kingdom have noted the statement formulated by the Government of the Republic of Korea on accession, under the title "RESERVATIONS". They are not however able to take a position on these purported reservations in the absence of a sufficient indication of their intended effect, in accordance with the terms of the Vienna Convention on the Law of Treaties and the practice of the Parties to the Covenant. Pending receipt of such indication, the Government of the United Kingdom reserve their rights under the Covenant in their entirety."

Declarations recognizing the competence of the Human Rights Committee under article 41[15]
(Unless otherwise indicated, the declarations were made upon ratification or accession).

ALGERIA

12 September 1989

[The Government of the Democratic People's Republic of Algeria] recognizes the competence of the Human Rights Committee referred to in article 28 of the Covenant to receive and consider communications to the effect that a State Party claims that another State Party is not fulfilling its obligations under the Covenant.

ARGENTINA

The instrument contains a declaration under article 41 of the Covenant by which the Government of Argentina recognizes the competence of the Human Rights Committee established by virtue of the International Covenant on Civil and Political Rights.

AUSTRIA

10 September 1978

[The Government of the Republic of Austria] declares under article 41 of the Covenant on Civil and Political Rights that Austria recognizes the competence of the Human Rights Committee to receive and consider communications to the effect that a State Party claims that another State Party is not fulfilling its obligations under the Covenant on Civil and Political Rights.

BELGIUM

5 March 1987

The Kingdom of Belgium declares that it recognizes the competence of the Human Rights Committee under article 41 of the International Covenant on Civil and Political Rights.

18 June 1987

The Kingdom of Belgium declares, under article 41 of the International Covenant on Civil and Political Rights, that it recognizes the competence of the Human Rights Committee established under article 28 of the Covenant to receive and consider communications submitted by another State Party, provided that such State Party has, not less than twelve months prior to the submission by it of a communication relating to Belgium, made a declaration under article 41 recognizing the competence of the Committee to receive and consider communications relating to itself.

CANADA

29 October 1979

"The Government of Canada declares, under article 41 of the International Covenant on Civil and Political Rights, that it recognizes the competence of the Human Rights Committee referred to in article 28 of the said Covenant to receive and consider communications submitted by another State Party, provided that such State Party has, not less than twelve months prior to the submission by it of a communication relating to Canada, made a declaration under article 41 recognizing the competence of the Committee to receive and consider communications relating to itself."

CHILE

7 September 1990

As from the date of this instrument, the Government of Chile recognizes the competence of the Human Rights Committee established under the International Covenant on Civil and Political Rights, in accordance with article 41 thereof, with regard to all actions which may have been initiated since 11 March 1990.

CONGO

6 July 1989

Pursuant to article 41 of the International Covenant on Civil and Political Rights, the Congolese Government recognizes, with effect from today's date, the competence of the Human Rights Committee to receive and consider communications to the effect that a State Party claims that another State party is not fulfilling its obligations under the above-mentioned Covenant.

CZECHOSLOVAKIA

12 March 1991

[The Czech and Slovak Federal Republic] recognizes the competence of the Human Rights Committee established on the basis of Article 28 of the Covenant to receive and consider communications to the effect that a State Party claims that another State Party is not fulfilling its obligations under the Covenant.

DENMARK[16]

19 April 1983

"[The Government of Denmark] recognizes, in accordance with Article 41 of the International

政府-在野 인권攻防 가열

獨自보고서 유엔에 제출 在野

"극단적주장만 수록" 비난 政府

民辯 "공개토론 是非가리자" 제안

재야인권단체가 독자적인 인권보고서를 작성,유엔인권이사회에 제출한뒤 이 보고서 내용을 공개하고 나서자 대검찰청이 이를 전면 반박하는 내용의 보도자료를 언론기관에 배포하고 재야인권단체가 다시 이에 대응해 정부측에 공개토론을 제안하는등 국내인권상황을 둘러싼 정부당국과 재야단체간의 공방이 가열되고 있다。

민주사회를 위한 변호사모임과 한국기독교교회협의회(KNCC)인권위원회는 지난2일 기자회견을 갖고 지난달8일 유엔에 제출한 자체 인권보고서를 공개, 정부측이 지난해 유엔인권이사회에 제출한 보고서의 내용을 반박하며 문제점을 지적했다。

재야쪽에서 이같은 움직임을 보이자 그동안 공식대응을 하지않던 정부는 이들 단체의 기자회견직전 재야측반박보고서를 비난하는 내용의 보도자료를 작성,각 언론기관에 배포했다。

대검은 이 보도자료를 통해 민변을 「극소수 과격소장변호사가 주도하는 단체로 이들의 반박보고서를 「일방적이고 극단적인 과격운동권의 주장을 원용한 것」이라고 원색적으로 비난했다。

대검은 또 반박보고서에는 「공산주의 위협이 완전히 없어졌다」「전투경찰대가 상설·활동해 사실상 항구적인 계엄상태에 놓여있다는 등의 내용이 포함되어있다면서 이는 「국내 안보상황에 대해 편향적시각을 견지하고있는 재야운동권의 진부한 논리를 그대로 원용한 것」이라고 주장했다。

대검측의 이같은 대응과 관련 민변은 3일 법무부에 공식서한을 보내 『공개적장소에서 공개적 방법으로 토론을 벌여 시시비비를 가릴것」을 제안하고 나섰다。

민변은 또 대검측의 보도자료에 대한 논평을 발표 『정부당국이 반박보고서에 「공산주의 위협이 완전히 사라졌다」는 내용이 들어있다고 주장했으나 이는 전혀 사실무근」이라면서 『이 부분은 실수로 포함된 것이기를 바란다』고 꼬집었다。

민변은 이와함께 『대검이 반박보고서의 내용중 「계엄상태에 놓여있다고 볼 수 있다」는 문구를 「계엄상태에 놓여있다」는 단정적 표현으로 바꿔 언론기관에 배포한 것은 반박보고서의 내용과 의도를 크게 왜곡한 것」이라고 주장, 『언론과 국민을 사이에 두고 더이상 무익한 논쟁을 벌이지말고 공개토론의 장에 나오라』고 촉구했다。

〈崔壽默〉

동아일보 19면 92.6.4.

0228

관리 번호	92-471

	분류번호	보존기간

발 신 전 보

번 호 : WGV-0870 920608 1536 FS 종별 :

수 신 : 주 제네바 대사. 총영사

발 신 : 장 관 (연이)

제 목 : 아국 인권규약(B) 최초보고서 심의

92.7.13-7.15간 귀지에서 개최되는 아국 인권규약(B) 최초보고서 심의와 관련, 귀직을 수석대표로, 본부, 귀관 및 법무부 담당관을 대표로 하는 대표단 임명을 추진중이니 참고바라며, 동 대표단에 포함할 귀관 직원을 보고바람. 끝.

(국제기구국장 김재섭)

검토필 (1992. 6 .30.)

보안 통제	

앙 고 재	92년 6월 8일	유엔2과	기안자 성명		과 장	심의관	국 장		차 관	장 관
							전결			

외신과통제

0229

관리번호	92-468

외 무 부

110-760 서울 종로구 세종로 77번지 / (02) 723-8934 / (02) 723-3505

문서번호 연이 20314- 1499

시행일자 1992.6.8.

수신 법무부장관

참조

취급		장 관
보존		
국 장	전결	
심의관		
과 장		
기안	김종훈	협조

제목 아국 인권규약(B) 최초보고서 심의

1. 연이 20314-1010(92.4.22), 1288(5.16) 및 인권 20314-125(92.5.8)와 관련입니다.

2. 아국 인권규약(B) 최초보고서 심의에 참가할 아국 대표단을 구성하고자 하오니 동 대표단에 포함할 귀부 직원을 추천하여 주시기 바랍니다. 끝.

검토필 (1992.6.30.)	

0230

인권보고서 심의대비 준비사항

1992. 6. 8.
외 무 부

1. 대표단 구성

o 6.15까지 대표단 구성

- 외무부(본부 및 주제네바 대표부), 법무부 관계관으로 구성

2. 준비자료

가. 수석대표 모두발언

o 보고서 개관 설명

- 국내 민주화 및 인권 개선상황 설명 포함

o 91.7월 보고서 제출 이후 규약관련 국내적 변경사항

- 법률 등의 제정 및 개정, 인권관련 협약 가입

- 헌법재판소 결정 및 법원 판례 변경

o 인권규약 이행과 관련한 고려사항(규약 적용의 제약 상황)

- 한반도 분단상황

- 최근 남북관계와 국가보안법 문제

o 향후 인권관련 조치계획

- 인권관련 협약 가입 등

- 인권보장기구 확충

- 인권관련 법규 개정

0231

나. 주요 답변자료

1) 작성시 고려사항

o 아국 보고서는 규약 이행을 위한 국내법규 및 제도에 대한 설명은 비교적 충실하므로, 민간단체들이 실제 적용상 문제점으로 지적한 사항에 대한 정부입장 구체설명 필요

- 국가보안법 등이 자의적으로 적용되고 있다는 민간단체 등의 주장

o 인권규약의 기본정신을 존중하는 바탕 위에서 아국 특수상황 설명

- 기본권 보장의 본질을 외면한 특수성 강조는 설득력이 적음

2) 주요 작성자료

가) 규약의 국내적 이행

o 규약과 국내법의 관계(후법우선원칙의 적용문제 등)

o 법원에서 규약의 규정을 원용할 수 있는지 및 하고 있는지 여부

- 국제협약이 재판과정에서 직접 원용된 사례 조사

나) 헌법기관의 견제와 균형에 관한 구체적 설명

o 헌법재판소, 법원의 역할

- 인권문제에 있어 행정부에 대한 견제기능 포함

다) 국가보안법 관련사항

o 국가보안법 존속의 필요성

o 사상, 표현의 자유와의 관계

o 국가보안법 적용의 자의성 주장에 대한 대응논리 및 사례

o 미전향 장기수 실태 및 NGO 거론 주요 장기수의 범법사실 설명

o 전향서 관계 해명

라) 헌법의 인권보장상 실효성

0232

마) 주요 인권관련 법규의 시행문제

o 집시법, 노동관계 법률(제3자 개입금지, 복수노조 금지, 공무원의 노동권 제한), 보안관찰법 등의 시행과 관련, 국내외 NGO등이 제기한 일부 규정상 문제 및 자의적 적용의 문제에 대한 구체적 설명

바) 재소자 인권보장

o 국내법규와 유엔채택 "피구금자 처우 최저기준규칙"과의 대비 검토자료

사) 규약 유보사항

o 유보조항에 관한 법적 설명

3. 기타 사항

o 아국 보고서 심의 관련 국내 홍보대책

- 심의전후 국내 홍보대책 사전수립
- 민변 등 심의 참관자의 심의내용 왜곡 홍보에 대한 대응방안 강구

4. 참고사항

o 인권이사회 위원 : 18인(위원장 : Pocar: 이태리)

o 심의일정

- 7.13.오후 제안설명 및 위원 질의
  7.14. 답변준비
  7.15.오후 답변 및 보충질의

o 최종평가

- 이사회 종료시 심의대상국 보고서 심의 최종평가서 채택

0233

민변 반대 보고서에서 제기된 문제에 대한 대응

가. 총 평

o 규약이행의 최대 장애요인은 남북 분단

- 북한을 반국가 단체로 규정하는 것은 유엔헌장 및 남북 합의서에 위배

준비사항

* 남북대화 현황 및 정부 입장
* 북한의 법적 지위
  - 국가보안법상 반국가 단체로 규정

o 헌법의 규범력 미약도 협약이행의 장애요인

- 정부, 법원 및 국민들은 헌법을 최고법으로 인정하기가 어려움.

준비사항

* 헌법의 국내법적 위치

o 국회 이외의 입법기관에서 현행 주요법률 제정

- 61년, 71년, 80년 3차례

준비사항

* 제6공화국 수립 이후 "민주악법" 개폐 실적 및 국회이외 입법기관에서 제정된 법률중 현재 발효중인 법률

o 국회는 행정부에 예속

0234

1

o 인권관련 대부분 법률은 규정의 모호성 및 추상성으로 죄형법정 주의 위배

- 국가보안법 및 노동관계법의 제3자 간섭 금지조항
- 형사관련 법률은 이중적으로 적용되고 있음.

o 수사기관 및 비밀경찰이 국가안보를 이유로 인권침해

- 안기부 및 기무사의 활동

o 규약과 국내법과의 관계

- 헌법 6조 1항의 해석상의 문제로 규약에 대하여 후법우선의 원칙이 적용될 수 있는 문제점 내포
- 법원은 규약을 직접 적용하려는 의도를 보이지 않음. (국가보안법 및 제3자 개입금지 관련)

준비사항

* 규약의 국내법적 위상 및 후법우선의 원칙의 적용문제
* 법원이 재판과정에서 국제협약을 적용한 사례

나. 인권침해시 구제

1) 구제제도의 문제점

o 수사 및 기소가 정치적 영향에 따라 불공정하게 집행됨.

- 수사기관 및 기소권에 관한 민주적 통제체제 필요

o 법원 또는 헌법재판소에 대한 청원의 비효율성

2) 긴급사태하의 기본권 제한

o 위수령 선포 사례(71.10월)

- 동 법의 위헌성("재해 또는 비상사태"의 모호성)

o 위수령 및 전투경찰 제도에 의해 계엄선포 없이 군대동원 가능

- 전투경찰이 항구적 조직이므로 남한은 항구적 계엄상태

준비사항

* 건국이후 계엄 또는 비상사태 선포 사례

* 전투경찰의 역할

3) 사법부 독립

o 사법부의 독립성에 대한 불신 만연

- 사법부가 검찰권에 종속

- 공안사건의 경우 대부분 검찰기소에 부합하는 판결이 있으며, 100%의 구속영장 발부, 구속적부심 및 보석청구 불허가 일반적

o 사법부 독립성 결여의 주요 원인은 과거 독재정권에 협력했던 법관이 존재하고 있으며, 남한의 사법제도 및 법관은 일제시대의 유산이며, 검사의 영향력 확대 때문임.

- 법관 선발의 문제점

준비사항

* 사법부 독립 및 헌법재판소 활동의 구체적 사례

0236

4) 피의자 권리보장

o 무죄추정 원칙

- 실제로는 피의자를 유죄로 추정하는 법률 및 관행이 상존

- 대부분 피의자는 구속상태에서 수사.재판을 받음.

o 공정한 재판의 권리

- 변호인 접견 제한, 피의자가 기소 및 증거의 내용파악 곤란, 궐석재판제도, 증인심문제도, 강제자백 등의 문제점

- 일반적으로 국가보안법 위반 사범들은 구속영장이 발부되지 않은 상태에서 불법 연행되어 외부와 단절상태하에서 최소한 48시간 이상 조사를 받고 자백을 강요당함.
(특히 안기부, 기무사 및 경찰 보안과 관할 사건)

- 안기부 수사의 경우 피의자는 안기부 지하실에 20일 이상 기간 억압적 분위기하에 구금

o 변호인의 피의자 접견시 감시 및 녹취 행위는 위헌(헌법재판소 결정)

o 남한에서는 변호인이 피의자 심문에 참여하지 못함.

준비사항

* 아국 보고서가 법률적.제도적 측면에서 인권보장 문제를 상세 설명한 반면 반대보고서는 적용상의 문제를 집중 언급한 바, 아국 현황 설명자료 필요

0237

다. 국가보안법

1) 국가보안법 개정의 문제점

o 북한 외 사회주의 국가와 접촉시 처벌조항을 삭제한 바, 종전에도 실제 적용되지 아니한 규정임.

o "국가의 안전.존립이나 자유민주적 기본질서를 위태롭게 한다는 정"의 제한을 추가하였으나 너무나 추상적 개념으로서 실제 적용상 아무런 변화 초래 못함.

o 법 시행전의 행위에 대한 벌칙은 종전 규정을 적용하여 법률의 변화에 따른 이익 보장을 규정한 규약 제15조에 위배

2) 반국가단체의 성격

o 반국가단체 관련조항(제3조) 및 이적단체 조항(7조 3항)은 규약 18조(사항의 자유), 19조(표현의 자유) 및 22조(결사의 자유)에 위배

3) 국가보안법 제4조(목적수행 간첩행위 등)

o 50여개 행위에 대하여 사형이 가능한 것은 규약 제6조 2항에 부합되는지 의문

o 국가기밀.군사기밀의 범위 및 기타 용어에 대한 대법원의 포괄적 해석은 표현의 자유 및 알권리를 보장한 규약 제19조에 위배
  - 임수경의 평양체류시 활동의 위법성 문제

0238

4) 국가보안법 제6조(잠입.탈출)

o "잠입.탈출", "반국가단체로부터 지령" 개념을 확대 해석 적용

- 임수경, 문익환은 공개적인 방문 및 귀환

- 북한 초청장은 대한적십자사로부터 국토통일원 허가하에 전대협이 접수

o 외국여행 및 귀환의 자유보장을 규정한 규약 제12조 2항, 4항에 위배

5) 국가보안법 제7조(찬양.고무 등)

o 금서(banned books) 지정숫자 매년 증가

- 당국의 금서목록 미공개로 일반인들은 금서여부 사전판단이 불가능한 현실

o 서사연 사건(1991.6.)의 문제점

- 이적표현 범죄사실중 대부분 박사.석사학위 논문 테제

- 문제의 테제들은 북한 주체사항에는 강력 반대 입장

o 홍근수 목사 및 박순경 교수사건

6) 국가보안법 제8조(회합.통신 등)

o 정기융 사건

- 재판부는 정목사가 북한으로부터 받았다는 지령의 내용, 일시, 장소, 방법 등 지령관련 구체적 범죄사실을 밝히지 못하였으나 유죄를 인정

- 영사(해외주재 안기부 요원으로 추정) 보고서를 피고측 변호인에 대한 반대심문 기회를 박탈하고 증거로 채택, 유죄 판결

- 모든 정보 및 사상추구권을 규정한 규약 제19조 2항 위배

7) 국가보안법 적용의 이중기준

o 문선명 사건과 문익환 사건

- 남북교류 협력에 관한 법률상 소정의 사건허가 또는 사후통보 없이 북한을 방문한 문선명에 대해 아무런 법적조치를 취하지 아니함.

o 한국정부의 대외적 자세와 국내적 입장의 차이

- 대외적으로는 북한을 독립국가(independent state) 및 통일을 향한 동반자(a partner in the course toward unification)로 인정하는 반면, 국내적으로는 국민들에게 북한을 "불법적 반국가 단체"로만 인식할 것을 요구하여 유엔헌장 및 남북합의서에 위배

o 한국정부 정책과 국가보안법의 상충

- 수년전 북한 및 공산권 국가 서적 등 자료공개정책을 표방 하였음에도 불구, 공개된 자료의 개인적 구입 및 KBS, MBC 방영 필림의 대학상영은 국가보안법의 위반으로 처벌

준비사항

* 국가보안법 존속의 필요성
* 국가보안법 적용 실태
* 반대보고서 내용에 대한 대응논리 및 자료

라. 사상 및 양심의 자유

1) 현 황

o 헌법상 사상의 자유 보장 규정이 없음.

- 자본주의 반대, 공산주의 또는 사회주의 지지의 자유는 없음.

o 국가보안법의 문제

o 미전향 장기수에 대한 전향서 징구의 문제

2) 보안관찰법의 문제

ㅇ 동법 시행령상의 준법서서 제출 의무

ㅇ 동법은 양심의 자유, 거주이전의 자유, 프라이버시 권리 등 규약 12, 17, 18조 위반

3) 종교교육의 문제점

ㅇ 초.중.고교의 경우 학교선택 및 학생선발의 자유가 없어 부모의 종교의 자유 위배

준비사항

* 보안관찰법의 주요 적용사례
* 전향서 징구에 대한 설명

마. 표현의 자유

1) 제3자 개입 금지

ㅇ 1980년 입법회의에서 채택된 노동조합법, 노동쟁의 조정법에 규정

ㅇ 노동운동가를 처벌함으로써 노동자를 고립시킴.

- 경영자측 인사 처벌사례 전무

ㅇ 홍영표 사건(1986년 대우자동차 해고자)

- 1989년 복직요구를 위해 복직자 대표로 회사협상에 참여한 바, 제3자 개입금지 위반으로 유죄판결

2) 공연, 영화, 음반 관련 검열제도

ㅇ 공연법, 영화법 등의 광범위한 사전검열로 예술과 표현의 자유가 극도로 제한

0241

3) 정기간행물 등록제도

o 전교조, 전민련, 언노련 간행물 발간 관련 유죄판결
  - 동 단체들은 등록신청 하였으나 불허됨.

4) 방송에서의 표현의 자유

o KBS, MBC 등의 인사 및 방송내용에서의 외부 간섭
o 중앙대생 이래창 변사사건 보도 관련 한겨레신문 이강순 기자 기소

5) 검인정 교과서 제도

6) 선거법상 표현의 자유 제한

o 집권당과 야당의 선거운동에 대한 차별적 법적용
o 국회의원 입후보자의 경제정책에 관한 경실련 조사 보고 공개금지 조치
  - 표현 및 정보의 자유 위반

준비사항

* 표현의 자유의 제한에 관한 구체적 [illegible]
  - 국가안전보장
  - 질서유지
  - 공공복리
* 제3자 개입금지 [illegible]정의 존치목적

0242

9

바. 집회의 자유

1) 실질적인 사전집회 허가제도

- o 집시법에 의거한 집회신고제도에도 불구, 집회 허가여부가 사실상 경찰의 자의적 판단에 따라 이뤄져 허가제로 운영
  - 90년도 1,285건 신고에 266건 불허 통보
- o 집시법상 심사기준이 광범위하여 사실상 모든 집회가 해당
- o 신청 불허에 대한 불복절차의 비현실성으로 사실상 허가제로 운영
- o 집회금지 이유의 문제점
  - 집회 개최자의 폭력시위 전력, 폭력시위화 위험성을 근거로 금지
  - 폭력시위 발생은 정부의 억압 및 집회 원천봉쇄가 직접 원인
- o 개선책 제시
  - 집시법중 과도한 규제내용 개정
  - 신고제도는 경찰 결정에 대한 불복절차가 실효성을 갖도록 개정
  - 원천봉쇄 금지
  - 사전에 불법집회로 규정하는 행위 금지
  - 해산방법 개선

준비사항

* 집회의 실태
  - 최근 시위관련 부상자 통계

0243

사. 참정권

o 노동조합의 정치참여 제한은 평등원칙 위배

- 기업주, 사기업 등의 정치활동을 인정, 정치자금 제공 가능 (정치자금법)

o 부재자투표의 부당성

- 군 부재자투표에 중앙선관위 직원 및 정당입회인 참관 불허

o 투표가치의 불평등성

- 유권자구의 불균형 : 구로갑 23만여명, 장흥 5만여명

아. 고문금지와 신체의 자유

1) 국가보안법 위반 관련자 문제

o 김근태 사건(전기고문), 권인숙 사건(성고문), 박종철 사건(물고문)등 사례열거

o 안기부의 불법행위

- 용의자 지하실 감금, 외부와의 연락차단, 공포분위기하의 수사
- 대통령 직속기관으로, 국회.감사원의 감사 및 검사의 구속장소 감찰에서 면제되며, 인권침해의 대표적 기관으로 비난받음.

o 법원은 안기부 작성 수사자료만으로 구속영장 발부

- 구속영장 발부전 피의자에 대한 신문 불가능

o 정부는 고문사례 발생을 대체로 부인하며, 검찰의 수사사례 희박

2) 고문피해 주장에 대한 대응

o 법원

- 고문학대에 의한 강요된 자백을 유죄증거로 인정

- 고문당했다는 입증책임의 전가, 자백과 장기간 구금 등과 인과 관계를 불인정하여 고문 등 근절의지 결여

o 수사기관

- "임의동행"이란 명목하에 인권침해 자행

- 국가보안법 위반사건을 피의자 자백에 의존하는 수사관행 상존

준비사항

* 고문사건과 관련한 정부의 주요 조치

* 고문과 관련한 법원의 입장에 대한 사례

자. 재소자의 처우

1) 재소자 실태의 문제점

o 피구금자 처우 최저기준 규칙에 미달

- 3평-5평의 방에 15-20명 수용

- 목욕은 주당 1회, 5분간 소량의 물만 제공

- 대부분 교도소 등 시설에 영양사, 요리사 부족

o 의료인원 부족으로 재소자 사망사례 발생

- 1990.3.17. 청주교도소 재소자 심재민 사망

- 진료지연, 중병호소 진찰요구 묵살

2) 재소자 징벌과 인권침해

o 행형법 규정을 무시한 교도관들의 고문, 폭력사태 심각

- 재갈, 수갑 등 각종 징벌장구 사용관련 규칙 미비

- 재소자들에 대한 보복적 수단으로 징벌 남용

o 재소자의 교통권 제한

o 각종 고문자행

- 마산교도소 배영태 사건 : 머리핀 고문 (hair pin torture)

- 목포교도소 한순민 사건 : 통닭 고문 (roast chicken torture)

준비사항

* 반대 보고서에서 제기된 주요사례의 진위와 유엔채택 "피구금자 처우 최저기준 규칙"과의 저촉여부 검토

차. 기 타

1) 국가기관의 사생활 침해

o 보안사의 민간인 사찰

o 우편물 검열

o 전화 도청

2) 여성 차별

o 민법개정에도 불구, 호주제도의 문제점 상존

o 여성취업시 차별

0246

3) 결사의 자유

o 국가보안법 반국가단체 결성 금지에 따라 반정부 또는 노동관계 단체 조직 제한

o 복수노조 금지의 문제

0247

관리 번호	92-483

원 본

외 무 부

종 별 :

번 호 : GVW-1145 일 시 : 92 0609 1900

수 신 : 장관(연이)

발 신 : 주 제네바 대사

제 목 : 인권보고서 심의

대: WGV-0870

대호, 대표단에 포함할 당관 직원으로 아래 2 명 건의함

0 참사관 문봉주

0 2 등서관 조현등. 끝

(대사 박수길-국장)

예고:92.12.31. 까지

검토필 (1992. 6 . 30.)	

국기국

PAGE 1

92.06.10 06:06

외신 2과 통제관 FM

0248

관리번호 92-519

외 무 부

110-760 서울 종로구 세종로 77번지 / (02) 723-8934 / (02) 723-3505

문서번호 연이 20314-1554
시행일자 1992.6.13.

수신 주제네바 대사
참조

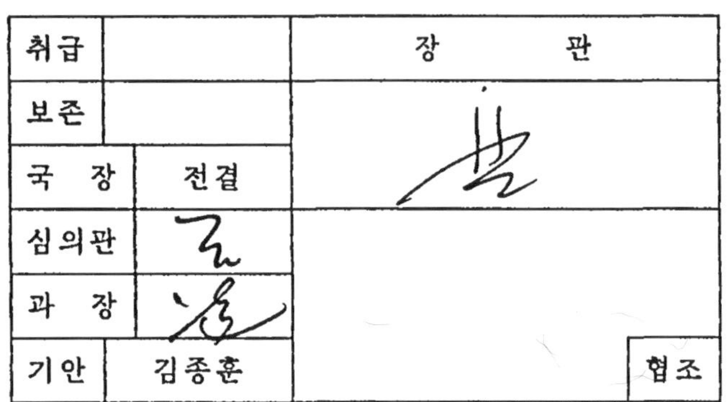

취급		장 관
보존		
국 장	전결	
심의관		
과 장		
기안	김종훈	협조

제목 인권보고서 심의대비 자료송부

연 : 연이 20314-117, 1411

1. 인권보고서 심의와 관련, 아래 자료를 별첨 송부합니다.

- 아 래 -

가. KNCC, 민변 "반박 보고서"(1부)

나. "반박 보고서"에서 제기된 쟁점별 진상 및 대응논리(안)(법무부 작성)(3부)

다. 쟁점별 대응자료(요약)(법무부 작성)(1부)

라. 인권보고서 심의대비 준비사항(외무부 작성)(1부)

2. 상기 자료를 검토하시고 심의준비에 관한 귀관 의견이 있을 경우 보고하여 주시기 바랍니다.

첨부 : 상기 자료. 끝.

검토필 (1992. 6. 30.)

0249

법무부 인권과

199 . . .

아래 문건을 수신자에게 전달하여 주시기 바랍니다.

제 목 :

수 신 : 국제연합2과 김 사무관님

(수신처 FAX NO: 723-3505)

발 신 : 법무부 인권과

표지포함 총 ___ 매

0250

Chairman
Human Rights Comittee
Center for Human Rights
Palais des Nations CH-1211
Genove 10

세계평화와 인류의 기본인권을 위해 노력하시는 귀하에게 진심으로 경의를 표합니다.

본인은 1953년 10월24일 창설된 국제인권옹호한국연맹 회장으로 한국정부가 작년 7월 귀위원회에 제출한 국제인권규약의 정치적.시민적 권리(B규약) 보고서에 대하여 한국기독교협의회(KNCC)와 민주사회를 위한 변호사모임(   )이 반박보고서를 작성, 제출한데 대해 깊은 관심을 표명하는 바입니다.

본인은 정부보고서나 KNCC.민변이 반박한 내용, 그리고 정부가 이에대해 세부적으로 해명.반박한 내용이 국내언론에 상세히 보도, 공개되어 그 내용을 알 수가 있었습니다.

본인은 KNCC.민변이 정부보고서에 대한 반박내용을 보면서 대한변협에서 발행한 90년도 인권보고서가"몇사람의 변호사들에 의해 논문형식이 됨에 따라 각 집필자의 주관이 개입됨은 불가피한 일이며, 따라서 인권상황을 보는 기본시각과 평가에 있어서 변호사 사이에서도 이론이 있었음"을 부기한 것을 상기하게 됩니다.

한국의 인권상황이 국제인권규약에 규정한 모든 부문에서 만족스럽다고는 할 수 없겠으나 6공화국 출범이래 많은 개선이 있었음은 인정할 수 있는 것이며 이번의 KNCC나 민변이 반박한 내용이 몇사람의 각자 주관에 따라 편향적 시각에서 우리의 인권실상을 왜곡함으로써 유엔등 국제사회에서 동보고서로 인하여 오해를 하게 되지나 않을까 우려합니다.

한국은 분단국가로서 부단한 침략위협에 대처해야 하는 등의 특수상황도 고려사항에서 제외할 수는 없을 것이므로 귀위원회에서 객관적인 판단에 정보를 제공하고자 참고도서를 보내는 바입니다.

감사합니다.

0251

92- 6-16 PM 1:53

International Human Rights League of Korea

Daihan-Ilbo Bldg, 7F # 340-2, 2Ka, Taepyung-Ro Chung-Ku,
Seoul, 100 KOREA. Tel : 776-4783-5, 776-8518 · 8625.

List of publications sent :

1. FACTS AND FICTION : HUMAN RIGHTS IN KOREA
2. THE HUMAN RIGHTS SITUATION IN NORTH KOREA
3. NORTH KOREA'S CRIMINAL LAW
4. RECENT DEVELOPEMENTS IN NORTH KOREA
5. THE OTHERS

0252

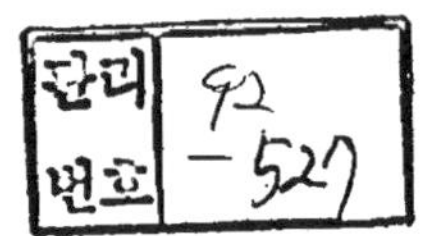

외 무 부

110-760 서울 종로구 세종로 77번지 / 전화 (02) 723-8934 / 전송 (02) 723-3505

문서번호 연이 20314- 1589

시행일자 1992.6.16.

취급		장 관
보존		
국 장	전결	
심의관		
과 장		
기안	김종훈	협조

수신 법무부장관

참조 인권과장

제목 국제인권규약(B) 최초보고서 심의 대비 자료

1. 인권 20314-172와 관련입니다.

2. 표제 보고서 심의에 대비한 답변자료중 당부 소관사항으로 90년 이후 인권관련 협약 가입실적 및 향후 가입계획을 아래와 같이 통보합니다.

- 아 래 -

가. 가입실적

o 아동권리에 관한 협약(Convention on the Rights of the Child)

- 91.11.20. 비준서 기탁
- 91.12.20. 아국에 대하여 발효

나. 향후 가입계획

o 난민지위에 관한 협약(Convention Relating to the Status of Refugees)와 난민지위에 관한 의정서(Protocol Relating to the Status of Refugees)

/ 계속 /

0253

- 92.6.5. 가입에 관한 대통령 재가
- 국회에 가입동의안 제출 준비중

O 고문방지협약(Convention against Torture and Other Cruel, Inhuman or Degrading Treatment or Punishment)
- 관계부처와 동 협약 가입문제 적극 검토중

3. 답변자료 작성과 관련, 당부 의견을 아래 통보하오니 참고하시기 바랍니다.

- 아 래 -

가. 작성시 고려사항

O 아국 보고서는 규약 이행을 위한 국내법규 및 제도에 대한 설명은 비교적 충실하므로, 국내의 민간단체들이 실제 운용상의 문제점으로 지적한 사항에 대한 정부입장 구체설명 필요
- 국가보안법 등이 자의적으로 적용되고 있다는 주장 등

O 인권규약의 기본정신을 옹호한다는 입장에서 아국 특수상황 설명 노력 필요
- 기본권 보장의 본질을 외면한 특수성 강조는 설득력이 적음.

나. 수석대표 기조발언에 포함되어야 할 사항

O 보고서 개관

O 91.7월 보고서 제출 이후 규약관련 국내적 변경사항

O 인권규약 적용의 제약상황
- 한반도 분단상황
- 최근 남북관계와 국가보안법 문제

O 향후 인권관련 조치 계획

다. ~~주요~~ 답변자료 포함사항

1) 규약의 국내법적 지위(모든 보고서 심의시 공통 질문사항)

O 규약 규정이 법원에서 직접 원용될 수 있는지 여부

O 법원 판결이 직접적으로 규약 규정에 근거한 사례 여부

/ 2 ...

0254

o 국내법과 규약이 상충될 경우 법원이 규약을 국내법에 우선하여 적용할 수 있는지 여부, 이 경우 동 국내법은 폐기되는지 여부

o 후법우선의 원칙이 규약에도 적용되는지 여부

2) 헌법기관의 견제와 균형에 관한 구체적 설명

o 헌법재판소, 법원의 역할

- 인권문제에 있어 행정부에 대한 견제기능 포함

3) 국가보안법 관련사항

o 국가보안법 존속의 필요성

o 사상, 표현의 자유와의 관계

o 북한의 국내법적 ~~위치~~ 지위

o 국가보안법 적용의 자의성 주장에 대한 대응논리 및 사례

o 미전향 장기수 실태 및 NGO 거론 주요 장기수의 범법사실 설명

o 전향서 관계 ~~해명~~

~~4) 헌법의 인권보장상 실효성~~

4) 주요 인권관련 법규의 시행문제

o 집시법, 노동관계 법률(제3자 개입금지, 복수노조 금지, 공무원의 노동권 제한), 보안관찰법 등의 시행과 관련, 국내외 NGO 등이 제기한 일부 규정상 문제 및 자의적 적용의 문제에 대한 구체적 설명

5) 재소자 인권보장

o 국내법규와 유엔채택 "피구금자 처우 최저기준규칙"과의 대비 검토자료

6) 규약 유보사항

o 유보조항에 관한 법적 설명

o 노동3권에 관한 A규약 제8조는 유보하지 않은 반면 B규약 제22조를 유보한 논거

- ILO 가입과 동 유보와의 상충성 여부. 끝.

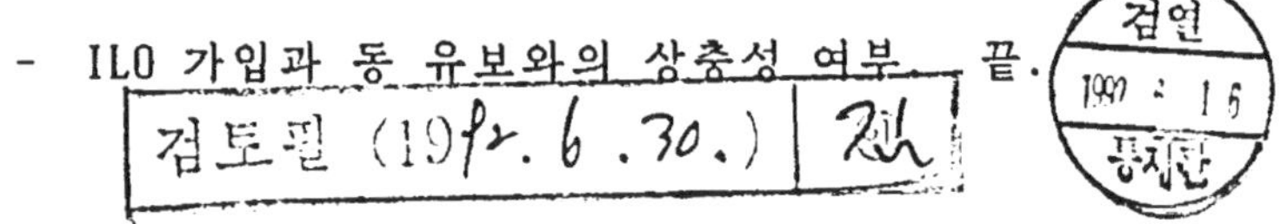

0255

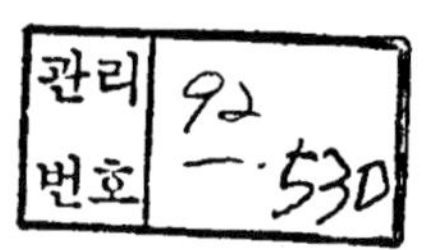

법 무 부

427-760 경기도 과천시 중앙동 1번지 / 전화 (02)503-7045 / 전송 (02)503-7046

문서번호 인권 20314-149
시행일자 1992. 6.

수신 외무부장관
참조

선결			지시	
접수	일자 시간	92.6.16	결재	
	번호	2322		
처리과			공람	
담당자				

제목 아국 인권규약(B규약) 최초보고서 심의대비

1. 연이 20314-1499 ('92.6.8)와 관련입니다.

2. 우리부에서는 아국의 인권규약(B규약) 최초보고서 심의에 참가할 대상자로 인권과장 부장검사 류국현(Senior Public Prosecutor, Yoo Kook-Hyun), 검사 정기용(Public Prosecutor, Chung Ki-Yong), 검사 최상관(Public Prosecutor, Choi Sang-Kwan)을 추천합니다. 끝.

청보필 (1992.6.30.)

법 무 부 장 관

0256

정 리 보 존 문 서 목 록					
기록물종류	일반공문서철	등록번호	2020110104	등록일자	2020-11-20
분류번호	734.23	국가코드		보존기간	영구
명 칭	시민적.정치적 권리에 관한 국제규약(B규약) 한국 최초 인권보고서 제출 및 심의, 1991-92. 전5권				
생 산 과	국제연합2과	생산년도	1991~1992	담당그룹	
권 차 명	V.4 1992.6.18-7.9				
내용목차	* 第45차 인권이사회. Geneva,1992.7.13-31 - 수석대표 : 박수길 주제네바대사 - 한국인권보고서 심의(심의기간:7.13-15)				

0001

UNITED
NATIONS

International covenant on civil and political rights

Distr.
GENERAL

CCPR/C/2/Rev.3
12 May 1992

Original: ENGLISH

HUMAN RIGHTS COMMITTEE

RESERVATIONS, DECLARATIONS, NOTIFICATIONS AND OBJECTIONS RELATING TO THE INTERNATIONAL COVENANT ON CIVIL AND POLITICAL RIGHTS AND THE OPTIONAL PROTOCOLS THERETO

Note by the Secretary-General

CONTENTS

Page

GE.92-15683/4499B

CONTENTS (continued)

CONTENTS (continued)

CONTENTS (continued) Page

Introduction

1. This document contains the texts of the reservations, declarations, notifications and objections made by States with respect to the International Covenant on Civil and Political Rights and the Optional Protocols thereto, as at 31 March 1992 and is based upon Multilateral Treaties deposited with the Secretary-General: Status as at 31 December 1991. 1/ As indicated in the introduction to that publication, the texts of declarations, reservations and objections are normally reproduced in full. Unless shown in quotation marks, the text is a translation by the Secretariat.

2. Part I of the present document contains the texts of reservations, declarations, notifications and objections made by States parties concerning the Covenant. Part II contains the texts concerning the Optional Protocols.

3. The organization of this document reflects a number of national and international developments that have occurred since the previous revision was issued in 1989. The developments in question are the following:

(a) Through the accession of the German Democratic Republic to the Federal Republic of Germany with effect from 3 October 1990, the two German States united to form one sovereign State. As from the date of unification, the Federal Republic of Germany acts in the United Nations under the designation of "Germany". The former German Democratic Republic had ratified the Covenant on 8 November 1973 and reservations it made at the time have been listed separately under the designation "Germany".

(b) On 22 May 1990 the People's Democratic Republic of Yemen and the Yeman Arab Republic merged to form a single sovereign State called the Republic of Yemen, with Sana'a as its capital. The People's Democratic Republic of Yemen had acceded to the Covenant on 9 May 1987 and reservations it made at the time have been reproduced under the designation "Yemen". The Yemen Arab Republic was not a State party to the Covenant.

(c) By a note transmitted by the Permanent Representative of the Russian Federation to the United Nations Office at Geneva on 26 December 1991, the Ministry for Foreign Affairs of the Russian Federation informed the Secretary-General that:

> "the membership of the Union of Soviet Socialist Republics in the United Nations and all of its bodies as well as the participation in all the conventions, agreements and other international legal instruments signed in the framework of the United Nations or under its auspices, is continued by the Russian Federation .... The Russian Federation remains responsible in full for all rights and obligations of the USSR in the United Nations, including the financial obligations".

Accordingly, all material emanating from the former Union of Soviet Socialist Republics has been listed in this publication under the designation "Russian Federation".

0006

I. INTERNATIONAL COVENANT ON CIVIL AND POLITICAL RIGHTS

A. General Information

Adopted by the General Assembly of the United Nations on 16 December 1966

Entry into force: 23 March 1976, in accordance with article 49, for all provisions except those of article 41; 28 March 1979 for the provisions of article 41, in accordance with paragraph 2 of the said article 41.

Registration: 23 March 1976, No. 14668.

Text: United Nations, Treaty Series, vol. 999, p. 171 and vol. 1057, p. 407 (procès-verbal of rectification of Spanish authentic text).

The Covenant was opened for signature at New York on 19 December 1966.

Participant	Signature	Ratification Accession a/
Afghanistan		24 January 1983 a/
Albania		4 October 1991 a/
Algeria	10 December 1968	12 September 1989
Angola		10 January 1992 a/
Argentina	19 February 1968	8 August 1986
Australia	18 December 1972	13 August 1980
Austria	10 December 1973	10 September 1978
Barbados		5 January 1973 a/
Belgium	10 December 1968	21 April 1983
Belarus	19 March 1968	12 November 1973
Benin		12 March 1992 a/
Bolivia		12 August 1982 a/
Brazil		24 January 1992 a/
Bulgaria	8 October 1968	21 September 1970
Burundi		9 May 1990 a/
Cambodia	17 October 1980	
Cameroon		27 June 1984 a/
Canada		19 May 1976 a/
Central African Republic		8 May 1981 a/
Chile	16 September 1969	10 February 1972
China 2/		
Colombia	21 December 1966	29 October 1969
Congo		5 October 1983 a/
Costa Rica	19 December 1966	29 November 1968
Côte d'Ivoire		26 January 1992 a/
Cyprus	19 December 1966	2 April 1969
Czech and Slovac Federal Republic	7 October 1968	23 December 1975
Democratic People's Republic of Korea		14 September 1981 a/

0007

Participant	Signature	Ratification Accession a/
Denmark	20 March 1968	6 January 1972
Dominican Republic		4 January 1978 a/
Ecuador	4 April 1968	6 March 1969
Egypt	4 August 1967	14 January 1982
El Salvador	21 September 1967	30 November 1979
Equatorial Guinea		25 September 1987 a/
Estonia		21 October 1991 a/
Finland	11 October 1967	19 August 1975
France		4 November 1980 a/
Gabon		21 January 1983 a/
Gambia		22 March 1979 a/
Germany, 4/	9 October 1968	17 December 1973
Grenada		6 September 1991 a/
Guinea	28 February 1967	24 January 1978
Guyana	22 August 1968	15 February 1977
Haiti		6 February 1991 a/
Honduras	19 December 1966	
Hungary	25 March 1969	17 January 1974
Iceland	30 December 1968	22 August 1979
India		10 April 1979 a/
Iran (Islamic Republic of)	4 April 1968	24 June 1975
Iraq	18 February 1969	25 January 1971
Ireland	1 October 1973	8 December 1989
Israel	19 December 1966	3 October 1991 a/
Italy	18 January 1967	15 September 1978
Jamaica	19 December 1966	3 October 1975
Japan	30 May 1978	21 June 1979
Jordan	30 June 1972	28 May 1975
Kenya		1 May 1972 a/
Lebanon		3 November 1972 a/
Liberia	18 April 1967	
Libyan Arab Jamahiriya		15 May 1970 a/
Lithuania		20 November 1991 a/
Luxembourg	26 November 1974	18 August 1983
Madagascar	17 September 1969	21 June 1971
Mali		16 July 1974 a/
Malta		13 September 1990 a/
Mauritius		12 December 1973 a/
Mexico		23 March 1981 a/
Mongolia	5 June 1968	18 November 1974
Morocco	19 January 1977	3 May 1979
Nepal		14 May 1991 a/
Netherlands	25 June 1969	11 December 1978
New Zealand	12 November 1968	28 December 1978
Nicaragua		12 March 1980 a/
Niger		7 March 1986 a/
Norway	20 March 1968	13 September 1972
Panama	27 July 1976	8 March 1977
Peru	11 August 1977	28 April 1978

0008

Participant	Signature	Ratification Accession a/
Philippines	19 December 1966	23 October 1986
Poland	2 March 1967	18 March 1977
Portugal	7 October 1976	15 June 1978
Republic of Korea		10 April 1990 a/
Romania	27 June 1968	9 December 1974
Russian Federation	18 March 1968	16 October 1973
Rwanda		16 April 1975 a/
Saint Vincent and the Grenadines		9 November 1981 a/
San Marino		18 October 1985 a/
Senegal	6 July 1970	13 February 1978
Somalia		24 January 1990 a/
Spain	28 September 1976	27 April 1977
Sri Lanka		11 June 1980 a/
Sudan		18 March 1986 a/
Suriname		28 December 1976 a/
Sweden	29 September 1967	6 December 1971
Syrian Arab Republic		21 April 1969 a/
Togo		24 May 1984 a/
Trinidad and Tobago		21 December 1978 a/
Tunisia	30 April 1968	18 March 1969
Ukraine	20 March 1968	12 November 1973
United Kingdom	16 September 1968	20 May 1976
United Republic of Tanzania		11 June 1976 a/
United States of America	5 October 1977	
Uruguay	21 February 1967	1 April 1970
Venezuela	24 June 1969	10 May 1978
Viet Nam		24 September 1982 a/
Yemen		9 February 1987 a/
Yugoslavia	8 August 1967	2 June 1971
Zaire		1 November 1976 a/
Zambia		10 April 1984 a/
Zimbabwe		13 May 1991 a/

B. Texts of reservations and declarations

(For objections to these declarations and reservations see section D)

AFGHANISTAN

[Original: Arabic]

Upon accession

The presiding body of the Revolutionary Council of the Democratic Republic of Afghanistan declares that the provisions of paragraphs 1 and 3 of article 48 of the International Covenant on Civil and Political Rights and provisions of paragraphs 1 and 3 of article 26 of the International Covenant on Economic, Social and Cultural Rights, according to which some countries cannot join the aforesaid Covenants, contradicts the international character of the aforesaid treaties. Therefore, in accordance with the equal right of all States to sovereignty, both Covenants should be left open for the purpose of the participation of all States.

ALGERIA

[Original: French]

<u>Upon ratification</u>

The Algerian Government interprets article 1, which is common to the two Covenants, as in no case impairing the inalienable right of all peoples to self-determination and to control over their natural wealth and resources.

It further considers that the maintenance of the state of dependence of certain territories referred to in article 1, paragraph 3, of the two Covenants and in article 14 of the Covenant on Economic, Social and Cultural Rights is contrary to the purposes and principles of the United Nations, to the Charter of the Organization and to the Declaration on the Granting of Independence to Colonial Countries and Peoples (General Assembly resolution 1514 (XV)).

The Algerian Government interprets the provisions of article 8 of the Covenant on Economic, Social and Cultural Rights and article 22 of the Covenant on Civil and Political Rights as making the law the framework for action by the State with respect to the organization and exercise of the right to organize.

The Algerian Government considers that the provisions of article 13, paragraphs 3 and 4, of the Covenant on Economic, Social and Cultural Rights can in no case impair its right freely to organize its educational system.

The Algerian Government interprets the provisions of article 23, paragraph 4, of the Covenant on Civil and Political Rights regarding the rights and responsibilities of spouses as to marriage, during marriage and at its dissolution as in no case impairing the essential foundations of the Algerian legal system.

AUSTRALIA

[Original: English]

<u>Upon ratification</u>

<u>Articles 2 and 50</u>*

Australia advises that, the people having united as one people in a Federal Commonwealth under the Crown, it has a federal constitutional system. It accepts that the provisions of the Covenant extend to all parts of

---

* See the notification of withdrawal of these reservations and declarations in section C.

0010

Australia as a Federal State without any limitations or exceptions. It enters a general reservation that article 2, paragraphs 2 and 3, and article 50 shall be given effect consistently with and subject to the provisions in article 2, paragraph 2.

Under article 2, paragraph 2, steps to adopt measures necessary to give effect to the rights recognized in the Covenant are to be taken in accordance with each State Party's Constitutional processes which, in the case of Australia, are the processes of a federation in which legislative, executive and judicial powers to give effect to the rights recognized in the Covenant are distributed among the federal (Commonwealth) authorities and the authorities of the constituent States.

In particular, in relation to the Australian States the implementation of those provisions of the Covenant over whose subject matter the federal authorities exercise legislative, executive and judicial jurisdiction will be a matter for those authorities; and the implementation of those provisions of the Covenant over whose subject matter the authorities of the constituent States exercise legislative, executive and judicial jurisdiction will be a matter for those authorities; and where a provision has both federal and State aspects, its implementation will accordingly be a matter for the respective constitutionally appropriate authorities (for the purpose of implementation, the Northern Territory will be regarded as a constituent State).

To this end, the Australian Government has been in consultation with the responsible State and Territory Ministers with the object of developing cooperative arrangements to coordinate and facilitate the implementation of the Covenant.

Article 10

Australia accepts the principle stated in paragraph 1 of article 10 and the general principles of the other paragraphs of that article, but makes the reservation that these and other provisions of the Covenant are without prejudice to laws and lawful arrangements, of the type now in force in Australia, for the preservation of custodial discipline in penal establishments.* In relation to paragraph 2 (a) the principle of segregation is accepted as an objective to be achieved progressively. In relation to paragraphs 2 (b) and 3 (second sentence) the obligation to segregate is accepted only to the extent that such segregation is considered by the responsible authorities to be beneficial to the juveniles or adults concerned.

Article 14

Australia accepts paragraph 3 (b) on the understanding that the reference to adequate facilities does not require provision to prisoners of all the facilities available to a prisoner's legal representative.*

Australia accepts the requirement in paragraph 3 (d) that everyone is entitled to be tried in his presence, but reserves the right to exclude an accused person where his conduct makes it impossible for the trial to proceed.*

Australia interprets paragraph 3 (d) of article 14 as consistent with the operation of schemes of legal assistance in which the person assisted is required to make a contribution towards the cost of the defence related to his capacity to pay and determined according to law, or in which assistance is granted in respect of other than indictable offences, only after having regard to all relevant matters.*

Australia makes the reservation that the provision of compensation for miscarriage of justice in the circumstances contemplated in paragraph 6 of article 14 may be by administrative procedures rather than pursuant to specific legal provisions.

Article 17*

Australia accepts the principles stated in article 17 without prejudice to the right to enact and administer laws which, in so far as they authorize action which impinges on a person's privacy, family, home or correspondence, are necessary in a democratic society in the interests of national security, public safety, the economic well-being of the country, the protection of public health or morals or the protection of the rights and freedoms of others.

Article 19*

Australia interprets paragraph 2 of article 19 as being compatible with the regulation of radio and television broadcasting in the public interest with the object of providing the best possible broadcasting services to the Australian people.

Article 20

Australia interprets the rights provided for by articles 19, 21 and 22 as consistent with article 20; accordingly, the Commonwealth and the constituent States, having legislated with respect to the subject matter of the article in matters of practical concern in the interests of public order (*ordre public*), the right is reserved not to introduce any further legislative provision on these matters.

Article 25*

The reference in paragraph (b) of article 25 to "universal and equal suffrage", is accepted without prejudice to law which provide that factors such as regional interest may be taken into account in defining electoral divisions, or which establish franchises for municipal and other local government elections related to the sources of revenue and the functions of such government.

Convicted persons

Australia declares that laws now in force in Australia relating to the rights of persons who have been convicted of serious criminal offences are generally consistent with the requirements of articles 14, 18, 19, 25 and 26 and reserves the right not to seek amendment of such laws.

0012

Discrimination and distinction

The provisions of articles 2, paragraph 1, and 24, paragraph 1, 25 and 26 relating to discrimination and distinction between persons shall be without prejudice to laws designed to achieve for the members of some class or classes of persons equal enjoyment of the rights defined in the Covenant. Australia accepts article 26 on the basis that the object of the provision is to confirm the right of each person to equal treatment in the application of the law.

Declaration

Australia has a federal constitutional system in which legislative, executive and judicial powers are shared or distributed between the Commonwealth and the constituent States. The implementation of the treaty throughout Australia will be effected by the Commonwealth, State and Territory authorities having regard to their respective constitutional powers and arrangements concerning their exercise.

AUSTRIA

[Original: German]

Upon ratification

1. Article 12, paragraph 4, of the Covenant will be applied provided that it will not affect the Act of 3 April 1919, State Law Gazette No. 209, concerning the Expulsion and the Transfer of Property of the House of Habsburg-Lorraine as amended by the Act of 30 October 1919, State Law Gazette No. 501, the Federal Constitutional Act of 30 July 1925, Federal Law Gazette No. 292, and the Federal Constitutional Act of 26 January 1928, Federal Law Gazette No. 30, read in conjunction with the Federal Constitutional Act of 4 July 1963, Federal Law Gazette No. 172.

2. Article 9 and article 14 of the Covenant will be applied provided that legal regulations governing the proceedings and measures of deprivation of liberty as provided for in the Administrative Procedure Acts and in the Financial Penal Act remain permissible within the framework of the judicial review by the Federal Administrative Court or the Federal Constitutional Court as provided by the Austrian Federal Constitution.

3. Article 10, paragraph 3, of the Covenant will be applied provided that legal regulations allowing for juvenile prisoners to be detained together with adults under 25 years of age who give no reason for concern as to their possible detrimental influence on the juvenile prisoner remain permissible.

4. Article 14 of the Covenant will be applied provided that the principles governing the publicity of trials as set forth in article 90 of the Federal Constitutional Law as amended in 1929 are in no way prejudiced and that:

(a) Paragraph 3, subparagraph (d) is not in conflict with legal regulations which stipulate that an accused person who disturbs the orderly conduct of the trial or whose presence would impede the questioning of another accused person, of a witness or of an expert can be excluded from participation in the trial;

(b) Paragraph 5 is not in conflict with legal regulations which stipulate that after an acquittal or a lighter sentence passed by a court of the first instance, a higher tribunal may pronounce conviction or a heavier sentence for the same offence, while they exclude the convicted person's right to have such conviction or heavier sentence reviewed by a still higher tribunal;

(c) Paragraph 7 is not in conflict with legal regulations which allow proceedings that led up to a person's final conviction or acquittal to be reopened.

5. Articles 19, 21 and 22 in connection with article 2, paragraph 1, of the Covenant will be applied provided that they are not in conflict with legal restrictions as provided for in article 16 of the European Convention for the Protection of Human Rights and Fundamental Freedoms.

6. Article 26 is understood to mean that it does not exclude different treatment of Austrian nationals and aliens, as is also permissible under article 1, paragraph 2, of the International Convention on the Elimination of All Forms of Racial Discrimination.

BARBADOS

[Original: English]

Upon accession

The Government of Barbados states that it reserves the right not to apply in full, the guarantee of free legal assistance in accordance with paragraph 3 (d) of article 14 of the Covenant, since, while accepting the principles contained in the same paragraph, the problems of implementation are such that full application cannot be guaranteed at present.

BELARUS

[Original: Belarussian]

Declaration made upon signature and confirmed upon ratification

The Byelorussian Soviet Socialist Republic declares that the provisions of paragraph 1 of article 26 of the International Covenant on Economic, Social and Cultural Rights and of paragraph 1 of article 48 of the International Covenant on Civil and Political Rights, under which a number of States cannot become parties to these Covenants, are of a discriminatory nature and considers that the Covenants, in accordance with the principle of sovereign equality of States, should be open for participation by all States concerned without any discrimination or limitation.

BELGIUM

[Original: French]

Upon ratification

Reservations

1. With respect to articles 2, 3 and 25, the Belgian Government makes a reservation, in that under the Belgian Constitution the royal powers may be exercised only by males. With respect to the exercise of the functions of the regency, the said articles shall not preclude the application of the constitutional rules as interpreted by the Belgian State.

2. The Belgian Government considers that the provision of article 10, paragraph 2 (a), under which accused persons shall, save in exceptional circumstances, be segregated from convicted persons is to be intepreted in conformity with the principle, already embodied in the standard minimum rules, for the treatment of prisoners [resolution (73) 5 of the Committee of Ministers of the Council of Europe of 19 January 1973], that untried prisoners shall not be put in contact with convicted prisoners against their will [rules 7 (b) and 85 (1)]. If they so request, accused persons may be allowed to take part with convicted persons in certain communal activities.

3. The Belgian Government considers that the provisions of article 10, paragraph 3, under which juvenile offenders shall be segregated from adults and be accorded treatment appropriate to their age and legal status refers exclusively to the judicial measures provided for under the regime for the protection of minors established by the Belgian Act relating to the protection of young persons. As regards other juvenile ordinary-law offenders, the Belgian Government intends to reserve the option to adopt measures that may be more flexible and be designed precisely in the interest of the persons concerned.

4. With respect to article 14, the Belgian Government considers that the last part of paragraph 1 of the article appears to give States the option of providing or not providing for certain derogations from the principle that judgements shall be made public. Accordingly, the Belgian constitutional principle that there shall be no exceptions to the public pronouncements of judgements is in conformity with that provision. Paragraph 5 of the article shall not apply to persons who, under Belgian law, are convicted and sentenced at second instance following an appeal against their acquittal of first instance or who, under Belgian law, are brought directly before a higher tribunal such as the Court of Cassation, the Appeals Court or the Assize Court.

5. Articles 19, 21 and 22 shall be applied by the Belgian Government in the context of the provisions and restrictions set forth or authorized in articles 10 and 11 of the Convention for the Protection of Human Rights and Fundamental Freedoms of 4 November 1950, by the said Convention.

Declarations

6. The Belgian Government declares that it does not consider itself obligated to enact legislation in the field covered by article 20, paragraph 1, and that article 20 as a whole shall be applied taking into account the rights to freedom of thought and religion, freedom of opinion and freedom of assembly and association proclaimed in articles 18, 19 and 20 of the Universal Declaration of Human Rights and reaffirmed in articles 18, 19, 21 and 22 of the Covenant.

7. The Belgian Government declares that it interprets article 23, paragraph 2, as meaning that the right of persons of marriageable age to marry and to found a family presupposes not only that national law shall prescribe the marriageable age but that it may also regulate the exercise of that right.

BULGARIA

[Original: English]

Upon ratification

The People's Republic of Bulgaria deems it necessary to underline that the provisions of article 48, paragraphs 1 and 3, of the International Covenant on Civil and Political Rights, and article 26, paragraphs 1 and 3, of the International Covenant on Economic, Social and Cultural Rights, under which a number of States are deprived of the opportunity to become parties to the Covenants, are of a discriminatory nature. These provisions are inconsistent with the very nature of the Covenants, which are universal in character and should be open for accession by all States. In accordance with the principle of sovereign equality, no State has the right to bar other States from becoming parties to a covenant of this kind.

CONGO

[Original: French]

Upon accession

Reservation

The Government of the People's Republic of the Congo declares that it does not consider itself bound by the provisions of article 11 ...

Article 11 of the International Covenant on Civil and Political Rights is quite incompatible with articles 386 ff. of the Congolese Code of Civil, Commercial, Administrative and Financial Procedure, derived from Act 51/83 of 21 April 1983. Under those provisions, in matters of private law, decisions or orders emanating from conciliation proceedings may be enforced through imprisonment for debt when other means of enforcement have failed, when the amount due exceeds 20,000 CFA francs and when the debtor, between 18 and 60 years of age, makes himself insolvent in bad faith.

CZECH AND SLOVAK FEDERAL REPUBLIC

[Original: Czech]

Upon signature

The Czechoslovak Socialist Republic declares that the provisions of article 48, paragraph 1, of the International Covenant on Civil and Political Rights are in contradiction with the principle that all States have the right to become parties to multilateral treaties governing matters of general interest.

Upon ratification

The provision of article 48, paragraph 1, is in contradiction with the principle that all States have the right to become parties to multilateral treaties regulating matters of general interest.

DENMARK

[Original: English]

Upon ratification

1. The Government of Denmark makes a reservation in respect of article 10, paragraph 3, second sentence. In Danish practice, considerable efforts are made to ensure appropriate age distribution of convicts serving sentences of imprisonment, but it is considered valuable to maintain possibilities of flexible arrangements.

2. (a) Article 14, paragraph 1, shall not be binding on Denmark in respect of public hearings. In Danish law, the right to exclude the press and the public from trials may go beyond what is permissible under this Covenant, and the Government of Denmark finds that this right should not be restricted.

(b) Article 14, paragraphs 5 and 7, shall not be binding on Denmark.

The Danish Administration of Justice Act contains detailed provisions regulating the matters dealt with in these two paragraphs. In some cases, Danish legislation is less restrictive than the Covenant (e.g. a verdict returned by a jury on the question of guilt cannot be reviewed by a higher tribunal, cf. para. 5); in other cases, Danish legislation is more restrictive than the Covenant (e.g. with respect to resumption of a criminal case in which the accused party was acquitted, cf. para. 7).

3. Reservation is further made to article 20, paragraph 1. This reservation is in accordance with the vote cast by Denmark in the sixteenth session of the General Assembly of the United Nations in 1961 when the Danish delegation, referring to the preceding article concerning freedom of expression, voted against the prohibition against propaganda for war.

FINLAND

[Original: English]

Upon ratification

Reservations

1. With respect to article 9, paragraph 3, of the Covenant, Finland declares that according to the present Finnish legislation the Administrative authorities may take decisions concerning arrest or imprisonment, in which event the case is taken up for decision in court only after a certain time lapse.

2. With respect to article 10, paragraphs 2 (b) and 3, of the Covenant, Finland declares that, although juvenile offenders are, as a rule, segregated from adults, it does not deem appropriate to adopt an absolute prohibition not allowing for more flexible arrangements.

3. With respect to article 13 of the Covenant, Finland declares that the article does not correspond to the present Finnish legislation regarding an alien's right to be heard or lodge a complaint in respect of a decision concerning his expulsion.*

4. With respect to article 14, paragraph 1, of the Covenant, Finland declares that under Finnish law a sentence can be declared secret if its publication could be an affront to morals or endanger national security.*

5. With respect to article 14, paragraph 3 (d), of the Covenant, Finland declares that the contents of this paragraph do not correspond to the present legislation in Finland inasmuch as it is a question of the defendant's absolute right to have legal assistance already at the stage of preliminary investigations.

6. With respect to article 14, paragraph 7, of the Covenant, Finland declares that it is going to pursue its present practice, according to which a sentence can be changed to the detriment of the convicted person, if it is established that a member or an official of the court, the prosecutor or the legal counsel have through criminal or fraudulent activities obtained the acquittal of the defendant or a substantially more lenient penalty, or if false evidence has been presented with the same effect, and according to which an aggravated criminal case may be taken up for reconsideration if, within a year, until then unknown evidence is presented, which would have led to conviction or a substantially more severe penalty.

7. With respect to article 20, paragraph 1, of the Covenant, Finland declares that it will not apply the provisions of this paragraph, this being compatible with the standpoint Finland already expressed at the sixteenth session of the United Nations General Assembly by voting against the prohibiton of propaganda for war, on the grounds that this might endanger the freedom of expression referred to in article 19 of the Covenant.

FRANCE

[Original: French]

Upon accession

Declarations and reservations

1. The Government of the Republic considers that, in accordance with Article 103 of the Charter of the United Nations, in case of conflict between its obligations under the Covenant and its obligations under the Charter (especially Articles 1 and 2 thereof), its obligations under the Charter will prevail.

2. The Government of the Republic enters the following reservation concerning article 4, paragraph 1: firstly, the circumstances enumerated in article 16 of the Constitution in respect of its implementation, in article 1 of the Act of 3 April 1978 and in the Act of 9 August 1849 in respect of the declaration of a state of siege, in article 1 of Act No. 55-385 of 3 April 1955 in respect of the declaration of a state of emergency and which enable these instruments to be implemented, are to be understood as meeting the purpose of article 4 of the Covenant; and, secondly, for the purpose of interpreting and implementing article 16 of the Constitution of the French Republic, the terms "to the extent strictly required by the exigencies of the situation" cannot limit the power of the President of the Republic to take "the measures required by circumstances".

3. The Government of the Republic enters a reservation concerning articles 9 and 14 to the effect that these articles cannot impede enforcement of the rules pertaining to the disciplinary regime in the armies.

4. The Government of the Republic declares that article 13 cannot derogate from chapter IV of Order No. 45-2658 of 2 November 1945 concerning the entry into, and sojourn in, France of aliens, nor from the other instruments concerning the expulsion of aliens in force in those parts of the territory of the Republic in which the Order of 2 November 1945 does not apply.

5. The Government of the Republic interprets article 14, paragraph 5, as stating a general principle to which the law may make limited exceptions, for example, in the case of certain offences subject to the initial and final adjudication of a police court and of criminal offences. However, an appeal against a final decision may be made to the Court of Cassation which rules on the legality of the decision concerned.

6. The Government of the Republic declares that articles 19, 21 and 22 of the Covenant will be implemented in accordance with articles 10, 11 and 16 of the European Convention for the Protection of Human Rights and Fundamental Freedoms of 4 November 1950.

However, the Government of the Republic enters a reservation concerning article 19 which cannot derogate from the monopoly of the French radio and television broadcasting system.*

7. The Government of the Republic declares that the term "war", appearing in article 20, paragraph 1, is to be understood to mean war in contravention of international law and considers, in any case, that French legislation in this matter is adequate.

8. In the light of article 2 of the Constitution of the French Republic, the French Government declares that article 27 is not applicable so far as the Republic is concerned. 5/

GAMBIA

[Original: English]

Upon accession

For financial reasons free legal assistance for accused persons is limited in our Constitution to persons charged with capital offences only. The Government of the Gambia therefore wishes to enter a reservation in respect of article 14, paragraph 3 (d), of the Covenant in question.

GERMANY**

[Original: German]

Upon ratification

1. Articles 19, 21 and 22 in conjunction with article 2, paragraph 1, of the Covenant shall be applied within the scope of article 16 of the Convention of 4 November 1950 for the Protection of Human Rights and Fundamental Freedoms.

2. Article 14, paragraph 3 (d), of the Covenant shall be applied in such manner that it is for the court to decide whether an accused person held in custody has to appear in person at the hearing before the court of review (Revisionsgericht).

3. Article 14, paragraph 5, of the Covenant shall be applied in such manner that:

(a) A further appeal does not have to be instituted in all cases solely on the grounds that the accused person - having been acquitted by the lower court - was convicted for the first time in the proceedings concerned by the appellate court;

** Through the accession of the German Democratic Republic to the Federal Republic of Germany with effect from 3 October 1990, the two German States united to form one sovereign State. As from the date of unification, the Federal Republic of Germany acts in the United Nations under the designation "Germany". The former German Democratic Republic ratified the Covenant on 8 November 1973.

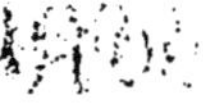

0020

(b) In the case of criminal offences of minor gravity the review by a higher tribunal of a decision not imposing imprisonment does not have to be admitted in all cases.

4. Article 15, paragraph 1, of the Covenant shall be applied in such manner that when provision is made by law for the imposition of a lighter penalty the hitherto applicable law may for certain exceptional categories of cases remain applicable to criminal offences committed before the law was amended. 6/

German Democratic Republic

[Original: English]

Upon ratification

The German Democratic Republic considers that article 48, paragraph 1, of the Covenant runs counter to the principle that all States which are guided in their policies by the purposes and principles of the United Nations Charter have the right to become parties to conventions which affect the interests of all States.

The German Democratic Republic has ratified the two Covenants in accordance with the policy it has so far pursued with the view to safeguarding human rights. It is convinced that these Covenants promote the worldwide struggle for the enforcement of human rights, which is an integral part of the struggle for the maintenance and strengthening of peace. On the occasion of the twenty-fifth anniversary of the Universal Declaration of Human Rights it thus contributes to the peaceful international cooperation of States, to the promotion of human rights and to the joint struggle against their violation by aggressive policies, colonialism and apartheid, racism and other forms of assaults on the right of the peoples to self-determination.

The Constitution of the German Democratic Republic guarantees the political, economic, social and cultural rights to every citizen independent of race, sex and religion. Socialist democracy has created the conditions for every citizen not only to enjoy these rights but also take an active part in their implementation and enforcement.

Such fundamental human rights as the right to peace, the right to work and social security, the equality of women, and the right to education have been fully implemented in the German Democratic Republic. The Government of the German Democratic Republic has always paid great attention to the material prerequisites for guaranteeing above all the social and economic rights. The welfare of the working people and its continuous improvement are the leitmotiv of the entire policy of the Government of the German Democratic Republic.

The Government of the German Democratic Republic holds that the signing and ratification of the two human rights Covenants by further Member States of the United Nations would be an important step to implement the aims for respecting and promoting the human rights, the aims proclaimed in the Charter of the United Nations.

GUINEA

[Original: French]

Upon ratification

In accordance with the principle whereby all States whose policies are guided by the purposes and principles of the Charter of the United Nations are entitled to become parties to covenants affecting the interests of the international community, the Government of the Republic of Guinea considers that the provisions of article 48, paragraph 1, of the International Covenant on Civil and Political Rights are contrary to the principle of the universality of international treaties and the democratization of international relations.

GUYANA

[Original: English]

Upon ratification

In respect of article 14, paragraph 3

While the Government of the Republic of Guyana accepts the principle of legal aid in all appropriate criminal proceedings, is working towards that end and at present applies it in certain defined cases, the problems of implementation of a comprehensive legal aid scheme are such that full application cannot be guaranteed at this time.

In respect of article 14, paragraph 6

While the Government of the Republic of Guyana accepts the principle of compensation for wrongful imprisonment, it is not possible at this time to implement such a principle.

HUNGARY

[Original: English]

Upon signature

The Government of the Hungarian People's Republic declares that paragraph 1 of article 26 of the International Covenant on Economic, Social and Cultural Rights and paragraph 1 of article 48 of the International Covenant on Civil and Political Rights according to which certain States may not become signatories to the said Covenants are of a discriminatory nature and are contrary to the basic principle of international law that all States are entitled to become signatories to general multilateral treaties. These discriminatory provisions are incompatible with the objectives and purposes of the Covenants.

0022

Upon ratification

The Presidential Council of the Hungarian People's Republic declares that the provisions of article 48, paragraphs 1 and 3, of ... the International Covenant on Civil and Political Rights, and article 26, paragraphs 1 and 3, of the International Covenant on Economic, Social and Cultural Rights are inconsistent with the universal character of the Covenants. It follows from the principle of sovereign equality of States that the Covenants should be open for participation by all States without any discrimination or limitation.

ICELAND

[Original: Icelandic]

The ratification was accompanied by reservations with respect to the following provisions

1. Article 8, paragraph 3 (a), in so far as it affects the provisions of Icelandic law which provide that a person who is not the main provider of his family may be sentenced to a term at a labour facility in satisfaction of arrears in support payments for his child or children.

2. Article 10, paragraph 2 (b), and paragraph 3, second sentence, with respect to the separation of juvenile prisoners from adults. Icelandic law in principle provides for such separation but it is not considered appropriate to accept an obligation in the absolute form called for in the provisions of the Covenant.

3. Article 13, to the extent that it is inconsistent with the Icelandic legal provisions in force relating to the right of aliens to object to a decision on their expulsion.

4. Article 14, paragraph 7, with respect to the resumption of cases which have already been tried. The Icelandic law of procedure has detailed provisions on this matter which it is not considered appropriate to revise.

5. Article 20, paragraph 1, with reference to the fact that a prohibition against propaganda for war could limit the freedom of expression. This reservation is consistent with the position of Iceland at the General Assembly at its sixteenth session.

Other provisions of the Covenant shall be inviolably observed.

INDIA

[Original: English]

Upon accession

I. With reference to [...] article 1 of the International Covenant on Civil and Political Rights, the Government of the Republic of India declares that the words 'the right of self-determination' appearing in [that article] apply only to the peoples under foreign domination and that these words do not apply to sovereign independent States or to a section of a people or nation - which is the essence of national integrity.

0023

II. With reference to article 9 of the International Covenant on Civil and Political Rights, the Government of the Republic of India takes the position that the provisions of the article shall be so applied as to be in consonance with the provisions of clauses (3) to (7) of article 22 of the Constitution of India. Further, under the Indian legal system, there is no enforceable right to compensation for persons claiming to be victims of unlawful arrest or detention against the State.

III. With respect to article 13 of the International Covenant on Civil and Political Rights, the Government of the Republic of India reserves its right to apply its law relating to foreigners.

IV. With reference to [...] articles 12, 19, paragraphs 3, 21 and 22 of the International Covenant on Civil and Political Rights, the Government of the Republic of India declares that the provisions of the said articles shall be so applied as to be in conformity with the provisions of article 19 of the Constitution of India."

IRAQ

[Original: English]

Upon signature and confirmed upon ratification

The entry of the Republic of Iraq as a party to the International Covenant on Economic, Social and Cultural Rights and the International Covenant on Civil and Political Rights shall in no way signify recognition of Israel nor shall it entail any obligation towards Israel under the said two Covenants. 7/

The entry of the Republic of Iraq as a party to the above two Covenants shall not constitute entry by it as a party to the Optional Protocol to the International Covenant on Civil and Political Rights.

Upon ratification

Ratification by Iraq ... shall in no way signify recognition of Israel nor shall it be conducive to entry with her into such dealings as are regulated by the said [Covenant]. 7/

IRELAND

[Original: English]

Upon ratification

Article 6, paragraph 5

Pending the introduction of further legislation to give full effect to the provisions of paragraph 5 of article 6, should a case arise which is not covered by the provisions of existing law, the Government of Ireland will have regard to its obligations under the Covenant in the exercise of its power to advise commutation of the sentence of death.

0024

Article 10, paragraph 2

Ireland accepts the principles referred to in paragraph 2 of article 10 and implements them so far as practically possible. It reserves the right to regard full implementation of these principles as objectives to be achieved progressively.

Article 14

Ireland reserves the right to have minor offences against military law dealt with summarily in accordance with current procedures which may not, in all respects, conform to the requirements of article 14 of the Covenant.

Ireland makes the reservation that the provision of compensation for the miscarriage of justice in the circumstances contemplated in paragraph 6 of article 14 may be by administrative procedures rather than pursuant to specific legal provisions.

Article 19, paragraph 2

Ireland reserves the right to confer a monopoly on or require the licensing of broadcasting enterprises.

Article 20, paragraph 1

Ireland accepts the principle in paragraph 1 of article 20 and implements it as far as it is practicable. Having regard to the difficulties in formulating a specific offence capable of ajudication at national level in such a form as to reflect the general principles of law recognized by the community of nations as well as the right to freedom of expression, Ireland reserves the right to postpone consideration of the possibility of introducing some legislative addition to, or variation of, existing law until such time as it may consider that such is necessary for the attainment of the objective of paragraph 1 of article 20.

Article 23, paragraph 4

Ireland accepts the obligations of paragraph 4 of article 23 on the understanding that the provision does not imply any right to obtain a dissolution of marriage.

ISRAEL

[Original: English]

Upon ratification

Declaration

Since its establishment, the State of Israel has been the victim of continuous threats and attacks on its very existence as well as on the life and property of its citizens.

These have taken the form of threats of war, of actual armed attacks, and campaigns of terrorism resulting in the murder of and injury to human beings.

In view of the above, the state of emergency which was proclaimed in May 1948 has remained in force ever since. This situation constitutes a public emergency within the meaning of article 4(1) of the Covenant.

The Government of Israel has therefore found it necessary, in accordance with the said article 4, to take measures to the extent strictly required by the exigencies of the situation, for the defence of the State and for the protection of life and property, including the exercise of powers of arrest and detention.

In so far as any of these measures are inconsistent with article 9 of the Covenant, Israel thereby derogates from its obligations under that provision.

Reservation

With reference to article 23 of the Covenant, and any other provision thereof to which the present reservation may be relevant, matters of personal status are governed in Israel by the religious law of the parties concerned.

To the extent that such law is inconsistent with its obligations under the Covenant, Israel reserves the right to apply that law.

ITALY

[Original: French]

Upon ratification

Article 9, paragraph 5

The Italian Republic, considering that the expression "unlawful arrest or detention" contained in article 9, paragraph 5, could give rise to differences of interpretation, declares that it interprets the aforementioned expression as referring exclusively to cases of arrest or detention contrary to the provisions of article 9, paragraph 1.

Article 12, paragraph 4

Article 12, paragraph 4, shall be without prejudice to the application of transitional provision XIII of the Italian Constitution, respecting prohibition of the entry into and sojourn in the national territory of certain members of the House of Savoy.

Article 14, paragraph 3

The provisions of article 14, paragraph 3 (d), are deemed to be compatible with existing Italian provisions governing trial of the accused in his presence and determining the cases in which the accused may present his own defence and those in which legal assistance is required.

0026

Article 14, paragraph 5

Article 14, paragraph 5, shall be without prejudice to the application of existing Italian provisions which, in accordance with the Constitution of the Italian Republic, govern the conduct, at one level only, of proceedings instituted before the Constitutional Court in respect of charges brought against the President of the Republic and its Ministers.

Article 15, paragraph 1

With reference to article 15, paragraph 1, last sentence: "If, subsequent to the commission of the offence, provision is made by law for the imposition of a lighter penalty, the offender shall benefit thereby", the Italian Republic deems this provision to apply exclusively to cases in progress.

Consequently, a person who has already been convicted by a final decision shall not benefit from any provision made by law, subsequent to that decision, for the imposition of a lighter penalty.

Article 19, paragraph 3

The provisions of article 19, paragraph 3, are interpreted as being compatible with the existing licensing system for national radio and television and with the restrictions laid down by law for local radio and television companies and for stations relaying foreign programmes.

JAPAN

[Original: English]

Upon ratification

... the Government of Japan declares that 'members ... of the police' referred to in ... paragraph 2 of article 22 of the International Covenant on Civil and Political Rights be interpreted to include fire service personnel of Japan.

LIBYAN ARAB JAMAHIRIYA

[Original: English]

Upon accession

The acceptance and the accession to this Covenant by the Libyan Arab Republic shall in no way signify a recognition of Israel or be conducive to entry by the Libyan Arab Republic into such dealings with Israel as are regulated by the Covenant. 7/

0027

LUXEMBOURG

[Original: French]

Upon ratification

Interpretative declarations

The Government of Luxembourg considers that article 10, paragraph 3, which provides that juvenile offenders shall be segregated from adults and accorded treatment appropriate to their age and legal status, refers solely to the legal measures incorporated in the system for the protection of minors, which is the subject of the Luxembourg Youth Welfare Act. With regard to other juvenile offenders falling within the sphere of ordinary law, the Government of Luxembourg wishes to retain the option of adopting measures that might be more flexible and be designed to serve the interests of the persons concerned.

The Government of Luxembourg declares that it is implementing article 14, paragraph 5, since that paragraph does not conflict with the relevant Luxembourg legal statutes, which provide that, following an acquittal or a conviction by a court of first instance, a higher tribunal may deliver a sentence, confirm the sentence passed or impose a harsher penalty for the same crime. However, the tribunal's decision does not give the person declared guilty on appeal the right to appeal that conviction to a higher appellate jurisdiction.

Reservations

The Government of Luxembourg further declares that article 14, paragraph 5, shall not apply to persons who, under Luxembourg law, are remanded directly to a higher court or brought before the Assize Court.

The Government of Luxembourg accepts the provision in article 19, paragraph 2, provided that it does not preclude it from requiring broadcasting, television and film companies to be licensed.

The Government of Luxembourg declares that it does not consider itself obligated to adopt legislation in the field covered by article 20, paragraph 1, and that article 20 as a whole will be implemented taking into account the rights to freedom of thought, religion, opinion, assembly and association laid down in articles 18, 19 and 20 of the Universal Declaration of Human Rights and reaffirmed in articles 18, 19, 21 and 22 of the Covenant.

MALTA

[Original: English]

Upon accession

Reservations

Article 13

The Government of Malta endorses the principles laid down in article 13. However, in the present circumstances it cannot comply entirely with the provisions of this article.

Article 14, paragraph 2

The Government of Malta declares that it interprets paragraph 2 of article 14 of the Covenant in the sense that it does not preclude any particular law from imposing upon any person charged under such law the burden of proving particular facts.

Article 14, paragraph 6

While the Government of Malta accepts the principle of compensation for wrongful imprisonment, it is not possible at this time to implement such a principle in accordance with article 14, paragraph 6, of the Covenant.

Article 19

The Government of Malta desiring to avoid any uncertainty as regards the application of article 19 of the Covenant declares that the Constitution of Malta allows such restrictions to be imposed upon public officers in regard to their freedom of expression as are reasonably justifiable in a democratic society. The Code of Conduct of public officers in Malta precludes them from taking an active part in political discussions or other political activity during working hours or on the premises.

The Government of Malta also reserves the right not to apply article 19 to the extent that this may be fully compatible with Act 1 of 1987 entitled "An Act to regulate the limitations on the political activities of aliens', and this in accordance with article 16 of the Convention of Rome (1950) for the protection of Human Rights and Fundamental Freedoms or with section 41 (2) (a) (ii) of the Constitution of Malta.

Article 20

The Government of Malta interprets article 20 consistently with the rights conferred by articles 19 and 21 of the Covenant but reserves the right not to introduce any legislation for the purposes of article 20.

Article 22

The Government of Malta reserves the right not to apply article 22 to the extent that existing legislative measures may not be fully compatible with this article.

MEXICO

[Original: Spanish]

Upon accession

Interpretative statements

Article 9, paragraph 5

Under the Political Constitution of the United Mexican States and the relevant implementing legislation, every individual enjoys the guarantees relating to penal matters embodied therein, and consequently no person may be unlawfully arrested or detained. However, if by reason of false accusation or complaint any individual suffers an infringement of this basic right, he has, *inter alia*, under the provisions of the appropriate laws, an enforceable right to just compensation.

Article 18

Under the Political Constitution of the United Mexican States, every person is free to profess his preferred religious belief and to practice its ceremonies, rites and religious acts, with the limitation, with regard to public religious acts, that they must be performed in places of worship and, with regard to education, that studies carried out in establishments designed for the professional education of ministers of religion are not officially recognized. The Government of Mexico believes that these limitations are included among those established in paragraph 3 of this article.

Reservations

Article 13

The Government of Mexico makes a reservation to this article, in view of the present text of article 33 of the Political Constitution of the United Mexican States.

Article 25, subparagraph (b)

The Government of Mexico also makes a reservation to this provision, since article 130 of the Political Constitution of the United Mexican States provides that ministers of religion shall have neither an active nor a passive vote, nor the right to form associations for political purposes.

MONGOLIA

[Original: English]

Declaration made upon signature and renewed upon ratifiction

[Same declaration, *mutatis mutandis*, as that made by the Byelorussian Soviet Socialist Republic, see page 9.]

0030

NETHERLANDS

[Original: English]

Upon ratification

Reservations

Article 10

The Kingdom of the Netherlands subscribes to the principle set out in paragraph 1 of this article, but it takes the view that ideas about the treatment of prisoners are so liable to change that it does not wish to be bound by the obligations set out in paragraph 2 and paragraph 3 (second sentence) of this article.

Article 12, paragraph 1

The Kingdom of the Netherlands regards the Netherlands and the Netherlands Antilles as separate territories of a State for the purpose of this provision.

Article 12, paragraphs 2 and 4

The Kingdom of the Netherlands regards the Netherlands and the Netherlands Antilles as separate countries for the purpose of these provisions.

Article 14, paragraph 3 (d)

The Kingdom of the Netherlands reserves the statutory option of removing a person charged with a criminal offence from the courtroom in the interests of the proper conduct of the proceedings.

Article 14, paragraph 5

The Kingdom of the Netherlands reserves the statutory power of the Supreme Court of the Netherlands to have sole jurisdiction to try certain categories of persons charged with serious offences committed in the discharge of a public office.

Article 14, paragraph 7

The Kingdom of the Netherlands accepts this provision only in so far as no obligations arise from it further to those set out in article 68 of the Criminal Code of the Netherlands and article 70 of the Criminal Code of the Netherlands Antilles as they now apply. They read:

1. Except in cases where court decisions are eligible for review, no person may be prosecuted again for an offence in respect of which a court in the Netherlands or the Netherlands Antilles has delivered an irrevocable judgement.

2. If the judgement has been delivered by some other court, the same person may not be prosecuted for the same offence in the case of (i) acquittal or withdrawal of proceedings or (ii) conviction followed by complete execution, remission or lapse of the sentence.

Article 19, paragraph 2

The Kingdom of the Netherlands accepts the provision with the proviso that it shall not prevent the Kingdom from requiring the licensing of broadcasting, television or cinema enterprises.

Article 20, paragraph 1

The Kingdom of the Netherlands does not accept the obligation set out in this provision in the case of the Netherlands.

Article 25 (c)

The Kingdom of the Netherlands does not accept this provision in the case of the Netherlands Antilles.*

Explanation

[The Kingdom of the Netherlands clarifies] that although the reservations [...] are partly of an interpretational nature, [it] has preferred reservations to interpretational declarations in all cases, since if the latter form were used doubt might arise concerning whether the text of the Covenant allows for the interpretation put upon it. By using the reservation form the Kingdom of the Netherlands wishes to ensure in all cases that the relevant obligations arising out of the Covenant will not apply to the Kingdom, or will apply, only in the way indicated.

NEW ZEALAND

[Original: English]

Upon ratification

Reservations

The Government of New Zealand reserves the right not to apply article 10, paragraph 2 (b), or paragraph 3, in circumstances where the shortage of suitable facilities makes the mixing of juveniles and adults unavoidable; and further reserves the right not to apply article 10, paragraph 3, where the interests of other juveniles in an establishment require the removal of a particular juvenile offender or where mixing is considered to be of benefit to the persons concerned.

The Government of New Zealand reserves the right not to apply article 14, paragraph 6, to the extent that it is not satisfied by the existing system for *ex gratia* payments to persons who suffer as a result of a miscarriage of justice.

The Government of New Zealand having legislated in the areas of the advocacy of national and racial hatred and the exciting of hostility or ill will against any group of persons, and having regard to the right of freedom of speech, reserves the right not to introduce further legislation with regard to article 20.

The Government of New Zealand reserves the right not to apply article 22 as it relates to trade unions to the extent that existing legislative measures, enacted to ensure effective trade-union representation and encourage orderly industrial relations, may not be fully compatible with that article."

NORWAY

[Original: English]

Upon ratification

Subject to reservations to article 6, paragraph 4,* article 10, paragraph 2 (b) and paragraph 3, "with regard to the obligation to keep accused juvenile persons and juvenile offenders segregated from adults" and to article 14, paragraphs 5 and 7, and to article 20, paragraph 1.

REPUBLIC OF KOREA

[Original: Korean]

Upon accession

The Government of the Republic of Korea [declares] that the provisions of paragraphs 5 and 7 of article 14, article 22 and paragraph 4 of article 23* of the Covenant shall be so applied as to be in conformity with the provisions of the local laws including the Constitution of the Republic of Korea.

ROMANIA

[Original: French]

Upon signature

The Government of the Socialist Republic of Romania declares that the provisions of article 48, paragraph 1, of the International Covenant on Civil and Political Rights are at variance with the principle that all States have the right to become parties to multilateral treaties governing matters of general interest.

Upon ratification

(a) The State Council of the Socialist Republic of Romania considers that the provisions of article 48, paragraph 1, of the International Covenant on Civil and Political Rights are inconsistent with the principle that multilateral international treaties whose purposes concern the international community as a whole must be open to universal participation.

0033

(b) The State Council of the Socialist Republic of Romania considers that the maintenance in a state of dependence of certain territories referred to in article 1, paragraph 3, of the International Covenant on Civil and Political Rights is inconsistent with the Charter of the United Nations and the instruments adopted by the Organization on the granting of independence to colonial countries and peoples, including the Declaration on Principles of International Law concerning Friendly Relations and Co-operation among States in accordance with the Charter of the United Nations, adopted unanimously by the United Nations General Assembly in its resolution 2625 (XXV) of 1970, which solemnly proclaims the duty of States to promote the realization of the principle of equal rights and self-determination of peoples in order to bring a speedy end to colonialism.

RUSSIAN FEDERATON

[Original: Russian]

Declaration made upon signature and confirmed upon ratification

[Same declaration, *mutatis mutandis*, as that made by the Byelorussian Soviet Socialist Republic, see page 9.]

SWEDEN

[Original: French]

Upon ratification

Sweden reserves the right not to apply the provisions of article 10, paragraph 3, with regard to the obligation to segregate juvenile offenders from adults, the provisions of article 14, paragraph 7, and the provisions of article 20, paragraph 1, of the Covenant.

SYRIAN ARAB REPUBLIC

[Original: French]

Upon accession

1. The accession of the Syrian Arab Republic to these two Covenants shall in no way signify recognition of Israel or entry into a relationship with it regarding any matter regulated by the said two Covenants.

2. The Syrian Arab Republic considers that paragraph 1 of article 26 of the Covenant on Economic, Social and Cultural Rights and paragraph 1 of article 48 of the Covenant on Civil and Political Rights are incompatible with the purposes and objectives of the said Covenants, inasmuch as they do not allow all States, without distinction or discrimination, the opportunity to become parties to the said Covenants.

TRINIDAD AND TOBAGO

[Original: English]

Upon accession

(i) The Government of the Republic of Trinidad and Tobago reserves the right not to apply in full the provision of paragraph 2 of article 4 of the Covenant since section 7 (3) of its Constitution enables Parliament to enact legislation even though it is inconsistent with sections (4) and (5) of the said Constitution.

(ii) Where at any time there is a lack of suitable prison facilities, the Government of the Republic of Trinidad and Tobago reserves the right not to apply article 10, paragraphs 2 (b) and 3, so far as those provisions require juveniles who are detained to be accommodated separately from adults.

(iii) The Government of the Republic of Trinidad and Tobago reserves the right not to apply paragraph 2 of article 12 in view of the statutory provisions requiring persons intending to travel abroad to furnish tax clearance certificates.

(iv) The Government of the Republic of Trinidad and Tobago reserves the right not to apply paragraph 5 of article 14 in view of the fact that section 43 of its Supreme Court of Judicature Act No. 12 of 1962 does not confer on a person convicted on indictment an unqualified right of appeal and that in particular cases, appeal to the Court of Appeal can only be done with the leave of the Court of Appeal itself or of the Privy Council.

(v) While the Government of the Republic of Trinidad and Tobago accepts the principle of compensation for wrongful imprisonment, it is not possible at this time to implement such a principle in accordance with paragraph 6 of article 14 of the Covenant.

(vi) With reference to the last sentence of paragraph 1 of article 15. - 'If, subsequent to the commission of the offence, provision is made by law for the imposition of a lighter penalty, the offender shall benefit thereby', the Government of the Republic of Trinidad and Tobago deems this provision to apply exclusively to cases in progress. Consequently, a person who has already been convicted by a final decision shall not benefit from any provision made by law, subsequent to that decision for the imposition of a lighter penalty. 8/

(vii) The Government of the Republic of Trinidad and Tobago reserves the right to impose lawful and or reasonable restrictions with respect to the right of assembly under article 21 of the Covenant.

(viii) The Government of the Republic of Trinidad and Tobago reserves the right not to apply the provision of article 26 of the Covenant in so far as it applies to the holding of property in Trinidad and Tobago, in view of the fact that licences may be granted to or withheld from aliens under the Aliens Landholding Act of Trinidad and Tobago.

UKRAINE

[Original: Russian]

Declaration made upon signature and confirmed upon ratification

[Same declaration, mutatis mutandis, as that made by the Byelorussian Soviet Socialist Republic, see page 9.]

UNITED KINGDOM OF GREAT BRITAIN AND NORTHERN IRELAND

[Original: English]

Upon signature

First, the Government of the United Kingdom declare their understanding that, by virtue of Article 103 of the Charter of the United Nations, in the event of any conflict between their obligations under article 1 of the Covenant and their obligations under the Charter (in particular, under Articles 1, 2 and 73 thereof) their obligations under the Charter shall prevail.

Secondly, the Government of the United Kingdom declare that:

(a) In relation to article 14 of the Covenant, they must reserve the right not to apply, or not to apply in full, the guarantee of free legal assistance contained in subparagraph (d) of paragraph 3 in so far as the shortage of legal practitioners and other considerations render the application of this guarantee in British Honduras, Fiji and St. Helena impossible;

(b) In relation to article 23 of the Covenant, they must reserve the right not to apply the first sentence of paragraph 4 in so far as it concerns any inequality which may arise from the operation of the law of domicile;

(c) In relation to article 25 of the Covenant, they must reserve the right not to apply:

(i) Subparagraph (b) in so far as it may require the establishment of an elected legislature in Hong Kong and the introduction of equal suffrage, as between different electoral rolls, for elections in Fiji; and

(ii) Subparagraph (c) in so far as it applies to jury service in the Isle of Man and to the employment of married women in the Civil Service of Northern Ireland, Fiji, and Hong Kong.

Lastly, the Government of the United Kingdom declare that the provisions of the Covenant shall not apply to Southern Rhodesia unless and until they inform the Secretary-General of the United Nations that they are in a position to ensure that the obligations imposed by the Covenant in respect of that territory can be fully implemented.

Upon ratification

Firstly the Government of the United Kingdom maintain their declaration in respect of article 1 made at the time of signature of the Covenant.

The Government of the United Kingdom reserve the right to apply to members of and persons serving with the armed forces of the Crown and to persons lawfully detained in penal establishments of whatever character such laws and procedures as they may from time to time deem to be necessary for the preservation of service and custodial discipline and their acceptance of the provisions of the Covenant is subject to such restrictions as may for these purposes from time to time be authorized by law.

Where at any time there is a lack of suitable prison facilities or where the mixing of adults and juveniles is deemed to be mutually beneficial, the Government of the United Kingdom reserve the right not to apply article 10, paragraphs 2 (b) and 3, so far as those provisions require juveniles who are detained to be accommodated separately from adults, and not to apply article 10, paragraph 2 (a), in Gibraltar, Montserrat and the Turks and Caicos Islands in so far as it requires segregation of accused and convicted persons.

The Government of the United Kingdom reserve the right not to apply article 11 in Jersey.

The Government of the United Kingdom reserve the right to interpret the provisions of article 12, paragraph 1, relating to the territory of a State as applying separately to each of the territories comprising the United Kingdom and its Dependencies.

The Government of the United Kingdom reserve the right to continue to apply such immigration legislation governing entry into, stay in the departure from the United Kingdom as they may deem necessary from time to time and accordingly, their acceptance of article 12, paragraph 4, and of the other provisions of the Covenant is subject to the provisions of any such legislation as regards persons not at the time having the right under the law of the United Kingdom to enter and remain in the United Kingdom. The United Kingdom also reserves a similar right in regard to each of its dependent territories.

The Government of the United Kingdom reserve the right not to apply article 13 in Hong Kong in so far as it confers a right of review of a decision to deport an alien and a right to be represented for this purpose before the competent authority.

The Government of the United Kingdom reserve the right not to apply or not to apply in full the guarantee of free legal assistance in subparagraph (d) of paragraph 3 of article 14 in so far as the shortage of legal practitioners renders the application of this guarantee impossible in the British Virgin Islands, the Cayman Islands, the Falkland Islands, the Gilbert Islands, the Pitcairn Islands Group, St. Helena and Dependencies and Tuvalu.

The Government of the United Kingdom interpret article 20 consistently with the rights conferred by articles 19 and 21 of the Covenant and having legislated in matters of practical concern in the interests of public order (ordre public) reserve the right not to introduce any further legislation. The United Kingdom also reserves a similar right in regard to each of its dependent territories.

The Government of the United Kingdom reserve the right to postpone the application of paragraph 3 of article 23 in regard to a small number of customary marriages in the Solomon Islands.

The Government of the United Kingdom reserve the right to enact such nationality legislation as they may deem necessary from time to time to reserve the acquisition and possession of citizenship under such legislation to those having sufficient connection with the United Kingdom or any of its dependent territories and accordingly their acceptance of article 24, paragraph 3, and of the other provisions of the Covenant is subject to the provisions of any such legislation.

The Government of the United Kingdom reserve the right not to apply subparagraph (b) of article 25 in so far as it may require the establishment of an elected Executive or Legislative Council in Hong Kong and subparagraph (c) of article 25 in so far as it relates to jury service in the Isle of Man.

Lastly, the Government of the United Kingdom declare that the provisions of the Covenant shall not apply to Southern Rhodesia unless and until they inform the Secretary-General of the United Nations that they are in a position to ensure that the obligations imposed by the Covenant in respect of that territory can be fully implemented.

VENEZUELA

[Original: Spanish]

Upon ratification

Article 60, paragraph 5, of the Constitution of the Republic of Venezuela establishes that: "No person shall be convicted in a criminal trial unless he has first been personally notified of the charges and heard in the manner prescribed by law. Persons accused of an offence against the res publica may be tried in absentia, with the guarantees and in the manner prescribed by law". Venezuela is making this reservation because article 14, paragraph 3 (d), of the Covenant makes no provision for persons accused of an offence against the res publica to be tried in absentia.

VIET NAM

[Original: Vietnamese]

Upon accession

The Government of the Socialist Republic of Viet Nam deems it necessary to declare that the provisions of article 48, paragraph 1, of the International Covenant on Civil and Political Rights, and article 26, paragraph 1, of the International Covenant on Economic, Social and Cultural Rights, under which a number of States are deprived of the opportunity to become parties to the Covenants, are of a discriminatory nature. The Government of the Socialist Republic of Viet Nam considers that the Covenants, in accordance with the principle of sovereign equality of States, should be open for participation by all States without any discrimination or limitation.

YEMEN

[Original: Arabic]

Upon accession

The accession of the People's Democratic Republic of Yemen to this Covenant shall in no way signify recognition of Israel or serve as grounds for the establishment of relations of any sort with Israel.

C. Notifications of withdrawal of certain reservations and declarations ***

AUSTRALIA

[Original: English]
[6 November 1984]

Withdrawal of certain reservations and declarations

... The Government of Australia notifies the Secretary-General of its decision to withdraw the reservations and declarations made upon ratification with the exception of the following reservations:

Article 10

"In relation to paragraph 2 (a) the principle of segregation is accepted as an objective to be achieved progressively. In relation to paragraphs 2 (b) and 3 (second sentence) the obligation to segregate is accepted only to the extent that such segregation is considered by the responsible authorities to be beneficial to the juveniles or adults concerned."

*** For the text of the reservations and declarations made by Governments upon ratification, see section B above.

Article 14

"Australia makes the reservation that the provision of compensation for miscarriage of justice in the circumstances contemplated in paragraph 6 of article 14 may be by administrative procedures rather than pursuant to specific legal provision."

Article 20

"Australia interprets the rights provided for by articles 19, 21 and 22 as consistent with article 20; accordingly, the Commonwealth and the constituent States, having legislated with respect to the subject matter of the article in matters of practical concern in the interests of public order (*ordre public*), the right is reserved not to introduce any further legislative provision on these matters."

Declaration

"Australia has a federal constitutional system in which legislative, executive and judicial powers are shared or distributed between the Commonwealth and the constituent States. The implementation of the treaty throughout Australia will be effected by the Commonwealth, State and Territory authorities having regard to their respective constitutional powers and arrangements concerning their exercise."

FINLAND

[Original: English]
[29 March 1985]

Withdrawal of some reservations made upon ratification

The Government of Finland notified the Secretary-General of its decision to withdraw the following reservations made upon ratification:

"3. With respect to article 13 of the Covenant, Finland declares that the article does not correspond to the present Finnish legislation regarding an alien's right to be heard or lodge a complaint in respect of a decision concerning his expulsion.

"4. With respect to article 14, paragraph 1, of the Covenant, Finland declares that under Finnish law a sentence can be declared secret if its publication could be an affront to morals or endanger national security."

The notification specifies that the withdrawal was effected because the relevant provisions of Finnish legislation have been amended to correspond fully to articles 13 and 14, paragraph 1, of the Covenant.

The said withdrawal took effect on 29 March 1985, the date of receipt of the notification.

[Original: English]
[26 July 1990]

Withdrawal of some reservations made upon ratification

The Government of Finland notified the Secretary-General of its decision to withdraw the following reservations made upon ratification:

"1. With respect to article 9, paragraph 3, of the Covenant Finland declares that according to the present Finnish legislation the administrative authorities may take decisions concerning arrest or imprisonment, in which event the case is taken up for decision in court only after a certain time lapse;

"5. With respect to article 14, paragraph 3 (d), of the Covenant, Finland declares that the contents of this paragraph do not correspond to the present legislation in Finland inasmuch as it is a question of the defendant's absolute right to have legal assistance already at the stage of preliminary investigations."

FRANCE

[Original: French]
[22 March 1988]

Withdrawal of a reservation made upon accession

The Government of France notified the Secretary-General of its decision to withdraw the following reservation, made upon accession:

"However, the Government of the Republic enters a reservation concerning article 19 which cannot derogate from the monopoly of the French radio and television broadcasting system."

The said withdrawal took effect on 22 March 1988, the date of receipt of the notification.

NETHERLANDS

[Original: English]
[20 December 1983]

Withdrawal of a reservation made by the Netherlands upon ratification

The Government of the Netherlands notified the Secretary-General of its decision to withdraw the reservation it had made upon ratification with regard to article 25 (c) of the Covenant (to the effect that the Netherlands did not accept that provision in the case of the Netherlands Antilles).

NORWAY

[Original: English]
[12 December 1979]

Withdrawal of a reservation

In a notification received by the Secretary-General on 12 December 1979, the Government of Norway withdrew the reservation formulated in respect of article 6, paragraph 4.

REPUBLIC OF KOREA

[Original: Korean]
[15 March 1991]

The Government of the Republic of Korea notified the Secretary-General of its decision to withdraw the reservation to paragraph 4 of article 23, made upon accession.

D. Objections and declarations concerning certain reservations and declarations ****

(Unless otherwise indicated, the objections were made upon ratification or accession)

ARGENTINA

[Original: Spanish]
[3 October 1983]

[The Government of Argentina makes a] formal objection to the [declaration] of territorial extension issued by the United Kingdom with regard to the Malvinas Islands (and dependencies), which that country is illegally occupying and refers to as the "Falkland Islands".

The Argentine Republic rejects and considers null and void the [said declaration] of territorial extension.

BELGIUM

[Original: French]
[6 November 1984]

[The Belgian Government] wishes to observe that the sphere of application of article 11 is particularly restricted. In fact, article 11 prohibits imprisonment only when there is no reason for resorting to it other than the fact that the debtor is unable to fulfil a contractual obligation.

**** For the text of the declarations or reservations referred to in this section, see section B above.

Imprisonment is not incompatible with article 11 when there are other reasons for imposing this penalty, for example when the debtor, by acting in bad faith or through fraudulent manoeuvres, has placed himself in the position of being unable to fulfil his obligations. This interpretation of article 11 can be confirmed by reference to the *travaux préparatoires* (see document A/2929 of 1 July 1955).

After studying the explanations provided by the Congo concerning its reservations, [the Belgian Government] has provisionally concluded that this reservation is unnecessary. It is its understanding that the Congolese legislation authorizes imprisonment for debt when other means of enforcement have failed when the amount due exceeds 20,000 CFA francs and when the debtor, between 18 and 60 years of age, makes himself insolvent in bad faith. The latter condition is sufficient to show that there is no contradiction between the Congolese legislation and the letter and the spirit of article 11 of the Covenant.

By virtue of article 4, paragraph 2, of the aforementioned Covenant, article 11 is excluded from the sphere of application of the rule which states that in the event of an exceptional public emergency, the States parties to the Covenant may, in certain conditions, take measures derogating from their obligations under the Covenant. Article 11 is one of the articles containing a provision from which no derogation is permitted in any circumstances. Any reservation concerning that article would destroy its effects and would therefore be in contradiction with the letter and the spirit of the Covenant.

Consequently, and without prejudice to its firm belief that Congolese law is in complete conformity with the provisions of article 11 of the Covenant, [the Belgian Government] fears that the reservation made by the Congo may, by reason of its very principle, constitute a precedent which might have considerable effects at the international level.

[The Belgian Government] therefore hopes that this reservation will be withdrawn and, as a precautionary measure, wishes to raise an objection to that reservation.

CZECH AND SLOVAK FEDERAL REPUBLIC

[Original: English]
[7 June 1991]

The Government of the Czech and Slovak Federal Republic considers the reservations entered by the Government of the Republic of Korea to the provisions of paragraphs 5 and 7 of article 14 and article 22 of the International Covenant on Civil and Political Rights as incompatible with the object and purpose of the Covenant. In the opinion of the Czechoslovak Government these reservations are in contradiction to the generally recognized principle of international law according to which a State cannot invoke the provisions of its own internal law as justificiation for its failure to perform a treaty.

0043

Therefore, the Czech and Slovak Federal Republic does not recognize these reservations as valid. Nevertheless the present declaration will not be deemed to be an obstacle to the entry into force of the Covenant between the Czech and Slovak Federal Republic and the Republic of Korea.

FRANCE

[Original: French]
[4 November 1980]

The Government of the Republic takes objection to the reservation entered by the Government of the Republic of India to article 1 of the International Covenant on Civil and Political Rights, as this reservation attaches conditions not provided for by the Charter of the United Nations to the exercise of the right of self-determination. The present declaration will not be deemed to be an obstacle to the entry into force of the Covenant between the French Republic and the Republic of India.

GERMANY

[Original: English]
[15 August 1980]

The Government of the Federal Republic of Germany strongly objects, ... to the declaration made by the Republic of India in respect of article 1 of the International Covenant on Economic, Social and Cultural Rights and of article 1 of the International Covenant on Civil and Political Rights.

The right of self-determination as enshrined in the Charter of the United Nations and as embodied in the Covenants applies to all peoples and not only to those under foreign domination. All peoples, therefore, have the inalienable right freely to determine their political status and freely to pursue their economic, social and cultural development. The Federal Government cannot consider as valid any interpretation of the right of self-determination which is contrary to the clear language of the provisions in question. It moreover considers that any limitation of their applicability to all nations is incompatible with the object and purpose of the Covenants.

[21 April 1982]

The Government of the Federal Republic of Germany objects to [reservation (i) by the Government of Trinidad and Tobago]. In the opinion of the Government of the Federal Republic of Germany it follows from the text and the history of the Covenant that the said reservation is incompatible with the object and purpose of the Covenant.

[Original: German]
[25 October 1990]

The Federal Republic of Germany states the following regarding the declarations made by Algeria upon deposit of its instrument of ratification to the International Covenant of 16 December 1966 on Economic, Social and Cultural Rights and the International Covenant of 16 December 1966 on Civil and Political Rights:

It interprets the declaration under paragraph 2 to mean that the latter is not intended to eliminate the obligation of Algeria to ensure that the rights guaranteed in article 8, paragraph 1, of the International Covenant on Economic, Social and Cultural Rights and in article 22 of the International Covenant on Civil and Political Rights may be restricted only for the reasons mentioned in the said articles and that such restrictions shall be prescribed by law.

It interprets the declaration under paragraph 4 to mean that Algeria, by referring to its domestic legal system, does not intend to restrict its obligation to ensure through appropriate steps equality of rights and responsibilities of spouses as to marriage, during marriage and at its dissolution.

[Original: German]
[24 May 1991]

The Federal Republic of Germany states the following regarding the declaration made by the Republic of Korea upon deposit of its instrument of accession to the International Covenant of 16 December 1966 on Civil and Political Rights:

It interprets the declaration to mean that the Republic of Korea does not intend to restrict its obligations under article 22 by referring to its domestic legal system.

NETHERLANDS

[Original: English]
[12 June 1980]

In the opinion of the Government of the Kingdom of the Netherlands it follows from the text and the history of the Covenant that [reservation (i) by the Government of Trinidad and Tobago] is incompatible with the object and purpose of the Covenant. The Government of the Kingdom of the Netherlands therefore considers the reservation unacceptable and formally raises an objection to it.

[12 January 1981]

The Government of the Kingdom of the Netherlands objects to the declaration made by the Government of the Republic of India in relation to article 1 of the International Covenant on Civil and Political Rights and article 1 of the International Covenant on Economic, Social and Cultural Rights, since the right of self-determination as embodied in the Covenants is conferred upon all peoples. This follows not only from the very language of article 1 common to the two Covenants but as well from the most authoritative statement of the law concerned, i.e. the Declaration on Principles of International Law concerning Friendly Relations and Co-operation among States in accordance with the Charter of the United Nations. Any attempt to limit the scope of this right or to attach conditions not provided for in the relevant instruments would undermine the concept of self-determination itself and would thereby seriously weaken its universally acceptable character.

[17 September 1981]

I. Reservation by Australia regarding articles 2 and 50

The reservation that article 2, paragraphs 2 and 3, and article 50 shall be given effect consistently with and subject to the provisions in article 2, paragraph 2, is acceptable to the Kingdom on the understanding that it will in no way impair Australia's basic obligation under international law, as laid down in article 2, paragraph 1, to respect and to ensure to all individuals within its territory and subject to its jurisdiction the rights recognized in the International Covenant on Civil and Political Rights.

II. Reservation by Australia regarding article 10

The Kingdom is not able to evaluate the implications of the first part of the reservation regarding article 10 on its merits, since Australia has given no further explanation on the laws and lawful arrangements, as referred to in the text of the reservation. In expectation of further clarification by Australia, the Kingdom for the present reserves the right to raise objection to the reservation at a later stage.

III. Reservation by Australia regarding Convicted Persons

The Kingdom finds it difficult, for the same reasons as mentioned in its commentary on the reservation regarding article 10, to accept the declaration by Australia that it reserves the right not to seek amendment of laws now in force in Australia relating to the rights of persons who have been convicted of serious criminal offences. The Kingdom expresses the hope that it will be possible to gain a more detailed insight into the laws now in force in Australia, in order to facilitate a definitive opinion on the extent of this reservation.

[Original: English]
[18 March 1991]

In the opinion of the Government of the Kingdom of the Netherlands, the interpretative declaration concerning article 23, paragraph 4 of the International Covenant on Civil and Political Rights (adopted by the General Assembly of the United Nations on 16 December 1966) must be regarded as a reservation to the Covenant. From the text and history of the Covenant it follows that the reservation with respect to article 23, paragraph 4 made by the Government of Algeria is incompatible with the object and purpose of the Covenant. The Government of the Kingdom of the Netherlands therefore considers the reservation unacceptable and formally raises an objection to it.

[This objection is] not an obstacle to the entry into force of [the Covenant] between the Kingdom of the Netherlands and Algeria.

[Original: English]
[10 June 1991]

In the opinion of the Government of the Kingdom of the Netherlands it follows from the text and the history of the International Covenant on Civil and Political Rights that the reservations with respect to articles 14, paragraphs 5 and 7 and 22 of the Covenant made by the Government of the Republic of Korea are incompatible with the object and purpose of the Covenant. The Government of the Kingdom of the Netherlands therefore considers the reservation unacceptable and formally raises objection to it. This objection is not an obstacle to the entry into force of this Covenant between the Kingdom of the Netherlands and the Republic of Korea.

PORTUGAL

[Original: English]
[26 October 1990]

The Government of Portugal hereby presents its formal objection to the interpretative declarations made by the Government of Algeria upon ratification of the International Covenants on Civil and Political Rights and on Economic, Social and Cultural Rights. The Government of Portugal having examined the contents of the said declarations reached the conclusion that they can be regarded as reservations and therefore should be considered invalid as well as incompatible with the purposes and object of the Covenants.

This objection shall not preclude the entry into force of the Covenants between Portugal and Algeria.

UNITED KINGDOM OF GREAT BRITAIN AND
NORTHERN IRELAND

[Original: English]
[28 February 1985]

The Government of the United Kingdom of Great Britain and Northern Ireland have no doubt as to their right, by notification to the Depositary under the relevant provisions of each of the above treaties, to extend the application of the Covenants in question to the Falkland Islands or to the Falkland Islands Dependencies, as the case may be.

For this reason alone, the Government of the United Kingdom are unable to regard the Argentine communications under reference as having any legal effect.

The Government of the United Kingdom of Great Britain and Northern Ireland rejects the statements made by the Argentine Republic, regarding the Falkland Islands and South Georgia and the South Sandwich Islands, when ratifying the International Covenant on Economic, Social and Cultural Rights and the International Covenant on Civil and Political Rights and when acceding to the Optional Protocol to the latter.

The Government of the United Kingdom of Great Britain and Northern Ireland has no doubt as to British sovereignty over the Falkland Islands and South Georgia and the South Sandwich Islands and its consequent right to extend treaties to those territories.

[Original: English]
[25 May 1991]

The Government of the United Kingdom have noted the statement formulated by the Government of the Republic of Korea on accession, under the title "RESERVATIONS". They are not however able to take a position on these purported reservations in the absence of a sufficient indication of their intended effect, in accordance with the terms of the Vienna Convention on the Law of Treaties and the practice of the Parties to the Covenant. Pending receipt of such an indication, the Government of the United Kingdom reserve their rights under the Covenant in their entirety.

E. Notifications under article 4, paragraph 3, of the Covenant

ALGERIA

[Original: French]
[19 June 1991]

In view of public disturbances and the threat of deterioration of the situation ... a state of siege has been proclaimed, beginning at midnight in the night of 4/5 June 1991, for a period of four months throughout Algerian territory.

The Government of Algeria subsequently specified that these disturbances had been fomented with a view to preventing the general elections to be held on 27 June 1991 and to challenge the ongoing democratic process; and that in view of the insurrectional situation which threatened the stability of the institutions, the security of the people and their property, and the normal operation of the public services, it had been necessary to derogate from the provisions of articles 9 (3), 12 (1), 17, 19 (2) and 21 of the Covenant.

The said state of siege was terminated throughout Algeria on 29 September 1991.

[14 February 1992]

(Dated 13 February 1992)

Issurance of Presidential Decree No. 92-44 of 9 February 1992 declaring a state of emergency throughout the national territory with effect from 9 February 1992 for a duration of 12 months. The notification stipulates that the decree was issued in view of the serious threats to public order and the safety of individuals over the preceding weeks, the growth of such threats during the month of February 1992 and the aggravation of the situation. The establishment of the state of emergency, which is aimed essentially at

0048

restoring public order, protecting the safety of individuals and property and ensuring the normal operation of institutions and public services, does not interfere with the democratic process inasmuch as the exercise of fundamental rights and freedoms continues to be guaranteed.

[24 March 1992]

(Dated 23 March 1992)

Clarification that the state of emergency declared on 9 February 1992 derogates specifically from paragraph 3 of article 9, paragraph 12 of article 12, article 17 and article 21 of the Covenant.

ARGENTINA

[Original: Spanish]
[7 June 1989]

(Dated 7 June 1989)

Proclamation of the state of siege throughout the national territory for a period of 30 days in response to events [attacks and looting of retail shops, vandalism, use of firearms] whose seriousness jeopardizes the effective enjoyment of human rights and fundamental freedoms by the entire community. (Derogation from articles 9 and 21.)

[12 July 1989]

(Dated 11 July 1989)

Termination of the state of siege as from 27 June 1989 throughout the national territory.

BOLIVIA

[Original: Spanish]
[1 October 1985]

(Dated 27 September 1985)

By Supreme Decree No. 21069, the Government of Bolivia declared a temporary state of siege throughout the country, with effect from 18 September 1985.

The notification specifies that the Government of Bolivia has been compelled to declare a temporary state of siege in order to discharge its obligation to ensure the maintenance of the rule of law, the constitutional system, democratic continuity and the safeguarding of the country's institutions and public order, these being essential to the life of the Republic and to the process of economic recovery initiated by the Government so as to save Bolivia from the scourge of hyperinflation, which had come to threaten the very life of the country.

The notification further specifies that the measure was adopted to counter the social unrest which sought to supplant the legitimately constituted authorities by establishing itself as an authority which publicly proclaimed the repudiation of the law and openly called for subversion, and to counter the occupation of State facilities and buildings and the interruption of services which are essential to the normal pursuit of all public activities.

[29 October 1985]

(28 October 1985)

In a complimentary notification dated 28 October 1985, received on 29 October 1985, the Government of Bolivia indicated that the provisions of the Covenant from which it is derogated from concern articles 9, 12 and 21.

[9 January 1986]

(6 January 1986)

On 9 January 1986, the Secretary-General received from the Government of Bolivia a notification dated 6 January 1986, made under article 4 of the above-mentioned Covenant, to the effect that, at the end of the constitutional period of 90 days, the Supreme Government had not found it necessary to prolong the emergency situation and that the guarantees and rights of citizens had been fully restored throughout the national territory, with effect from 19 December 1985 and advising that, accordingly, the provisions of the Covenant were again being implemented in accordance with the stipulations of its relevant articles.

[29 August 1986]

(28 August 1986)

The notification indicates that the state of emergency was proclaimed because of serious political and social disturbances, inter alia: a general strike in Potosi and Druro which paralysed illegally those cities; the hyperinflationary crisis suffered by the country; the need for rehabilitation of the Bolivian mining structures; the subversive activities of the extreme left; the desperate reaction of the drug trafficking mafia in response to the Government's successful campaign of eradication; and in general plans aiming to overthrow the constitutional Government.

[28 November 1986]

(Dated 28 November 1986)

Notification, identical in essence, mutatis mutandis, as that of 9 January 1986; with effect from 29 November 1986.

[17 November 1989]

(Dated 16 November 1989)

Proclamation of a state of siege throughout the Bolivian territory. The notification indicates that this measure was necessary to restore peace which had been seriously breached owing to demands of an economic nature, but with a subversive purpose that would have put an end to the process of economic stabilization. The provisions of the Covenant from which it is derogated from concern articles 9, 12 and 21 of the Covenant.

[22 March 1990]

(Dated 18 March 1990)

Termination of the state of emergency as from 15 February 1990.

CHILE

[Original: Spanish]
[7 September 1976]

Chile signed the Covenant on Civil and Political Rights and ratified it on 10 February 1972. This Covenant entered into force internationally on [23] March 1976.

[Chile] has been under a state of siege for reasons of internal defence since 11 March 1976; the state of siege was legally proclaimed by Legislative Decree No. 1.369.

The proclamation was made in accordance with the constitutional provisions concerning state of siege, which have been in force since 1925, in view of the inescapable duty of the government authorities to preserve public order and the fact that there continue to exist in Chile extremist seditious groups whose aim is to overthrow the established Government.

As a consequence of the proclamation of the state of siege, the rights referred to in articles 9, 12, 13, 19 and 25 (b) of the Covenant on Civil and Political Rights have been restricted in Chile.

Derogation from these rights is expressly authorized by article 4, paragraph 1, of the Covenant.

[14 November 1984]

Under Supreme Decree No. 1.200 of 6 November 1984, the Government declared a state of siege throughout Chilean territory until 4 February 1985, with the prior agreement of the Government Junta and in keeping with the terms of article 40, paragraph 2, and the fifteenth Transitional Provision, (B), (4), of the Constitution of the Republic.

The reasons that have required application of this emergency measure under the Constitution lie in the unprecedented escalation of terrorism, which has recently caused the country the loss of many human lives, a great deal of property, both public and private, and substantial harm to the economy.

The terrorist action itself has been combined with subversive preparations for a general stoppage of the activities of the nation and with a very large number of illegal acts involving a broad range of offences punishable under Chilean criminal law which was already in existence before the present Government.

Under the declaration of the state of siege, the President of the Republic may order the transfer of persons from one place to another within Chilean territory, to urban areas in each instance; house arrest or custody of persons in places which are not prisons or in others which are not intended for the detention or imprisonment of common criminals; and expel persons from Chilean territory. He may, in addition, restrict freedom of movement and prohibit specified persons from entering and leaving the country. Similarly, he may suspend or restrict exercise of the right of assembly and freedom of information and opinion; restrict exercise of the rights of association and trade-union membership and impose censorship on correspondence and communications.

None of the powers conferred by the Constitution on the President of the Republic affects the rights and guarantees set forth in articles 6, 7, 8, 11, 15, 16 and 18 of the Covenant.

Similarly, they do not affect obligations under international law nor do they involve discrimination solely on the ground of race, colour, sex, language, religion or social origin.

The officially proclaimed grave internal disturbances referred to above will require the adoption of measures strictly required by the exigencies of the situation, within the context of the Constitution and the laws of the Republic, in order to restore public order in the country and to ensure that the life of the nation proceeds normally.

Once these essential aims have been achieved, the provisions from which a temporary derogation has been made will become fully operative and the States parties will be informed accordingly.

(Dated 17 June 1985)

... By Supreme Decree No. 795 of 14 June 1985, the Government of Chile, using the powers granted to it by the Political Constitution, has decided to lift the state of siege which was in force in the country ... .

The Government of Chile took this decision after having evaluated the general situation in the country and finding, on the basis of a thorough review of the entire period during which the state of siege was in force, that there had been a considerable decline in the consequences of subversive acts, which had been affecting increasingly broader sectors of national activity and had made it necessary to declare the state of siege in November 1984.

[23 September 1986]

(Dated 16 September 1986)

By Decree No. 1.037, the Government of Chile declared a state of siege throughout the national territory from 8 September to 6 December 1986. The Decree stipulates that its provisions shall remain in force from its publication in the Official Gazette, which took place on 8 September, until 6 December 1986, and for as long as circumstances warrant.

The constitutional basis for such a measure is to be found in articles 39, 40 and 41 of the Constitution of the Republic which, in this connection, provide that "in the event of internal war or unrest, the President of the Republic may, with the approval of Congress, declare all or part of the national territory to be under a state of siege" ... .

The Government of Chile established categorically that this extraordinary measure will be applied for the reasonable period required by the circumstances; its application will not alter the commitment of the Chilean authorities to continue to promote the political and institutional process embodied in the Political Constitution of the State.

With regard to the rights the exercise of which will be affected by the state of siege ... the rights set forth in articles 9, 12, 13 and 19 of the Covenant on Civil and Political Rights will be restricted. The rights set forth in articles 6, 7, 8 (paras. 1 and 2), 11, 15, 16 and 18 of the Covenant will not be affected.

[29 October 1986]

(Dated 28 October 1986)

The Secretary-General received from the Government of Chile a notification dated 28 October 1986, made under article 4 of the Covenant, to the effect that by various Decrees the above-mentioned state of siege had been lifted in the following areas:

By Decree No. 1074 of 26 September 1986, published in Official Gazette No. 22584 of 30 September 1986, in the 11th Region.

By Decree No. 1155 of 16 October 1986, published in Official Gazette No. 32600 of 18 October 1986 in the 12th Region (with the exception of the commune of Punta Arenas), in the Province of Chiloé in the 10th Region, and in the Province of Parinacota in the 1st Region.

[20 November 1986]

(Dated 20 November 1986)

The Secretary-General received from the Government of Chile, on 20 November 1986, a notification made under article 4 of the Covenant, to the effect that the state of siege had also been lifted, on 11 November 1986, in the Provinces of Cardenal Caro in the 6th Region, Arauco in the 8th Region and Palena in the 10th Region.

0053

[29 January 1987]

(Dated 20 January 1987)

The Secretary-General received from the Government of Chile a notification made under article 4 of the Covenant, informing him that the circumstances which had prompted the state of siege had completely changed, and that accordingly the said state of siege had not been renewed and had therefore ceased throughout Chile as of 6 January 1987.

[31 August 1988]

(Dated 31 August 1988)

The Secretary-General received from the Government of Chile a notification, dated 31 August 1988 made under article 4 of the Covenant, which informed him of the termination of the state of emergency and of the state of danger of disturbance of the domestic peace in Chile as from 27 August 1988, pursuant to the provisions of Supreme Decrees Nos. 1197 and 1198, respectively, both of the Ministry of the Interior, thereby bringing to an end all states of exception in the country, which is now in a situation of full legal normality.

COLOMBIA

[Original: Spanish]
[18 July 1980]

The Government, by Decree 2131 of 1976, declared that public order had been disturbed and that all of the national territory was in a state of siege, the requirements of the Constitution having been fulfilled, and that in the face of serious events that disturbed the public peace, it had become necessary to adopt extraordinary measures within the framework of the legal regime provided for in the National Constitution for such situations (art. 121 of the National Constitution).

The events disturbing the public peace that led the President of the Republic to take that decision are a matter of public knowledge. Under the state of siege (art. 121 of the National Constitution) the Government is empowered to suspend, for the duration of the state of siege, those provisions that are incompatible with the maintenance and restoration of public order.

On many occasions the President of the Republic has informed the country of his desire to terminate the state of siege when the necessary circumstances prevail.

It should be observed that, during the state of siege in Colombia, the institutional order has remained unchanged, with the Congress and all public bodies functioning normally. Public freedoms were fully respected during the most recent elections, both the election of the President of the Republic and the election of members of elective bodies.

[11 October 1982]

By Decree No. 1674 of 9 June 1982, the state of siege was terminated on 20 June 1982.

0054

[11 April 1984]

(Dated 30 March 1984)

The Government of Colombia had declared a breach of the peace and a state of siege in the territory of the Departments of Caquetá, Huila, Meta and Cauca in response to the activities in those Departments of armed groups which were seeking to undermine the constitutional system by means of repeated public disturbances.

Further to Decree No. 615, Decrees Nos. 666, 667, 668, 669 and 670 had been enacted on 21 March 1984 to restrict certain freedoms and to take other measures aimed at restoring public order. (For the provisions which were derogated from, see in fine notification of 8 June 1984 hereinafter.)

[8 June 1984]

(Dated 7 May 1984)

The Government of Colombia indicated that it had, through Decree No. 1038 of 1 May 1984, declared a state of siege in the territory of the Republic of Colombia owing to the assassination in April of the Minister of Justice and to recent disturbances of the public order that occurred in the cities of Bogotá, Cali, Barranquilla, Medellín, Acevedo (Department of Santander), Giraldo (Department of Antioquia) and Miraflores (Comisaría of Guaviare).

Pursuant to the above-mentioned Decree No. 1038, the Government had issued Decrees Nos. 1039 and 1040 of 1 May 1984 and Decree No. 1042 of 2 May 1984, restricting certain freedoms and enacting other measures to restore public order. (Following inquiries made by the Secretary-General, in keeping with the purpose of article 4, paragraph 3, of the Covenant, as to which articles of the Covenant were being derogated from, the Government of Colombia, in a communication dated 23 November 1984, which was received by the Secretary-General on that date, indicated that the decrees affected the rights referred to in articles 12 and 21 of the Covenant.)

[12 December 1984]

(Dated 11 December 1984)

Termination of derogation from article 21.

[13 August 1991]

(Dated 9 August 1991)

Termination as of 7 July 1991 of the state of siege and of the measures adopted on 1 and 2 May 1984 which were still in force throughout the national territory.

ECUADOR

[Original: Spanish]
[12 May 1983]

The Government declared the extension of the state of emergency as from 20 to 25 October 1982 by Executive Decree No. 1252 of 20 October 1982 and derogation from article 12, paragraph 1, owing to serious disorders brought about by the suppression of subsidies, and termination of the state of emergency by Executive Decree No. 1274 of 27 October 1982.

[20 March 1984]

Derogation from articles 9, paragraphs 1 and 2; 12, paragraphs 1 and 3; 17; 19, paragraph 2, and 21 in the provinces of Napo and Esmeraldas by Executive Decree No. 2511 of 16 March 1984.

[29 March 1984]

Termination of the state of emergency by Executive Decree No. 2537 of 27 March 1984 owing to destruction and sabotage in the area.

[17 March 1986]

(Dated 14 March 1986)

Proclamation of the state of emergency in the provinces of Pichincha and Manabí. The state of emergency was declared on 14 March 1986 due to the acts of subversion and armed uprising by a high-ranking officer no longer in active service, backed by extremist groups.

The articles of the Covenant being derogated from are 12, 21 and 22, it being understood that no Ecuadorian may be exiled or subjected to restricted residence outside the capitals of the provinces or to a region other than the one in which he lives.

[19 March 1986]

(Dated 18 March 1986)

Termination of the state of emergency. The state of emergency was lifted on 17 March 1986.

[29 October 1987]

(Dated 28 October 1987)

Declaration of a state of national emergency throughout the national territory, effective as of 28 October 1987. (Derogation from articles 9 (1) and (2); 12 (1) and (2); 19 (2); and 21.)

The notification states that this measure was made necessary as a result of an illegal call for a national strike which would lead to acts of vandalism, offences against persons and property and would disrupt the peace of the State and the proper exercise of the civic rights of Equadorians.

[30 October 1987]

Termination of the state of emergency throughout the national territory as from 0 hour on 29 October 1987.

[3 June 1988]

(Dated 1 June 1988)

Declaration of a state of national emergency throughout the national territory, effective as of 9 p.m. on 31 May 1988. (Derogation from articles 9 (1) and (2); 12 (1) and (2); 19 (2); and 21.)

The notification states that this measure is the necessary legal response to the 24 hour strike called for by the United Workers Front, which would result in acts of vandalism, violation of the security of persons and attacks on public and private property.

(Dated 2 June 1988)

Termination of the state of emergency throughout the national territory as from 1 June 1988.

EL SALVADOR

[Original: Spanish]
[14 November 1983]

(Dated 3 November 1983)

The Government has declared an extension for a period of 30 days of the suspension of constitutional guarantees by Legislative Decree No. 329 dated 28 October 1983. The constitutional guarantees have been suspended in accordance with article 175 of the Political Constitution because of disruption of public order.

[24 January 1984]

(Dated 23 January 1984)

1. The provisions of the Covenant from which derogation is made are articles 12 and 19 by Decree No. 329 of 28 August 1983, and article 17 (in respect of interference with correspondence).

2. The constitutional guarantees were first suspended by Decree No. 155 dated 6 March 1980, with further extensions of the suspension for a total of 24 months. Decree No. 155 was modified by Decree No. 999 dated 24 February 1982, which expired on 24 March 1982. By Decree No. 1089

dated 20 April 1982, the Revolutionary Government Junta again suspended the constitutional guarantees. By Legislative Decree No. 7 dated 20 May 1982, the Constituent Assembly extended the suspension for an additional period of 30 days. The said Legislative Decree No. 7 was itself extended several times until the adoption of the above-mentioned Decree No. 329 dated 28 October 1983, which took effect on that date.

3. The reasons for the adoption of the initial suspension decree (No. 155 of 6 March 1980) were the same as for the adoption of the subsequent decrees.

[18 June 1984]

(Dated 14 June 1984)

By Legislative Decree No. 28 of 27 January 1984, the Government of El Salvador introduced a change to the effect that political parties would be permitted to conduct electoral campaigns, and were thus authorized to engage in partisan campaigning and electoral propaganda activities. The said Decree was extended for successive 30-day periods until the promulgation of Decree No. 97 of 17 May 1984, which rescinded the aforementioned change allowing political parties to conduct electoral campaigns.

The provisions of the Covenant from which derogation is made are articles 12, 19, 17 (in respect of interference with correspondence) and 21 and 22. As regards article 22, the suspension refers to the right to association in general, but does not affect the right to join professional associations (the right to form and join trade unions).

[2 August 1985]

(Dated 31 July 1985)

[...] the Government of El Salvador has for successive periods extended martial law by the following legislative decrees: Decrees No. 127 of 21 June 1984, No. 146 of 19 July 1984, No. 175 of 24 August 1984, No. 210 of 18 September 1984, No. 234 of 21 October 1984, No. 261 of 20 November 1984, No. 277 of 14 December 1984, No. 322 of 18 January 1985, No. 335 of 21 February 1985, No. 351 of 14 March 1985, No. 386 of 18 April 1985, No. 10 of 21 May 1985, No. 38 of 13 June 1985, and the most recent, Decree No. 96 of 11 July 1985 which extended the martial law for an additional period of 30 days beyond that date.

The provisions of the Covenant that are thus suspended are those of articles 12, 17 (in respect of interference with correspondence) and 19, paragraph 2.

The notification specifies that the reasons for the suspension of constitutional guarantees continue to be those originally indicated, namely: the need to maintain a climate of peace and tranquility, which had been disturbed through the commission of acts designed to create a state of instability and social unrest which affected the economy and the public peace by persons seeking to obstruct the process of structural change, thus seriously disrupting public order.

[19 December 1989]

(Dated 13 November 1989)

Suspension for a period of 30 days as from 12 November 1990 of various constitutional guarantees. (Derogation from articles 12, 17, 19, 21 and 22 of the Covenant.)

The notification indicates that this measure became necessary owing to the use of terror and violence by the Frente Farabundo Marti to obtain political authority, in complete disregard of previous elections.

ISRAEL

[Original: English]
[3 October 1991]

Since its establishment, the State of Israel has been the victim of continuous threats and attacks on its very existence, as well as on the life and property of its citizens.

These have taken the form of threats of war, of actual armed attacks, and campaigns of terrorism resulting in the murder of and injury to human beings.

In view of the above, the State of Emergency which was proclaimed in May 1948 has remained in force ever since. This situation constitutes a public emergency within the meaning of article 4 (1) of the Covenant.

The Government of Israel has therefore found it necessary, in accordance with the said article 4, to take measures to the extent strictly required by the exigencies of the situation, for the defence of the State and for the protection of life and property, including the exercise of powers of arrest and detention.

In so far as any of these measures are inconsistent with article 9 of the Covenant, Israel thereby derogates from its obligations under that provision.

NICARAGUA

[Original: Spanish]
[4 June 1980]

The Governing Junta for National Reconstruction of the Republic of Nicaragua, by Decree No. 383 of 29 April 1980, rescinded the National Emergency Act promulgated on 22 July 1979 and revoked the state of emergency extended by Decree No. 365 of 11 April 1980.

[14 April 1982]

Suspension of articles 1 to 5, 8, paragraph 3, 10, 12 to 14, 17, 19 to 22, 26 and 27 in accordance with Decree No. 996 of 15 March 1982 (national emergency) from 15 March to 14 April 1982.

Extension to the suspension to 14 May 1982.

[8 June 1982]

Extension of the suspension to 14 June 1982.

[26 August 1982]

Suspension of the above-mentioned articles of the Covenant in accordance with Decree No. 1082 of 26 July 1982 from 26 July 1982 to 26 January 1983.

[14 December 1982]

Extension of the suspension to 30 May 1983.

[8 June 1984]

Extension of the state of emergency for 50 days beginning on 31 May 1984 and derogation from articles 2, paragraph 3, 9, 12, 14, 19, paragraphs 2 and 3, and 21 of the Covenant.

[1 August 1984]

(Dated 10 June 1984)

Extension of the state of emergency until 30 May 1984 by Decree 1255 of 26 May 1984 and derogations from articles 1 to 5, 8, paragraph 3, 9, 10, 12, 13, 14, 19 to 22, 26 and 27.

[22 August 1984]

(Dated 2 August 1984)

Extension of the state of emergency until 20 October 1984 and derogation from articles 2, paragraph 3, 9 and 14 of the Covenant by Legislative Decree No. 1477 of 19 July 1984.

(Dated 9 August 1984)

Derogation from the implementation of articles 2, paragraph 3, 9 and 14 of the Covenant from 6 August to 20 October 1984, in respect of persons committing or suspected of committing the offences referred to in articles 1 and 2 of the Act concerning the Maintenance of Order and Public Security.

[13 November 1985]

(Dated 11 November 1985)

... In accordance with article 4 of the International Covenant on Civil and Political Rights, [the] Government [of Nicaragua] has been obliged, as a result of the foreign aggression to which it is being subjected, to suspend the application of certain of the provisions of the Covenant throughout the national territory, for a period of one year starting on 30 October 1985.

The reasons for this suspension are well known: the Government of the United States of America, against the express will of the majority of the world's Governments and peoples and in violation of the norms of international law, has continued its unjust, unlawful and immoral aggression against the Nicaraguan people and their revolutionary Government.

The political and diplomatic efforts exerted by [the] Government [of Nicaragua], by the nations of the Contadora Group and by other peace-loving countries to change this criminal and aggressive policy of the Government of the United States have all proved fruitless.

United States troops and warships on continuous manoeuvres and deployment in the areas adjacent to Nicaragua offer a constant threat of direct military intervention.

Thousands of patriots have given up their precious and irrecoverable lives in combat, or have been murdered in the defence of the fatherland.

Tens of thousands of families have been forced to abandon their lands and homes; enormous resources have had to be devoted to defence at the expense of consumption, production and civilian investment.

Hundreds of millions of dollars worth of material goods and productive capacity have been destroyed through direct action by bands of mercenaries and sabotage by the United States Central Intelligence Agency. These factors, together with the commercial blockage and the economic crisis in the developing countries, have resulted in a serious deterioration in the living conditions of our people.

The Government of the United States, instead of scaling down its aggression, has in the past few months intensified it, supplying the bands of mercenaries with more and improved weapons so that they can go on committing murder, destroying productive infrastructure through terrorist attacks, in short, bringing more pain, grief, death and economic difficulties to the Nicaraguan people. This intensification of terrorist acts is due in part to the fact that the United States Government has started to distribute to the counter-revolutionary bands the $27 million that was authorized by the United States Congress in June 1985 as "humanitarian aid".

... The following provisions of the Covenant [are suspended] throughout the national territory for the period of one year, starting on 30 October 1985: article 8, paragraph 3; article 9; article 10, except paragraph 1; article 12, paragraphs 2 and 4; article 14, except paragraphs 2 and 5 and subparagraphs (a), (b), (d) and (g) of paragraph 3; article 17; article 19; article 21 and article 22.

Article 2, paragraph 2, remains in force for those rights that have not been suspended, and paragraph 3 of the same remains in force for all those offences which do not affect national security and public order.

[30 January 1987]

(Dated 29 January 1987)

Comandante Daniel Ortega Saavedra, the President of the Republic of Nicaragua, owing to the continuation and escalation of the military, political and economic aggression to which the Nicaraguan Government and people are subjected by the Government of the United States; and by virtue of the powers conferred on him by the Political Constitution of Nicaragua promulgated on 9 January 1987; as from that date has re-established the state of national emergency by Decree No. 245, pursuant to article 185 of the new Constitution of the Republic.

Consequently, in compliance with article 4 (3) of the International Covenant on Civil and Political Rights, the following provisions of the Covenant have been suspended throughout the territory of Nicaragua until 8 January 1988:

Article 2 (3) is suspended in respect of acts which undermine national security and public order and of the rights and guarantees set forth in those provisions of the Covenant which have been suspended;

Article 9, although the recourse referred to in paragraph 4 is suspended solely for offences against national security and public order. Article 12 and article 14 (3) (c); article 17, in so far as it relates to home and correspondence, with the other rights remaining in effect; and articles 19, 21 and 22.

This exceptional measure is aimed at preserving national security and public order and is in force for one year, subject to renewal.

[13 May 1987]

(Dated 8 April 1987)

The Secretary-General received the following notification from the Government of Nicaragua:

A state of national emergency has been established in the Republic of Nicaragua, in accordance with article 4 of the Covenant, under which the following provisions thereof are suspended throughout the territory of Nicaragua for a period of one year, as of 28 February 1987:

Article 2, paragraph 3, in which we draw a distinction between administrative amparo which is suspended in respect of the rights and guarantees provided in the Covenant, which have been suspended, and the remedy of habeas corpus, which is not applicable to offences against national security and public order;

Article 9. It should be understood that the remedy referred to in paragraph 4 is suspended solely in respect of offences against national security and public order;

Article 12, regarding the right of residence, liberty of movement and freedom to enter and leave the country;

Article 14, paragraph (3) (c), regarding the right to be tried without undue delay;

Article 17, in respect of the inviolability of the home and correspondence, with the other rights remaining in effect;

Article 19, paragraphs (1) and (2), regarding the right to hold opinions and freedom of expression.

[8 February 1988]

(Dated 4 February 1988)

On 8 February 1988, the Secretary-General received, in the name of the Government of Nicaragua a notification dated 4 February 1988, made under article 4 of the Covenant, which reads as follows:

By Decree No. 297 of 19 January 1988, the Government of Nicaragua has lifted the state of emergency in force in the country, thus re-establishing the full enjoyment of all rights and guarantees of Nicaraguans laid down in the Constitution of Nicaragua.

With the lifting of the state of emergency, the following rights shall enter into force: the right to strike, assemble and demonstrate; the right to freedom of expression and of movement within the country; and the right to the inviolability of domicile and correspondence.

Despite the continuing unlawful war which the United States of America has imposed on Nicaragua, the Government has decided to lift the state of emergency as a reflection of its unilateral decision to comply fully with the commitments made by the Presidents of the Central American Republics in the agreements signed in Guatemala City on 7 August 1987 and the Declaration signed in Alajuela, Costa Rica, on 16 January 1988.

Also on behalf of peace, by Decree No. 296 of 16 January 1988, the Government repealed Decree/Law No. 1233 of 11 April 1983 on the Anti-Somozan People's Courts, as a result of which the jurisdiction of those courts shall revert to the judicial branch. With this measure, article 159 of the Constitution, which lays down that the courts of Nicaragua shall form a unified system whose highest body is the Supreme Court of Justice, is fully complied with.

Moreover, with a view to facilitating the administration of justice during the emergency created by the aggression imposed on the country, the executive branch empowered the Supreme Court of Justice, by Decrees Nos. 299 and 300 of 20 January 1988, to establish, abolish or combine district and local courts and to establish appellate courts in regions I, V and VI and in special areas I and II, where the war of aggression has particularly taken its toll.

PANAMA

[Original: Spanish]
[12 June 1987]

(Dated 11 June 1987)

On 12 June 1987, the Secretary-General received from the Government of Panama a notification dated 11 June 1987, made under article 4 of the above-mentioned Covenant, to the effect that the Government of Panama had declared a state of emergency throughout the territory of the Republic of Panama.

The notification specified that the state of emergency was declared since, on 9 and 10 June 1987, there were outbreaks of violence, clashes between demonstrators and units of defence forces, and incitement to violence by individuals and political groups resulting in personal injury and considerable material damage. The measure was taken with a view to restoring law and order and safeguarding the life, the dignity and the property of Panamanian nationals and of foreigners living in Panama.

The notification further specified that this exceptional measure will apply as long as reasons for the disruption of law and order remain. The articles of the Covenant being derogated from are articles 12, paragraph 1; 17, with regard only to the inviolability of correspondence; 19 and 21.

[1 July 1987]

(Dated 30 June 1987)

The Secretary-General received a notification from the Government of Panama on 1 July 1987, which informed him that by Legislative Assembly resolution of 30 June 1987 all constitutional guarantees suspended 19 days ago have been reinstated ... . In the text of the resolution reinstating the aforementioned guarantees, the Legislative Assembly stated that "at national level there has been a marked improvement in the situation which prompted the declaration of the state of emergency and the suspension of individual guarantees" and that "the country is now facing foreign aggression through the United States Senate".

PERU

[Original: Spanish]
[22 March 1983]

(Dated 18 March 1983)

First notification:

The Government has declared the extension of the state of emergency in the Provinces of Huanta, La Mar, Cangallo, Víctor Fajardo, Huamanga, in the Department of Ayacucho, Andahuaylas in the Department of Apurímac, and

0064

Angaraes, Tayacaja and Acobamba, in the Department of Huancavelica, for a period of 60 days from the date of the issue of the Supreme Decree No. 003-83-IN of 25 February 1983.

Suspension of the constitutional guarantees provided for in paragraphs 7, 9, 10 and 20 (g) of article 2 of the Political Constitution of Peru, which relate to the inviolability of the home, liberty of movement in the national territory, the right of peaceful assembly and the right to liberty and security of person.

Second notification:

Extension of a state of emergency in the Department of Lima by Supreme Decree No. 005-83-IN of 9 March [1983], and suspension for a period of five days of the constitutional guarantees provided for in paragraphs 9, 10 and 20 (g) of article 2 of the Political Constitution of Peru relating to liberty of movement in the national territory, the right of peaceful assembly and the right to liberty and security of persons.

[4 April 1983]

Suspension of the state of emergency as from 14 March 1983. In a communication received by the Secretary-General on 4 April 1983, the Government of Peru specified that the state of emergency extended by Supreme Decree No. 003-83-IN of 25 February 1983 was originally proclaimed by Supreme Decree No. 026-81-IN of 12 October 1981. It further specified that the provisions of the Covenant from which derogation was made by reason of the proclamation of the state of emergency were articles 9, 12, 17 and 21.

[3 May 1983]

(Dated 27 April 1983)

Extension of derogations for a further 60 days by Supreme Decree No. 014-83-IN of 22 April 1983.

[2 June 1983]

(Dated 28 May 1983)

Extension of the state of emergency for a period of three days in Lima and in the Province of Callao by Supreme Decree No. 020-83 of 25 May 1983.

(Dated 31 May 1983)

Extension of the state of emergency for a period of 60 days throughout the Republic by Supreme Decree No. 022-83 of 30 May 1984.

0065

[9 August 1983]

(Dated 8 August 1983)

Further extension of the state of emergency in its national territory for 60 days by Supreme Decree No. 036-83 of 2 August 1983.

[29 September 1983]

Termination as from 9 September 1983 of the state of emergency and of the derogations with the exceptions of the Departments of Huancavelica, Ayacucho and Apurímac.

[9 November 1983]

(Dated 3 November 1983)

Extension of the state of emergency in the Provinces of Huanta, La Mar, Cangallo, Víctor Fajardo y Huamanga (Department of Ayacucho), Andahuaylas (Department of Apurímac), Angaraes, Tayacaja and Acobamba (Department of Huancavelica) by Supreme Decree No. 054-83 of 22 October 1983.

[20 December 1983]

(Dated 19 December 1983)

Extension of the state of emergency in the Provinces of Lucanas and Ayacucho (department of Ayacucho) and the Province of Huancavelica (Department of Huancavelica) by Supreme Decree No. 061-83-IN of 6 December 1983.

[13 February 1984]

(Dated 31 January 1984)

Extension of the state of emergency for 60 days in the Provinces of Huanta, La Mar, Cangallo, Víctor Fajardo y Huamanga (Department of Ayacucho), Andahuaylas (Department of Apurímac), Angaraes, Tayacaja and Acobamba (Department of Huancavelica), and in the Districts of Querobamba and Cabana (Department of Ayacucho), and throughout the Provinces of Lucanas (Department of Ayacucho) and Huancavelica (Department of Huancavelica) by Supreme Decree No. 061-83-IN of 6 December 1983.

[28 March 1984]

(Dated 26 March 1984)

Extension of state of emergency throughout Peru from 21 to 23 March 1984.

[14 May 1984]

(Dated 19 April 1984)

Continuation of the state of emergency for a period of 60 days in the Provinces of Huanta, La Mar, Cangallo, Víctor Fajardo, Huamanga and Lucanas (Department of Ayacucho); Andahuaylas and Chincheros (department of Apurímac); Angaraes, Tayacaja, Acobamba, Huancavelica and Castrovirreyna (Department of Huancavelica) by Decree No. 031-84-IN of 17 April 1984 and derogations from articles 9, 12, 17 and 21 of the Covenant.

[18 June 1984]

(Dated 15 June 1984)

Declaration of a state of emergency for a period of 30 days, starting from 8 June 1984, in the whole of the territory of the Republic of Peru and derogations from articles 9, 12, 17 and 21 of the Covenant.

[9 August 1984]

(Dated 12 July 1984)

Extension of the state of emergency as at 8 July 1984, for a period of 30 days, throughout the territory of the Republic of Peru and derogations from articles 9, 12, 17 and 21.

[14 August 1984]

Extension of the state of emergency throughout Peru for a period of 60 days, starting from 7 August 1984 and extension of the said derogations.

[25 October 1984]

(Dated 22 October 1984)

By Supreme Decree No. 052-84-IN of 5 October 1984, termination of the state of emergency in the territory of the Republic excepting the following provinces and departments, where the state of emergency has been extended for 60 days as of 5 October 1984:

- Department of Huánuco; Province of Mariscal Cáceres (Department of San Martín); Provinces of Huanta, La Mar, Cangallo, Víctor Fajardo, Huamanga and Lucanas (Department of Ayacucho); Provinces of Andahuaylas and Chincheros (Department of Apurímac); Provinces of Angaraes, Tayacaja, Acobamba, Huancavelica and Castrovirreyna (Department of Huancavelica), and derogations from articles 9, 12, 17 and 21 of the Covenant in the above-mentioned departments and provinces.

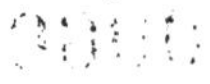

[21 December 1984]

(Dated 19 December 1984)

By Supreme Decree No. 063-84-IN, the Government of Peru had extended the state of emergency as at 3 December 1984, for a period of 60 days, in the Departments of Huánuco and San Martín and the Province of Mariscal Cáceres. The said extension had been declared owing to the continued terrorist acts of violence and sabotage in those regions and, as a result, the Government of Peru continued to derogate from articles 9, 12, 17 and 21 of the Covenant.

(Dated 21 December 1984)

By Supreme Decree No. 065-84-IN, the Government of Peru had found it necessary to extend the state of emergency for a period of 60 days, starting from 7 December 1984, in the following provinces:

Department of Ayacucho

- Cangallo, Huamanga, Huanta, La Mar, Lucanas, Víctor Fajardo, Huancasancos and Vilcashuamán;

Department of Huancavelica

- Acobamba, Angaraes, Castrovirreyna, Huancavelica, Tayacaja and Huaytará;

Department of Apurímac

- Andahuaylas and Chincheros.

The notification specifies that the extension of the state of emergency was decided because of the continued terrorist acts of violence and sabotage in the said provinces and that it was necessary to continue to derogate from articles 9, 12, 17 and 21 of the Covenant.

[8 February 1985]

(Dated 7 February 1985)

By Supreme Decree No. 001-85-IN, extension of the state of emergency as of 3 February 1985 in the Department of San Martín, including the Province of Tocache and excluding the Province of Mariscal Cáceres, and Huánuco, excluding the Provinces of Puerto Inca and Pachitea. The said extension had been declared owing to the continued terrorist acts of violence and sabotage in those regions and, as a result, the Government of Peru continued to derogate from articles 9, 12, 17 and 21 of the Covenant.

0068

[12 April 1985]

(Dated 9 April 1985)

By Supreme Decree No. 012-85-IN, extension of the state of emergency as of 1 April 1985 in the Department of San Martín, including the Province of Tocache, and in the Department of Huánuco, except in the Provinces of Puerto Inca and Pachitea.

The said extension has been declared owing to the continued terrorist acts of violence and sabotage in those regions and, as a result, the Government of Peru continued to derogate from articles 9, 12, 17 and 21 of the Covenant.

[18 June 1985]

(14 June 1985)

By Supreme Decree No. 020-85-IN, the state of emergency in the Province of Pasco (Department of Pasco) has been declared for a period of 60 days, starting from 10 May 1985.

By Supreme Decree No. 021-85-IN, the state of emergency in the Department of San Martín, including the Province of Tocache and in the Department of Huánuco, except in the Provinces of Puerto Inca and Pachitea, has been extended for a period of 60 days, starting from 1 June 1985.

By Supreme Decree No. 022-85-IN, the state of emergency in the Province of Daniel Alcides Carrión (Department of Pasco) has been extended for a period of 60 days, starting from 4 June 1985.

By Supreme Decree No. 023-85-IN, the state of emergency has been extended for a period of 60 days starting from 5 June 1985 in the following provinces:

<u>Department of Ayacucho</u>

- Cangallo, Huamanga, Huanta, La Mar, Lucanas, Víctor Fajardo, Huancasancos and Vilcashuamán;

<u>Department of Huancavelica</u>

- Acobamba, Angaraes, Castrovirreyna, Huancavelica, Tayacaja, Huaytará and Churcampa;

<u>Department of Apurímac</u>

- Andahuaylas and Chincheros

The above-mentioned notifications specify that the state of emergency had been declared or extended as indicated above owing to the continued terrorist acts of violence and sabotage.

As a result, articles 9, 12, 17 and 21 of the Covenant are being or are still derogated from in the regions in question for the said periods of time.

0069

[24 July 1985]

(Dated 23 July 1985)

By Supreme Decree No. 031-85, the state of emergency in the Province of Pasco (Department of Pasco) has been extended for a period of 60 days, starting from 10 July 1985.

[6 August 1985]

(Dated 31 July 1985)

By Supreme Decree No. 033-85-IN, the state of emergency in the Province of Yauli (Department of Junín) has been declared for a period of 12 days, starting from 19 July 1985.

[12 August 1985]

(Dated 12 August 1985)

By Supreme Decree No. 042-85-IN, the state of emergency has been extended for a period of 60 days starting from 6 August 1985 in the following provinces and departments:

(i) Province of Tocache (Department of San Martín);

(ii) Department of Huánuco, except the Provinces of Puerto Inca and Pachitea;

(iii) Province of Daniel Alcides Carrión (Department of Pasco);

(iv) Provinces of Cangallo, Huamanga, Huanta, La Mar, Lucanas, Víctor Fajardo, Huancasancos and Vilcashuamán (Department of Ayacucho);

(v) Provinces of Acobamba, Angaraes, Castrovirreyna, Huancavelica, Andahuaylas and Chincheros (Department of Apurímac).

As a result, articles 9, 12, 17 and 21 of the Convention are being or are still derogated from in the regions in question for the said periods.

[13 December 1985]

(Dated 11 December 1985)

Extension of the state of emergency for a period of 60 days in the following provinces, in accordance with Decree No. 052-85-IN, as of 5 December 1985 (derogation from articles 9, 12, 17 and 21 of the Covenant), owing to continued terrorist actions in the said regions:

- Provinces of Cangallo, Huamanga, Huanta, La Mar, Víctor Fajardo, Huancasancos and Vilcashuamán (Department of Ayacucho);

- Provinces of Acobamba, Angaraes, Castrovirreyna, Huancavelica, Tayacaja, Huaytará and Churcampe (Department of Huancavelica);
- Provinces of Huaycabamba, Huamalíes, Dos de Mayo and Ambo (Department of Huánuco);
- Province of Chincheros (Department of Apurímac).

[13 December 1985]

(Dated 11 December 1985)

On 5 December 1985, the Government of Peru terminated the state of emergency in the following areas:

Department of Ayacucho (Province of Lucanas);

Department of Apurímac (Province of Andahuaylas);

Department of San Martín (Province of Tocache);

Department of Huánuco (Provinces of Marañón, Leoncio Prado and Huánuco);

Department of Pasco (Province of Daniel Alcides Carrión).

[21 February 1986]

(Dated 14 February 1986)

By Supreme Decree No. 001-86, the Government of Peru has extended the state of emergency as of 5 February 1986 for a period of 60 days in the following provinces:

Department of Ayacucho (Provinces of Cangallo, Huamanga, Huanta, La Mar, Víctor Fajardo, Huancasancos and Vilcashuamán);

Department of Huancavelica (Provinces of Acobamba, Castrovirreyna, Huancavelica, Tayacaja, Huaytará, Churcampa and Angaraes);

Department of Huánuco (Provinces of Huaycabamba, Huamalíes, Dos de Mayo and Ambo);

Department of Apurímac (Province of Chincheros).

By Supreme Decree No. 002-86, the Government of Peru has declared a state of emergency in the city of Lima and the Constitutional Province of Callao for a period of 60 days starting from 7 February 1986.

The notifications specify that the state of emergency has been extended or declared as indicated above owing to the continued or increased terrorist acts of violence and sabotage.

As a result, articles 9, 12, 17 and 21 of the Covenant are being or are still derogated from in the regions in question for the said periods of time.

[24 April 1986]

(Dated 14 April 1986)

By Supreme Decree No. 004-86-IN, the Government of Peru has extended the state of emergency as of 3 April 1986 for a period of 60 days in the following provinces:

Department of Ayacucho (Provinces of Cangallo, Huamanga, Huanta, La Mar, Víctor Fajardo, Huancasancos and Vilcashuamán);

Department of Huancavelica (Provinces of Acobamba, Angaraes, Castrovirreyna, Huancavelica, Tayacaja, Huaytará and Churcampa);

Department of Apurímac (Province of Chincheros);

Department of Huánuco (Provinces of Huaycabamba, Huamalíes, Dos de Mayo and Ambo).

By Supreme Decree No.005-86-IN, the Government of Peru has extended the state of emergency in the city of Lima and the Constitutional Province of Callao for a period of 60 days as of 3 April 1986.

The notifications specify that the said extensions have been declared as indicated above owing to the continued or increased terrorist acts of violence and sabotage.

As a result, articles 9, 12 17 and 21 of the Covenant continue to be derogated from in the regions in question for the said periods of time.

[5, 9 and 23 June 1986]

(Dated, respectively, 4, 6 and 20 June 1986)

I

The Government of Peru has declared or extended a state of emergency as follows:

By Supreme Decree No. 012-86-IN, the state of emergency in the city of Lima and the Constitutional Province of Callao has been extended for a period of 60 days, starting from 2 June 1986.

II

By Supreme Decree No. 013-86-IN, the state of emergency has been extended for a period of 60 days, starting from 4 June 1986 in the following provinces:

Department of Ayacucho (Provinces of Cangallo, Huamanga, Huanta, La Mar, Víctor Fajardo, Huancasancos and Vilcashuamán);

Department of Huancavelica (Provinces of Acobamba, Angaraes, Castrovirreyna, Huancavelica, Tayacaja, Huaytará and Churcampa);

Department of Apurímac (Province of Chincheros);

Department of Huánuco (Provinces of Huaycabamba, Huamalíes, Dos de Mayo and Ambo).

III

By Supreme Decree No. 015-86-IN, a state of emergency has been declared for a period of 60 days, starting from 18 June 1986, in the Provinces of Daniel Alcides Carrión and Pasco (Department of Pasco).

[5 August 1986]

(30 July 1986)

By a notification dated 30 July 1986 and received on 5 August 1986, the Government of Peru specified that the said extensions and declaration of a state of emergency had been declared owing to the continuation or occurrence of terrorist acts and sabotage.

As a result, articles 9, 12, 17 and 21 of the Covenant are being or still being derogated from in the regions in question for the said periods of time.

[6 August 1986]

(Dated 5 August 1986)

By Supreme Decree No. 019-86-IN, extension of the state of emergency in the Province of Lima and the Constitutional Province of Callao for a period of 30 days, starting from 2 August 1986.

[8 August 1986]

(Dated 7 August 1986)

By Supreme Decree No. 020-86-IN, for a period of 60 days starting from 3 August 1986, extension of the state of emergency in the same provinces as under notification of 18 June 1985 and the Department of Huánuco (Province of Huaycabamba, Huamalíes, Dos de Mayo and Ambo).

[25 August 1986]

(Dated 19 August 1986)

By Supreme Decree No. 023-86-IN, extension of the state of siege in the Provinces of Daniel Alcides Carrión and Pasco (Department of Pasco) for a period of 60 days, starting from 19 August 1986.

[5 September 1986]

(Dated 4 September 1986)

By Supreme Decree No. 026-86-IN the Government of Peru has extended the state of emergency in the Constitutional Province of Callao for a period of 60 days as of 1 September 1986.

[8 October 1986]

(Dated 3 October 1986)

By Supreme Decree No. 029-86-IN, extension of the state of emergency for a period of 60 days, starting on 1 October 1986, in the same provinces as those indicated under the notification of 8 August 1986 (see above).

[22 October and 5 November 1986]

(Dated 17 October and 3 November 1986)

In two notifications to the Secretary-General, the Government of Peru extended a state of emergency as follows:

By Supreme Decree No. 03-86-IN, in the Provinces of Daniel Alcides Carrión and Pasco (Department of Pasco) for a period of 60 days, starting from 16 October 1986.

By Supreme Decree No. 032-86-IN, in the Province of Lima and the Constitutional Province of Callao for a period of 60 days, starting from 29 October 1986.

[18 December 1986]

(Dated 16 December 1986)

By Supreme Decree No. 036-86-IN the Government of Peru extended the state of emergency in the Provinces of Daniel Alcides Carrión and Pasco for a period of 60 days as of 14 December 1986.

[2 February 1987]

(Dated 30 January 1987)

Extension of the state of emergency for a period of 60 days as from 25 January 1987 in the Provinces of Lima and Callao.

(Dated 2 February 1987)

Extension of the state of emergency for a period of 60 days as from 29 January 1987 in the Provinces stated in notification of 13 December 1985.

Both notifications specify that the said extensions for the state of emergency had been declared owing to the continued terrorist acts of violence and sabotage.

[4 March 1987]

(Dated 23 February 1987)

Extension of state of emergency in the Provinces of Daniel Alcides Carrión and Pasco for a period of 60 days as of 13 February 1987.

[3 April 1987]

(Dated 2 April 1987)

The Government of Peru extended the state of emergency for a period of 60 days in the following Provinces:

Department of Ayacucho (Provinces of Cangallo, Huamanga, Huanta, La Mar, Víctor Fajardo, Huancasancos, Vilcashuaman and Sucre);

Department of Apurímac (Province of Chincheros); and

Department of Huánuco (Province of Ambo and District of Monzón of the Province of Huamalíes).

[1 and 8 June 1987]

(Dated 26 May 1987)

I

Extension of the state of emergency in the Provinces of Lima and Callao for a period of 30 days as of 26 May 1987.

II

Extension of the state of emergency for a period of 60 days, as of 26 May 1987, in the following Provinces:

Department of Ayacucho (Provinces of Cangallo, Huamanga, Huanta, La Mar, Víctor Fajardo, Huacasancos, Vilcashuamán and Sucre);

Department of Huancavelica (Provinces of Acobamba, Angaraes, Castrovirreyna, Huancavelica, Tayacaja, Huaytará and Churcampa);

Department of Apurímac (Provinces of Chincheros);

Department of Huánuco (Province of Ambo and District of Monzón of the Province of Humalíes).

[18 June 1987]

(Dated 8 June 1987)

Extension of the state of emergency in the Provinces of Daniel Alcides Carrión and Pasco for a period of 60 days as of 8 June 1987.

[24 June and 23 July 1987]

(Dated 24 June and 20 July 1987)

Notifications that the state of emergency in the Provinces of Lima and Callao had been extended for a period of 30 days, starting from 20 June 1987 and 20 July 1987.

[23 July 1987]

(Dated 20 July 1987)

The Government of Peru declared a state of emergency for a period of 60 days, starting from 14 July 1987, in the following areas:

Province of Leoncio Prado and District of Cholón;

Department of Huánuco (Province of Marañón);

Department of San Martín (Provinces of Mariscal Cáceres and Tocache);

The notification specified that the state of emergency had been declared owing to the continuing acts of terrorism and sabotage in those regions.

[4 August 1987]

(Dated 25 July 1987)

The Government of Peru declared a state of emergency for a period of 60 days, starting from 25 July 1987, in the following areas:

Department of Ayacucho (Provinces of Cangallo, Huamanga, Huanta, La Mar, Víctor Fajardo, Huancasancos, Vilcashuamán and Sucre);

Department of Huancavelica (Provinces of Acobamba, Angaraes, Castrovirreyna, Huancavelica, Tayacaja, Huaytara and Churcampa);

Department of Apurímac (Province of Chincheros);

Province of Ambo and District of Monzón of the Province of Humalíes.

The notification specified that the state of emergency had been declared owing to the continuing acts of terrorism and sabotage in those regions.

[13 and 27 August 1987]

(Dated 7 and 19 August 1987)

The Government of Peru, through two notifications, declared or extended a state of emergency as follows:

A state of emergency in the Provinces of Daniel Alcides Carrión and Pasco (Department of Pasco) had been declared for a period of 60 days, starting from 7 August 1987.

The state of emergency in the Provinces of Lima and Callao had been extended for a period of 30 days, starting from 19 August 1987.

[23 September 1987]

(Dated 13 and 21 September 1987)

I

Extension of state of emergency for a period of 60 days, starting on 13 September 1987, in the following areas:

Department of Huánuco (Province of Leoncio Prado and District of Chólon of the Province of Marañón);

Department of San Martín (Provinces of Mariscal Cáceres and Tocache).

II

Extension of state of emergency in the Provinces of Lima and Callao for a period of 30 days starting on 21 September 1987.

[9 October 1987]

(Dated 3 and 5 October 1987)

In two notifications to the Secretary-General, the Government of Peru had, on the one hand, declared a state of emergency for a period of 60 days, starting from 23 September 1987, in the Provinces of Abancay, Aymares, Antabamba, Andahuaylas and Grau (Department of Apurímac) and, on the other hand, extended the state of emergency in the Provinces of Danial Alcides Carrión and Pasco for 60 days as of 5 October 1987.

[4 November 1987]

(Dated 23 October 1987)

Extension of the state of emergency in the Provinces of Lima and Callao for a period of 30 days as of 21 October 1987.

[23 December 1987]

(Dated 19 December 1987)

Extension of state of emergency in the Provinces of Lima and Callao for a period of 30 days as of 17 December 1987.

[22 January 1988]

(Dated 20 January 1988)

In two notifications to the Secretary-General, the Government of Peru had, on the one hand, extended the state of emergency in the Provinces of Lima and Callao for a period of 30 days as of 16 January 1988 and, on the other hand, extended the state of emergency for a period of 30 days, starting from 17 January 1988, in the following Provinces:

Department of Ayacucho (Provinces of Cangallo, Huamanga, Huanta, La Mar, Víctor Fajardo, Huacasancos, Vilcashuamán and Sucre);

Department of Huancavelica (Provinces of Acobamba, Angaraes, Huancavelica, Tayacaja, Huaytará and Churcampa);

Department of Apurímac (Provinces of Chinceros);

Department of Huánuco (Provinces of Ambo and District of Monzón of the Province of Humalíes).

[1 and 8 February 1988]

(Dated 22 January and 4 February 1988)

In two notifications to the Secretary-General, the Government of Peru extended a state of emergency as follows:

By Supreme Decree No. 001-88-IN, the state of emergency has been extended for a period of 60 days, starting from 8 January 1988, in the following Provinces:

Department of Huánuco (Province of Leoncio Prado and District of Chólon of the Province of Marañón);

Department of San Martín (Provinces of Moyobamba, Bellavista, Huallaga, Lamas, Picota, Rioja, San Martín, Mariscal Cáceres and Tocache).

By Supreme Decree No. 005-88-IN, the state of emergency has been extended for a period of 60 days, starting from 2 February 1988, in the Provinces of Daniel Alcides Carrión and Pasco (Department of Pasco).

[11 and 29 March 1988]

(Dated 20 and 21 March 1988)

In two notifications to the Secretary-General, the Government of Peru extended a state of emergency as follows:

By Supreme Decree No. 010-88-IN, the state of emergency has been extended for a period of 60 days, starting from 9 March 1988 in the following Provinces:

Provinces of Moyobamba, Bellavista, Huallaga, Lamas, Picota, Rioja, San Martín, Mariscal Cáceres and Tocache (Department of San Martín);

Province of Leoncio Prado and District of Cholón of the Province of Marañón (Department of Huánuco).

By Supreme Decree No. 0014-88-IN, the state of emergency has been extended for a period of 60 days, starting from 17 March 1988 in the following Provinces:

Provinces of Abancay, Aymares, Antabamba, Andahuaylas and Grau (Department of Apurímac).

[8 April 1988]

(Dated 4 April 1988)

By Supreme Decree No. 0015-88-IN, the Government of Peru extended the state of emergency in the Provinces of Daniel Alcides Carrión and Pasco for a period of 60 days starting from 2 April 1988.

[19 April 1988]

(Dated 21 March 1988)

By Supreme Decree No. 017-88-IN, the Government of Peru extended the state of emergency in the Provinces of Lima and Callao for a period of 60 days as of 15 April 1988.

[2 May 1988]

(Dated 28 April 1988)

By Supreme Decree No. 019-88-IN, the Government of Peru extended the state of emergency in the Province of Castrovirreyna (Department of Huancavelica) for a period of 20 days as of 27 April 1988.

[23 May 1988]

(Dated 19 May 1988)

By Supreme Decree No. 021-88-IN, the Government of Peru extended the state of emergency for a period of 60 days, as of 15 May 1988, in the following areas:

0079

Department of Ayacucho (Provinces of Cangallo, Huamanga, Huanta, La Mar, Víctor Fajardo, Huancasancos, Vilcashuamán and Sucre);

Department of Huancavelica (Provinces Acobamba, Angaraes, Huancavelica, Tayacaja, Huaytará, Churcapa and Castrovirreyna);

Department of Apurímac (Provinces of Chincheros, Abancay, Aymares, Antabamba, Andahuaylas and Grau);

Department of Huánuco (Province of Ambo, and District of Monzón of the Province of Humalíes).

[27 June 1988]

(Dated 7 June 1988)

By Supreme Decree No. 0022-88-IN, the Government of Peru extended the state of emergency in the Provinces of Daniel Carrión and Pasco, for a period of 43 days, starting on 1 June 1988.

[27 June 1988]

(Dated 16 June 1988)

In three notifications to the Secretary-General, the Government of Peru extended a state of emergency as follows:

By Supreme Decree No. 0024-88-IN, the state of emergency has been extended for a period of 30 days, starting 15 June 1988, in the Province of Cotabambas (Department of Apurímac);

By Supreme Decree No. 0025-88-IN, the state of emergency has been extended for a period of 30 days, starting 14 June 1988, in the Provinces of Lima and Callao;

By Supreme Decree No. 0026-88-IN, the state of emergency has been extended for a period of 29 days, starting 15 June 1988, in the following areas:

Department of San Martín (Provinces of Moyobamba, Bellavista, Huallaga, Lamas, Picota, Rioja, San Martín, Mariscal Cáceres and Tocache);

Department of Huánuco (Province of Marañón).

[22 July 1988]

(Dated 19 July 1988)

In two notifications to the Secretary-General, the Government of Peru extended a state of emergency as follows:

By Supreme Decree No. 0028-88-IN, the state of emergency has been extended for a period of 60 days, starting 14 July 1988, in the Provinces of Lima and Callao;

By Supreme Decree No. 0029-88-IN, the state of emergency has been extended for a period of 60 days, starting 14 July 1988, in the following areas:

Department of Apurímac;

Department of Huancavelica;

Department of San Martín;

Department of Ayacucho (Provinces of Cangallo, Huamanga, La Mar, Víctor Fajardo, Huancasancos, Huanta, Vilcashuamán and Sucre);

Department of Huánuco (Provinces of Ambo and Leoncio Prado; Districts of Monzón of the Province of Huamalíos and Cholón of the Province of Marañón.

[15 September 1988]

(Dated 13 September 1988)

By Supreme Decree No. 035-88-IN, the Government of Peru extended a state of emergency for a period of 60 days, as of 7 September 1988, in the following departments, provinces and districts:

Department of Apurímac;

Department of Huancavelica;

Department of San Martín;

Department of Ayacucho (Provinces of Cangallo, Huamanga, La Mar, Víctor Fajardo, Huancasancos, Huanta, Vilcashuamán and Sucre);

Department of Pasco (Provinces of Daniel Alcides Carrión and Pasco);

Department of Huánuco (Provinces of Ambo and Leoncio Prado); District of Monzón (Province of Huamalíes); and District of Cholón (Province of Marañón);

Department of Lima (Province of Lima and Constitutional Province of Callao).

[21 December 1988]

(Dated 8 December 1988)

By Supreme Decree No. 035-87-IN, the Government of Peru extended the state of emergency in the Provinces of Lucanas, Parinacochas and Páucar del Sara Sara in the Department of Ayacucho, and the Provinces of Pachitea, Huánuco, Dos de Mayo, Huamalíes and Marañón in the Department of Huánuco for 60 days as of 18 September 1988.

0081

[9 January 1989]

(Dated 5 January 1989)

Extension of the state of emergency for sixty (60) days from 3 January 1989 in the Departments of Apurímac, Huancavelica, San Martín, Junín, Pasco, Ayacucho, Huánuco and Lima, the province of Lima and the Constitutional Province of Callao.

[8 March 1989]

(Dated 6 March 1989)

Extension of the state of emergency for sixty (60) days from 4 March 1989 in the following Departments and Provinces:

The Department of Apurímac (with the exception of the Province of Andahuaylas), the Departments of Huancavalica, San Martín, Junín, Pasco, Ayacucho, Huánuco and Lima, the province of Lima and the Constitutional Province of Callao.

[4 August 1989]

(Dated 2 August 1989)

Extension of the state of emergency for a period of 30 days from 31 July 1989 in the Department of Ucayali and the Province of Ucayali-Contamaná of the Department of Loreto.

[15 August 1989]

(Dated 14 August 1989)

Proclamation of the state of emergency for a period of 30 days from 9 August 1989 in the Province of Huarochirí of the Department of Lima.

[7 June 1990]

(Dated 7 June 1990)

Proclamation of the state of emergency for a period of 30 days, with effect from 31 May 1990, in the province of Lima, Department of Lima, and in the Consitutional Province of Callao.

Suspension of the individual rights provided for in articles 9 and 21 of the Covenant.

0082

POLAND

[Original: English]
[29 January 1982]

... in connection with the proclamation of martial law by the Council of State of the Polish People's Republic, as based on article 33, paragraph 2, of Poland's Constitution, there has been temporary derogation from or limitation of application of provisions of articles 9, 12, paragraphs 1 and 2, 14, paragraphs 5, 19, paragraphs 2, 21 and 22) of the Covenant, to the extent strictly required by the exigencies of the situation ...

Temporary limitation of certain rights of citizens has been prompted by the supreme national interest. It was caused by the exigencies of averting a civil war, economic anarchy as well as destabilization of State and social structures ....

The restrictive measures in question are of a temporary nature. They have already been considerably cut back and along with the stabilizing of the situation, will be successively terminated.

[22 December 1982]

Based on the law passed by the Diet (Seym) of the Polish People's Republic of 18 December 1982 concerning special legal regulation in time of suspension of martial law, derogation from articles 9, 12, paragraphs 1 and 2, 21 and 22 of the Covenant has been terminated as of 31 December 1982.

By terms of the same law and as a result of earlier successive measures, restrictions in the application of provisions of the Covenant which are still derogated from, namely article 14, paragraph 5, and article 19, paragraph 2, have also been considerably reduced.

For instance, with reference to article 14, paragraph 5, of the Covenant emergency procedures have been lifted in relation to crimes and offences committed in social conflicts out of political motivations, they have only been retained with regard to crimes most dangerous to the State's basic economic interests as well as to the life, health and property of its citizens.

[25 July 1983]

Termination of derogations as of 22 July 1983.

RUSSIAN FEDERATION

[Original: Russian]
[18 October 1988]

(Dated 13 October 1988)

[Owing to] nationalistic clashes in the Soviet Union in the Nagorno-Karabach Autonomous Region and the Agdam district of the Azerbaijan Soviet Socialist Republic [and to] contraventions of public order, accompanied in a number of cases by the use of weapons, [which] have unfortunately resulted in casualties and damage to the property of the State and of private individuals [and owing to the attack of] some State institutions ... a state of emergency has been temporarily imposed, and a curfew is in effect, in the Nagorno-Karabakh Autonomous Region and the Agdam district of the Azerbaijan SSR, as of 21 September 1988. The state of emergency has been imposed in order to restore public order, protect citizens' individual and property rights and enforce strict compliance with the law, in accordance with the powers conferred by the Presidium of the Supreme Soviet of the USSR.

While the state of emergency is in force, demonstrations, rallies, meetings and strikes are banned. The movements of civilians and vehicles are restricted between 9 p.m. and 6 a.m. These restrictions represent a partial departure from the provisions of articles 12 and 21 of the International Covenant on Civil and Political Rights. Steps to ensure the safety of civilians and maintain public order are being taken by units of the militia and the armed forces. The local and central organs of power and government are taking steps to normalize the situation; and an elucidation effort is in progress, with the aim of preventing criminal acts and incitement to national hatred.

The Soviet Union will continue to abide strictly by its international obligations arising out of the International Covenant on Civil and Political Rights.

Further information will be provided as concerns the date on which the state of emergency is lifted after the normalization of the situation.

[17 January 1990]

(Dated 15 January 1990)

Proclamation of the state of emergency as from 11 p.m. local time on 15 January 1990, in the territory of the Nagorno-Karabkh autonomous region, the regions of the Azerbaijan SSR adjacent thererto, the Gorissa region of the Armenian SSR and the border zone along the state frontier between the USSR and the territory of the Azerbaijan SSR. The state of emergency was proclaimed owing to incitement by extremist groups which are organizing disorder, stirring up dissension and hostility between nationalities, and which do not hesitate to mine roads, open fire in inhabited areas and take hostages. Articles 9, 12, 19, 21 and 22 of the Covenant were accordingly suspended.

[25 January 1990]

(Dated 29 January 1990)

Proclamation of the state of emergency, as from 20 January in the city of Baku and application to that territory of the Decree adopted by the Presidium of the Supreme Soviet of the USSR on 15 January 1990, in the light of massive disorder organized by criminal extremist forces to overthrow the Government, and also with a view to ensure the protection and security of citizens. Articles 9, 12, 19, 21 and 22 of the Covenant are accordingly suspended.

[26 March 1990]

(Dated 23 March 1990)

Establishment of the state of emergency as from 12 February 1990 in Dushanbe (Tadzhik SSR) because of widespread disorder, arson and other criminal acts which resulted in a threat to the citizens. Articles 9, 12 and 21 of the Covenant were accordingly suspended.

SRI LANKA

[Original: English]
[21 May 1984]

Proclamation of a state of emergency throughout Sri Lanka, and derogation as a consequence from articles 9, paragraph 3, and 14, paragraph 3 (b), of the Covenant as of 18 May 1983.

[23 May 1984]

The Government of Sri Lanka specified that the Emergency Regulations and Special Laws were temporary measures necessitated by the existence of an extraordinary security situation and that it was not intended to continue with them longer than was absolutely necessary.

[16 January 1989]

(Dated 13 January 1989)

Termination of the state of emergency as from 11 January 1989.

[29 August 1989]

(Dated 18 August 1989)

Establishment of the state of emergency for a period of 30 days as from 20 June 1989 and derogation from provisions of article 9 (2).

The notification specifies that the state of emergency was declared in view of the progressive escalation of violence, acts of sabotage and the disruption of essential services throughout the country as from the termination of the state of emergency on 11 January 1989 (see previous notification of 16 January 1989).

SUDAN

[Original: English]

(Dated 21 August 1991)

Notification that a state of emergency was declared on 30 June 1989 when the Revolution for National Salvation took power, in order to ensure security and safety of the country, particularly in view of the political and military situation existing in the southern part of the country. Emergency regulations were issued to complement the provisions of Constitutional Decree no. 2, which established the state of emergency.

[14 February 1992]

(Dated 13 February 1992)

Clarification received that the state of emergency declared from 30 June 1989 derogates specifically from article 2 and article 22, paragraph 1.

SURINAME

[Original: English]

(Dated 5 December 1986)

By General Decree A-22 of 1 December 1986, the Government of Suriname proclaimed a state of emergency for a part of the territory of the Republic of Suriname. The decree reads as follows:

Article 1

1. The State of Emergency is being proclaimed for the part of the territory of the Republic of Suriname, comprising the districts of Marowijne, Commewijne, Para, Brokopondo and that part of the district of Sipaliwini situated between the Marowijne River and 56° west longitude.

2. The territory mentioned in the previous paragraph may be expanded by the Government if necessary.

Article 2

The State of Emergency will remain in force until lifted by decree.

Article 3

The instruction given and measures taken on account of the State of Emergency shall be applicable to anyone being outside of the area mentioned in article 1, paragraph 1, and of whom it has become evident that he conspires with or provides support to persons case quo agencies undertaking violent actions in the area for which the State of Emergency has been proclaimed.

Article 4

1. During the State of Emergency, special measures may be taken and instructions given by decision of the military authority in derogation of the existing legislation, taking into consideration the national security, the property, integrity and freedom of persons falling under operation of this decree.

2. Each decision of the military authority taken in conformity with this decree has the same force of law as a decree containing generally binding provisions enacted in the usual manner.

Article 5

Any generally binding instruction issued on the basis of this decree and emanating from the military authority shall be made known to the public in the usual manner.

Article 6

1. This decree shall be published in the Official Gazette of the Republic of Suriname.

2. It shall furthermore be published by the news media in Suriname.

3. It shall take effect as from 2 December 1986 at 00.00 hours.

[18 March 1991]

Termination, as from 1 September 1989, of the state of emergency declared on 1 December 1986 in the territory of the districts of Marowijne, Commewijne, Para, Brolopondo and in part of the territory of the district of Sípaliwini (between the Marowijne river and 56° west. The articles of the Covenant being derogated from were articles 12, 21 and 22.

TRINIDAD AND TOBAGO

[Original: English]
[6 November 1990]

(Dated 15 August 1990)

Proclamation of state of emergency in the Republic of Trinidad and Tobago as from 28 July 1990 for a period of ninety days and derogation from articles 9, 12, 21 and 14 (3).

TUNISIA

[Original: French]

(Dated 6 February 1984)

Further to serious events in Tunisia endangering the lives of the inhabitants, the Tunisian Government was compelled to declare a state of emergency by Decree No. 84-1, of 3 January 1984.

The declaration was made under pre-existing regulations and it scrupulously respects the provisions of the Covenant, more particularly articles 6, 7, 8, paragraphs 1 and 2, 11, 13, 16 and 18.

Decree No. 78-50 of 26 January 1978, governing a state of emergency relates only to the following matters:

1. Prohibition of the movement of persons or vehicles during specific hours of the night, though the curfew was ended on 15 January 1984;

2. Prohibition of all strikes or lock-outs;

3. Control of people's residence and, in particular, local banishment of any person attempting to interfere with the actions of the public authorities in any way;

4. Power to cammandeer persons and property needed for the proper operation of the public services of vital interest to the nation;

5. Power to order that arms and ammunition legally held by physical persons be given up for the period of the state of emergency;

6. Closure of any public place and, in particular, entertainment halls, licensed premises and places of assembly of all kinds;

7. Power to order the entering and searching of premises by day and by night; and

8. Control of publication and broadcasting.

The above-mentioned measures may be enforced at the discretion of the administrative authority notwithstanding the existence of the provisions of the Decree in question.

These regulations for the state of emergency have been issued pursuant to the provisions of the Tunisian Constitution.

Decree No. 78-50 of 26 January 1978 has been applied on one occasion in the past, at least in principle. On 26 January 1978 a state of emergency was declared in application of the Decree, but it was not extended and the Decree was not actually applied because the country promptly returned to normal, for which reason the Tunisian Government did not at the time inform the States parties to the Covenant of the application of the Decree. Lastly, the state of emergency automatically terminates on 3 February 1984, pursuant to article 2 of the above-mentioned Decree of 1978, but the Head of State wished to confirm this end to the state of emergency by an official communiqué.

UNITED KINGDOM OF GREAT BRITAIN AND NORTHERN IRELAND

[Original: English]
[17 May 1976]

The Government of the United Kingdom notify other States parties to the present Covenant, in accordance with article 4, of their intention to take and continue measures derogating from their obligations under the Covenant.

There have been in the United Kingdom in recent years campaigns of organized terrorism related to Northern Irish affairs which have manifested themselves in activities which have included murder, attempted murder, maiming, intimidation and violent civil disturbances and in bombing and fire-raising which have resulted in death, injury and widespread destruction of property. This situation constitutes a public emergency within the meaning of article 4, paragraph 1, of the Covenant. The emergency commenced prior to the ratification by the United Kingdom of the Covenant and legislation has, from time to time, been promulgated with regard to it.

The Government of the United Kingdom have found it necessary (and in some cases continue to find it necessary) to take powers, to the extent strictly required by the exigencies of the situation, for the protection of life, for the protection of property and the prevention of outbreaks of public disorder, and including the exercise of powers of arrest and detention and exclusion. In so far as any of these measures is inconsistent with the provisions of articles 9, 10, paragraphs 2, 10, paragraphs 3, 12, paragraphs 1, 14, 17, 19, paragraphs 2, 21 or 22 of the Covenant, the United Kingdom hereby derogates from its obligations under those provisions.

[22 August 1984]

Termination forthwith of derogations from articles 9, 10, paragraphs 2, 10, paragraphs 3, 12, paragraphs 1, 14, 17, 19, paragraphs 2, 21 and 22 of the Covenant.

[23 December 1988]

[The Government of the United Kingdom of Great Britain and Northern Ireland] have found it necessary to take or continue measures derogating in certain respects from their obligations under article 9 of the Covenant. (For the reasons of that decision, see paragraph 2 of a previous notification of 17 May 1976, which continue to apply).

Persons reasonably suspected of involvement in terrorism connected with the affairs of Northern Ireland, or of offences under the legislation and who have been detained for 48 hours may be, on the authority of the Secretary of State, further detained without charge for periods of up to five days.

Notwithstanding the judgement of 29 November 1988 by the European Court of Human Rights in the case of Brogan and Others, the Government has found it necessary to continue to exercise the powers described above but to the extent strictly required by the exigencies of the situation to enable necessary inquiries and investigations properly to be completed in order to decide whether criminal proceedings should be instituted. [This notice is given] in so far as these measures may be inconsistent with article 9 (3) of the Covenant.

[31 March 1989]

(Dated 23 March 1989)

Replacement as from 22 March 1989, of the measures indicated in the previous notification of 23 December 1988 by section 14 of and paragraph 6 of Schedule 5 to the Prevention of Terrorism (Temporary Provisions) Act 1989, which make comparable provision.

[18 December 1989]

(Dated 12 December 1989)

The Government of the United Kingdom have [previously] found it necessary to take and continue [various measures], derogating in certain respects from obligations under article 9 of the International Covenant on Civil and Political Rights.

On 14 November 1989 the Home Secretary announced that the Government had concluded that a satisfactory procedure for the review of detention of terrorist suspects involving the judiciary had not been identified and that the derogation notified under article 4 of the Covenant would therefore remain in place for as long as circumstances require.

URUGUAY

[Original: Spanish]
[30 July 1979]

[The Government of Uruguay] has the honour to request that the requirement laid down in article 4, paragraph 3, of the International Covenant on Civil and Political Rights should be deemed to have been formally fulfilled with regard to the existence and maintenance in Uruguay of a public emergency as referred to in article 4, paragraph 1.

This emergency situation, the nature and consequences of which match the description given in article 4, namely that they threaten the life of the nation, is a matter of universal knowledge, and the present communication might thus appear superfluous in so far as the provision of substantive information is concerned.

This issue has been the subject of countless official statements at both the regional and the international level.

None the less, my Government wishes both to comply formally with the above-mentioned requirement and to reiterate that the emergency measures which it has taken, and which comply strictly with the requirements of article 4, paragraph 2, are designed precisely to achieve genuine, effective and lasting protection of human rights, the observance and promotion of which are the essence of our existence as an independent and sovereign nation.

Notwithstanding what has been stated above, the information referred to in article 4, paragraph 3, concerning the nature and duration of the emergency measures will be provided in more detailed form when the report referred to in article 40 of the Covenant is submitted, so that the scope and evolution of these measures can be fully understood.

VENEZUELA

[Original: Spanish]
[12 April 1989]

(Dated 17 March 1989)

Establishment of emergency measures and derogation from articles 9, 12, 17, 19 and 21 throughout Venezuela. The notification stipulates that derogation was effected due to a series of serious breaches of the peace having taken place throughout Caracas and in other cities in the country and outbursts of violence, acts of vandalism and violations of the security of Venezuelan individuals and households, leading to loss of life and the destruction of much property, thus causing a further deterioration in the economic situation of the country.

(Dated 31 March 1989)

Re-establishment as from 22 March 1989 of the constitutional safeguards which had been suspended as stated in the previous notification of 17 March 1989.

[14 February 1992]

(Dated 11 February 1992)

Notification of the temporary suspension in all the territory of Venezuela of a number of constitutionally protected liberties and freedoms as a result of the issuance of Council of Ministers Decree 2086 on 4 February 1992, which was subsequently ratified by a joint session of the National Congress on the same day. The decree specifies the suspension of guarantees provided for under paragraphs 1, 2, 6 and 10 of article 60 of the Constitution as well as articles 62, 64, 66, 71, 92 and 115, thereby derogating from articles 9, 12, 17, 19 and 21 of the Covenant. The notification stipulates that the decree was issued to facilitate the restoration of public order following military activity directed against the constitutional and democratic Government of President Carlos Andres Perez.

[25 February 1992]

(Dated 21 February 1992)

Promulgation of Council of Ministers Decree No. 2097 providing for the partial restoration of guarantees suspended on 4 February 1992. Specifically, articles 64, 66 and 92 of the Constitution relating to freedom of movement, freedom of expression and the right to strike were restored throughout the national territory.

YUGOSLAVIA

[Original: English]
[17 April 1989]

(Dated 14 April 1989)

Derogation from articles 12 and 21 of the Covenant in the Autonomous Province of Kosovo as from 28 March 1989. The measure became necessary because of disorders which led to the loss of human lives and which had threatened the established social system. This situation which represented a general danger was a threat to the rights, freedoms and security of all the citizens of the Province, regardless of nationality.

[30 May 1989]

(Dated 29 May 1989)

Termination of the derogation from the provisions of article 12 of the Covenant in the Autonomous Province of Kosovo as from 21 May 1989. The right of public assembly [article 21] continues to be temporarily suspended but only as concerns demonstrations. This is aimed at protecting public order, peace and the rights of citizens, regardless of nationality.

[20 March 1990]

(Dated 19 March 1990)

As of 21 February 1990 and owing to the escalation of disorders which had led to the loss of human lives, the movement of persons in Kosovo was prohibited from 9 p.m. to 4 a.m.; thereby derogating from article 12; and public assembly was prohibited for the purpose of demonstration, thereby derogating from article 21. The Government of Yugoslavia further indicated that the measure derogating from article 12 had been terminated as of 10 March 1990.

[26 April 1990]

(24 April 1990)

Termination of the state of emergency with effect from 18 April 1990.

F. Declarations recognizing the competence of the Human Rights Committee under article 41 of the Covenant 9/

(Unless otherwise indicated, the declarations were made upon ratification or accession)

General information

The States which have made the declaration under article 41 of the Covenant are as follows:

State party	Valid from	Valid until
Algeria	12 September 1989	Indefinitely
Argentina	8 August 1986	Indefinitely
Austria	10 September 1978	Indefinitely
Belgium	5 March 1987	Indefinitely
Canada	29 October 1979	Indefinitely
Chile	11 March 1990	Indefinitely
Congo	7 July 1989	Indefinitely
Czech and Slovak Federal Republic	20 March 1991	Indefinitely
Denmark	23 March 1976	Indefinitely
Ecuador	24 August 1984	Indefinitely
Finland	19 August 1975	Indefinitely
Gambia	9 June 1988	Indefinitely
Germany	28 March 1979	27 March 1996
Hungary	7 September 1988	Indefinitely
Iceland	22 August 1979	Indefinitely
Ireland	8 December 1989	Indefinitely
Italy	15 September 1978	Indefinitely
Luxembourg	18 August 1983	Indefinitely
Malta	13 September 1990	Indefinitely
Netherlands	11 December 1978	Indefinitely
New Zealand	28 December 1978	Indefinitely
Norway	23 March 1976	Indefinitely
Peru	9 April 1984	Indefinitely
Philippines	23 October 1986	Indefinitely
Poland	25 September 1990	Indefinitely
Republic of Korea	10 April 1990	Indefinitely
Russian Federation	1 October 1991	Indefinitely
Senegal	5 January 1981	Indefinitely
Spain	25 January 1985	25 January 1993
Sri Lanka	11 June 1980	Indefinitely
Sweden	23 March 1976	Indefinitely
United Kingdom of Great Britain and Northern Ireland	20 May 1976	Indefinitely
Zimbabwe	20 August 1991	Indefinitely

0093

ALGERIA

[12 September 1989]

The Government of the Democratic People's Republic of Algeria declares, pursuant to article 41 of the Covenant, that it recognizes the competence of the Human Rights Committee referred to in article 28 of the Covenant to receive and consider communications to the effect that a State party claims that another State party is not fulfilling its obligations under the Covenant.

ARGENTINA

The instrument contains a declaration under article 41 of the Covenant by which the Government of Argentina recognizes the competence of the Human Rights Committee established by virtue of the International Covenant on Civil and Political Rights.

AUSTRIA

[10 September 1978]

[The Government of the Republic of Austria] declares under article 41 of the Covenant on Civil and Political Rights that Austria recognizes the competence of the Human Rights Committee to receive and consider communications to the effect that a State party claims that another State party is not fulfilling its obligations under the Covenant on Civil and Political Rights.

BELGIUM

[18 June 1987]

The Kingdom of Belgium declares, under article 41 of the International Covenant on Civil and Political Rights, that it recognizes the competence of the Human Rights Committee established under article 28 of the Covenant to receive and consider communications submitted by another State party, provided that such State party has, not less than 12 months prior to the submission by it of a communication relating to Belgium, made a declaration under article 41 recognizing the competence of the Committee to receive and consider communications relating to itself.

CANADA

[29 October 1979]

The Government of Canada declares, under article 41 of the International Covenant on Civil and Political Rights, that it recognizes the competence of the Human Rights Committee referred to in article 28 of the said Covenant to receive and consider communications submitted by another State party, provided that such State party has, not less than 12 months prior to the submission by it of a communication relating to Canada, made a declaration under article 41 recognizing the competence of the Committee to receive and consider communications relating to itself.

CHILE

[7 September 1990]

By virtue of the powers vested in me by the Political Constitution of the Republic, I hereby declare that, as from the date of this instrument, the Government of Chile recognizes the competence of the Human Rights Committee established under the International Covenant on Civil and Political Rights, in accordance with article 41 thereof, with regard to all actions which may have been initiated since 11 March 1990.

CONGO

[7 July 1989]

Pursuant to article 41 of the International Covenant on Civil and Political Rights, the Congolese Government recognizes, with effect from today's date, the competence of the Human Rights Committee to receive and consider communications to the effect that a State party claims that another State party is not fulfilling its obligations under the above-mentioned Covenant.

CZECH AND SLOVAK FEDERAL REPUBLIC

[12 March 1991]

The Czech and Slovak Federal Republic declares, in accordance with article 41 of the International Covenant on Civil and Political Rights, that it recognizes the competence of the Human Rights Committee established on the basis of article 28 of the Covenant to receive and consider communications to the effect that a State party claims that another State party is not fulfilling its obligations under the Covenant.

DENMARK

[19 April 1983] 10/

[The Government of Denmark] recognizes, in accordance with article 41 of the International Covenant on Civil and Political Rights, opened for signature in New York on 19 December 1966, the competence of the Committee referred to in article 41 to receive and consider communications to the effect that a State party claims that another State party is not fulfilling its obligations under the Covenant.

ECUADOR

[6 August 1984]

... The Government of Ecuador recognizes the competence of the Human Rights Committee to receive and consider communications to the effect that a State party claims that another State party is not fulfilling its obligations under the aforementioned Covenant, as provided for in paragraph 1 (a), (b), (c), (d), (e), (f), (g) and (h) of that article.

This recognition of competence is effective for an indefinite period and is subject to the provisions of article 41, paragraph 2, of the International Covenant on Civil and Political Rights.

FINLAND

[19 August 1975]

Finland declares, under article 41 of the International Covenant on Civil and Political Rights that it recognizes the competence of the Human Rights Committee referred to in article 28 of the said Covenant, to receive and consider communications to the effect that a State party claims that another State party is not fulfilling its obligation under this Covenant.

GAMBIA

[9 June 1988]

The Government of the Gambia hereby declares that the Gambia recognizes the competence of the Human Rights Committee to receive and consider communications to the effect that a State party claims that another State party is not fulfilling its obligations under the present Covenant.

GERMANY 11/

[24 March 1986] 12/

The Federal Republic of Germany, in accordance with article 41 of the said Covenant, recognizes for a further five years from the date of expiry of the declaration of 28 March 1981 the competence of the Human Rights Committee to receive and consider communications from a State party in so far as that State party has recognized in regard to itself the competence of the Committee and as corresponding obligations have been assumed under the Covenant by the Federal Republic of Germany and by the State party concerned.

[10 May 1991]

The Federal Republic of Germany, in accordance with article 41 of the said Covenant, recognizes for a further five years from the date of expiry of the declaration of 24 March 1986 the competence of the Human Rights Committee to receive and consider communications from a State party in so far as that State party has recognized in regard to itself the competence of the Committee and as corresponding obligations have been assumed under the Covenant by the Federal Republic of Germany and by the State party concerned.

HUNGARY

[7 September 1988]

The Hungarian People's Republic declares, under article 41 of the International Covenant on Civil and Political Rights, that it recognizes the competence of the Human Rights Committee established under article 28 of the Covenant to receive and consider communications to the effect that a State party claims that another State party is not fulfilling its obligations under the Covenant.

0096

ICELAND

[22 August 1979]

The Government of Iceland ... recognizes, in accordance with article 41 of the International Covenant on Civil and Political Rights, the competence of the Human Rights Committee referred to in article 28 of the Covenant to receive and consider communications to the effect that a State party claims that another State party is not fulfilling its obligations under the Covenant.

IRELAND

The Government of Ireland hereby declares that in accordance with article 41 they recognize the competence of the said Human Rights Committee established under article 28 of the said Covenant.

ITALY

[15 September 1978]

The Italian Republic recognizes the competence of the Human Rights Committee, elected in accordance with article 28 of the Covenant, to receive and consider communications to the effect that a State party claims that another State party is not fulfilling its obligations under the Covenant.

LUXEMBOURG

[18 August 1983]

The Government of Luxembourg recognizes, in accordance with article 41, the competence of the Human Rights Committee referred to in article 28 of the Covenant to receive and consider communications to the effect that a State party claims that another State party is not fulfilling its obligations under the Covenant.

MALTA

Furthermore, the Government of Malta declares that under article 41 of this Covenant it recognizes the competence of the Human Rights Committee to receive and consider communications submitted by another State party, provided that such other State party has, not less than 12 months prior to the submission by it of a communication relating to Malta, made a declaration under article 41 recognizing the competence of the Committee to receive and consider communications relating to itself.

NETHERLANDS

[11 December 1978]

The Kingdom of the Netherlands declares under article 41 of the International Covenant on Civil and Political Rights that it recognizes the competence of the Human Rights Committee referred to in article 28 of the Covenant to receive and consider communications to the effect that a State party claims that another State party is not fulfilling its obligations under the Covenant.

NEW ZEALAND

[28 December 1978]

The Government of New Zealand declares under article 41 of the International Covenant on Civil and Political Rights that it recognizes the competence of the Human Rights Committee to receive and consider communications from another State party which has similarly declared under article 41 its recognition of the Committee's competence in respect to itself except where the declaration by such a State party was made less than 12 months prior to the submission by it of a complaint relating to New Zealand.

NORWAY

[31 August 1972]

Norway recognizes the competence of the Human Rights Committee referred to in article 28 of the Covenant, to receive and consider communications to the effect that a State party claims that another State party is not fulfilling its obligations under the Covenant.

PERU

[9 April 1984]

Peru recognizes the competence of the Human Rights Committee to receive and consider communications to the effect that a State party claims that another State party is not fulfilling its obligations under the Covenant on Civil and Political Rights, in accordance with article 41 of the said Covenant.

PHILIPPINES

The Phillipine Government, in accordance with article 41 of the said Covenant recognizes the competence of the Human Rights Committee, set up in the aforesaid Covenant, to receive and consider communications to the effect that a State party claims that another State party is not fulfilling its obligations under the Covenant.

POLAND

[25 September 1990]

The Republic of Poland recognizes, in accordance with article 41, paragraph 1, of the International Covenant on Civil and Political Rights, the competence of the Human Rights Committee to receive and consider communications to the effect that a State party claims that another State party is not fulfilling its obligations under the Covenant.

REPUBLIC OF KOREA

[The Government of the Republic of Korea] recognizes the competence of the Human Rights Committee under article 41 of the Covenant.

0098

RUSSIAN FEDERATION

[1 October 1991]

The Union of Soviet Socialist Republics declares that, pursuant to article 41 of the International Covenant on Civil and Political Rights, it recognizes the competence of the Human Rights Committee to receive and consider communications submitted by another State party, in respect of situations and events occurring after the adoption of the present declaration, provided that the State party in question has, not less than 12 months prior to the submission by it of such a communication, recognized in regard to itself the competence of the Committee, established in article 41, in so far as obligations have been assumed under the Covenant by the USSR and by the State concerned.

SENEGAL

[5 January 1981]

The Government of Senegal declares, under article 41 of the International Covenant on Civil and Political Rights, that it recognizes the competence of the Human Rights Committee referred to in article 28 of the said Covenant to receive and consider communications submitted by another State party, provided that such State party has, not less than 12 months prior to the submission by it of a communication relating to Senegal, made a declaration under article 41 recognizing the competence of the Committee to receive and consider communications relating to itself.

SPAIN

[21 December 1988] 13/

The Spanish Government declares under article 41 of the International Covenant on Civil and Political Rights that it recognizes, for a period of five years as from the date of deposit of this declaration, the competence of the Human Rights Committee to receive and consider communications to the effect that a State party claims that another State party is not fulfilling its obligations under this Covenant.

SRI LANKA

[11 June 1980]

The Government of the Democratic Socialist Republic of Sri Lanka declares under article 41 of the International Covenant on Civil and Political Rights that it recognizes the competence of the Human Rights Committee to receive and consider communications to the effect that a State party claims that another State party is not fulfilling its obligations under the Covenant, from another State party which has similarly declared under article 41 its recognition of the Committee's competence in respect to itself.

SWEDEN

[26 November 1971]

Sweden recognizes the competence of the Human Rights Committee referred to in article 28 of the Covenant to receive and consider communications to the effect that a State party claims that another State party is not fulfilling its obligations under the Covenant.

UNITED KINGDOM OF GREAT BRITAIN AND NORTHERN IRELAND

[20 May 1976]

The Government of the United Kingdom declares under article 41 of this Covenant that the United Kingdom recognizes the competence of the Human Rights Committee to receive and consider communications submitted to another State party, provided that such other State party has, not less than 12 months prior to the submission by it of a communication relating to the United Kingdom made a declaration under article 41 recognizing the competence of the Committee to receive and consider communications relating to itself.

ZIMBABWE

[20 August 1991]

Pursuant to article 41 of the International Covenant on Civil and Political Rights, the Government of the Republic of Zimbabwe recognizes the competence of the Human Rights Committee to receive and consider communications to the effect that a State party claims that another State party is not fulfilling its obligations under the above-mentioned Covenant.

Territorial application

Participant	Date of notification	Territories
Netherlands	11 December 1978	Netherlands Antilles
United Kingdom	20 May 1976	The Bailiwick of Guernsey, the Bailiwick of Jersey, the Isle of Man, Belize, Bermuda, the British Virgin Islands, the Cayman Islands, the Falkland Islands and Dependencies, Gibraltar, the Gilbert Islands, Hong Kong, Montserrat, the Pitcairn Group, St. Helena and Dependencies, the Solomon Islands, the Turks and Caicos Islands and Tuvalu

II. OPTIONAL PROTOCOLS TO THE INTERNATIONAL COVENANT ON CIVIL AND POLITICAL RIGHTS

A. OPTIONAL PROTOCOL

1. General information

Adopted by the General Assembly of the United Nations on 16 December 1966

Entry into force: 23 March 1976, in accordance with article 9.

Registration: 23 March 1976, No. 14668.

Text: United Nations, Treaty Series, vol. 999, p. 171.

The Protocol was opened for signature at New York on 19 December 1966.

Participant	Signature	Ratification, accession a/
Algeria		12 September 1989 a/
Angola		10 January 1992 a/
Argentina		8 August 1986 a/
Australia		25 September 1991 a/
Austria	10 December 1973	10 December 1987
Barbados		5 January 1973 a/
Benin		12 March 1992 a/
Bolivia		12 August 1982 a/
Bulgaria		26 March 1992 a/
Cameroon		27 June 1984 a/
Canada		19 May 1976 a/
Central African Republic		8 May 1981 a/
China 14/		
Colombia	21 December 1966	29 October 1969
Congo		5 October 1983 a/
Costa Rica	19 December 1966	29 November 1968
Cyprus	19 December 1966	
Czech and Slovak Federal Republic		12 March 1991 a/
Denmark	20 March 1968	6 January 1972
Dominican Republic		4 January 1978 a/
Ecuador	4 April 1968	6 March 1969
El Salvador	21 September 1967	
Equatorial Guinea		25 September 1987 a/
Estonia		21 October 1991 a/
Finland	11 December 1967	19 August 1975
France		17 February 1984 a/
Gambia		9 June 1988 a/
Guinea	19 March 1975	
Honduras	19 December 1966	
Hungary		7 September 1988 a/

0101

Participant	Signature	Ratification, accession a/
Iceland		22 August 1979 a/
Ireland		8 December 1989
Italy	30 April 1976	15 September 1978
Jamaica	19 December 1966	3 October 1975
Libyan Arab Jamahiriya		16 May 1989 a/
Lithuania		20 November 1991
Luxembourg		18 August 1983 a/
Madagascar	17 September 1969	21 June 1971
Malta		13 September 1990 a/
Mauritius		12 December 1973 a/
Mongolia		16 April 1991 a/
Nepal		14 May 1991 a/
Netherlands	25 June 1969	11 December 1978
New Zealand		26 May 1989 a/
Nicaragua		12 March 1980 a/
Niger		7 March 1986 a/
Norway	20 March 1968	13 September 1972
Panama	27 July 1976	8 March 1977
Peru	11 August 1977	3 October 1980
Philippines	19 December 1966	22 August 1989
Poland		7 November 1991 a/
Portugal	1 August 1978	3 May 1983
Republic of Korea		10 April 1990 a/
Russian Federation		1 October 1991 a/
Saint Vincent and the Grenadines		9 November 1981 a/
San Marino		18 October 1985 a/
Senegal	6 July 1970	13 February 1978
Somalia		24 January 1990 a/
Spain		25 January 1985 a/
Suriname		28 December 1976 a/
Sweden	29 September 1967	6 December 1971
Togo		30 March 1988 a/
Trinidad and Tobago		14 November 1980 a/
Ukraine		25 July 1990 a/
Uruguay	21 February 1967	1 April 1970
Venezuela	15 November 1976	10 May 1978
Yugoslavia	14 March 1990	
Zaire		1 November 1976 a/
Zambia		10 April 1984 a/

2. Texts of reservations and declarations

(Unless otherwise indicated, the declarations and reservations were made upon ratification or accession).

0102

AUSTRIA 15/

The Republic of Austria ratifies the Optional Protocol to the International Covenant on Civil and Political Rights on the understanding that, further to the provisions of article 5 (2) of the Protocol, the Committee provided for in article 28 of the Covenant shall not consider any communication from an individual unless it has been ascertained that the same matter has not been examined by the European Commission of Human Rights established by the European Convention for the Protection of Human Rights and Fundamental Freedoms.

DENMARK 15/

With reference to article 5, paragraph 2 (a), the Government of Denmark makes a reservation with respect to the competence of the Committee to consider a communication from an individual if the matter has already been considered under other procedures of international investigation.

FRANCE

Declaration

France interprets article 1 of the Protocol as giving to the Committee the competence to receive and consider communications from individuals subject to the jurisdiction of the French Republic who claim to be victims of a violation by the Republic of any of the rights set forth in the Covenant which results either from acts, omissions, developments or events occurring after the date on which the Protocol entered into force for the Republic, or from a decision relating to acts, omissions, developments or events after that date.

With regard to article 7, the accession of France to the Optional Protocol should not be interpreted as implying any change in its position concerning the resolution referred to in that article.

Reservation

France makes a reservation to article 5, paragraph 2 (a), specifying that the Human Rights Committee shall not have competence to consider a communication from an individual if the same matter is being examined or has already been considered under another procedure of international investigation or settlement.

ICELAND 15/

Iceland ... accedes to the said Protocol subject to a reservation, with reference to article 5, paragraph 2, with respect to the competence of the Human Rights Committee to consider a communication from an individual if the matter is being examined or has been examined under another procedure of international investigation or settlement. Other provisions of the Covenant shall be inviolably observed.

IRELAND

Article 5, paragraph 2

Ireland does not accept the competence of the Human Rights Committee to consider a communication from an individual if the matter has already been considered under another procedure of international investigation or settlement.

ITALY 15/

The Italian Republic ratifies the Optional Protocol to the International Covenant on Civil and Political Rights, it being understood that the provisions of article 5, paragraph 2, of the Protocol mean that the Committee provided for in article 28 of the Covenant shall not consider any communication from an individual unless it has ascertained that the same matter is not being and has not been examined under another procedure of international investigation or settlement.

LUXEMBOURG

Declaration

The Grand Duchy of Luxembourg accedes to the Optional Protocol to the International Covenant on Civil and Political Rights on the understanding that the provisions of article 5, paragraph 2, of the Protocol mean that the Committee established by article 28 of the Covenant shall not consider any communications from an individual unless it has ascertained that the same matter is not being examined or has not already been examined under another procedure of international investigation or settlement.

MALTA

Declarations

1. Malta accedes to the Optional Protocol to the International Covenant on Civil and Political Rights, on the understanding that the provisions of article 5, paragraph 2, of the Protocol mean that the Committee established by article 28 of the Covenant, shall not consider any communication from an individual unless it has ascertained that the same matter is not being examined or has not already been examined under another procedure of international investigation or settlement.

2. The Government of Malta interprets article 1 of the Protocol as giving the Committee the competence to receive and consider communications from individuals subject to the jurisdiction of Malta who claim to be victims of a violation by Malta of any of the rights set forth in the Covenant which results either from acts, omissions, developments or events occuring after the date on which the Protocol enters into force for Malta, or from a decision relating to acts, omissions, developments or events after that date.

NORWAY 15/

Article 5, paragraph 2

The Committee shall not have competence to consider a communication from an individual if the same matter has already been examined under other procedures of international investigation or settlement.

POLAND

The Republic of Poland decides to accede to the aforementioned Protocol while making a reservation that would exclude the procedure set out in article 5, paragraph 2 (a) in cases where the matter has already been examined under another international procedure of international investigation or settlement.

RUSSIAN FEDERATION

The Union of Soviet Socialist Republics, pursuant to article 1 of the Optional Protocol, recognizes the competence of the Human Rights Committee to receive and consider communications from individuals subject to the jurisdiction of the Union of Soviet Socialist Republics, in respect of situations or events occurring after the date on which the Protocol entered into force for the USSR.

The Soviet Union also proceeds from the understanding that the Committee shall not consider any communications unless it has been ascertained that the same matter is not being examined under another procedure of international investigation or settlement and that the individual in question has exhausted all available domestic remedies.

SPAIN

The Spanish Government accedes to the Optional Protocol to the International Covenant on Civil and Political Rights, on the understanding that the provisions of article 5, paragraph 2, of that Protocol mean that the Human Rights Committee shall not consider any communication from an individual unless it has ascertained that the same matter has not been or is not being examined under another procedure of international investigation or settlement.

SWEDEN 15/

On the understanding that the provisions of article 5, paragraph 2, of the Protocol signify that the Human Rights Committee provided for in article 28 of the said Covenant shall not consider any communication from an individual unless it has ascertained that the same matter is not being examined or has not been examined under another procedure of international investigation or settlement.

VENEZUELA

[Same reservation as that made by Venezuela in respect of article 14, paragraph 3 (d), of the International Covenant on Civil and Political Rights: see chapter I, section B]

Territorial application

Participant	Date of receipt of the notification	Territories
Netherlands	11 December 1978	Netherlands Antilles

B. SECOND OPTIONAL PROTOCOL AIMING AT THE ABOLITION OF THE DEATH PENALTY

1. General information

Adopted by the General Assembly of the United Nations
on 15 December 1989

Entry into force: 11 July 1991, in accordance with article 8 (1)

Registration: 11 July 1991, No. A/14668

Text: (not yet reproduced in the United Nations Treaty Series)

The Second Optional Protocol was opened for signature at New York on 15 December 1989

Participant	Signature	Ratification, accession a/
Australia		2 October 1990 a/
Austria	8 April 1991	
Belgium	12 July 1990	
Costa Rica	14 February 1990	
Denmark	13 February 1990	
Finland	13 February 1990	4 April 1991
Germany	13 February 1990	
Honduras	10 May 1990	
Iceland	30 January 1991	2 April 1991
Italy	13 February 1990	
Luxembourg	13 February 1990	12 February 1992
Netherlands	9 August 1990	27 February 1991
New Zealand	22 February 1990	22 February 1990
Nicaragua	21 February 1990	
Norway	13 February 1990	5 September 1991
Portugal	13 February 1990	17 October 1990
Romania	15 March 1990	27 February 1991
Spain	23 February 1990	11 April 1991
Sweden	13 February 1990	11 May 1990
Uruguay	13 February 1990	
Venezuela	7 June 1990	

2. Texts of reservations and declarations

SPAIN

Pursuant to article 2, Spain reserves the right to apply the death penalty in the exceptional and extremely serious cases provided for in Fundamental Act No. 13/1985 of 9 December 1985 regulating the Military Criminal Code, in wartime as defined in article 25 of that Act.

0106

Notes

1/ United Nations publication, Sales No. E.92.V.4.

2/ Signed on behalf of the Republic of China on 5 October 1967.

With reference to the above-mentioned signature, communications have been addressed to the Secretary-General by the Permanent Representatives or Permanent Missions to the United Nations of Bulgaria, the Byelorussian Soviet Socialist Republic, Czechoslovakia, Mongolia, Romania, the Ukrainian Soviet Socialist Republic, the Union of Soviet Socialist Republics and Yugoslavia, stating that their Governments did not recognize the said signature as valid since the only Government authorized to represent China and to assume obligations on its behalf was the Government of the People's Republic of China.

In letters addressed to the Secretary-General in regard to the above-mentioned communications, the Permanent Representative of China to the United Nations stated that the Republic of China, a sovereign State and Member of the United Nations, had attended the twenty-first regular session of the General Assembly of the United Nations and contributed to the formulation of, and signed the Covenants and the Optional Protocol concerned, and that "any statements or reservations relating to the above-mentioned Covenants and Optional Protocol that are incompatible with or derogatory to the legitimate position of the Government of the Republic of China shall in no way affect the rights and obligations of the Republic of China under these Covenants and Optional Protocol".

3/ With respect to the signature by Democratic Kampuchea the Secretary-General received, on 5 November 1980, the following communication from the Government of Mongolia:

"The Government of the Mongolian People's Republic considers that only the People's Revolutionary Council of Kampuchea as the sole authentic and lawful representative of the Kampuchean people has the right to assume international obligations on behalf of the Kampuchean people. Therefore the Government of the Mongolian People's Republic considers that the signature of the Human Rights Covenants by the representative of so-called Democratic Kampuchea, a regime that ceased to exist as a result of the people's revolution in Kampuchea, is null and void.

"The signing of the Human Rights Covenants by an individual, whose regime during its short period of reign in Kampuchea exterminated about 3 million people and thus grossly violated the elementary norms of human rights, each and every provision of the Human Rights Covenants, is a regrettable precedent, which discredits the noble aims and lofty principles of the Charter of the United Nations, the very spirit of the above-mentioned Covenants, and gravely impairs the prestige of the United Nations."

Thereafter, similar communications were received from the Governments of the following States on the dates indicated:

State	Date of receipt
German Democratic Republic	11 December 1980
Poland	12 December 1980
Ukrainian SSR	16 December 1980
Hungary	19 January 1981
Bulgaria	29 January 1981
Union of Soviet Socialist Republics	18 February 1981
Byelorussian SSR	18 February 1981
Czechoslovakia	10 March 1981

4/ With the following declaration: "... The said Covenant shall also apply to Berlin (West) with effect from the date on which it enters into force for the Federal Republic of Germany except as far as Allied rights and responsibilities are affected."

In this connection, the Secretary-General received on 5 July 1974 a communication from the Government of the Union of Soviet Socialist Republics which states in part as follows:

By reason of their material content, the International Covenant on Civil and Political Rights and the International Covenant on Economic, Social and Cultural Rights of 19 December 1966 directly affect matters of security and status. With this in mind the Soviet Union considers the statement made by the Federal Republic of Germany concerning the extension of the operation of these Covenants to Berlin (West) to be illegal and to have no force in law, since, under the Quadripartite Agreement of 3 September 1971, the treaty obligations of the Federal Republic of Germany affecting matters of security and status may not be extended to the Western Sectors of Berlin.

Communications identical in essence, *mutatis mutandis*, were received from the Governments of the German Democratic Republic (12 August 1974) and of the Ukrainian Soviet Socialist Republic (16 August 1974).

In this regard, the Governments of France, the United Kingdom and the United States of America, in a communication received on 5 November 1974, made the following declaration:

"The Governments of France, the United Kingdom of Great Britain and Northern Ireland and the United States of America wish to bring to the attention of the States parties to the Covenants that the extension of the Covenants to the Western Sectors of Berlin received the prior authorization, under established procedures, of the authorities of France, the United Kingdom and the United States on the basis of their supreme authority in those Sectors.

"The Government of France, the United Kingdom and the United States wish to point out that the International Covenant on Economic, Social and Cultural Rights and the International Covenant on Civil and Political Rights, the primary purpose of both of which is the protection of the rights of the individual, are not treaties which 'by reason of their material content, directly affect matters of security and status'.

"As for the references to the Quadripartite Agreement of 3 September 1971 which are contained in the communication made by the Government of the Union of Soviet Socialist Republics referred to in the Legal Counsel's note, the Governments of France, the United Kingdom and the United States wish to point out that, in a communication to the Government of the Union of Soviet Socialist Republics, which is an integral part (annex IV A) of the Quadripartite Agreement, they reaffirmed that, provided that matters of security and status were not affected, international agreements and arrangements entered into by the Federal Republic of Germany might be extended to the Western Sectors of Berlin. For its part the Government of the Union of Soviet Socialist Republics, in a communication to the Governments of France, the United Kingdom and the United States which is similarly an integral part (annex IV B) of the Quadripartite Agreement, affirmed that it would raise no objection to such extension.

"In authorizing the extension of the Covenants to the Western Sectors of Berlin, as mentioned above, the authorities of France, the United Kingdom and the United States took all necessary measures to ensure that the Covenants could not be applied in the Western Sectors of Berlin in such a way as to affect matters of security and status. Accordingly, the application of the Covenants to the Western Sectors of Berlin continues in full force and effect."

In a communication received on 6 December 1974, the Government of the Federal Republic of Germany stated in part:

"By their note of 4 November 1974, circulated to all States parties to either of the Covenants by C.N.306.1974.TREATIES-7 of 19 November 1974, the Governments of France, the United Kingdom and the United States answered the assertions made in the communication of the Government of the Union of Soviet Socialist Republics referred to above. The Government of the Federal Republic of Germany shares the position set out in the note of the three Powers. The extension of the Covenants to Berlin (West) continues in full force and effect."

On the same subject, the Secretary-General received the following communications:

Union of Soviet Socialist Republics (13 February 1975)

The Soviet Union deems it essential to reassert its view that the extension by the Federal Republic of Germany of the operation of the International Covenant on Civil and Political Rights and the International Covenant on Economic, Social and Cultural Rights of 19 December 1966 to Berlin (West) is illegal as stated in the note dated 4 July 1974 addressed to the Secretary-General (C.N.145.1974.TREATIES-3) of 5 August 1974.

France, United Kingdom of Great Britain and Northern Ireland and United States of America (8 July 1975 - in relation to the declarations by the German Democratic Republic and the Ukrainian Soviet Socialist Republic received on 12 and 16 August 1974, respectively)

"The communications mentioned in the notes listed above refer to the Quadripartite Agreement of 3 September 1971. This Agreement was concluded in Berlin between the Governments of the French Republic, the Union of Soviet Socialist Republics, the United Kingdom of Great Britain and Northern Ireland and the United States of America. The Governments sending these communications are not parties to the Quadripartite Agreement and are therefore not competent to make authoritative comments on its provisions.

The Governments of France, the United Kingdom and the United States wish to bring the following to the attention of the States parties to the instruments referred to in the above-mentioned communications. When authorizing the extension of these instruments to the Western Sectors of Berlin, the authorities of the three Powers, acting in the exercise of their supreme authority, ensured in accordance with established procedures that those instruments are applied in the Western Sectors of Berlin in such a way as not to affect matters of security and status.

Accordingly, the application of these instruments to the Western Sectors of Berlin continues in full force and effect.

The Governments of France, the United Kingdom and the United States do not consider it necessary to respond to any further communications of a similar nature by States which are not signatories to the Quadripartite Agreement. This should not be taken to imply any change in the position of those Governments in this matter."

Federal Republic of Germany (19 September 1975 - in relation to the declarations by the German Democratic Republic and the Ukrainian Soviet Socialist Republic received on 12 and 16 August 1974, respectively):

"By their note of 8 July 1975, disseminated by Circular Note ... C.N.198.1975.TREATIES-6 of 13 August 1975, the Governments of France, the United Kingdom and the United States answered the assertions made in the communications referred to above. The Government of the Federal Republic of Germany, on the basis of the legal situation set out in the note of the three Powers, wishes to confirm that the application in Berlin (West) of the above-mentioned instruments extended by it under the established procedures continues in full force and effect.

"The Government of the Federal Republic of Germany wishes to point out that the absence of a response to further communications of a similar nature should not be taken to imply any change of its position in this matter."

5/ In this connection, the Secretary-General received on 23 April 1982 from the Government of the Federal Republic of Germany the following declaration with regard to the declaration made by France concerning article 27 of the said Covenant.

The Federal Government refers to the declaration on article 27 made by the French Government and stresses in this context the great importance attaching to the rights guaranteed by article 27. It interprets the French declaration as meaning that the Constitution of the French Republic already fully guarantees the individual rights protected by article 27.

0110

6/ See also footnote 4.

7/ In two communications received by the Secretary-General on 10 July 1969 and 23 March 1971 respectively, the Government of Israel declared that it "has noted the political character of the declaration made by the Government of Iraq on signing and ratifying the above Covenants. In the view of the Government of Israel, these two Covenants are not the proper place for making such political pronouncements. The Government of Israel will, in so far as concerns the substance of the matter, adopt towards the Government of Iraq an attitude of complete reciprocity."

Identical communications, mutatis mutandis, were received by the Secretary-General from the Government of Israel on 9 July 1969 in respect of the declaration made on accession by the Government of the Syrian Arab Republic, and on 29 June 1970 in respect of the declaration made on accession by the Government of Libya. In the latter communication, the Government of Israel moreover stated that the declaration concerned "cannot in any way affect the obligations of the Libyan Arab Republic already existing under general international law".

8/ In a communication received by the Secretary-General on 31 January 1979, the Government of Trinidad and Tobago confirmed that paragraph (vi) constituted an interpretative declaration which did not aim to exclude or modify the legal effect of the provisions of the Covenant.

9/ See "Entry into force", chap. I, sect. A.

10/ A previous declaration received on 6 April 1978 expired on 23 March 1983.

11/ In a communication accompanying the declaration, the Government of the Federal Republic of Germany indicated that in this connection it wished to recall the reservations made by the Federal Republic upon ratification with regard to articles 19, 21 and 22 in conjunction with article 2, paragraph 1, and with regard to articles 14, paragraph 3, 14, paragraph 5, and 15, paragraph 1 of the said Covenant, and the reservation in favour of Allied rights and responsibilities contained in the declaration (see footnote 4), also made upon ratification, on the application of the Covenant to Berlin (West).

12/ A previous declaration, received on 28 March 1981, expired on 28 March 1986.

13/ A previous declaration, received on 25 January 1985, expired on 25 January 1988.

14/ See footnote 2.

15/ See text of the declaration by the State party recognizing the competence of the Human Rights Committee under article 41 of the Covenant in chapter I, section F.

Index

---

* Reservations or declarations were withdrawn.

Articles of the Covenant	States parties which made reservations, declarations or notifications
Art. 10, para. 3	Australia, Austria, Belgium, Denmark, Finland, Luxembourg, Netherlands, New Zealand, Norway, Sweden, Trinidad and Tobago, United Kingdom
Art. 11	Congo, United Kingdom
Art. 12	India
Art. 12, para. 1	Netherlands, United Kingdom
Art. 12, para. 2	Netherlands, Trinidad and Tobago
Art. 12, para. 4	Austria, Italy, Netherlands, United Kingdom
Art. 13	Finland*, France, Iceland, India, Malta, Mexico, United Kingdom
Art. 14	Austria, France, Ireland
Art. 14, para. 1	Belgium, Denmark, Finland*
Art. 14, para. 2	Malta
Art. 14, para. 3	Australia*, Austria, Barbados, Finland, Gambia, Germany, Guyana, Italy, Netherlands, United Kingdom, Venezuela
Art. 14, para. 5	Austria, Belgium, Denmark, France, Germany, Italy, Luxembourg, Netherlands, Norway, Republic of Korea, Trinidad and Tobago
Art. 14, para. 6	Australia, Guyana, Malta, New Zealand, Trinidad and Tobago
Art. 14, para. 7	Austria, Denmark, Finland, Iceland, Netherlands, Norway, Republic of Korea, Sweden
Art. 15, para. 1	Germany, Italy, Trinidad and Tobago
Art. 17	Australia*
Art. 18	Mexico

Articles of the Covenant	States parties which made reservations, declarations or notifications
Art. 19	Austria, Belgium, France*, Germany, Malta
Art. 19, para. 2	Australia*, Ireland, Luxembourg, Netherlands
Art. 19, para. 3	India, Italy
Art. 20	Australia, Belgium, Luxembourg, Malta, New Zealand, United Kingdom
Art. 20, para. 1	Belgium, Denmark, Finland, France, Iceland, Ireland, Luxembourg, Netherlands, Norway, Sweden
Art. 21	Austria, Belgium, France, Germany, India, Trinidad and Tobago
Art. 22	Algeria, Austria, Belgium, France, Germany, India, Malta, New Zealand, Republic of Korea
Art. 22, para. 2	Japan
Art. 23	Israel
Art. 23, para. 2	Belgium
Art. 23, para. 3	United Kingdom
Art. 23, para. 4	Algeria, Ireland, Republic of Korea*, United Kingdom
Art. 24, para. 1	Australia*
Art. 24, para. 3	United Kingdom
Art. 25	Australia*, Belgium
Art. 25 (b)	Australia*, Mexico, United Kingdom
Art. 25 (c)	Netherlands*, United Kingdom
Art. 26	Australia*, Austria, Trinidad and Tobago
Art. 27	France

Articles of the Covenant	States parties which made reservations, declarations or notifications
Art. 41	Austria, Canada, Denmark, Ecuador, Finland, Germany, Iceland, Italy, Luxembourg, Netherlands, New Zealand, Norway, Peru, Senegal, Spain, Sri Lanka, Sweden, United Kingdom
Art. 48, para. 1	Afghanistan, Belarus, Bulgaria, Czech and Slovak Federal Republic, German Democratic Republic, Guinea, Hungary, Mongolia, Romania, Russian Federation, Syrian Arab Republic, Ukraine, Viet Nam
Art. 48, para. 3	Afghanistan, Bulgaria
Art. 50	Australia*
Art. 1	France
Art. 5, para. 2	Denmark, France, Iceland, Italy, Luxembourg, Norway, Spain, Sweden
Art. 7	France

외 무 부

110-760 서울 종로구 세종로 77번지 / 전화 (02) 723-8934 / 전송 (02) 723-3505

문서번호 연이 20314-

시행일자 1992.6.18.

수신 건 의

참조

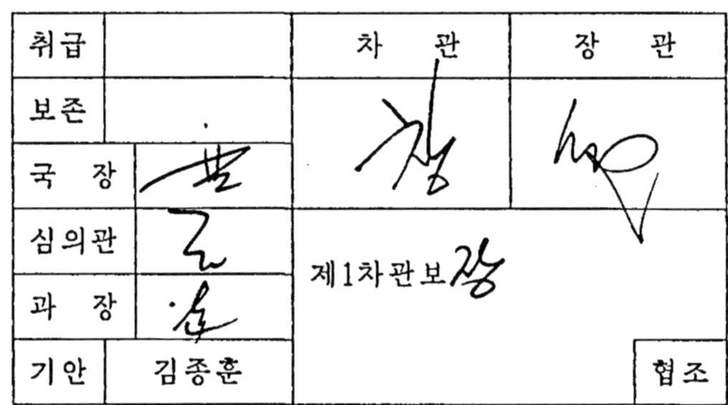

취급		차 관	장 관
보존			
국 장			
심의관		제1차관보	
과 장			
기안	김종훈		협조

제목 인권규약(B) 아국 최초보고서 심의

아국이 91.7월 제출한 "시민적.정치적 권리에 관한 국제규약" 최초보고서에 대한 심의가 92.7.13-7.31간 제네바에서 개최되는 제45차 인권이사회에서 있을 예정인 바, 동 심의에 참가할 정부대표단을 아래와 같이 임명할 것을 건의하오니 재가하여 주시기 바랍니다.

- 아 래 -

1. 심의기간 : 92.7.13-7.15. (필요시 7.16까지 연장)

2. 대표단 구성

   o 수석대표 : 박수길 주제네바 대사

   o 대 표 :

   (외무부) 문봉주 주제네바대표부 참사관

   정달호 외무부 국제연합2과장

   김종훈 외무부 국제연합2과 서기관

   조현동 주제네바대표부 2등서기관

/ 계속 /

0116

(법무부)　　류국현　법무부 인권과장

정기용　법무부 인권과 검사

최상관　법무부 인권과 검사(파견)

3. 심의일정

o 7.13. 수석대표 기조연설

인권위원(18인) 질의

o 7.14. 답변 준비

o 7.15. 질의에 대한 답변

인권위원 논평

4. 출장기간 : 92.7.8-7.18(10박 11일). 끝.

0117

인권규약(B) 아국 최초보고서 심의개요

1. 보고서 심의 개요

가. 인권이사회 구성

o 총 18명의 위원으로 구성

- 의 장 : Pocar 위원(이태리)

o 명 단 : 별첨 참조

나. 심의 방법

o 공개회의로서 일반인도 방청 가능

- 대한변협에서 2-3명 대표 파견 예정

o 아래 절차에 따라 심의 진행

7.13.

- 수석대표 기조발언(30분 이내)

- 위원 질의(2시간)

7.14.

- 답변준비를 위하여 휴회

7.15.

- 질의에 대한 답변(2시간)

- 위원의 논평(observation)(1시간)

* 필요시 7.16. 회의속개

* 이사회 폐회직전에 국가별 종합평가(comment) 채택

2. 준비사항

o 수석대표 기조발언

- 외무부, 법무부 협의 작성

o 예상질의 답변자료

- 법무부에서 관계부처와 협의 작성

0118

[첨 부]

인권이사회 위원(18인) 명단

Mr. Francisco Jose Aguilar Urbina (코스타리카)

Mr. Janos Fodor (헝가리)

Mrs. Rosalyn Higgins (영국)

Mr. Rajsoomer Lallah (모리셔스)

Mr. Andreas V. Mavrommatis (사이프러스)

Mr. Rein A. Mullerson (러시아)

Mr. Fausto Pocar (이태리) (의장)

Mr. Alejandro Serrano Caldera (니카라과)

Mr. S. Amos Wako (케냐)

Mr. Nisuke Ando (일본)

Ms. Christine Chanet (프랑스)

Mr. Vojin Dimitrijevic (유고)

Mr. Omran El-Shafei (에집트)

Mr. Kurt Herndl (오스트리아)

Mr. Birame Ndiaye (세네갈)

Mr. Julio Prado Vallejo (에쿠아돌)

Mr. Waleed Sadi (요르단)

Mr. Bertil Wennergren (스웨덴)

0119

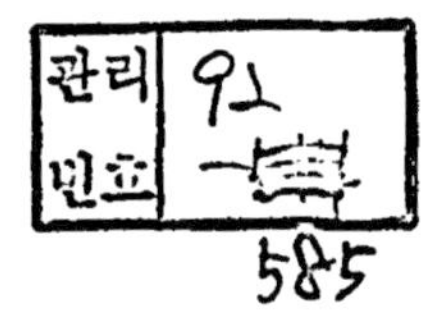

외 무 부

110-760 서울 종로구 세종로 77번지 / 전화 (02) 723-8934 / 전송 (02) 723-3505

문서번호 연이 20314-1640
시행일자 1992.6.19.

수신 법무부장관
참조 인권과장

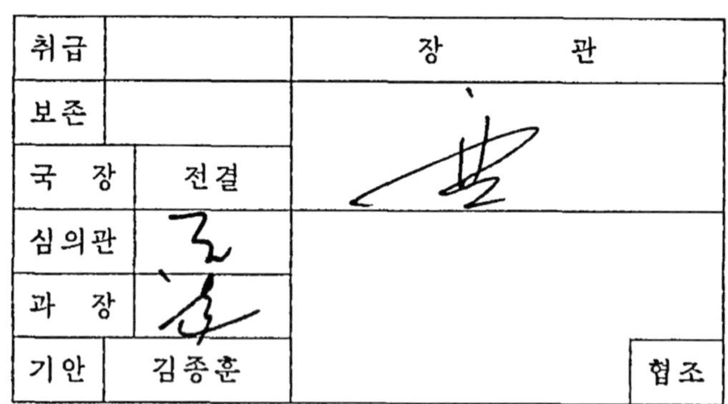

취급		장 관
보존		
국 장	전결	
심의관		
과 장		
기안	김종훈	협조

제목 아국 인권규약(B) 최초보고서 심의

제45차 인권이사회에서의 아국 최초보고서 심의에 참가할 정부대표단을 아래와 같이 임명하였으니 귀부소속 직원의 출장에 필요한 조치를 취하여 주시기 바랍니다.

- 아 래 -

o 수석대표 : 박수길 주제네바 대사

검토필 (1992. 6. 30.)

o 대 표 :

(외무부) 문봉주 주제네바대표부 참사관
정달호 외무부 국제연합2과장
김종훈 외무부 국제연합2과 서기관
조현동 주제네바대표부 2등서기관

(법무부) 류국현 법무부 인권과장
정기용 법무부 인권과 검사
최상관 법무부 인권과 검사(파견). 끝.

0120

관리 번호	92-544

	분류번호	보존기간

발 신 전 보

번 호 : WGV-0939 920619 1134 WH 종별 :

수 신 : 주 제네바 대사. 총영사

발 신 : 장 관 (연이)

제 목 : 인권규약 최초보고서 심의

1. 第45차 인권이사회에서의 아국 최초보고서 심의에 참가할 정부대표단을 아래와 같이 임명하였으니 인권사무국에 적의 통보바람.

o 수석대표 : 박수길 주제네바 대사

o 대 표 :

(외무부) 문봉주 참사관

정달호 유엔2과장

김종훈 유엔2과 서기관

조현동 서기관

(법무부) 류국현 인권과장

(Senior Public Prosecutor, Yoo Kook Hyun)

정기용 인권과 검사

(Public Prosecutor, Chung Ki Yong)

최상관 인권과 검사

(Choi Sang Kwan)

2. 본부 대표단은 심의대비 사전준비를 위하여 7.8경 귀지도착 예정인 바, 상세일정은 추후 통보함. 끝.

검토필 (1992. 6. 30.)

(국제기구국장 김재섭)

보안 통제	

앙 고 재	92년 6월 19일	유엔2과	기안자 성명		과 장	심의관	국 장		차 관	장 관
			김종훈				전결			

외신과통제

0121

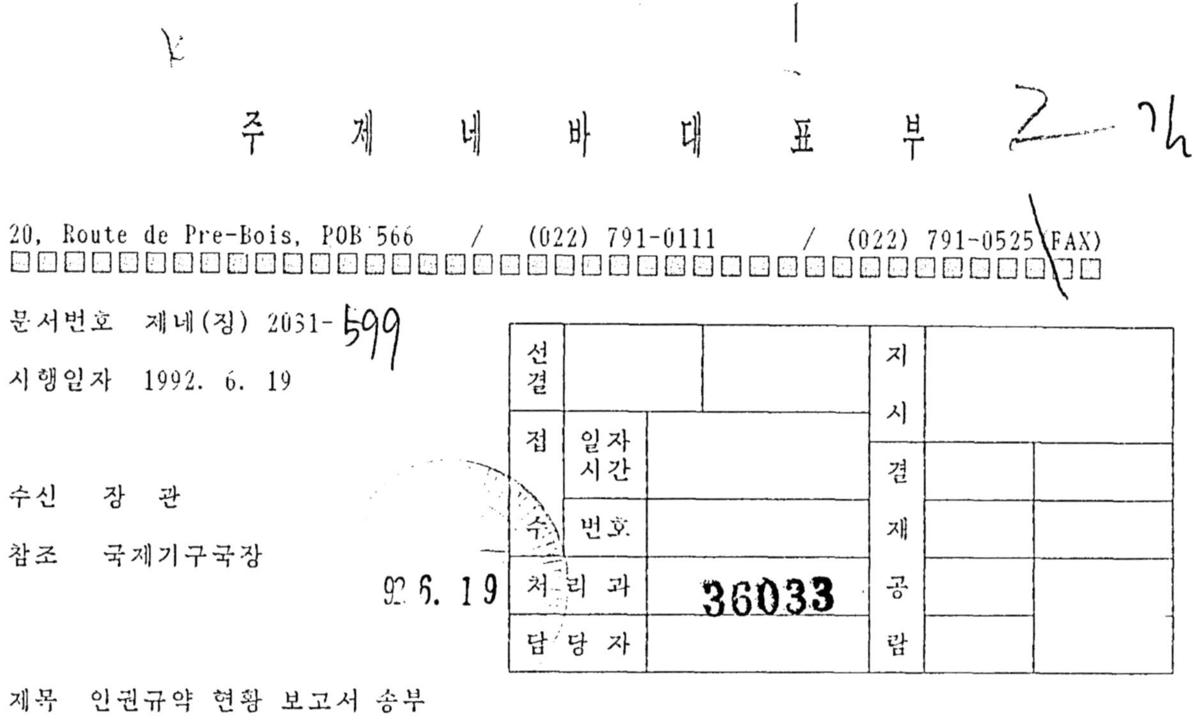

주 제 네 바 대 표 부

20, Route de Pre-Bois, POB 566 / (022) 791-0111 / (022) 791-0525 (FAX)

문서번호 제네(정) 2031-599

시행일자 1992. 6. 19

수신 장 관

참조 국제기구국장

선결			지시	
접수	일자 시간	92. 6. 19	결재	
	번호			
처리과		36033	공람	
담당자				

제목 인권규약 현황 보고서 송부

인권사무국에서 발간한 시민적, 정치적 권리규약의 91. 12. 31. 현재 각국별 Status 현황 보고서를 별첨 송부합니다.

첨부 : 상기 보고서 1부. 끝.
(CCPR/C/2/Rev.3)

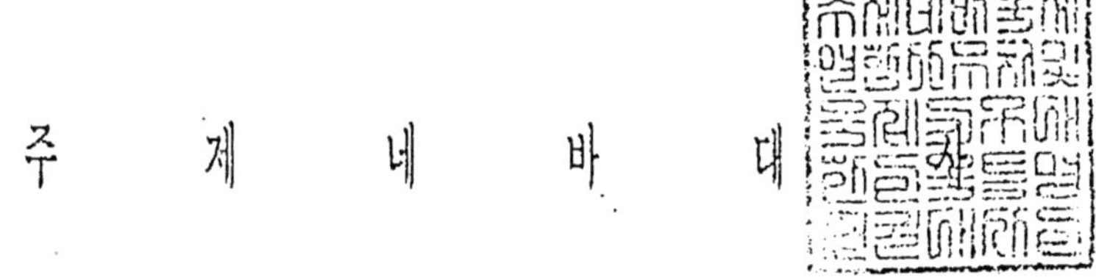

주 제 네 바 대 사

0122

외 무 부

110-760 서울 종로구 세종로 77번지 / 전화 (02) 723-8934 / 전송 (02) 723-3505

문서번호 연이 20314- 162
시행일자 1992.6.24.

수신 법무부장관
참조

취급		장 관
보존		
국 장	전결	
심의관		
과 장		
기안	김종훈	협조

제목 인권규약 보고서 심의

1. 인권규약 보고서 심의와 관련, 인권사무국 공한(별첨)에서는 심의 대상국이 관계법률을 사전에 제출하여 줄것을 요망하고 있으며, 이에 따라 당부는 주제네바 대표부를 통해 우리나라 헌법을 이미 제출하였는 바, 다른 주요 법률을 제출하는 문제에 대한 귀부 의견을 조속히 통보하여 주시기 바랍니다.

2. 주요 법률을 제출할 경우에는 동 법률의 영문본(최신 개정사항 포함)을 송부하여 주시기 바랍니다.

첨부 : 사무국 공한사본 1부. 끝.

검열 1992. 6. 25

0123

발 신 전 보

분류번호	보존기간

번 호 : WGV-0976 920627 1415 DG 종별 : 암호송신

수 신 : 주 제네바 대사. ~~총영사~~ (문봉주 참사관님)

발 신 : 장 관 (유엔2과 정달호)

제 목 : 업 연

1. 기조발언 실무 초안을 우선 송부하니 준비에 활용하시기 바랍니다.

2. 답변자료(국문 최종본)는 금 파편 송부하였으며, 영문 자료는 내주 초 지급 송부할 예정임을 참고 바랍니다. 끝

첨부: 발언문안. 끝

WGV(F)-255

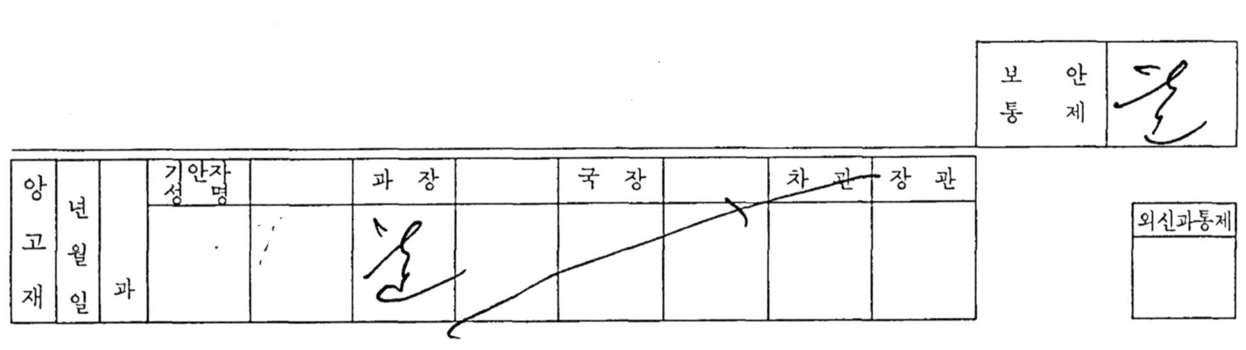

앙고재	년월일	과	기안자 성명		과 장		국 장		차 관	장 관

보안통제

외신과통제

0124

[서　　언]

대한민국은 국민의 인권보장을 보다 확고히 하고 국제적으로 보편적인 인권 신장을 위한 노력에 참여하기 위해 「경제적.사회적.문화적 권리에 관한 규약」과 함께 「시민적.정치적 권리에 관한 국제규약」에 가입하기로 하고, 1990년 4월 10일 유엔에 각각 가입서를 기탁함으로써 1990년 7월 10일부터 동 2개 규약에의 당사국이 되었습니다. 1991년 7월 「시민적.정치적 권리에 관한 국제규약」 제41조에 따라 대한민국의 인권보장에 관한 최초보고서를 제출한데 이어 오늘 우리 보고서의 심의가 있게 된 것을 의의깊게 생각하며, 대한민국 정부의 대표로서 우리의 보고서를 소개하고 설명드릴 수 있는 기회를 갖게 된 것을 매우 기쁘게 생각합니다.

[보고서 개관]

우리 정부는 보고서를 작성하는데 있어서 아래와 같은 사항에 유의하였습니다. 첫째로, 보고서의 체제와 내용이 인권이사회에서 채택한 보고서 작성에 관한 일반지침(General Guidelines)에 부합되도록 노력하였으며, 조문별 주해(General Comment)에서 요구하는 정보를 가급적 상세히 기술하려고 하였습니다. 이를 위하여 모든 정부 관계부처가 참여한 협의체를 구성하여 분야별로 세심한 협의 과정을 거쳐 보고서를 작성하였습니다.

둘째로, 우리나라의 법체제가 성문법 체제임을 감안, 인권보장을 위한 법적. 제도적 설명에 중점을 두면서, 헌법재판소의 결정, 법원의 판결 및 정부의 조치 등을 함께 기술하여 아국의 인권보장 실태에 대한 이해를 돕고자 하였습니다.

셋째로, 대한민국의 인권보장이 1988년 제6공화국 출범을 계기로 대폭적인 개선을 이루어 왔음을 고려하여, 보고서는 88년 이후의 인권보장 실태에 촛점을 맞추었습니다.

[제6공화국의 민주화 노력]

먼저 제6공화국 헌법하에서 이룩한 민주화와 인권신장을 위한 조치에 대하여 간략한 설명을 드리고자 합니다.

제6공화국 헌법은 자유선거에 의한 국민의 대통령 직접 선출, 국회의 국정 감사권 부활 등 국회의 권한강화, 법관 임명절차 개선 등을 통한 사법부의 독립 보장, 헌법 재판소 신설, 언론.출판에 대한 허가.검열제의 금지를 통한 언론의 자유의 최대한 보장 등으로 민주주의 실현과 인권보장을 위한 제도적 장치를 강화하였습니다. 또한 보고서에서 상세히 밝혔듯이 보다 확실한 인권보장을 위하여 기본권 조항을 대폭 강화하였습니다. 특히 처벌, 강제노역, 체포, 구속, 압수 수색에 있어서의 적법 절차를 명문화함으로써 신체의 자유에 대한 제한 요건을 더욱 엄격하게 하고, 형사피의자와 피고인의 권리를 확대하였습니다.

이와 같은 헌법정신을 적극 반영하여 정부는 형사사법절차와 관련된 각종 법령 및 제도와 수사관행을 개선하고 형행제도를 획기적으로 개선하는 한편, 법률구조 사업을 적극 전개하고 출입국관리 제도를 개선하는 등 실질적인 인권보호에 최선의 노력을 경주해 왔습니다.

뿐만 아니라, 88년 이전에 제정된 집회 및 시위에 관한 법률, 국가보안법 등 인권을 제약할수 있다는 면에서 논란이 많았던 법령들에 대하여는 일부 내용을 개정하는 한편, 법집행의 요건을 더욱 엄격히 함으로써 인권침해의 소지를 불식 하도록 하였습니다.

2

0126

또한 헌법수호와 기본권 보장을 목적으로 신설된 헌법재판소의 주요활동으로써 위헌법률 심판제도와 함께 헌법소원제도가 활발히 운용됨으로써 공권력에 의한 기본권 침해에 대하여 국민이 직접 심판청구의 주체가 되어서 그 시정과 구제를 할 수 있게 되었음은 인권보장에 있어서의 실질적 진전으로서 그 의의가 매우 크다고 할 수 있습니다.

민주화에 있어 또 하나의 획기적인 일은 지방자치제도의 확립이라고 하겠습니다. 헌법에는 오래전 부터 지방자치를 규정하고 있었으나 1960년대 초에 잠시 실시되다가 중단된 이후 30여년만에 처음으로 91년 3월 및 6월에 전국적으로 두차례의 지방자치 단체 의회 선거를 실시하여 각급 지방자치단체 의회가 구성되어 활동중이며, 이는 국민의 참정권을 대폭 확대한 것이라고 하겠습니다.

이러한 과정을 통해, 대한민국에는 국민의 자유와 권리가 힘에 억눌리던 과거의 어두운 권위주의 시대가 청산되고, 법위 지배가 자리잡은 가운데 국민의 인권을 완벽하게 보장하고 법을 통해 정의를 실현 할 수 있는 진정한 자유민주주의가 구현되고 있는 것입니다.

1990년 7월 인권규약에의 가입도 이러한 민주화의 진전과정에서 이루어진 것으로서 인권보장에 대한 대한민국의 의지를 대내외적으로 재확인한 것이라고 평가할 수 있습니다. 나아가「시민적, 정치적 권리에 관한 국제 인권규약」제 41조에 따른 선언을 하고 동 규약의 「선택의정서」에도 가입하였음은 개인의 인권을 실질적으로 보장하기 위하여 한걸은 더 나아간 것으로서 인권의 신장을 위한 대한민국의 확고한 자세를 보여준것이라고 하겠습니다.

규약가입 이후 동 규약의 내용이 전국민에게 널리 알려질 수 있도록 정부는 모든 노력도 다해 왔습니다. 정부는 규약의 내용, 인권이사회의 주요결정 사례집 등을 번역.발간하여 전국에 널리 배포하였고, 검찰.경찰.교도소 등 인권관련 업무 담당직원을 비롯한 각급 공무원에게 규약의 주요내용을 포함한 적법절차의 준수 등에 관한 직무교육을 실시하여 이들의 직무수행에 있어 규약의 정신 및 내용을 철저히 실천하도록 하였습니다.

[규약의 국내법적 수용]

규약은 대한민국 국회의 동의를 얻어 비준.공포됨으로써 별도의 국내입법 없이 헌법에 의해 국내법과 같은 효력을 갖기 때문에 규약에 규정된 모든 권리는 헌법에 의해 보장하고 있다고 하겠습니다.

규약에 규정된 모든 권리는 이미 헌법에 대부분 그대로 규정되어 있어 규약은 헌법과 함께 대한민국의 인권법 체계의 주축을 이룬다고 할 수 있으며 이점에서 헌법재판소가 1991년 4월 위헌심판사건의 결정에서 규약 제18조 2항을 직접 원용한 것은 주목할만 합니다.

대한민국은 규약을 비준하면서 국내법의 규정이 규약과 완전히 일치하지 않은 부분에 대해서는 이의 적용을 어느정도 유보한 바 있습니다. 그 의도는 해당조항인 제14조 5항(상소권 보장), 제14조 7항(일사부조리 또는 이중처벌금지) 및 제22조 (결사의 자유)에 규정한 권리를 인정하지 않는다는 뜻이 아니라, 국내법에 규정된 일부 제한을 유지한다는 뜻이며, 크게 보아 규약의 기본 취지에서 벗어나지 않는 것으로 보고 있습니다.

[보고서 제출 이후의 진전사항]

대한민국은 91년 9월 17일 오랜 숙원이었던 국제연합에 가입함으로써 유엔헌장의 규정에 따라 국내적, 국제적으로 인권보장을 위한 노력을 더욱 강화하는 계기를 마련하였으며, 이어 91년 12월 8일 국제노동기구에 가입 함으로써 노동권의 보장을 위한 국제적 노력에도 동참하게 되었습니다. 또한 1991년 12월 20일 "아동의 권리에 관한 협약(Convention on the Rights of Child)"을 비준함으로써 동 협약의 당사국이 되었고 현재 "난민지위에 관한 협약 및 의정서"에 가입하기 위한 행정부내의 절차를 완료하고 국회의 동의를 위해 가입안을 국회에 제출할 예정입니다.

이러한 제도적 개선에 못지않게, 실질적으로 인권 보장을 제고하는 움직임이 사회 전반에 걸쳐 많이 나타나고 있습니다. 헌법 재판소와 법원에 의한 인권침해 시정 사례가 늘어나고있으며, 이러한 추세와 함께 많은 민간인권 단체에 의한 인권신장 운동이 활발히 전개되고 있음은 매우 바람직한 방향이라고 보겠습니다.

[규약 이행상의 요인과 장애]

규약의 이행에 영향을 주는 큰 요인으로써 남북한 관계의 현실을 잘 이해하는 것은 매우 필요한 일입니다.

남한과 북한은 하나의 민족이 1945년 서로 다른 정치적 이념에 따라 분단 되었으며 그 이후 1950년 동족상잔의 전쟁을 겪은이래 이념적으로 뿐 아니라 군사적으로도 서로 대치 하고있는 긴장된 상황에 있습니다. 이러한 상황하에서도 양측은 평화적인 방법에 의한 통일을 위해 서로간에 대화를 추진해 오고 있으며, 그 결과로 지난 2월 「남북한 사이의 화해와 불가침 및 교류 협력에 관한 합의서」가 체결 되었으며, 이를 토대로 양측은 각분야 별로 서로 거리를 좁혀가기 위한 협의를 계속해 오고있습니다.

그러나 통일에의 염원에 따른 남북한 대화의 진전에도 불구하고, 대한민국은 1950년 북한 공산주의 침략에 의해 자유민주주의 사회가 공산화 될번했던 역사적 경험과 그 이후에도 각종 도발과 파괴적 테러행위 및 사회혼란 조성 등 끊임없이 계속되어온 북한의 남한체제 전복기도와 가공할 만한 전쟁준비로 인해 북한을 국가안보에 대한 위협적 존재로 인식하고 있습니다.

따라서 정부는 북한과의 대화를 통하여 한반도 평화와 통일을 위한협의를 적극 추진하면서, 동시에 북한의 적화통일 기도와 이러한 기도에 부응하여 자유민국주의 체제를 위해하려는 세력을 견제하는 노력을 계속하여야 하는 입장에 놓여 있습니다.

자유민주주의 체제에 대한 위협으로부터 국가의 안전을 보호하기 위해 제정된 법률로서 국가보안법을 들 수 있겠습니다. 국가보안법에 대해서는 최근들어 남북간의 교류와 접촉이 확대됨에 따라 국내 일각에서 개정 내지 폐지해야 한다는 주장이 대두되고 있으나, 북한의 태도에 기본적인 변화가 없는 현 상황에서는 이를 존치하여야 한다는 것이 우리의 입장입니다. 북한이 대남 적화혁명 의도를 포기하고 현재의 남북한 대화가 잘 진전되어 한반도에 진정한 평화가 정착되면 국가보안법도 불필요하게 될것으로 봅니다.

[인권 신장을 위한 앞으로의 계획]

정부는 국제노동기구 가입을 계기로 동 기구산하 제협약에의 가입을 추진 중이며, 근로자 단체와 사용자 단체를 대표하는 동수의 위원과 공익을 대표하는 위원으로 구성된 노동관계법 연구위원회를 통해 복수노조 허용등 노동관계 국내법의 개선을 위한 검토를 진행하고 있습니다.

정부는 개인의 기본적 인권을 최대한 보장하는 방향으로 죄형법정주의의 형법규범 명시와 영장 실질 심사제 도입등을 주요 내용으로 하는 형법과 형사 소송법의 개정안을 작성하였으며 이를 금번 국회에 제출할 예정으로 있습니다.

나아가 정부는 고문에 의한 인권침해의 예방을 보다 공고히 하기위해 「고문방지 협약」에도 가입하기로 원칙적인 방침을 정하고 관계부처간 가입을 위한 세부 사항을 협의중에 있습니다.

대한민국은 헌법과 규약에 규정된 인권보장의 정신이 국민의 일상 생활속에 올바로 구현될 수 있도록 제도와 관행을 개선하는 노력을 계속함과 동시에 인권 보장을 위한 국제적인 노력에도 적극 동참해나갈 것입니다.

[결　　어]

끝으로, 우리 보고서의 심의가 인권 보장을 향상하기 위한 건설적인 대화의 과정인 만큼, 본인의 설명이 위원 여러분들에게 한국의 인권 보장 실태를 이해하는데 도움이 되기를 기대하면서 여러분들의 코멘트와 질문에 성실하게 답변드리고자 합니다. 감사합니다. 끝.

6

0130

제45차 유엔인권이사회
대한민국 수석대표 발언자료(안)

1992. 6.

법 무 부 연 구 반

0131

대한민국은 1990년 4월 10일 국제인권규약, 즉 경제적.사회적 및 문화적 권리에 관한 국제규약(A규약)과 시민적 및 정치적 권리에 관한 국제규약(B규약) 및 선택의정서의 가입서를 국제연합 사무총장에게 기탁하여 동 규약은 동년 7월 10일 발효되었다. 이에 따라 대한민국 정부는 B규약 최초보고서를 1991년 7월 31일 국제연합 인권이사회에 제출한 바 있다.

B규약 최초보고서는 대한민국 정부가 동 규약에 가입함에 따라 시민적 및 정치적 권리에 관한 일반적 사항 (General Comments)과 27개 조문별 개별적 사항 (Information in relation to each of the articles of the Covenant)을 망라하여 작성하였는 바, 자의적인 체포.억류의 금지 등 기본적인 신체적 자유권은 물론 정신적 자유권의 보장과 관련된 각종 법률, 헌법재판소의 결정, 법원의 판결 및 각종 인권보호제도 등과 정부의 조치 및 성취된 진전사항들에 관하여 상세히 기술하려고 노력하였다.

국제인권규약과 국내법과의 관계에서 대한민국 정부는 규약이 대한민국 헌법과 상충되지 않는 것으로 판단하였으며, 규약에 규정된 모든 권리는 대한민국 헌법에 의하여 보장된다.
규약은 대한민국 국회의 동의를 얻어 비준.공포됨으로써 별도의 국내 입법없이 국내법과 같은 효력을 갖게 되었는 바, 단지 대한민국 고유의 관습 또는 매우 중요한 정책목표에 기초하여 이루어진 법률적 제도 및 관행으로서 규약과 상충되는 부분인 상소권보장 조항과 일사부재리 조항 및 결사의 자유 관련조항에 대하여는 규약의 비준시 유보하였다.

대한민국 헌법이 보장하는 기본적 인권은 원칙적으로 대한민국의 국적을 가지지 아니한 외국인에게도 평등하게 적용된다. 선거권이나 피선거권과 같이 대한민국의 국적을 보유할 것을 전제로 하는 것이 분명한 권리를 제외한 여타의 규약상 권리는 대한민국의 주권이 미치는 영토내에 거주하거나 일시 체류하는 모든 외국인에게도 대한민국 국민과 동등하게 보장된다.

그리고, 개인의 기본권을 실질적으로 보장하기 위하여 인권이사회에 대한 당사국의 문제제기권을 인정하는 B규약 선택조항을 수락하고, 개인의 청원권을 인정하는 선택의정서에도 가입하였음을 주목할 필요가 있다.

국제인권규약의 가입은, 대한민국 정부로 하여금 인권의 보편적 존중이라는 국제적 노력에 적극 호응하고 국내적으로 인권보장에 대한 인식을 한층 더 제고하는 계기를 마련하도록 촉구하는 중요한 역사적 계기가 되었다.

대한민국 정부는 규약가입후 국제인권규약의 내용이 전국민에게 널리 알려질 수 있도록 많은 노력을 기울여 왔다.
규약가입 사실에 대해 국내의 각 언론이 이를 일제히 보도하여 큰 의미를 부여하였으며, B규약 내용. 인권이사회의 주요결정사례집 등을 번역. 발간하여 전국에 널리 배포하였고, 검찰.경찰.교도소 등 인권관련업무 담당직원을 비롯한 각급 공무원에게 규약의 주요내용을 포함한 적법절차 준수 등 이들의 직무수행에 있어 규약의 정신이 철저히 실천되도록 하기 위한 여러가지 형태의 직무교육이 실시되었다.

또한 매년 12.10. 세계인권선언기념일을 전후하여 인권주간을 설정, 기념식을 거행하고 무료인권상담 실시, 인권심포지엄 개최 등 인권의식 고취를 위하여 다양한 행사를 전개하고 있다.

국내외 인권단체들은 개방적이고 적극적인 언론보도를 통하여 모든 국내인권관련 문제들에 관해 각자의 다양한 견해를 발표하고, 국내인권 신장 및 상황평가 문제들에 있어서 상반된 입장에서 폭넓은 논쟁을 계속하여 왔다.

극소수의 편향된 시각의 소유자들은, 국가보안법을 표현 및 양심의 자유를 본질적으로 침해하는 악법이라고 매도하면서 실정법 위반자들에 대한 정부의 엄정한 법집행을 마치 인권침해인양 왜곡하고, 정치범.양심수라는 자의적이고 모호한 개념을 사용, 그 범주안에 폭력계급혁명을 기도한 반국가사범. 방화범. 화염병폭력시위 등을 포함시켜 왜곡 발표함으로써 국내 인권상황에 대해 오해를 유발토록 하고, 극소수자들의 편향된 시각하에서의 주장이 마치 국민전체의 의사인양 과대포장하여 발표해 오고 있다.

그러나, 6공화국 출범이후 국내 인권상황이 대폭 향상되었고, 각종 인권관련 법률과 제도 및 그 운용실태 등을 인권선진국들과 비교해 볼 때 손색이 없다는 사실은 논란의 여지가 없이 국내외적으로 인정받고 있고, 이와 같은 인권문제에 관한 폭넓은 시비는 오히려 인권관련정책의 수립.시행에 있어 국내외 다양한 견해를 수렴하려는 정부의 노력을 입증해 주는 좋은 예인 것이다.

현재, 대한민국 정부는 개인의 기본적 인권을 최대한 보장하는 방향으로 죄형법정주의의 형법규범 명시와 영장실질심사제 도입 등 형법과 형사소송법의 개정안을 작성하여 국회에 제출할 예정이고, 노동분야에서 복수노조문제도 이를 허용하는 방향으로 행정부내 실무적 검토가 시작되고 있으며, 관련법령중 급격한 경제.사회.윤리적 여건 변화에 따라 사회현실에 맞지 않게 된 부분에 대해서는 이를 전향적인 자세로 검토하여 개선을 추진해 나가고 있다.

대한민국은 동.서간의 화해와 화합으로 특징지워지는 새로운 국제질서가 형성되어 가는 가운데, 1991년 9월 17일 국제연합에 가입하여 정식 회원국이 됨에 따라 유엔헌장상에 규정된 의무를 수락하고, 이러한 의무를 이행할 능력과 의사를 가진 평화애호국임을 명실공히 국제사회에 천명함과 동시에 인권관련 등 주요 국제문제에 관한 의사결정에 참여함으로써 인권향상은 물론 국가간의 협력증진에도 크게 기여할 수 있게 되었다.

법치주의를 지향함에 있어 가장 중요한 가치척도는 인권이며, 법치주의를 바탕으로 한 민주화 실천과제의 요체는 인권의 옹호와 신장이다.

대한민국 정부는 1988년 제6공화국 출범이후 인권보장에 대한 강한 의지를 거듭 천명해 왔으며, 실제로 제6공화국 헌법도 보다 확실한 인권보장을 위해 기본권 조항을 대폭 강화하고 있다.

적법절차규정을 명문화함으로써 신체의 자유에 대한 제한요건을 더욱 엄격하게 하고, 형사피의자와 피고인의 권리를 확대하는 한편 언론의 비판과 감시기능의 활성화를 통해 인권침해행위를 예방할 수 있도록 언론.출판에 대한 허가. 검열제 금지조항을 신설하였으며, 나아가 법관의 임명절차를 크게 개선, 사법부의 독립을 더욱 확고히 하는 제도적 장치를 마련해 놓았고, 아울러 헌법재판소를 신설하여 행정부를 견제하고 사법권의 독립과 국민의 기본권을 뒷받침함에 있어 중요한 역할을 수행하도록 하였다.

이와 같이 헌법정신을 적극 반영, 인권신장의 기반을 구축하기 위하여 정부가 형사사법절차와 관련된 각종 법령 및 제도와 수사관행을 개선하고 행형제도를 획기적으로 개선하는 한편, 나아가 법률구조사업을 적극 전개하고 출입국관리제도를 개선하는 등 실질적 인권보호에 최선의 노력을 경주해 왔다.

특히 과거에 제정된 집회및시위에관한법률, 국가보안법 등 논란이 많았던 인권관련법령들에 대하여 여.야 합의로 손질을 가하여 법집행 요건을 더욱 엄격히 하는 등 인권침해의 소지를 불식하는 법적.제도적 장치를 강구하였다.

헌법수호와 기본권 보장목적으로 신설된 헌법재판소는 1991년 4월 1일 민법의 명예훼손사죄광고 위헌심판사건에서 결정문에 B규약 제18조 제2항을 인용함으로써 직접적으로 규약의 법원성을 인정하였고, 기본권 보장의 핵심적 제도인 헌법소원제도를 도입함으로써 공권력에 의한 기본권 침해에 대하여 국민이 직접 심판청구의 주체가 되어서 그 시정과 구제를 가능케 하였는데, 이는 실질적 기본권 보장이념의 구현이라는 점에 의의가 크다.

또한 1991년 12월에는 『아동의 권리에 관한 협약 - Convention on the Rights of Child』에 가입하였고, 현재 『국제난민협약 및 난민의정서』의 가입서 기탁을 위하여 국회의 동의절차만을 남겨 놓고 있으며, 나아가 『고문방지협약 - Convention against Torture and Other Cruel, Inhuman or Degrading Treatment or Punishment』에의 가입 문제도 전향적으로 검토하고 있다.

이와 같이 국제인권규약은 대한민국 인권법 체계의 중심에서 구심점으로서의 역할을 담당하면서, 국민들 모두에게 실질적인 인권보장기능을 수행하고 있다.

대한민국의 법집행과 인권상황을 보다 정확히 이해하기 위하여는 제2차 세계대전 이후 마지막으로 남아 있는 냉전의 현장인 남북분단 및 그 대치상황에 대한 명확한 인식이 전제되어야 한다.

대한민국은 1945년 해방후 외세에 의해 남북으로 분단되면서 이데올로기적으로 대립하게 되고, 그 과정에서 북한이 도발한 6.25전쟁으로 3년간 피비린내나는 동족상잔의 비극을 겪었으며, 이때 유엔이 개입하여 최초로 유엔군이 투입되기에 이르렀다.
그리고 1953년 동란후 40여년 동안 동서로 뻗은 길이 155마일의 휴전선 하나를 사이에 두고 유엔군과 한국군은 세계에서 가장 호전적이고 폐쇄적인 약 100만명에 달하는 북한군과 대치하여 왔는데, 휴전선과 서울은 불과 40킬로미터 거리로 북한 장거리포의 사정거리에 놓여 있어 안보상 중대한 위협에 처해 있다.

북한은 유엔에 가입한 후에도 계속하여 우리의 자유민주주의체제를 파괴하기 위한 대남무력적화통일노선을 고수하면서·크고 작은 군사적 도발을 감행하는 등 긴장관계를 늦추지 않고 있다.

이와 같은 남.북 분단 및 군사대치상황이 인권문제를 평가하는데 기준이 되는 것은 아니지만 한반도의 특수한 현실을 이해하는 배경으로서 중요한 의미를 갖는다.
호전적인 북한공산세력이 무력적화혁명노선을 고수한 채 무력혁명기회만을 노리고 있는 절박한 상황에서, 자유민주주의체제를 전복시키기 위하여 그들의 사주로 발생하는 불법소요, 과격노사분규 등 각종 사회혼란행위들이 국민들에게 미치는 심대한 충격에 대해서는 한반도 상황에 대한 충분한 이해가 전제되어야만 진정한 평가가 가능하다.

북한의 무력도발 위협에 대처하고, 국가의 안전과 국민의 생존 및 자유를 확보하기 위하여 자위적이고 방어적인 수단으로 제정된 법률이 바로 국가보안법이다.
국가보안법은 1948년 제정이래 그 필요성과 존재 당위성에 관하여 그 동안 많은 논란이 있어 왔고, 최근들어 남.북간의 교류접촉이 확대됨에 따라 일부 재야단체로부터 개.폐지 주장이 다시 대두되고 있는 것이 현실이다.

그러나, 대부분의 국민들은 국가보안법이 6.25전쟁 등 대한민국 정부 수립의 혼란기를 틈탄 공산주의자들의 국가변란기도를 제압하고 정치적 변혁기마다 자유민주주의체제를 전복코자 획책한 북한 공산주의자들을 척결해 온 제도적 장치로서, 지금도 대남무력적화혁명노선을 포기하지 않고 있는 호전적인 북한 공산세력으로부터 대한민국의 안전과 국민의 생존권을 보호하기 위해서 반드시 필요하다는 인식을 갖고 있다.

대다수 국민들이 갖고 있는 북한의 호전성 및 무력남침에 대한 우려는 한반도 분단의 역사적 특수상황에서 기인하는 것 뿐만 아니라, 바로 지난 5월 22일 제7차 남북고위급회담이 끝난 직후 비무장지대 군사분계선 남방 1km지점에 북한의 무장간첩을 침투시켜 UN군과 한국군에 의해 사살된 사건과, 국제원자력기구(IAEA)의 지속적인 핵사찰 속에서도 핵무기 개발을 강행하고 있는 것 등 일련의 사건들을 통해서도 그 원인을 이해할 수 있다.

어느 국가이건 자체의 생존을 확보하기 위한 자위적 방어권은 어떠한 경우라도 부인될 수 있다.
세계 어느 국가를 보더라도 그 명칭은 서로 다르지만 모두 국가의 안전을 확보하기 위한 법률을 마련해 놓고 있다.
본질적으로 관용의 체제인 자유민주주의체제를 유지하는데 가장 취약한 지역이 전세계에서 바로 한반도이다.

다만, 앞으로 북한의 태도가 근본적으로 변화되어 대남적화혁명노선이 완전히 포기되고 한반도에 평화공존체제가 완전히 구축된다면 상호주의 원칙아래 북한의 각종 호전적인 안보관련법령 개폐와 함께 국가보안법의 개폐문제도 논의될 수 있다.

최근 남.북한은 군사적대치 상황속에서도 민족통일을 위한 접촉을 진행한 결과 남.북한 합의서 채택 및 발효, 이산가족 상호방문 합의, 한반도 비핵화공동선언채택 등을 이루었다.

이와 같은 외형적 성과에도 불구하고 남.북관계가 종래 대결구조에서 평화공존의 상태로 이행되었다고 단정할 수는 없다. 이는 북한이 유엔에 가입신청서를 내면서까지 『하나의 조선』 논리를 포기한 것이 아니라고 공언하는 등 평화를 선언하면서도 기존의 대남적화혁명노선에 아무런 태도변화가 없음을 명백히 한 사실에서도 입증이 된다 할 것이다.

또한 최근 국제원자력기구(IAEA)의 북한 핵사찰 결과 북한은 중간단계의 시험시설도 없이 불완전한 상태에서 대형핵재처리시설을 건설중에 있으며, 원자탄 생산원료인 플루토늄도 이미 추출한 사실이 확인되었고, 남북한 뿐만 아니라 인류의 공동이익에 부합하는 철저한 남북한 상호 핵 사찰을 계속 회피하여 전세계적으로 핵 긴장상태를 야기하고 있다.

그러므로 국제사회는 북한이 진정으로 대남적화전략을 포기하고 성실하게 평화통일을 위한 노력을 기울여 나가도록 계속 촉구하면서 핵안전협정 보조약정을 조속히 체결하여 IAEA의 정식사찰과 남북한 상호 사찰을 성실히 이행토록 하는 한편, 인권최악의 국가로서 현재 10만명이 넘는 정치범을 구금하고 있는 북한의 인권상황 개선에도 지속적인 관심을 가지고 예의 주시해야 할 것이다.

진정한 인권보장은 법과 질서가 잘 준수되는 안정된 사회에서만 가능하다. 법질서 파괴는 곧 사회의 불안을 가져오고 이는 더 나아가 대다수 국민들이 생존권을 지켜나가는 데 있어 커다란 장애가 되기 때문이다. 종래에는 법질서 파괴자들이 인권을 앞세워, 법질서를 수호하려는 정부의 엄정한 법집행 노력과 대다수 국민들의 지지를 인권탄압으로 왜곡 선전하고, 화염병이나 사제폭탄을 사용하여 공공기관을 습격하는 등 폭력을 행사하여 왔다.

대한민국은 법치주의의 기틀을 뒤흔드는 폭력파괴행위, 그리고 자유민주주의체제를 전복하려는 일부 극렬세력들에 단호히 대처하여 자유민주주의체제를 수호하고 사회의 공동약속인 법과 질서를 확립함으로써 참다운 인권신장을 이룩해 나갈 것이다.

그리고, 앞으로도 새 헌법에 담긴 인권보장의 정신이 국민의 일상생활 속에 올바로 구현될 수 있도록 제도와 관행을 지속적으로 개선함과 동시에 인권보장을 위한 국제적 노력에 적극 동참해 나갈 것이다.

끝으로, 우리는 오늘 대한민국 정부가 제출한 B규약 최초보고서에 대한 심의를 갖을 수 있도록 준비해 준신 여러분께 감사를 드리며, 이 자리가 생산적인 토론의 장으로서 한국의 인권상황과 모든 인권관련 과제들에 대한 서로의 이해에 도움이 되는 뜻깊은 회의가 되기를 바라며, 많은 건설적인 대화들이 나누어지기를 희망한다.

외 무 부

110-760 서울 종로구 세종로 77번지 / 전화 (02) 723-8934 / 전송 (02) 723-3505

문서번호 연이 20314-165
시행일자 1992.6.27
24664

수신 주제네바대사
참조

취급		장 관
보존		
국 장	전결	
심의관		
과 장		
기안	김 종 훈	협조

제목 인권규약 최초보고서 심의관련 아국법령 제출

연 : 연이 20314-1346

인권 규약 최초보고서 심의와 관련, 아국이 기 제출한 헌법외에 아래 아국관계 법령을 인권사무국에 제출하여 주시기 바랍니다.

- 아 래 -

1. 민법
2. 형법
3. 형사소송법
4. 헌법재판소법
5. 법률 구조법
6. 행형법
7. 국가보안법
8. 집회 및 시위에 관한 법률
9. 노동조합법
10. 근로기준법

첨부 : 1. 헌법재판소법(영문).

0142

2. 행형법(영문). 끝.

0143

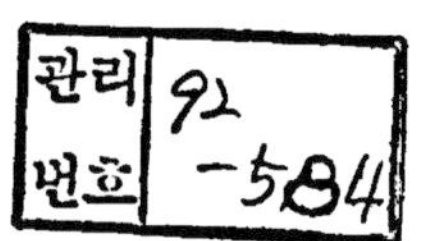

외 무 부

110-760 서울 종로구 세종로 77번지 / 전화 (02) 723-8934 / 전송 (02) 723-3505

문서번호 연이 20314-1674
시행일자 1992.6.27

수신 주제네바대사
참조

취급		장 관
보존		
국 장	전결	
심의관		
과 장		
기안	김 종 훈	협조

제목 인권규약 최초보고서 심의대비

인권규약 최초보고서 심의에 대비, 법무부에서 작성한 설명자료등을 별첨 송부합니다.

첨부 : 1. B규약 최초보고서 심의대비 설명자료 2부.

2. B규약 최초보고서 심의관련 쟁점별 진상 및 대응자료 2부. 끝

검토필 (1992. 6. 30.)

0144

원 본

외 무 부

종 별 : 지 급

번 호 : GVW-1295 일 시 : 92 0629 1920

수 신 : 장관(연이 정달호 과장)

발 신 : 주 제네바 대사(문봉주 참사관)

제 목 : 업연

대: WGV-0976

연: GVW-0995

1. 대호 기조 발언 초안 관련, 연호로 보고한바와 같이 인권 사무국측은 보고서제출 이후의 진전사항을 상세히 설명하는 것이 좋겠다는 의견을 제시 하였음을 고려, 보고서 제출 이후의 진전사항을 좀더 상세히 설명(작년 7월 이후 민법, 가족법등 각종 국내법 개정 현황 설명등) 하는것이 필요할 것으로 봄.

2. 대사님의 문의사항인바 작년 보고서 제출시 인용한 각종 국내법중 그후 개정된 법령, 법규가 있으면 그 명칭 및 주요 내용(즉 보고서에 설명한 내용과 달라진 부분)을 금일중 당관에 알려 주기 바람. 끝

국기국

92.06.30 02:56 FN

외신 1과 통제관

0145

	분류번호	보존기간

발 신 전 보

번 호 : WGV-0985 920630 1607 FX　　종별 : 암호송신

수 신 : 주 제네바 대사. ~~총영사~~ (문봉주 참사관님)

발 신 : 장 관 (유엔2과 정달호)

제 목 : 업 연

대 : WGV-0976

91.7월 보고서 제출후 국내법령중 개정된 내용은 아래와 같으나 동 법령 내용은 아국 보고서에서 인용되지 않은것 임을 참고바람.

1. 즉결 심판에 관한 절차법 (91.11. 22개정)
   - o 불출석 심판 청구권 인정

2. 보안 관찰법(91.11. 22개정)
   - o 국가보안법의 개정 취지를 반영, 국가보안법 개정전에 처벌 받은 자는 보안관찰 처분대상에서 제외

3. 형사 보상법 시행령(91.6. 19개정)
   - o 형사 보상금을 2배 이상 인상하여 형사 피고인 및 피의자의 인권을 보장

4. 범죄 피해자 구조법 시행령(91.6.19)
   - o 범죄 피해 구조금을 2배 인상. 끝.

보안 통제	

앙고재	년월일	과	기안자 성명		과 장		국 장		차 관	장 관

외신과통제

0146

원 본

외 무 부

종 별 :

번 호 : GVW-1300 일 시 : 92 0630 1830

수 신 : 장관(연이 정달호 과장)

발 신 : 주제네바대사(문봉주참사관)

제 목 : 업연

대: GVW-0976

1. 대호 모두 연설문 실무초안 내용중 5-6 페이지를별첨과 갑이 수정하는 것이 좋겠다는 것이대사님의 의견인바, 이를 반영하여 주시기 바람.

2. 아울러 5페이지 상단 둘째줄 '헌법재판소와법원에 의한 인권침해' 앞에 ....등 구체적사례 열거요망하여 6페이지 하단 결어는 원문대로유지바람.

첨부:(GVW(F)-0405)

끝

(대사 박수길-국장)

국기국

PAGE 1

92.07.01 04:53 DG

외신 1과 통제관

0147

주 제 네 바 대 표 부

번 호 : GVW(F) - 0405 년월일 : 20630 시간 : 1830

수 신 : 장 관 (연이 정달호 과장)

발 신 : 주 제네바대사 (문봉주 참사관)

제 목 : GVW-1300 첨부

보 안	
통 제	

총 2 매(표지포함)

외신과	
통 제	

405-3-1

0148

〈규약 이행상의 요인과 장애〉

규약의 이행에 영향을 주는 큰 요인으로써 남북한 관계의 현실을 잘 이해하는 것은 매우 필요한 일입니다.

남한과 북한은 하나의 민족이 1945년 서로 다른 정치적 이념에 따라 분단되었으며 그이후 1950년 동족상잔의 전쟁을 겪은이래 이념적으로 뿐 아니라 군사적으로서 서로 대치하고 있는 긴장된 상황에 있습니다. 이러한 상황하에서 양측은 겨우 작년부터 평화적인 방법에 의한 통일을 위해 본격적으로 서로간에 대화를 추진해 오고 있으며, 그 결과로 지난 2월〈남북한 사이의 화해와 불가침 및 교류 협력에 관한 합의서〉가 체결되었고, 이를 토대로 양측은 각분야별로 서로 거리를 좁혀가기 위한 협의를 계속해 오고 있습니다.

A

그러나 작금에 시작된 남북한간의 대화는 통일의 장정을 위한 첫걸음에 불과합니다. 대한민국은 1950년 북한 공산주의 침략에 의해 자유민주주의 사회가 공산화 될뻔했던 역사적 경험과 그이후에도 계속 있어났던 KAL기 폭파사건등 국가적 테러행위와 군사적 도발행위에 깊은 경각심을 갖지 않을 수 없습니다. 그리고 냉전체계가 붕괴된 오늘에도 한반도에는 평화 협정 아닌 휴전협정이 존속되고 있으며 남북간에 150만의 군대가 대치하고 있다는 사실을 또한 우리는 한시도 잊을 수가 없는 것입니다.
따라서 정부는 북한 형제와의 대화를 통하여 한반도 평화와 통일을 위한 협의를 적극 추진하면서, 동시에 북한의 기도(DESIGN ON KOREA)와 이러한 기도에 편승하여 자유 민주주의 체제를 위해하려는 세력을 견제하는 노력을 계속하여야 하는 입장에 놓여 있습니다.

자유민주주의 체제에 대한 위협으로부터 국가의 안전을 보호하기 위해 제정된 법률로서 국가보안법을 들 수 있겠습니다. 국가보안법에 대해서는 최근들어 남.북간의 교류와 접촉이 확대됨에 따라 국내 일각에서 개정 내지 폐지해야 한다는 주장이 대두되고 있으나, 북한의 태도에 기본적인 변화가 없는 현 상황에서는 이를 존치

0149

405-3-2

하여야 한다는 것이 대다수 우리 국민의 입장입니다. 앞으로 한반도내에서 휴전체제가 남북간의 평화체제로 대치되고 어느 일방이 타방을 병탄하려는 의도를 확고히 포기한 경우에는 국가보안법 같은 안보관계법도 자연이 폐기될 것입니다.

〈인권 신장을 위한 앞으로의 계획〉

정부는 국제노동기구 가입을 계기로 동 기구산하 제협약에의 가입을 추진중이며 근로자 단체와 사용자 단체를 대표하는 동수의 위원과 공익을 대표하는 위원으로 구성된 노동관계법 연구위원회를 통해 복수노조 허용등 노동관계 국내법의 개선을 위한 검토를 진행하고 있습니다.

정부는 개인의 기본적 인권을 최대한 보장하는 방향으로 죄형법정주의의 형법규범 명시와 영장 실질 심사제 도입등을 주요 내용으로 하는 형법과 형사소송법의 개정안을 작성하였으며 이를 금번 국회에 제출할 예정으로 있습니다.

나아가 정부는 고문에 의한 인권침해의 예방을 보다 공고히 하기 위해 〈고문방지 협약〉에도 가입하기로 원칙적인 방침을 정하고 관계부처간 가입을 위한 세부사항을 협의중에 있습니다.

대한민국은 헌법과 규약에 규정된 인권보장의 정신이 국민의 일상 생활속에 올바로 구현될 수 있도록 제도와 관행을 개선하는 노력을 계속함과 동시에 인권보장을 위한 국제적인 노력에도 적극 동참해나갈 것입니다.

이러한 맥락에서 대한민국정부는 내년 6월 비엔나에서 개최 예정인 세계인권회의의 성공적인 결실에 큰 기대를 갖고 있습니다. 동 회의를 통해 세계적으로 인권 보호의 차원을 한단계 높일 수 있는 계기가 되고, 시민적 정치적 권리규약등 모든 국제인권 협약의 보다 보편적인 이행이 가능해 지기를 희망하고 있으며 이를 위해 대한민국 정부도 동 세계회의에 적극 참여할 계획입니다.

B

405-3-3 0150

원 본

외 무 부

2 7h.

종 별 :

번 호 : GVW-1327 일 시 : 92 0703 1030

수 신 : 장관(연이,정달호과장)

발 신 : 주 제네바 대사(문봉주 참사관)

제 목 : 업연

당관에서 각종 인권단체의 한국관련 자료를 참조 작성한 예상 질문을 별첨 송부하니 김서기관 출발시 동 질문에 대한 영문 답변자료도 함께 지참토록 준비 바람.

첨부: 질문자료 2매. 끝

(GVW(F)-412)

국기국

PAGE 1

92.07.03 19:07 CO

외신 1과 통제관 ✓

0151

주제네바대표부

번호 : GVW(F) - 412 　　　　년월일 : 20703 　　　시간 : 1630

수신 : 장 관(연이)

발신 : 주제네바대사

제목 : GVW-1327 첨부

보 안 통 제	

총 3 매(표지포함)

외신관 통 제	

412 - 3 - 1 　　　　　　　0152

예 상 질 문

0 한국이 인권규약에 가입했지만 한반도의 특수상황을 전제로한 보안관계 법령들은 여전히 한국의 헌법 및 인권규약에 배치되는 인권제한 요소들을 포함하고 있으며 실제로 이러한 인권침해 사례들이 아직도 발생하고 있다는 주장이 있음.
그렇다면 인권규약 가입이 실제 한국국민 개개인의 인권보호 차원에서 기여하는 바가 무엇인지 ?

0 한국정부의 설명에 따르면 남.북간에 확실한 평화 보장이 선행되지 않으면 국가보안법등 보안관계법령들은 계속 유지될수 밖에 없다고 보는데, 정부가 이러한 정치적, 이념적 상황에 얽매이지 않고 국민의 기본적 인권보호 차원에서 문제된 법령들을 폐지 또는 개선할 계획은 없는 것인지 ?

0 인권 규약 가입이후 국가보안법 위반 사건의 통계와 동법에 의해 현재 구속 수감중인 정치 사상범의 숫자는 얼마나 되는지 ?

0 입법부가 정부의 부당한 인권침해 행위에 대해 견제할 수 있는 메카니즘이 어떤 것이며, 실제로 이행된 사례가 있는지 ?

0 전통적인 여성차별 제도 개선을 위해 여러가지 입법 조치가 있었다고는 하나, 실제로 사회 관행상 아직도 많은 여성차별 행위가 공공연히 존재하고 있는바 정부가 이런 문제 해결을 위해 구체적으로 어떤 정책을 시행하고 있는지 ?

0 보트피플등 주변국으로부터 정치적 망명을 요청해오는 경우 이를 어떻게 처리하고 있으며 또한 구체적인 사례가 있는지 ?

6-12-3-2

0153

0 한국은 낙태를 법률로 금지하고 있으나 전통적인 남성우위의 사회풍습에 따라 남아 선호 현상이 남아 있고 이로 인해 불법적인 낙태행위가 계속 되고 있다하는데 이는 인권차원에서 큰 문제가 아닌지 ? 실제로 10세 이하 어린이의 남녀 비율 통계는 ?

0 한국 형법상의 국가 모욕죄(insult or defame) 는 헌법과 규약이 보장하는 표현의 자유에 대한 제한이 아닌지 ?

0 보고서에는 86-90년간 29명의 경찰관등 공무원이 고문혐의로 기소되었다고 기록되어 있으나 이들에 대한 재판 결과등 보다 세부적인 기록이 결여 되어 있음.

0 피구금자들에 대한 수사관의 고문 또는 가혹 행위에 대해 피해자가 직접 고소를 제기하는 것이 현실적으로 곤란한 경우가 많다고 보는데, 고문방지를 위한 별도의 Mechanism 은 없는지 ?

0 91.11 한국정부가 Kooijmans UN 고문문제 Special Rapporteur 제출한 사로맹 사건 관련자들에 대한 고문행위 관련 답변자료 내용은 매우 단순하고 불명확한 점이 많은바 further information 요망

0 개정 이전의 구 "국가보안법" 위반으로 장기 복역중인 정치범, 양심수에 대해서는 정치적 변화, 적용법의 개정등 제반 여건 변동에 따라 재심의 기회가 부여되는 것이 타당하지 않은지 ?

4 12 - 3 - 3

0154

인권보고서 심의대비 검토사항

1992.7.3.
([illegible])

1. 준비자료

o 수석대표 기조연설문

o 예상질의 답변자료(국.영문)

- 추가 영문자료 포함

o 기본법령(국.영문)

o 아국관련 인권보고서

2. 사전 검토사항

o 홍보대책

- 심의 이전 및 심의결과에 대한 정부차원의 홍보 여부
- 민변 등의 홍보활동에 대한 대응조치

o 아국에 대한 이사회 권고사항 대응방안

- 홍보대책과 관련 검토 필요

o 대표단 출발전 주요사항 청와대 보고

3. 기타사항

o 제네바에서의 사전 준비작업

- 7.9(목) : 준비상황 점검을 위한 대표단 회의
- 7.10(금) : 예상질의에 대한 최종 점검
- 7.11(토) : 답변자료 등 준비

0155

인권보고서 심의대비 준비자료(추가)

1992. 7. 3.
외 무 부

1. 추가로 준비하여야 할 자료(국.영문)

가. 제22조 등 일부 유보조항 철회 의사

　o A규약 제8조는 유보를 하지 않은 반면 제22조를 유보한 근거

나. 장기 좌익수의 주요 범법 사례

다. 북한주민에 대한 국적부여 문제

라. 외국인의 출입국 자유에 대한 제한규정 예시

마. 외국인 거주 현황

바. 노동조합 관련 현황

사. 사실혼에 대한 보호규정

아. 여성에 대한 실질적 차별 사례 및 정부대책

2. 영문화가 필요한 자료

가. 안기부의 역할 및 수사시 인권보장을 위한 제도적 장치(대응자료 p17-18)

나. 외국인의 국내법상 지위(대비설명자료 p137-139)

다. 고문사례 발생 방지를 위한 구체적 조치(대비설명자료 p81-83)

라. 사회보호법 및 보안관찰법상 규정의 이중처벌 해당 여부

　o 보안관찰법 내용 추가 필요(대비설명자료 p184-185)

바. 부인의 국적 선택권(대비설명자료 p199)

사. 집회 및 시위에 관한 법률(대응자료 p141-142)

3. 기타 검토사항

가. 개정 국가보안법 부칙의 규약 제15조 1항 위배 여부

0156

수 신 : 법무부 인권과 정기용 검사님

발 신 : 외무부 유엔2과 김종훈

추가준비자료

o 낙태에 대한 법규정 및 정부입장과 남아선호 경향과 관련, 아동의 남여 비율

o 형법상 국가모독죄가 표현의 자유에 대한 제한이 아닌지 여부

o 보고서상 고문혐의로 기소된 29명의 공무원에 대한 재판 결과

o 인권규약 가입 이후 국가보안법 위반사건 및 수형자 통계. 끝.

총 1 매

0157

사 전 홍 보 (안)

1. 인권이사회 심의 사실 소개 :
   - 대표단 파견내용 포함
2. 심의의 목적 및 경위
3. 기조발언 요지
4. 심의결과 반영의사
5. 홍보기관 : 외무부, 법무부
   * 보고서 첨부 여부

상 부 보 고 (안)

1. 기조발언 요지
2. 향후 계획 확인
   - 노동법 개정, 고문방지협약 가입
   * 유보관련 개선 여부 검토
3. 홍보계획
   - 사전 및 사후 홍보

0158

외 무 부

110-760 서울 종로구 세종로 77번지 / 전화 (02) 723-8934 / 전송 (02) 723-3505

문서번호 연이 20314- 181
시행일자 1992.7.4.
25336

수신 주제네바대사
참조

취급		장 관
보존		
국 장	전결	
심의관		
과 장		
기안	김종훈	협조

제목 국.영문 법령집 송부

제45차 인권이사회에 참가하는 아국 대표단용으로 국.영문 법령집을 별첨 송부합니다.

첨부 : 1. 법전 1부.
2. Laws of the Republic of Korea(I-III) 각 1부. 끝.

0159

국제社會 평가 받는다

13일부터 유엔人權理事會

政府 보고서 제출 단일案件 채택
民辯 반박書…「양심수」등 논란일듯

韓國人權 몇점일까

우리나라가 국제인권규약에 가입(90년7월)하고 최초보고서를 제출(91년7월)한뒤 처음으로 국내 인권문제를 단일의제로 올리는 45차 유엔 인권이사회(13~15일, 스위스 제네바)를 앞두고 국내 인권문제에 관한 국제적인 평가에 관심이 모아지고 있다.

특히 이번 이사회는 우리나라가 제출한 보고서를 토대로 청문식의 집중적인 검토·토론작업을 벌일 것으로 예상돼 국내인권문제가 국제무대에 개방되는 계기는 물론 국내 제도 변화의 전기가 될것으로 보인다.

이에따라 정부는 지금까지 소극적·수세적 입장에서 다뤄오던 인권문제를 공개적인 논의대상에 내놓고 국제사회의 다양한 견해와 비판·평가를 수용하겠다는 전향적인 자세를 보이고있다.

정부는 특히 국내외 인권단체등이 집중적으로 거론했던 시국사범의 처우등에 관한 갖가지 문제가 강도높게 제기될 것으로 예상, 이에대해 80년대 후반이래 개선된 법률·제도를 구체적으로 제시하는 과정에서 각국의 편견을 불식할수 있을 것으로 기대하고 있다.

이와함께 근로자의 지위·여성차별해소등 非정치적분야의 기본권보장제도도 적극적으로 알려 논의의 폭을 넓힌다는 계획도 세웠다.

정부는 최초보고서가 27개조항 3백12개항목에 걸쳐 각분야의 인권보장 장치를 포괄적으로 기술하고 있어 이미 유엔에서 「성실한 보고서」란는 사전 평가가 나오고 있다고 밝히고 있다.

그러나 이번 회의에는 民辯과 KNCC가 공동으로 반박보고서를 제출, 이에대한 이사국의 판단과 평가도 주목된다.

반박보고서는 정부보고서에 대한 전체적인 평가에서 『정부와 법원은 인권을 보장하는 조항들을 축소해석하고 인권을 제한하는 규정들을 넓게 해석해 많은 인권침해를 정당화해왔고 반면에 인권침해를 예방하고 침해된 권리를 구제하기 위한 효율적인 제도는 마련돼 있지 않다』고 주장하고 있다.

이와 관련해 법무부당국자는 『반박보고서는 어디까지나 참고자료일뿐 이를 근거로한 논쟁은 별로 없을 것』이라며 『오히려 인권상황에 대한 내부비판의 자유가 허용된다는 점을 국제사회에 인식시킬수 있어 정부입장에 도움이 되는 측면도 있다』고 밝혔다.

예컨대 美國의 경우 인권보고서 제출때마다 수백건의 반박보고서가 제출됐고 日本등 다른 가입국들도 대부분 반박보고서를 통한 공개비판을 경험해왔다는 것이 정부의 설명이다.

비교적 이른 시기인 81년「규약」에 가입한 北韓의 경우는 83년 최초보고서를 냈으나 84년 열린 인권이사회에 반박보고서가 접수되지 않아 오히려 내부비판의 자유가 없다는 이유로 「폐쇄적」이란는 비판을 받았다는 것이다.

각국 반박보고서는 美國의 경우 흑백인종차별문제, 日本은 在日한국인등 외국인차별정책·내부무역장벽, 英國은 귀족에의해 운영되는 상원구성의 문제등을 거론해왔다.

어쨌든 정부는 6共들어 각종 민주화조치로 인권상황이 급신장했다는 자신감을 이번 회의를 통해 공식적으로 확인하려는 입장이다.

〈李夏慶기자〉

0160

중앙일보 22면 92.7.3. 22면

"수사과정 가혹행위 근절"

鄭검찰총장 지시

鄭錄永검찰총장은 3일 우리나라의 국제인권규약 가입 2주년을 맞아 수사과정에서 적법절차를 준수하고 피의자 인권을 철저히 보호하라고 전국검찰에 시달했다.

鄭총장은 『계속된 인권침해행위 근절작업에도 불구하고 아직까지 수사과정에서 적법절차를 제대로 지키지 않거나 가혹행위시비가 일고 있는 것은 유감』이라며 『앞으로 인권침해 행위가 발생할 경우에는 당사자는 물론, 감독자와 기관장 모두에게 책임을 묻겠다』고 말했다.

鄭총장은 특히 사건수사에서의 적법절차를 철저히 준수, 피의자 검거및 압수수색, 조사등 수사단계별로 구속영장 또는 압수수색영장을 반드시 제시할 뿐만 아니라 피의자에게 변호인선임권및 진술거부권이 있음을 고지토록 했으며, 폭언이나 폭행등 가혹행위가 없도록 했다.

92. 7. 4

0161

	분류번호	보존기간

발 신 전 보

번 호 : WGV-1026 920706 1927 FQ 종별 : 암호송신

수 신 : 주 제네바 대사. ~~총영사~~

발 신 : 장 관 (연이)

제 목 : 제45차 인권이사회 참가

표제회의 참가 본부 대표단이 아래 일정으로 귀지 도착 예정이니 숙소로 싱글 5실 예약바람.

- 법무부 대표단 및 김종훈 서기관 : 7.8(수) 21:50 SR-729편
- 정달호 과장 : 7.9(목) 22:15 SR-545편. 끝.

(국제기구국장 김재섭)

보안통제	

앙고재	92년 7월 6일	유엔2과	기안자 성명		과 장	심의관	국 장		차 관	장 관

외신과통제

0162

관리 번호	92-615

	분류번호	보존기간

발 신 전 보

번 호 : WGV-1023 920706 1834 FQ 종별 : 지급

수 신 : 주 제네바 대사. 총영사 (문봉주 참사관)

발 신 : 장 관 (유엔2과 정달호)

제 목 : 업 연

1. 홍보관련 아래와 같이 검토중임을 참고하시고, 의견 있으시면 회보 바랍니다.

   가. 사전홍보 : 규약발효 2주년(7.10)에 맞추어 7.9.오후 우리 보고서 심의 및 관련사항 언론 브리핑

   나. 사후홍보

   o 특파원 현지 참관시 : 수석대표의 브리핑 및 보도자료 배포

   o 특파원 현지 불참시 : 현지작성 보도자료의 본부송부를 통해 보도

2. 또한 회의종료 후 심의결과(필요시 향후 대책 포함)를 특별보고로 상부 보고코자 함.(문안은 현지에서 작성 Fax 송부)

3. (수정) 보완된 영문 답변자료는 대표단이 지참코자 함을 참고바람. 끝.

검토필 (1992. .30.)

예고 : 독후 파기

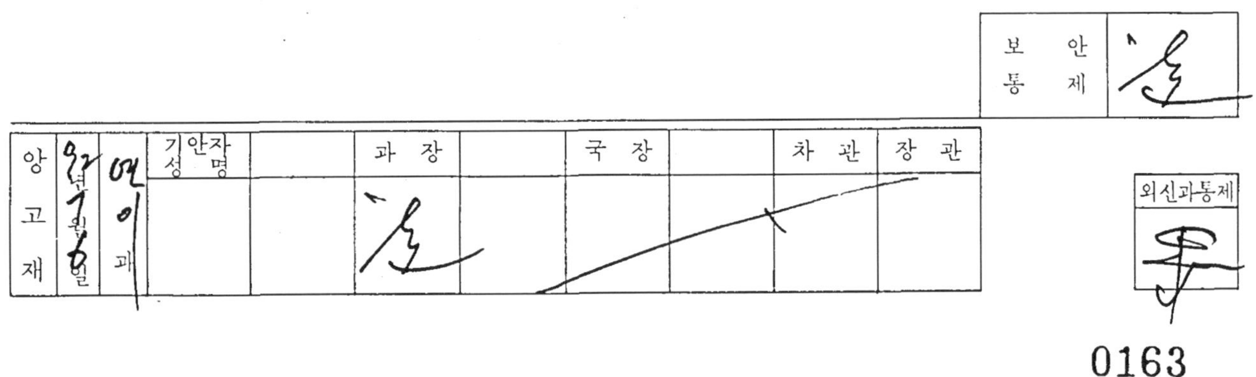

보안 통제	

앙 고 재	92년 7월 6일	연이과	기안자 성명		과 장		국 장		차 관	장 관

외신과통제

0163

관리번호	92-620

원 본

외 무 부

종 별 : 지 급

번 호 : GVW-1345 일 시 : 92 0706 1830

수 신 : 장관(연이 정달호 과장)

발 신 : 주 제네바 대사(문봉주 참사관)

제 목 : 업연

1. 대호 아국대표 기조발언 영문안을 별첨과 같이 수정하였는바 고견 회시 바람.

2. 답변자료에 이인모건 추가 바람.

3. 1 차로 송부해준 영문답변 자료의 영문 표현을 REFINE 해가지고 오는 것이 좋겠다는 것이 대사님의 의견이니 참고 바람.

4. 현지 외국 언론에 대한 홍보계획은 없는지 알려주시기 바람.

첨부: 영문안 1 부

(GVW(F)-0419). 끝

(대사 박수길-국장)

예고:92.12.31. 까지

국기국

PAGE 1

92.07.07 03:12

외신 2과 통제관 FM

0164

관리 번호	92-619

원 본

외 무 부

종 별 :

번 호 : GVW-1348 일 시 : 92 0706 2320

수 신 : 장관(연이)

발 신 : 주 제네바 대사

제 목 : 인권보고서 심의

대: WGV(F)-0263

1. 대호 인권관계 본직연설 초안을 별첨과 같이 수정하였으니 참고 바람.

2. 수정 이유는 국가보안법의 존재 이유에 관련된 남북관계 설명에서 북의 도발정책을 지나치게 부각시킴으로서 인권회의에서 아국이 불필요하게 대결적이라는 인상을 줄 필요가 없다는 점, 기타 외국어 법률용어 사용에 일관성을 기하는데 있었음을 첨언함. 끝

(대사 박수길-국장)

첨부: GVW(F)-0421

예고:92.12.31. 까지

검토필 (1992.8.30.)

국기국

PAGE 1

92.07.07 06:16

외신 2과 통제관 BZ

0165

2 가

주 제 네 바 대 표 부

번 호 : GVW(F) - 0421 년월일 : 20706 시간 : 2320

수 신 : 장 관 (연이)

발 신 : 주 제네바대사

제 목 : 첨부

보 안	
통 제	

총 12 매(표지포함)

외신과	
통 제	

421-12-1

0166

Republic of Korea
13 July, 1992

Introductory Remarks by
Ambassador Park Soo Gil

1) **Introduction**

It is a distinct pleasure and honour for me to present the Initial Report of the Republic of Korea for consideration by the Human Rights Committee.

The Republic of Korea acceded to the International Covenant on Civil and Political Rights and the International Covenant on Economic, Social and Cultural Rights in 1990 to consolidate the protection of human rights in Korea and to join the international effort to promote human rights throughout the world. In this regard, I believe that the consideration of our first Report pursuant to Article 40 of the Covenant is an important event for Korea as it will show our endeavours and achievements on our way to reaching Korea's human rights goals.

At the same time I fully hope and expect that this forum will provide us an excellent opportunity to engage in a constructive dialogue concerning how Korea can better fulfill its commitments to the International Covenant. The scrutiny of the Initial Report by the internationally renowned human rights advocates here today will encourage my government to continue its undertaking to enhance the human rights of the Korean people.

With this in mind, I take great pleasure in introducing the Report to the Committee.

Let me start by making a few points concerning the preparation of this Report. First, great efforts were made to ensure that the structure and contents of the Report complied with the general guidelines set out by the Committee. In accordance with the guidelines, and the explanatory notes, we sought to include as much information as possible so that a full picture would emerge of the protection of human rights in Korea. The research undertaken to produce the Report was compiled by an inter-ministerial working group composed of members from the Government agencies involved in the protection of human rights. This working group was responsible for drafting the Report, and did so through in-depth discussions on every aspect of human rights protection.

Second, in view of the fact that the laws of the Republic of Korea are based on the Civil Law system of written laws, the emphasis of the Report is on the explanation of the legal and institutional aspects concerning the protection of human rights. Decisions of the Constitutional Court and other courts, as well as relevant administrative measures are also described to complement the institutional aspects.

Third, noting that there has been great progress in the protection of human rights since the inauguration of the current government in early 1988, the Report focuses on the developments since that time.

2) **Human Rights Promotion under the current Constitution.**

I would now like to turn to the substantive part of the Report, the status of civil and political rights in the Republic of Korea. Under the current Constitution, as revised on 29 October 1987, institutional devices were strengthened to fully embody genuine democratic principles, and to better enhance the protection of human rights and fundamental freedoms in Korea.

The revised Constitution provides for the election of the President of the Republic of Korea through direct popular vote, instead of the system of indirect vote practised under the previous Constitution. This change increases the right of the people to participate directly in presidential politics. The Constitutional changes also strengthen the power and authority of the National Assembly to check and balance the Administrative branch by reinstating for example, the Assembly's power to review the Administration's actions.

In the area of justice, the current Constitution has made the independence of the judiciary more effective by improving the procedure for appointing judges. Another important change made in this area is the establishment of the Constitutional Court, which works as a crucial guarantor of human rights.

In addition, the constitutional provisions dealing with human rights and fundamental freedoms were amended to further protect and enhance these rights. For example, to further guarantee the liberty and security of persons, the lawful procedures to be followed in the event of arrest or detention have been written into the Constitution itself. The Constitution also strengthens the rights of criminal suspects and defendants.

To put these constitutional provisions into practice, the Republic of Korea has amended the relevant laws and regulations that deal with the administration of criminal justice, and improved the related procedures and practices. The government has also made improvements in the penal administration in accordance with the spirit and the letter of the Constitution. We have also instituted legal aid programmes so that poorer citizens receive the full protection of the law and improved the regulations and practices relating to immigration control to further facilitate the right to liberty of movement.

Moreover, amendments have been made to the National Security Law and the Act concerning Assembly and

Demonstration which had been often the subject of controversy. The application of these laws has been strictly limited in order to eliminate any room for misinterpretation or abuse.

It is also worth mentioning that individuals may now make direct petitions to the Constitutional Court to redress infringements of fundamental rights committed by the State. More than thirty cases of human rights infringements have been redressed since the establishment of the petition system and the Constitutional Court in 1989.

Another important democratic development is the introduction of a system allowing greater autonomy to local governments. Local autonomy, although written into the Constitution in 1961, had not been implemented except during a brief period in the early sixties. However, in December 1991 and March 1992, two rounds of legislative council election were held nationwide for the first time in nearly thirty years. These local assemblies, created through popular elections and functioning actively, represent another step in the expansion of political rights of the people.

Mr. Chairman, I am pleased to report that completely free from authoritarian tinges of the past, our people live now under the rule of law in a democracy. Rights and fundamental freedoms are protected, and safeguards are in place to ensure that these fundamental freedoms are guaranteed. The seed of liberal democracy has taken root at all levels of our society, and we, the Korean people are enjoying the fruits of our freedom.

Accession to the Covenants is an important part of these democratic processes. Only a true democracy feels free to open its doors to public scrutiny and to participate at the international level to protect and promote human rights at

421-12-5

home and abroad. In this respect it is noted that we have made a declaration recognizing the competence of the Committee under Article 41 of the Covenant and have acceded to the Optional Protocol to the Covenant as well. As you know, this means that people are now under international protection in addition to the extensive domestic protections provided by our Constitution.

Since accession to the aforementioned instruments, the government of the Republic of Korea has made every effort to publicize their contents. The texts have been translated and published in the Korean language, along with a compilation of this Committee's proceedings and decisions. Measures have also been taken to educate law enforcement officials so that they act in accordance with the provisions and procedures set forth in the Covenant, and in the Constitution. It is my personal opinion that these texts are now widely known in Korea, and will be known in greater detail as a result of this forum's work over the next three days.

3) **Accommodation of the Covenant as a law of the land under the Constitution**

All of the rights provided for in the Covenant are guaranteed by the Republic of Korea's Constitution, as our Constitution stipulates that all treaties duly concluded and promulgated shall have the same effect as the domestic laws of the Republic of Korea.

Since virtually all of the rights in the Covenant are likewise provided for in the Constitution, I can say that the Covenant, together with the Constitution, forms the centrepiece of the human rights law of the Republic of Korea. In this respect, it is noteworthy that the Constitutional Court invoked Article 18, Paragraph 2 of the Covenant in an 1 April 1991 decision on the

421-12-6

constitutionality of a provision of the Civil Code.

The Republic of Korea maintains three reservations to the Covenant, with regard to specific provisions that conflict with domestic laws; namely, paragraphs 5 and 7 of Article 14, and Article 22. These reservations are only partial in nature and are not intended to disavow the specific rights provided for in the Covenant. Instead they seek to maintain limitations prescribed in the relevant domestic laws as explained in detail in the Report. My government firmly believes that these reservations do not represent a derogation from the basic principles embodied in the Covenant.

4) Developments Since the Submission of the Report

The Republic of Korea's admission to the United Nations in September 1991 provided additional momentum to my government's efforts to promote universal human rights in accordance with the Charter of the United Nations. By subsequently joining the International Labour Organization as a full-fledged member in December 1991, the Republic of Korea strongly endorsed international endeavours to ensure the protection of fundamental rights relating to trade union activities.

Furthermore, the Republic of Korea ratified the Convention on the Rights of the Child in December 1991 and is on the threshold of becoming a party to the Convention Relating to the Status of Refugees and its Protocol, pending the consent of the National Assembly.

While I place great significance on my government's international commitments to human rights, no less importance should be placed on the actions of individuals and groups within Korea that have worked hard to enhance the protection of human rights. I believe that it is a positive step, and a display of confidence in the due process of law that the number of human rights cases being brought to courts is on the increase. Corresponding to this trend, private human rights groups are increasing their efforts to monitor the protection of human rights. Clearly these actions are eloquent evidence that Korea is moving in a desirable direction, and has succeeded in creating a favorable atmosphere for the redress of human rights complaints.

5) **Factors and Difficulties Affecting the Implementation of the Covenant**

One of the most important factors affecting the implementation of the Covenant is the tense situation resulting from the division of Korean peninsula. Following its liberation from Japanese colonial rule in 1945, Korea was caught between two opposing ideologies. The Northern aggression in 1950 brought about untold misery upon Korean people and further cemented the division of the nation. Since the Korean war, the two parts of Korea have confronted one another militarily as well as ideologically across the 38th parallel.

Under these circumstances, it was not until last year following the collapse of the Cold War that the two sides managed to engage in a serious dialogue, and to begin to seek a way to reunify the nation peacefully. As a result, the Agreement on Reconciliation, Non-aggression and Exchanges and Cooperation was concluded between the two Koreas in February this year. This Agreement has led to a series of regular consultations which will narrow the distances separating the two Koreas in every field of life.

Nevertheless, the dialogue has just begun and we have seen nothing more than the first cautious step along the long road to reunification. It is natural that a country that

421-12-8

has had the unforgettable experience of nearly being overthrown by an invasion, cannot easily relax its guard against another aggression.

It is also noted that armed forces totalling 1.5 million are in a military stand-off along the 38th Parallel and that the Armistice Agreement has still not been replaced by a peace agreement, despite the end of the Cold War.

Accordingly, the Republic of Korea, while it proceeds in earnest with the dialogue for peace and reunification, must make efforts to guard against subversive forces intent on impairing the integrity of the liberal democratic system of the Republic of Korea particularly when North Korea still maintains a clause in the preamble of the platform of the Korean Workers party declaring as its basic policy the "realization of the people's revolution for national liberation in South Korea," - namely the communization of the whole Korean peninsula.

It is in this context that Korea finds itself in a dilemma. While North Korea has to be a crucial dialogue partner on such issues as peace, cooperation and exchanges and unification, it is an entity which continues to pose a clear and present danger to the security of the South Korea because of its strategy of destabilizing the state of the Republic of Korea. It is for this reason that the National Security Law, which was adopted by the Republic of Korea as a means to protect the security of the state and the integrity of the system, still finds its raison d'être.

Amid the recent trend of expanding South-North contacts and exchanges, a call for abolishing the National Security Law is being made in some quarters. However, the overwhelming majority of the people in the Republic of Korea believe that the law should be maintained to safeguard the Republic from subversive activities. It is my firm belief that when the Armistice Agreement is replaced by a peace agreement and the South-North relations are normalized, the National Security Law will close its function.

In the meantime, the government of the Republic of Korea remains determined to eliminate any room for possible infringement of human rights resulting from the application of this law, beyond the restrictions permitted by the Constitution and the Covenant.

This determination has been expressed by the government through its incorporation into the National Security Law in May 1991 of portions of a 1990 Constitutional Court decision limiting the scope of the National Security Law. The Court decision provides clearer and narrower definitions on such concepts as "endangering national security and survival" and "endangering the basic liberal democratic order" in strict observance of the constitutional provisions.

6) **Future Programmes for the Promotion of Human Rights**

As part of its future programme to further promote universal human rights, my government has decided to accede to the Convention against Torture and Other Cruel, Inhuman or Degrading Treatment or Punishment and has embarked on consultations among the relevant ministries to formulate an accession plan.

Furthermore, my government is in the final stages of drafting amendments to the Penal Code and the Code of Penal Procedure to reinforce the principle of "nullum crimen sine lege" and to introduce measures for more effective review of the warrants. we expect that these amendments will be enacted by the National Assembly by the end of this year.

On the other hand, my government, as a new member of the

ILO, is now preparing to accede to various conventions concluded under the auspices of this organization. In addressing domestic labour issues, I take pleasure in reporting to you that my government has set up a working group consisting of an equal number of representatives from workers, employers and the government, respectively, for the purpose of streamlining labour-related domestic laws and thus enhancing the rights of workers. This working group is also considering an amendment to the Labour Union Act to allow multiple unions in a single workplace, which is prohibited under the present Act.

The Republic of Korea will thus continue its endeavours to improve its institutions and practices relevant to human rights so that the spirit and principles for the protection of human rights embodied in its Constitution and in the Covenant will be further incorporated into the daily life of the Korean people.

My government will also take an active part in protecting and promoting human rights at the international and regional levels. In this context, the government of the Republic of Korea has high expectations for the fruitful outcome of the World Conference on Human Rights which will be held next June in Vienna. The government believes that this conference will add momentum to enhancing the universal protection of human rights and that as a result of this conference all human rights instruments will be implemented more effectively and on a wider basis. To this end the government of the Republic of Korea will participate actively in the forthcoming World Conference.

In conclusion, I hope that the explanations and statements given above will be of some assistance to you in fully understanding the status of the protection of human rights in the Republic of Korea. As I believe this exercise is a process of constructive dialogue between the distinguished members of the Committee and my government, I shall be pleased to answer, to the best of my knowledge, any comments and questions you may have. Thank you.

인권규약 보고서 심의 대비

예상질의 답변자료

92. 7.

외 무 부

0178

- 차 례 -

0179

분야별 예상 질의사항

I. 일반적 사항

1. 규약의 국내법적 지위

A-1　　o 규약규정이 법원에서 직접 원용될 수 있는지 여부 및 있을 경우 그 사례

A-2　　o 국내법과 규약이 상충될 경우 법원이 규약을 국내법에 우선하여 적용할 수 있는지 여부

A-3　　o 후법우선의 원칙이 규약에도 적용되는지 여부

A-4　　o 제22조 등 일부 유보조항 철회 의사

- A규약 제8조는 유보를 하지 않은 반면 제22조를 유보한 근거

2. 국가보안법

B-1　　o 국가보안법

B-2　　o 표현의 자유와의 관계

B-3　　o 양심.결사의 자유와의 관계

B-4　　o 국가보안법의 적용상의 문제

B-5　　o 국가기밀의 범위

B-6　　o 개정 국가보안법 부칙의 규약 제15조 1항 위배 여부

- 헌법재판소에 헌법소원 등 제소사례 여부

B-7　　o 정치범

B-8　　o 장기좌익수

B-9　　o 장기좌익수의 범법유형

0180

B-10　o 장기좌익수의 전향문제

B-11　o 이인모 문제

B-12　o 비상입법기구 제정 법률의 합헌성

B-13　o 안전기획부 활동

Ⅱ. 조문별 예상 질문사항

1. 제1조 (민족자결권)

1-1　o 아파타이트 정책

2. 제2조 (평등권, 권리침해의 구제)

2-1　o 외국인 권리의 평등보장을 위한 조치

2-2　o 외국인 체류 현황

2-3　o 외국인 출입국 자유에 대한 제한 규정

3. 제3조(여성지위)

3-1　o 여성에 대한 실질적 평등보장

3-2　o 여성지위 향상을 위한 제반조치

3-3　o 부인의 국적선택권

4. 제4조 (비상사태)

4-1　o 비상사태시의 인권제한 범위 및 절대적 기본권의 내용

4-2　o 헌법 제37조상의 "국가안전보장", "질서유지", "공공복리"의 개념 및 구체적 사례

0181

5. 제5조 (기본권의 보장)

6. 제6조 (생명권)

6-1　　o 사형문제에 대한 정부 입장

7. 제7조 (고문)

7-1　　o 고문방지를 위한 제도적 장치

7-2　　o 공무원 가혹행위에 대한 처벌 현황

7-3　　o 고문피해자에 대한 보상 현황

7-4　　o 강요된 자백의 효력

8. 제8조 (강제노동)

9. 제9조 (신체의 자유)

9-1　　o 영장주의의 예외

　　　　- 임의동행의 문제 포함

9-2　　o 수사과정에서의 변호인 접견권 제한

9-3　　o 공안사건 피의자 구속의 남용

9-4　　o 구속남용

9-5　　o 법원의 판결에 의하지 아니한 신체의 자유 제한 사례 및 구체절차

9-6　　o 보안관찰법, 보호관찰법의 신체의 자유 제한 문제

0182

10. 제10조 (재소자 인권)

10-1 o 재소자에 대한 징벌 및 징벌결정에 대한 불복절차

10-2 o 사상전향제도와 부당한 처우

10-3 o 재소자의 교통권 보장

10-4 o 미결수용자의 처우

10-5 o 피구금자 처우 최저기준 규칙 등 국제법규에 관한 법집행 관리 교육 현황

11. 제11조 (채무불이행)

12. 제12조 (거주이전의 자유)

12-1 o 외국인 입국거부자의 불복절차 및 현황

13. 제13조 (외국인의 강제퇴거)

13-1 o 외국인 강제퇴거 현황

13-2 o 강제퇴거 결정에 대한 불복절차

14. 제14조 (재판의 권리)

14-1 o 특별법원의 유형

14-2 o 군사법원에서의 민간인 재판

14-3 o 군사법원에서의 피고인 권리 보장

14-4 o 공개재판원칙의 예외

14-5 o 사회보호법 및 보안관찰법상 규정의 이중처벌 해당 여부

0183

15. 제15조 (형벌불소급)

16. 제16조 (법률 행위능력)

16-1　　o 미성년자의 행위능력 제한

17. 제17조 (프라이버시 권리보호)

17-1　　o 사실혼에 대한 보호규정

17-2　　o 가정 또는 가족의 개념 및 범위

17-3　　o 사생활의 비밀보장을 위한 조치

- 정보유출로 인한 사생활의 보호 및 침해시 구제

17-4　　o 통신의 자유

18. 제18조 (양심.종교의 자유)

18-1　　o 종교현황

18-2　　o 종교의 자유에 대한 제한 사례

18-3　　o 양심적 병역거부

19. 제19조 (표현의 자유, 알권리)

19-1　　o 표현물 심의와 공연.음반 등에 대한 사전 심의

19-2　　o 언론 및 출판 활동의 보장

20. 제20조 (전쟁선동금지)

0184

21. 제21조 (집회의 자유)

21-1 ㅇ 집회 및 시위의 자유의 보장

21-2 ㅇ 집회.시위에 대한 신고제도

22. 제22조 (결사의 자유)

22-1 ㅇ 노동조합의 정치활동 금지

22-2 ㅇ 노동관계법상 제3자 개입금지

22-3 ㅇ 교원노조활동

22-4 ㅇ 노동조합 현황

22-5 ㅇ 노동조합 설립절차

22-6 ㅇ 복수노조금지

22-7 ㅇ 공무원 노조 현황

22-8 ㅇ 정당해산 사유 및 사례

23. 제23조 (가정의 보호)

23-1 ㅇ 사실혼에 대한 보호규정

24. 제24조 (아동의 권리)

24-1 ㅇ 아동의 국외입양절차

24-2 ㅇ 아동의 국적취득 보장

25. 제25조 (참정권)

25-1 ㅇ 공무담임권의 제한

26. 제26조 (사회보장)

0185

27. 제27조 (소수민 보호)

27-1　　o 소수민족을 위한 교육 현황

27-2　　o 귀화자의 권리 보장

0186

답 변 자 료

I. 일반적 사항

B-1　　O 국가보안법

B-2　　O 표현의 자유와의 관계

B-3　　O 양심.결사의 자유와의 관계

B-4　　O 국가보안법의 적용상의 문제

B-5　　O 국가기밀의 범위

B-7　　O 정치범

B-8　　O 장기좌익수

B-12　　O 비상입법기구 제정 법률의 합헌성

B-15　　O 안전기획부 활동

II. 조문별 답변자료

1-1　　O 아프타이트 정책

2-1　　O 외국인 권리의 평등보장을 위한 조치

2-2　　O 외국인 체류 현황

3-1　　O 여성에 대한 실질적 평등보장

7-4　　O 강요된 자백의 효력

9-2　　O 수사과정에서의 변호인 접견권 제한

9-3　　O 공안사건 피의자 구속의 남용

9-4　　O 구속남용

10-1　　O 재소자에 대한 징벌 및 징벌 결정에 대한 불복절차

10-2　　O 사상전향제도와 부당한 처우

0187

21-1　　o 집회 및 시위의 자유의 보장

21-2　　o 집회.시위에 대한 신고제도

22-1　　o 노동조합의 정치활동 금지

22-2　　o 노동관계법상 제3자 개입금지

0188

The National Security Law

A. Overview

- North Korea's goal of communizing the South by force poses a continued threat to the security of the Republic of Korea. The National Security Law(NSL) remains an indispensable legal instrument for safeguarding our democratic system against such threat.

- The restriction of fundamental human rights under the NSL shall be strictly limited to the extent necessary to preserve our national security. The Constitution provides that the fundamental human rights may be restricted by law only when necessary for "national security, the maintenance of law and order, or for public welfare", in so far as no essential aspect of these rights shall be violated. This basic principle is acknowledged by the Covenant.

- The NSL has been strictly enforced against anti-state activities such as agitation for violent revolution and subversive acts to imperil national security and the survival of the basic free and democratic order.

0189

B. Freedom of Expression

o As for the allegation that Art. 7 of the NSL excessively limits the freedoms of speech, press, art, creation, or education, theoretical and empirical studies do not provide any evidence to date in support of this allegation. On the contrary, this allegation has proved to be predicated on purely erroneous assumptions, findings, and legal interpretations.

o It does not intervene in the free exchange of ideas. This is not within the scope or the purpose of the NSL. Only those who imperil national security by engaging in subversive activities and thereby destroying the peaceful fabric of our society are the ones convicted by NSL.

o The standard of punishment is applied equally to the freedoms of speech, press, art, writing, and academic research. Thus, it can be said that the freedom of education is guaranteed without restriction. However, if any person intentionally commits an anti-state act under the justification of academic research which endangers national security, his act obviously exceeds such limits. In such a case, therefore, it is inevitable that he should be punished according to the provisions of the National Security Law.

0190

C. Freedom of Conscience, Freedom of Association

- o The assertion that freedom of conscience is limited by Article 10 (Failure to inform) and that freedom of association is limited by Article 3 (Anti-state organization) and Article 7 (Enemy-benefitting organization) is ill-founded.

- o The purpose of Article 10 is not to reveal a person's thoughts or ethics but simply to give information on the objective facts which he has acquired. In this sense, it does not infringe upon freedom of conscience. Article 10 applies the same logic as that of a punishment against a witnesses who refuses to give testimony.

- o The activities prohibited under Article 3 and Article 7 are only those of anti-state organizations and enemy-benefitting organizations which endanger national security. The formation of such kind of subversive organizations is generally prohibited in any country's law.

0191

D. Concerning the Problems in Relation to the Application of the National Security Law

- o The Government of the Republic of Korea interprets and applies the provisions of the National Security Law very strictly in accordance with the spirit of the Constitution which declares the principle of minimum restrictions on fundamental rights and within the purpose of the National Security Law. Thus, there is no room for human rights violations caused by abuses of the NSL.

- o The government of the Republic of Korea applies the provisions of the National Security Law only to activities obviously endangering national security or the survival of the basic liberal democratic order, activities such as instigation of violent revolution or other attempts to displace the legitimate government which go beyond the acceptable boundaries of such rights.

- o Accordingly, the courts focuse its examination on whether the activity of the accused actually instigated or advocated violence to make a decision on the indictment on a strict interpretation.

- o The Constitutional Court has rigorously interpreted the provision concerning activities that "endanger national security or survival of the basic liberal democratic order," thus eliminating any room for abuse of the NSL.
  - Activities endangering national security or survival means, on the one hand, explicit communist activities which treaten or infringe upon the independence of the Republic of Korea or infiltrate into the territory or try to destroy and paralyze the operation of the Constitution, the laws, or constitutionally created institutions.

0192

- Activities endangering the basic liberal democratic order means, on the other hand, the activities which make it difficult to maintain the majority rule exclusive of violence and arbitrariness and the legal order based on principles of liberty and equality. They also include those activities which destroy the current system of respect for human rights, the separation of powers, the parliamentary system, the plural party system, the electoral system, a political and economic order based on private ownership of property and the market economy, and the independence of the judiciary.

o Therefore, the assertion that the goverment of the Republic of Korea interpret and apply the National Security Law in an exceedingly broad and arbitrary fashion seems to come from a distortion of the truth.

- Under the Natinal Security Law, a person would not be punished even though he harbors or expresses socialist ideas as long as it does not endanger national security.
- Simple criticisms directed against the government, the unification movement, academic research, or unharmful activities in the fields of speech, publication, art, and writing are not subject to punishment.
- Visits to North Korea or contacts with persons of North Korea for the purpose of unification exchanges and cooperation is allowed if they are approved by the government under the Special Act Governing intra-Korean Exchanges and Cooperations. In this case, the National Security Law would not be applied.

0193

o The essence of the problem is that anti-state activists, harboring subversive ulterior motives, present themselves as democratic figures acting under the justification of academic research or the unification movement attempting to stir up disruptive activities and mislead the public.

0194

E. <u>Secret under NSL</u>

- o Today, modern war is defined as all-out war. Thus, state secrets, vital to the strength and performance of military operations, encompass not only military secrets in the strict sense of the term, but also all secret matters in the fields of politics, the economy, society, culture, etc. Hence, they should be safeguarded from anti-state organizations so that they may not undermine the capability of our military forces.

- o Even if information is made public, it is reasonable to regard the act of collecting such information for the enemy as an espionage activity. Thus, a person who collects such information shall be prosecuted under the National Security Law insofar as he or she has the intention of providing it to North Korea.

- o According to Article 4(1) (ii) of the National Security Law, in the event that a cell of any anti-state organization, or a person who has been under instructions from such organization, has detected, collected, divulged, transmitted or intermediated state secrets designed to effect purposes such as social upheaval or political revolution, he or she will be duly prosecuted.

0195

Political Prisoners

o People in certain segments of our society have been insisting that "political prisoners" must be realeased without condition.

- They appear to include a wide range of offenders, including those who violate the NSL, such as spies, those who initiate street demonstrations by throwing rocks and Molotov cocktails or by wielding steel pipes, those who destroy and burn public building, public facilities, public vehicles, police equipment, and even those who injure or kill policemen, those who occupy the president's office of their universities, destroy the materials within, those who use physical violence on their teachers, those who destroy or set fire to important facilities at their workplace, those who confine, use violence on, or intimidate their co-workers and employers, and even those who injure or kill their co-workers.

o It is claimed that the worsening situation of human rights in Korea is vividly shown by the steady increase in the number of political prisoners. Their argument is based on the farfetched assumption that offenders of security-related laws, such as the NSL, are all political prisoners, irrespective of their specific criminal activities.

o Yet, as we examined above, such argument is absolutely illogical, groundless, and unjustifiabel. The criteria they use to classify political prisoners are totally contradictory, highly arbitrary, and completely subjective. They are unacceptable.

0196

o In order to have a free and democratic society, no country can tolerate those who negate the very existence of law and order. Law and order are the products of consensus among the constituents who support society. No society can allow outrightly to let law-breakers who deny law and order to go about with impunity.

o The number of so-called political prisoners may fluctuate in accordance with the number of sabotage attempts of such subversives. Someone asserts that the increase of such prisoners is the indicia in determining the situation of human rights in our country. In light of the above, such assertions would appear to be unjust and unreasonable.

0197

Long-Term Leftist Inmates

o Long-term leftist inmates are criminals who were tried and sentenced and are now serving their terms according to law. They committed anti-state crimes such as attempting to overthrow the government of the Republic of Korea and thereby creating casualties.

o It is highly likely that they will break the law again when they are released.

- Even elderly inmates may resume covert espionage in connection with currently operating underground spy organizations in South Korea, thus posing a direct threat to our society.

o Accordingly, their general release is not to be considered.

- However, some aged inmates and some ailing ones were released by suspending their sentences. Release will continue to be granted on a case-by-case basis in consideration of service records and humanitarian concerns.

0198

Constitutionality of Laws Enacted by Non-elected Legislatures

- o It is understood that previously non-elected legislatures were instituted as emergency measures in order to deal with certain crises.
  - The possibility of military confrontation with North Korea was greatly heightened by extreme social unrest and constant military provocation.

- o Since the inauguration of the sixth Republic, the National Assembly organized a special committee for the revision and repeal of alleged illegitimate laws enacted by the above non-elected legislatures.
  - The number of illegitimate laws was estimated at about 700. Of those, approximately 200 laws were revised or repealed and the remainder were approved.

0199

Role of the National Security Planning Agency

- o In Korea, neither illegitimate investigation agencies nor secret police organizations exist. The National Security Planning Agency(the "Agency"), the Security Division of National Police Headquarters, and the Military Security Command lawfully investigate National Security Law violation cases in accordance with relevant empowering laws.

- o The National Security Planning Agency collects domestic security information regarding communist and subversive activities and conducts investigations in only a limited number of cases, such as National Security Law violation cases. When National Security Law violation cases are investigated and decided, the Agency does not actually exercise its co-ordination power over other investigation agencies, even though it is empowered to do so by law. Such other agencies conduct investigations and make decisions independently of the Agency.

- o Satisfactory means of control over the Agency have been secured. The controlling means at the disposal of the National Assembly include budget reviews, accountability of the Chief of the Agency, and regular and special inspections. The Board of Audit audits the Agency.

0200

Article 1 (Right to Self-Determination)

Apartheid

o The Republic of Korea, in the firm belief that apartheid constitutes a crime against the conscience and dignity of mankind, reaffirms its support for the efforts of the South African people and the international community to establish, through peaceful means, a united, non-racial and democratic society in South Africa in which all people, irrespective of race, colour, sex or creed, will enjoy the same fundamental human rights.

o In this regard, the Government of the Republic of Korea welcomes the recent favourable developments in South Africa, which will foster a climate fully conducive to a peaceful settlement of the problems through negotiation. The Korean Government believes that these developments are positive steps toward the elimination of all forms of racial discrimination and the establishment of a united, democratic and non-racial society in South Africa.

o In November 1991 and January 1992, responding to the ongoing efforts pursued by the South African Government, Korea lifted some of the sanctions against South Africa which had been imposed since 1978. The measures taken to that effect include the following;

- Sports and cultural exchanges as well as the establishment of business relations are allowed;

0201

- Private enterprises are allowed to set up branches in South Africa;
- Investment and other financial activities by corporations with government investment are allowed;
- Trade missions and direct air services are allowed.

o The Korean Government believes that removal of the sanctions will contribute to enhancing the welfare of the black community and also to the regional development of southern Africa.

o Notwithstanding the above-mentioned measures, Korea has not established diplomatic or consular relations with South Africa. Furtheremore, the ban on the trade of oil and military items with South Africa remains in effect, along with the ban on any activities that may help the country develop or manufacture nuclear weapons.

o The Korean Government, as an expression of its support for and solidarity with the people of South Africa, since 1978 has provided financial assistance to the United Nations trust funds and programmes for southern Africa and is fulfilling its pledge of US$ 1 million pledged in 1987 to the Action for Resisting Invasion, Colonialism and Apartheid Fund.
The Republic of Korea fully supports the noble and untiring efforts of the Special Committee against Apartheid and other relevant bodies of the United Nations to achieve the lofty goal of eliminating all forms of racial discrimination and apartheid.

0202

Status of Foreigners under Korean Laws

- o Regardless of whether any specific provisions exist in the Constitution or not, the fundamental human rights are equally guaranteed to all foreigners, with the exception of the rights which require Korean nationality as a condition for enjoyment.

- o Article 10 of the Constitution provides that every person is entitled to basic respect as a human being and to the pursuit of happiness.

- o The right to freedom is a right granted to everyone, including foreigners. However, certain rights such as freedom of residence and movement(Article 14), freedom of speech and press(Article 4), and freedom of assembly and association(Article 21) may be restricted for reasons of national security.

- o Pursuant to relevant laws such as the Exit and Entry Control Act, the freedom of exit and entry may be restricted under certain circumstances. A foreigner may be deported if the requirements for deportation provided for in Article 45 of the Exit and Entry Control Act are met.

- o Certain restrictions apply to foreigners' rights to the occupation of land and ownership of property rights, including mining rights. The Alien Land Acquisition Act places restrictions, through provisions in the Presidential Decree, on the rights to and on the basis of principles of reciprocity(Article 2 of the Act). The Mining Act prohibits, in principle, a foreigner or foreign corporation from gaining mining rights(Article 6 of the Act).

0203

o The right to political activities such as the right to participate in elections, the right to be elected to office, and the right to vote are rights guaranteed only to Korean nationals and are not allowed to foreigners.

o As part of the guarantee of the fundamental human rights, foreigners are entitled to claim the rights such as the right to pursue happiness (Article 10), equality rights(Article 11), the right to personal liberty (Article 12), and the right to a fair trial(Article 27). The right to claim government compensation is allowed only if a reciprocal treatment agreement exists with the home country of the foreigner(Government Compensation Act, Article 7).

o The right of everyone to an adequate standard of living does not fully apply, in principle, to foreigners. Some rights, such as environmental rights and sanitation rights, apply to a limited degree.

0204

Number of Foreign Nationals in Korea

o As of 31 December 1991, the number of foreign nationals residing in Korea in 51,021.

Foreign nationals residing in Korea	
Chinese	23,464
Americans(United States)	14,922
Japanese	5,725
Other nationalities	6,910
Total	51,021

o Since 1 January 1991, 86 people have been naturalized of whom 74 persons are of Chinese origin.

0205

Article 3 (Status of Women)

Status of Women at the de facto level

o The Government of the Republic of Korea has taken positive steps to enhance women's status on both governmental and private levels as explained in the Report in detail. With the initiation of the Sixth Republic of Korea, government policies emphasized systematically ensuring women's participation in social and economic activities, and on expanding welfare facilities for women.

o In spite of advances and changes for the status of women, there are a lot of problems to be tackled. These problems have continued to increase despite the Government's implementation of economic and social development plans.

- The unemployment rate of women in higher academic careers still remains high.
- Most female workers are still engaged in low-wage jobs where they are subject to employment or wage discrimination.
- Although the participation of married women in economic activities is continuously increasing, the supply of public childcare facilities for children of low-income female workers falls short of the sharply growing demand.
- Improvement of women-related laws and systems have failed to yield substantial results or to enhance the position of women.

0206

- Though it is difficult and thus time-consuming to completely eliminate entrenched traditions of discrimination against women, and to fully realize equal participation of women in every field, the Government endeavours to work to promote conditions in which women can improve their status.

- This must be done not only at the de jure level but also at the de facto level. Only in this way women can fully demonstrate their capabilities and contribute to society on an equal footing with men. Specifically, the Government is trying to eliminate persistent, stereotyped concepts based on traditional sex roles and provide a climate conducive to women's full participation in society.

- In the future, various efforts should be exerted to implement the plans in the Long-Term Perspective on National Development Toward the Year 2000 which was adopted in 1986. This would be in accordance with the guidelines suggested by the United Nations in the Nairobi Forward Looking Strategies for the Advancement of Women, which promotes the development of women's capacity, the utilization of women's resources, and a more healthy family life.

0207

Involuntary confession

o Article 12(7) of the Constitution and Article 309 of the Code of Criminal Procedure provide that any confession extracted by torture, violence, threat or unjustifiably prolonged detention, or which is suspected to have been made involuntarily, shall not be admitted as evidence of guilt. In compliance with these provisions, the courts carefully examine whether confessions have been made voluntarily or not. In fact, it is so difficult to determine whether or not a confession has been made against the will of the defendant that the courts shall not admit confessions into evidence unless the voluntariness of the confession is proved beyond a reasonable doubt.

o The Supreme Court ruled that confession was not made against the will of defendants because they made statements that they were interrogated at the prosecutor's office in a free atmosphere without any violence treatment or threat of violence and the contents of the confessions were in line with the objective facts extracted from other evidence.
(84-DO-1846, October 23, 1984)

o On the other hand, the Supreme Court determined that it was doubtful whether confessions made before the public prosecutor were made voluntarily because of unduly prolonged detention and ill-treatment, such as in the case against Song Gi-Sub and several other persons who violated the National Security Law. Consequently, the Supreme Court reversed the lower court's decision twice and returned it for retrial. After that, the appellate court examined 8 more witnesses and found that the

0208

defendants could not deny the charges against them when investigative officials presented enough objective evidence to prove the charges, such as instructions from North Korea for their espionage activities, etc., during the interrogation. Accordingly, the court acknowledged that the confessions were made voluntarily.

Participation of the Defence Counsel During the Investigation

- o The Code of Criminal Procedure of the Republic of Korea, adopting a significant portion of the adversarial system of Anglo-American law, provides the right to remain silent and the right to assistance from defence counsel for the suspect during the investigation stage and guarantees the idea of equality of the parties.
  - The suspect may designate his own defence counsel and communicate with him.
  - The defence counsel may participate in the execution of the search and seizure warrant and the preservation of evidence procedure and the review of the legality of arrest examination.

- o However, criminal investigation requires sophisticated investigative techniques and should be conducted principally in secret. Until the investigation has ended, the secrecy of the investigation is to be abided by.

- o The suspect's right to defence counsel is fully protected by guaranteeing his right to communicate with the defence counsel insofar as it does not hamper the investigation.

0210

Rates of Release on Review of Legality of Arrest and on Bail

o Public security-related cases involve activities endangering national survival and security or the basic free and democratic order, and violent assemblies and demonstrations with Molotov cocktails and so on. The cases pose a serious threat to national peace and order, and have a great impact on society. The probability that the suspect may escape or destroy evidence in those cases is higher than that in ordinary criminal cases.

o Consequently, it is natural that the rates of issuance of warrant and indictment under detention in cases related with public security are higher than those of ordinary criminal case, which are mostly trifling administrative law violations, traffic accidents, and minor assault and battery cases. For that reason, the public security-related are classified as felonies across the globe.

o The Court will consider the seriousness of a case, the probability that the suspect may escape or destroy evidence, and bad influences upon society in the event of release as important factors in executing a review of legality of arrest and bail systems. It is, therefore, a matter of course that the release of public security-related criminals is less likely than that of ordinary minor crime offenders.

0211

Abuse of Arrest

- The objective of the administration of criminal justice is to compromise and harmonize two conflicting goals, namely, the protection of society through the prevention of crime and the guarantee of human rights through due process of the law.

- To realize this objective, the principle of non-detention interrogation which our country has adopted in the law enforcement system is a compromise scheme. Under this principle, only a small fraction of criminal cases are eligible for arrest warrants.

- The criteria considered by the court are the seriousness of the crime, the risk that the accused will flee or will obstruct or attempt to obstruct justice or interfere with a prospective witness.

- The ratio of the number of accused under arrest to the total number of accused has dramatically declined. In 1980, the ratio was 14.7%, but it decreased to 8.7% in 1990, and to 7.9% in 1991. A significant number of those arrested are released through bail hearing or a review of the legality of the arrest. Consequently, the number of accused set free before first judgment has increased sharply. The ratio of those released to the total arrested was 24% in 1991, compared to 21% in 1990.

- The maximum period of detention in our country is fairly short compared to that of other countries. A reasonable detention period should be allowed to investigators lest they rely on confessions or only perfunctorily investigate the elements of the crime. A reasonable detention period

0212

still allows the guarantee of human rights since it enables investigators to employ scientific investigative methods and to gather extensive evidence concerning defences and extenuating circumstances.

* Maximum detention period in foreign countries:
  - Germany : 6 months,
  - Frances : 1 year for felony cases, 4 months for misdemeanor cases,
  - Japan : 20 days in the prosecution office, 25 days for security-related law violators are allowed respectively.
  - the United States : There is no limit to the detention period provided that the investigator reports to the court every other week if the detention continues more than 10 days. Those who report should show grounds for extension of the detention period.

0213

Disciplinary Punishments and Procedure of Appeal

o Disciplinary procedures are extensively detailed in the laws concerning penal administration. Prisoners violating the internal rules of the prison are investigated by prison officers. After a thorough investigation, their cases are transferred to the disciplinary committee. The committee examines the violation and determines the punishment accordingly. The use of restraining instruments requires the prior permission of the chief of the prison. The use of restraining instruments is strictly limited to cases where the prisoner made an attempt to escape, commit suicide, incite unrest, or use violence.

o Where it is no longer necessary to do so, the use of restraining instruments becomes unwarranted. Undue extensions of the application of such instruments have not yet been reported to date.

o Disciplinary punishment is decided by the disciplinary committee, which is composed of three to five senior officials of the prison. The disciplinary committee summons the accused prisoner, questions the accused and witnesses, and examines the evidence. Not until the accused has had a sufficient opportunity to defend himself is the decision of the committee handed down.

o The accused prisoner can appeal the decision of the committee by filing a petition with circuit inspectors, who represent the Minister of Justice. He may also file an administrative complaint or suit through his relatives. His right to appeal is systematically and judicially guaranteed.

0214

Conversion of Beliefs and Discriminatory Treatment

o The purposes of correctional education of inmates lies in the prevention of another offenses and the rehabilitation of inmates through repentance for their past wrongdoing and the cultivation of sound civic ethics.

- Long-term leftist inmates also receive correctional education including study tours of outside world. The education provides them the opportunity to realize the falsity of their ideologies which are the motivating cause of their crimes.
- At the same time, the abandonment of their communist beliefs remains completely at their own choice. They are not forced to convert because forced conversion is of no use.

o All inmates receive equal treatment. Unconverted leftist inmates enjoy equal rights including the right to meet relatives and friends, to receive correspondence, and to read newspapers.

o Unconverted leftist inmates are regarded as being likely to repeat crimes because they strongly retain viewpoints which justify their past behavior.

- They do not satisfy the general requirements of the parole system, which takes into account their record, behavior, and ability to adapt themselves to society.

0215

Guarantee of Freedom of Assembly and Demonstration

o the Act concerning Aseembly and Demonstration guarantees peaceful and legal assemblies and demonstrations while limiting them, as little as possible, so as to maintain social order. In particular, the amendment of 1989 more clearly defines the concept of prohibited assemblies and demonstrations, rejecting arbitrary interpretations of the law and thus fully guaranteeing the freedoms of assembly and peaceable demonstration.

o In the course of assembly and demonstration in Korea it is common scene that, under the leadership of demonstration organizers, demonstrators hurl firebombs and stones at the police officer, while police vehicles and stations, as well as other public agencies, are often attacked, resulting in much damage to persons and property. It should be noted that firebombs are offensive, as opposed to defensive, weapons.

0216

The Notice System of Assembly and Demonstration

- o Upon the receipt of notice of an assembly or demonstration, the police examines whether the object of the assembly violates the principles underlying our liberal democratic order, such as whether it will occur in a prohibited time and place, and whether it will disrupts traffic. So long as it does not fall under the regulations prohibiting such acts, the assembly or demonstration can proceed.

- o However, if it is definite that such assemblies or demonstrations will endanger public safety through acts of organized violence, a prohibition notice is issued in the cause of mainainance of order. In determining the possibility of violence caused by assembly or demonstration, the entire situation is taken into account with regard to the purpose of the assembly or demonstration, the past record of violent demonstrations by the organizer, the disposition of the participants and the capability of control over the participants by the organizer, the preparation of demonstration equipment, and demonstration plans such as attacks on public agencies.

- o It cannot be accepted that assemblies or demonstrations are prohibited simply because they result in anti-government activities or because the organizer has a past record of violent anti-government demonstrations.

0217

o In order to prevent the excessive issuances of prohibition notices, the Korean government established on June 1, 1991, the Assembly and Demonstration Judging Committee. It has also issued more objective standards on the appropriateness of prohibition so that human rights are not unnecessarily trampled upon in the enforcement of the law.

Prohibition of Political Activities of Labor Unions

o Whether or not political activities of labor unions will be permitted, and to what degree they are permissible, are issues to be decided on a country-to-country basis after careful consideration of various factors including history and practices of labor unions and different legislation.

o Labor unions are autonomous organizations created for the purposes of securing and advancing minimun labor conditions and promoting the social and economic status of laborers. Its political function is nothing more than a means to accomplish such purposes.

o Since Korean labor unions have a history of only some forty odd years, they can easily become subject to a particular party or be reduced to mere instruments of the party if unions are allowed to participate in political activities.

- This may lead to conflict and divisions among laborers stemming from differences of ideological and political opinion.
- When a union cannot afford to raise strike funds, the permission to provide political funds can make the union insolvent.
- Therefore, current law prohibits labor unions from supporting a particular political party or conducting activities to help a particular person get elected, collecting political funds and providing political funds.

0219

o However, even under existing laws, labor unions can submit proposals to the government, the National Assembly, and political parties with regard to the enactment and revision of the related laws and systems. They may lobby, endeavor to form public opinion, and act as a political pressure group to get support. Their members may individually joint a party and support a particular candidate.

0220

Labor-Third Party Intervention

o Since collective bargaining negotiations affect the economic interests of the concerned parties in labor relations, such negotiations should be settled on the basis of factors which constitute the labor relations themselves.

- When labor disputes arise, they may cause permanent damage to management and the laborers themselves may have to suffer salary reductions corresponding to the actual duration of the labor dispute.
- In the event that a third party were to intervene in the labor dispute, labor relations may become distorted by the particular political ideology of the third party.

o Therefore, the main factors in the labor dispute, such as the initiation, manner, and level of the dispute, should be determind independently by the immediately concerned parties.

o Labor-related Acts prohibit third party intervention only if there is a possibility that such intervention might distort the labor relations by manipulating, instigating, or obstructing the concerned parties. The Acts do not prohibit laborers from obtaining support from specialists such as private lawyers, etc.

o The government guarantees that a trade union could be supported by the Federation of Korean Trade Unions(FKTU) or by one of its affiliated industrial federations through an amendment of the labor-related acts on December 31, 1986.

0221

- It does not violate the Covenant because Article 19(3)[a] of the Convenant provides that the right to freedom of expression may be subject to certain restrictions on the rights of others.

o Article 13-2 of The Labor Dispute Adjustment Law juxtaposes intervening activities - "any other act to influence the parties concerned" and "manipulating, instigating and obstructing". In light of the structure of said provision, the term "any other act to influence the parties concerned" is obviously interpreted as intervening activities that might cause the same result as caused by "manipulating, instigating, obstructing". Thus, It can be said that the above provision does not violate the principle of legality[nullum crimen sine lege]. (Constitutional Court Decision, 89-Hunga-103)

0222

I. 일반적 사항

B-1/5 국가보안법

가. 일반적 설명

o 남북대화와 교류.협력의 진전에도 불구하고 무력적화노선을 고수하고 있는 북한의 존재는 여전히 절박한 체제에 대한 위협으로 인식됨.

- 이에 따라 한국정부는 북한의 체재전복기도에 적극적으로 대처하여 국가안보를 수호하기 위하여 국가보안법을 유지

o 국가보안법에 의하여 한국국민의 기본적 권리가 부분적으로 제한되고 있는 것은 사실임.

- 그러나, 표현의 자유, 결사의 자유 등은 국가의 안전보장을 위하여 그 본질적인 부분을 침해하지 않은 한 법률로서 이를 제한할 수 있음. 이는 인권규약과 한국헌법에서도 인정되고 있는 기본원칙임.
- 국가보안법도 이러한 법이론에 따라 국가안보를 위하여 필요한 최소한도로 기본권을 제한하고 있어 인권침해의 여지는 없음.

o 한국정부는 기본권에 내재된 본질적 한계를 일탈하여 폭력혁명을 선동하고 자유민주주의 체제의 전복을 기도하는 등 명백히 국가의 존립.안전, 자유민주적 기본질서를 저해하는 반국가적 행위에 엄격하게 한정하여 동 법을 적용

0223

B-7 정치범

o 한국에서 일부 인사들이 소위 정치범이라고 주장하는 범법자들은 실정법 위반자들로서 대부분 아래와 같이 분류될 수 있음.

- 간첩 등 국가보안법 위반사범
- 돌멩이와 화염병을 투척하고 쇠파이프를 휘두르는 등 불법가두시위를 주도한 자
- 공공기관에 화염병을 투척하고 시설물을 파괴하며 방화까지 한 극렬 행위자
- 화염병과 신나로 경찰장비에 불을 지르고 심지어 경찰관을 상해하거나 죽음에까지 이르게 한 자
- 학내분규시 총장실을 점거하고 시설을 파괴하거나 스승을 폭행한 반인륜적 파렴치 행위자
- 사업장내의 중요 시설물을 파괴.방화하거나 동료 근로자 혹은 사용자를 감금.폭행.협박하고 동료 근로자를 사상케 한 자들임.

o 어떠한 사회라도 수단과 방법을 가리지 않고 질서와 체제를 파괴하려는 책동을 용납하지 아니하며, 국민의 총의에 기초한 실정법을 위반하여 국가의 안전에 위해를 가한 자는 그 정치적 의견과는 관계없이 처벌되는 것이 일반적임.

o 국가보안법 위반사범 등을 소위 정치범이라고 분류하고 그 숫자가 많아 마치 한국의 인권상황이 악화된 것으로 주장하는 것은 맞지 않음.

0224

B-8 장기좌익수

o 미전향 장기좌익수들은 한국정부의 전복을 기도하고 인명을 살상하는 등 반국가적 행위를 자행한 자들로서 적법한 사법절차에 따라 형이 선고되어 집행중인 자임.

o 미전향 좌익수들을 석방할 경우에는 여전히 재범의 위험성이 상존함.
  - 비록 고령이라 하더라도 현재 남한내에서 활동중인 지하간첩 조직과 연계하여 지하간첩활동을 재개할 위험성이 충분

o 따라서, 현재로서는 동인들에 대한 일괄 석방을 고려하고 있지 않음.
  - 다만, 노령자와 질병자에 대해서는 인도적 차원에서 형집행 정지로 석방한 바가 있으며, 앞으로도 행형성적을 참고하고 인도적 고려를 병행해서 석방여부를 개별적으로 결정하게 될 것임.

0225

B-12 비상입법기구 제정 법률의 합헌성

o 국회 이외의 비상입법기구 구성은 시대상황을 고려한 비상조치로 이해

- 군사적 대치가 지속되는 긴박한 안보상황 속에서 극심한 사회혼란으로 북한의 무력행사 가능성 증대

o 제6공화국 출범이후 국회에서 특별위원회를 구성, 법률 개폐작업

- 법률 700여건 개폐여부 일괄심의 - 200여건 개폐 완료

0226

제2조(평등권)

2-1 외국인 권리의 평등보장을 위한 조치

o 헌법에 명문의 규정이 있든 없든, 국적을 보유할 것을 전제로 하는 것이 분명한 권리를 제외한 규약상의 모든 권리는 외국인에게도 동등하게 보장됨.

- 선거권, 피선거권, 공무담임권, 국민표결권 등 정치적 활동권은 국민만의 권리로서 외국인에게는 불인정

o 외국인의 출입국은 보장되나 출입국관리법 등 관계법규에 의거, 일정한 경우 출입국 자유 제한

- 외국인은 출입국관리법 제45조에 의거, 강제퇴거 가능

o 직업선택의 자유(헌법 제15조), 토지소유권, 광업권 등 재산권에 있어서는 내국인보다 많은 제한을 받음.

- 외국인토지법에는 상호주의 원칙에 따라 대통령령에 의거, 토지 관련 권리향유에 제한을 규정(동법 제2조)
- 광업법에는 외국인.외국법인의 광업권 향유를 원칙적으로 금지 (동법 제6조)

o 기본권을 보장하기 위한 기본권으로서 행복추구권(제10조), 평등권 (제11조), 신체의 자유(제12조), 재판받을 권리(제27조) 등과 결부된 청구권은 외국인에게도 인정

- 국가배상청구권은 외국인이 피해자인 경우 상호보증이 있는 때 한하여 인정(국가배상법 제7조)

0227

제7조 (고문)

7-4 강요된 자백의 효력

o 강요에 의한 자백이나 자백이 피고인에게 불리한 유일한 증거인 때는 유죄의 증거로 사용하지 못함.

o 법원에서도 폭행, 협박에 의한 자백이나 장기간의 신체구속으로 인한 자백은 증거능력 불인정

0228

제9조 (신체의 자유)

9-2 수사과정에서의 변호인 참여

o 수사단계에서 피의자는 변호인 선임권, 선임된 변호인과의 접견.통신권이 보장되며, 또한 변호인은 압수.수색영장의 집행, 증거보전절차 및 구속적부심 심문 등의 참가권이 보장

o 그러나 범죄수사의 특수성으로 고도의 기술 필요하며 밀행 원칙, 수사기밀 준수가 필수적임.

o 수사에 지장이 없는 범위내에서 변호인 접견, 통신권을 최대한 보장하며 피의자 방어권을 보호

0229

9-3 공안사건 피의자 구속의 남용

o 공안관련 사건은 국가의 안전.존립이나 자유민주적 기본질서를 위태롭게 하거나 화염병을 투척하는 등 폭력 집회.시위를 개최하여 국가의 안녕 질서를 위태롭게 하는 등 그 사안이 중대하고 사회적으로 미치는 영향이 지대할 뿐만 아니라 도주나 증거인멸의 우려가 일반 형사사건 보다 더욱 큰 것으로 보이며, 세계의 모든 국가가 공안관련 사범을 중죄로 분류하고 있음.

o 따라서 공안관련 사건의 구속율과 구속기소율이 사소한 행정법규 위반 사범, 교통사고, 가벼운 폭력사건 등이 대부분을 차지하고 있는 일반 형사사범의 구속율과 구속기소율보다 높은 것은 당연한 것임.

o 법원이 구속적부심과 보석제도를 운용함에 있어서도 결국 사안의 중요성, 도주 및 증거인멸의 우려, 석방할 경우 사회에 미칠 악영향 등이 중요한 고려요소가 될 것인 바, 공안관련 사범의 석방율이 일반형사사법 중 죄질이 가벼운 사범의 석방율보다 낮은 것은 사안의 성격에 비추어 당연한 것이며, 법의 남용에 의한 것이 아님.

0230

9-4 구속남용

o 수사권 행사는 불구속수사가 원칙

- 구속수사는 도주나 증거인멸 우려, 죄질 특히 나쁜 경우 한함.
- 구속사건 비율은 전체사건대비 80년 14.7%, 90년 8.7%, 91년 7.9%로 매년 감소추세
- 1심 선고전 석방비율은 구속자중 90년 21%, 91년 24%가 구속적부심, 보석으로 석방

o 구속기간이 외국의 예에 비해 장기간 아님.

- 독일 6월, 프랑스 중죄 1년, 경죄 4월, 미국 10일 이상 구속시 격주 1회 법원 보고 외 구속기간 제한 없음.

o 어느 정도 수사기간 확보는 오히려 인권보장에 도움.

- 과학적 수사 및 광범위한 정상.양형자료 관련 수사 가능

0231

제10조(재소자 인권)

10-1 재소자에 대한 징벌 및 징벌결정에 대한 불복절차

o 재소자에 대한 규율 및 징벌

- 징벌의 요건, 종류, 기간, 징벌의 심리와 피징벌자의 자기변명의 기회 부여 등 모든 절차는 법무부 규칙으로 엄격히 규정

  (행형법 제45조, 제46조, 재소자 규율 및 징벌에 관한 규칙)

- 징벌을 집행하기 전 재소자에 대하여 의사검진을 실시하며, 징벌집행 중에도 수시로 검진을 실시, 건강이상시 즉시 징벌집행을 중지하거나 면제

  (행형법시행령 제145조-제148조)

- 재소자의 도주, 소요, 폭행, 자살 등을 방지하기 위하여 필요한 때에는 계구를 사용하며, 그 종류와 사용방법, 사용할 수 있는 기간 등을 법령으로 엄격히 규제

  (행형법 제14조, 동 시행령 제45조, 제46조)

o 징벌은 징벌위원회(3-5인 간부 교도관으로 구성)에서 의결

- 피조사자 소환, 신문, 증거조사 및 증인신문 절차를 거치며, 방어할 수 있는 충분한 기회 부여

o 수형자가 이의를 제기하고자 할 때는 법무부장관을 대리한 순열관에게 청원하거나, 행정상의 이의 신청 및 행정소송 제기 가능

0232

10-2 사상전향제도와 부당한 처우

o 수형자에 대한 교정교육의 목적은 자신의 과오를 반성하고 건전한 국민 정신을 함양하여 재범을 방지하고 사회에 다시 복귀할 수 있도록 하는 것임.

- 장기좌익수에 대하여도 범죄의 원인과 동기를 제공한 사상적 오류를 깨닫고 자유민주사회에 합류할 수 있도록 사회참관 등 교정교육을 실시
- 공산주의 신념의 포기는 전적으로 자신들의 자유로운 의사에 맡기고 있으며, 강요에 의한 전향은 아무런 의미가 없으므로 전향을 강요 하지는 않음.

o 모든 재소자는 규정에 따라 동일한 처우를 받고 있으며, 미전향 좌익수에 대해서도 접견, 서신수발, 신문열독 등 모든 권리 보장

o 다만, 미전향 좌익수들은 자신들의 과오를 반성하지 않은 채 오히려 이를 정당화하려는 태도를 고수하고 있어 여전히 재범의 위험성이 있다고 판단

- 따라서, 재소자의 수형성적, 생활태도, 사회적응능력 여부 등을 종합 평가하는 가석방제도의 일반적인 요건을 충족하지 못하여 가석방의 은전을 받지 못하고 있음.

0233

제21조(집회의 자유)

21-1 집회 및 시위의 자유의 보장

o 한국정부는 집회의 자유를 보장한 헌법규정에 의거하여 집회 및 시위에 관한 법률을 제정.시행하고 있음.

- 동 법은 평화적이고 적법한 집회 및 시위를 최대한 보장하는 한편 사회질서를 유지하는데 필요한 최소한도의 범위내에서 이를 제한하고 있음.
- 특히 1989년 개정된 법률은 금지되는 집회 및 시위의 개념을 더욱 명백히 규정하여 자의적인 법 해석에 따른 인권침해의 여지를 배제 하였음.

o 한국에서의 집회.시위 형태를 보면, 집회.시위주최자의 주도하에 조직적으로 준비된 수백 내지 수천개의 화염병과 돌, 쇠파이프 등이 시위를 저지하려는 경찰관을 향하여 던져지고, 경찰관 폭행에 사용되며, 경찰서, 파출소 등 공공기관과 경찰차량도 기습 대상이 되는 등 폭력 시위가 오히려 일반적 양태로서, 이로 인하여 막대한 인명과 재산피해가 발생하고 있음.

- 화염병은 분명히 단순한 자위수단이 아니며 인명살상.방화의 무기로 쓰이는 공격적인 것임.
- 세계 그 어느 국가에서도 찾아보기 어려운 화염병의 사용은 한국에서 평화적인 집회.시위문화를 정착시키는데 큰 장애요인으로 작용하고 있음.

0234

21-2 집회.시위에 대한 신고제도

o 경찰은 집회.시위에 관한 신고가 있을 경우 집회의 목적이 금지된 시간. 장소에서 개최되는지 여부, 교통소통에 현저한 지장을 초래하는 것인지 여부 등을 검토하여 동 법의 금지규정에 위배되지 않는한 원칙적으로 이를 허용하고 있음.

o 다만, 집단적인 폭력을 행사하여 공공의 안녕질서에 직접적인 위협을 가할 것이 명백한 집회.시위일 경우에는 질서유지를 위하여 금지통고를 하고 있음.

- 집회.시위의 폭력성을 판단함에 있어서는 집회.시위의 내용, 주최자의 폭력시위 전력, 참가자들의 성향과 그들에 대한 주최자의 통제능력, 화염병, 돌, 쇠파이프 등 시위용품 준비상태, 공공기관 기습을 비롯한 시위계획 등을 종합적으로 고려하여 금지여부를 신중히 결정
- 단지 집회.시위의 내용이 반정부적이라거나 그 주최자가 반정부적 인사 또는 폭력시위의 전력이 있다는 이유만으로 무조건 집회.시위를 금지하는 것은 아님.

o 금지통고제도의 남용을 방지하기 위하여 1991.6.1부터 지방경찰청, 경찰서 별로 사회 각계인사가 참여하는 집회.시위 심사위원회를 구성하고, 금지사유별 심사기준과 내용을 보다 객관화하는 등 법집행 과정에서 인권침해의 여지가 없도록 노력하고 있음.

0235

第22조 (결사의 자유)

22-1 노동조합의 정치활동 금지

o 노동조합의 정치활동을 허용할 것인지 여부와 그 허용의 정도는 노동조합의 역사, 노동조합 운용실태 등 제반여건을 고려하여 그 나라에 알맞는 제도를 선택하여야 할 것이며 각국의 입법례도 각기 상이한 것으로 알고 있음.

o 노동조합은 근로자가 자주적으로 단결하여 근로조건의 유지.개선과 경제적.사회적 지위향상을 도모하려는 목적으로 조직된 단체로서 정치적 기능은 이를 위한 수단에 불과

o 한국은 노동조합의 역사가 40여년에 불과하여 정치활동을 허용할 경우에는 노동조합이 특정정당에 예속되거나 정치적 도구로 전락할 우려가 있고 이념과 정치적 견해 차이로 인한 노동조합 구성원간의 대립.분열을 초래할 우려가 있을 뿐만 아니라 노동조합이 파업기금조차 제대로 마련하지 못하는 실정에서 정치자금 제공을 허용할 경우 조합재정이 부실해질 우려가 있음.

- 현행법은 공직선거에 있어서의 특정정당 지지 또는 특정인 당선을 위한 행위, 정치자금 모금 및 제공행위를 금지

o 그러나, 현행법하에서도 정부.국회 및 정당에 대한 각종 건의, 관련법령.제도의 제.개정 건의 및 청원, 지지 확보를 위한 로비활동, 여론조성, 정치적 압력 단체로서의 활동 등의 정치적 기능은 광범위하게 보장되고 있으며 조합원들이 개인적으로 정당가입, 특정후보 지지 등의 정치활동을 할 수 있음.

0236

22-2 노동관계법상 제3자 개입 금지

o 단체협약에 의하여 정하여질 사항은 노동관계 당사자 사이의 경제적 이해관계에 관한 것이므로 당사자 사이에 존재하는 갖가지 요인에 의하여 결정되어야 할 것임.

- 쟁의행위에 의하여 사용자로서는 기업의 정상적인 운영을 방해받게 되고, 근로자로서는 쟁의기간중 보수에 관한 불이익을 받게되는 등 손해의 위험을 스스로 부담해야 함.
- 제3자가 이에 개입할 경우에는 근로자의 임금 및 근로조건의 향상과는 관계없이 제3자의 특정한 세계관이나 정치적 이념에 의하여 왜곡될 우려가 있으므로 쟁의행위의 여부와 그 방법.정도의 선택은 노동관계 당사자의 책임아래 자주적으로 결정되어야 할 것임.

o 노동관계법은 제3자가 노동관계 당사자를 조종.선동.방해.개입하는 등 정상적인 노사관계를 왜곡시키는 간섭행위를 금지하는 것일 뿐이고 근로자들이 변호사.공인노무사 등 전문가의 조력을 받는 것을 차단하는 것은 아니며, 정부는 86.12.31. 법률개정을 통하여 노동조합의 상급 단체인 한국노총과 산업별 연합단체의 조직적인 지원을 받을 수 있도록 하고 있음.

- 인권규약 제19조 제3항(a)도 타인의 권리에 관한 표현의 자유는 법률로 제한할 수 있다고 규정하고 있으므로 인권규약과 배치되는 것은 아님.

0237

o 노동관계법의 "기타 이에 영향을 미칠 목적으로 개입하는 행위"라는 구성요건은 조종.선동.방해 등의 행위와 병렬적으로 규정되어 있어 적어도 조종.선동.방해 등의 결과에 준하는 영향을 미칠 목적으로 그에 준하는 정도의 간섭행위를 하는 것을 의미하는 것이 해석상 명백하므로 죄형법정주의에 위배된다고도 할 수 없음.(헌법재판소, 89헌가 103호)

0238

외 무 부

WGVF-0263 920703 1507 WG

번 호 : 년월일 : 시간 :

수 신 : 주 제네바 대사(총영사) (문봉주 참사관)

발 신 : 외무부장관(정 달 호)

제 목 : 이사회 기조 발언문

보 안 통 제	

1. 영문번역을 별첨합니다.

2. 부분적으로 국문에도 수정을 가하였읍니다.(국문별첨-수정부분 밑줄표시)

외신과 통 제	

3. 송부한 자료중 영문으로 되지않은 부분도 영역 작업중 임을 참고 바랍니다. 끝.

총 / 매(표지포함)

0239

오부2540 되돌림

인권이사회 아국대표 기조발언문(안)

- 92.7.13 박수길 주제네바 대사 -

[서 언]

인권이사회의 심의를 위하여 대한민국의 최초보고서를 이자리에서 소개하게 된 것을 영광으로 생각합니다.

대한민국은 국민의 인권보장을 보다 확고히 하고, 보편적인 인권신장을 위한 국제적 노력에 동참하기 위해 1990년 「경제적.사회적.문화적 권리에 관한 규약」과 「시민적.정치적 권리에 관한 규약」에 가입한 바 있습니다. 오늘 규약 40조에 따른 대한민국의 최초보고서 심의는 한국의 인권보장 목표 달성을 위한 노력과 성과를 보여줄 수 있는 중요한 기회라고 생각합니다.

동시에, 이 자리가 한국이 국제규약을 보다 더 잘 이행할 수 있는 방안에 관한 건설적인 대화의 기회가 되고 또한 오늘 국제적으로 인권분야에서 탁월한 위원 여러분들의 우리 보고서 심의가 우리 정부로 하여금 국민의 인권신장을 위한 노력을 계속해 나가는데 있어 큰 격려가 될 것으로 기대합니다. 이러한 점에서, 본 이사회에 우리 보고서를 소개하게 된 것을 기쁘게 생각합니다.

우리 정부는 보고서를 작성하는데 있어서 아래와 같은 사항에 유의하였습니다. 첫째로, 보고서의 체제와 내용이 인권이사회에서 채택한 보고서 작성에 관한 일반지침에 부합되도록 노력하였으며, 일반지침과 주해에 따라 한국의 인권보장에 관한 전반적 사항이 기술될 수 있도록 가능한 많은 정보를 포함하려고 노력하였습니다. 이를 위하여 모든 정부 관계부처가 참여한 협의체를 구성하여 인권보장의 모든 측면에 관한 세심한 협의 과정을 거쳐 보고서를 작성하였습니다.

둘째로, 우리나라의 법체제가 성문법 체계임을 감안, 인권보장을 위한 법적. 제도적 설명에 중점을 두면서, 헌법재판소의 결정, 법원의 판결 및 정부의 조치 등을 함께 기술하여 제도적 설명을 보완토록 하였습니다.

1

0240

셋째로, 인권보장이 1988년 현정부의 출범을 계기로 대폭적인 개선을 이루어 왔음을 고려하여, 보고서는 88년 이후의 개선상황에 촛점을 맞추었습니다.

[현 헌법하에서의 인권신장]

이제, 대한민국의 시민적, 정치적 권리에 관한 보고서의 실질적인 내용에 관하여 말씀드리겠습니다.

1987.10.29에 개정된 현 헌법은 민주주의 실현과 인권보장을 위한 제도적 장치를 강화하였습니다. 개정된 헌법은 구헌법하에서의 간접선거에 의한 대통령 선출방법을 직접선거로 바꿈으로서 대통령제 하에서 국민의 참정권을 높이는 한편 국회의 국정감사권을 부활하여 행정부에 대한 국회의 견제기능을 강화하였습니다.

사법분야에 있어서는 법관의 임명절차 개선을 통해 사법부의 독립을 보다 효과적으로 보장토록 하였습니다. 이 분야에서의 또다른 중요한 변화는 헌법재판소를 설치하여 인권 보장기관으로서 핵심적인 역할을 담당토록 한 것입니다.

나아가, 보다 확실한 인권보장을 위하여 헌법상 기본권 조항을 대폭 개정, 강화하였습니다. 특히 신체의 자유에 대한 제한요건을 더욱 엄격하게 하기 위해 체포 또는 구속에 있어서의 적법 절차를 헌법조문에 명문화하였고, 형사피의자와 피고인의 권리도 확대하였습니다.

정부는 이와 같은 헌법정신을 적극 반영하여 형사사법절차와 관련된 각종 법령 및 제도와 수사관행을 개선하고 행형제도를 획기적으로 개선하였습니다. 아울러 가난한 시민들이 완전한 법의 보호를 받을 수 있도록 법률구조사업을 적극 전개하고 이동의 자유를 촉진하기 위해 출입국 관리와 관련된 규정과 관행을 개선하였습니다.

뿐만 아니라, 집회 및 시위에 관한 법률, 국가보안법 등 88년 이전에 제정된 것으로서 논란이 많았던 법령들에 대하여는 그 내용을 개정하는 한편, 법적용을 더욱 엄격히 제한함으로써 해석상의 오류와 남용의 소지를 불식하도록 하였습니다.

또한 공권력에 의한 기본권 침해를 시정하기 위해 국민이 헌법재판소에 직접 제소할 수 있게 된 것은 인권보장에 있어서 실질적 진전으로서 그 의의가 매우 크다고 할 수 있습니다. 헌법재판소와 헌법소원제도가 89년 수립된 이래 인권 침해를 구제한 사례가 30여건이 넘는다는 사실이 이를 잘 뒷받침 해주고 있습니다.

민주화에 있어 또 하나의 획기적인 일은 지방자치제도의 확대실시라고 하겠습니다. 1961년 이래로 헌법에 규정하고는 있었으나 1960년대 초에 잠시 실시되다가 중단된 지방자치제는 이후 30여년만인 91년 3월 및 6월에 전국적으로 두차례의 지방자치단체 의회선거 실시를 통하여 확립되고 있습니다. 현재 전국적으로 각급 지방자치단체 의회가 구성되어 활동중인 바, 이는 국민의 참정권을 확대하는 또 하나의 진전이라고 할 수 있습니다.

의장님,

이제 우리 국민은 과거의 권위주의적 요소가 청산됨으로써 민주주의의와 법치주의하에 생활하고 있는 것을 말씀드리고자 합니다. 권리와 기본적 자유가 보장되고, 이러한 기본적 자유의 보장을 확실히 하기 위한 제도도 정착되었습니다. 자유민주주의 씨앗은 우리사회의 모든 부문에 뿌리내려, 우리 대한민국 국민은 자유의 열매를 향유하고 있습니다.

인권규약에의 가입은 이러한 민주화 과정의 중요한 부분이라고 하겠습니다. 진정한 민주주의만이 공개적인 토의에 관해서도 자유롭게 문호를 개방할 수 있고, 대내외적인 인권보장 및 신장을 위한 국제노력에도 동참할 수 있는 것입니다. 이러한 점에서 대한민국이 제41조에 의한 이사회의 권능을 인정하는 선언을 하고 동 규약의 「선택의정서」에도 가입하였음은 주목할만 합니다. 여러분이 아시다시피 이는 국민의 인권이 헌법에 의한 광범한 국내적 보호뿐 아니라, 이제는 국제적 보호하에 있음을 의미하는 것입니다.

인권규약 가입 이래 대한민국 정부는 동 규약의 내용이 널리 알려질 수 있도록 모든 노력을 다해 왔습니다. 규약의 내용은 인권이사회의 회의경과와 결정 사례집과 함께 번역, 발간되었습니다. 또한 각급 법집행 공무원에게 직무교육을 실시하여 이들의 직무 수행에 있어 규약과 헌법의 규정 및 절차를 철저히 이행하도록 하였습니다. 이렇게 규약의 내용이 현재 우리나라에서 널리 알려져 있지만, 이번 3일간의 보고서 심의를 통해 보다 더 상세하게 알려질 것이라고 생각합니다.

[규약의 국내법적 수용]

우리 헌법은 적법하게 체결.공포된 모든 조약은 대한민국의 국내법과 같은 효력을 갖는다고 규정하고 있기 때문에 규약에 규정된 모든 권리는 헌법에 의해 보장되고 있습니다.

실제로 규약에 규정된 모든 권리는 이미 헌법에 대부분 그대로 규정되어 있어 규약은 헌법과 함께 대한민국 인권법의 주축을 이룬다고 할 수 있습니다. 이점에서 헌법재판소가 1991년 4월 1일 민법조항의 위헌심판사건 결정에서 규약 제18조 2항을 직접 원용한 것은 주목할만 합니다.

대한민국은 국내법에 저촉되는 일부 규정, 즉 규약 제14조 5항, 7항과 제22조를 유보한 바 있습니다. 이러한 유보는 그 성격상 단지 부분적인 것이고 규약에 규정된 특정권리를 인정하지 않으려는 의도가 아니라, 보고서에 상세히 설명되어 있듯이, 관련 국내법에 규정된 일부 제한을 유지한다는 뜻입니다. 우리 정부는 이러한 유보가 규약의 기본 원칙에서 벗어나지 않는 것으로 믿고 있습니다.

[보고서 제출 이후의 진전사항]

91년 9월 대한민국의 국제연합 가입은 유엔헌장에 따라 보편적 인권신장을 위한 우리 정부의 노력을 강화하는 계기를 마련하였습니다. 이어 91년 12월 국제노동기구에 정회원으로 가입함으로써 노동권의 보장을 위한 국제적 노력에도 동참하게 되었습니다. 또한 1991년 12월 "아동의 권리에 관한 협약"을 비준하였으며, 현재 "난민지위에 관한 협약 및 의정서"에 가입하기 위한 행정부내의 절차를 완료하고 국회의 동의를 남겨놓고 있습니다.

본인은 인권에 대한 우리 정부의 국제적 공약에 큰 중요성을 부여하였으나, 인권보장을 신장하고자 노력하는 한국내 개인 및 단체의 움직임에도 같은 중요성이 부여되어야 합니다. 법원에 제기되는 인권침해 시정사건의 수가 증가하고 있다는 것은 매우 긍정적이며, 적법절차에 대한 신뢰감을 나타내는 것이라고 할 수 있습니다. 이러한 추세와 함께, 민간 인권단체들이 인권보장 감시 노력을 증가시키고 있습니다. 이러한 추세는 한국이 바람직스러운 방향으로 가고 있으며, 대한민국이 인권침해 시정을 위한 여건을 조성하는데 성공한 것임을 분명하게 보여주고 있습니다.

[규약 이행상의 요인과 장애]

규약의 이행에 영향을 주는 가장 큰 하나의 요인은 한반도의 분단으로부터 야기되는 긴장 상태입니다.

1945년 일제 식민지에서 해방된 후, 한국은 서로 다른 적대적 이념에 휘말리게 되었으며 그 이후 한국민은 1950년 북한의 남침으로 말할 수 없는 불행을 겪었고 분단은 더욱 굳어 졌습니다. 그 이래로 남북한은 38선을 따라 이념적으로 뿐 아니라 군사적으로도 서로 대치하고 있는 것입니다.

이러한 상황하에서 냉전체재의 붕괴에 따라 양측은 겨우 작년부터 진지한 대화를 시작하여 민족을 평화적으로 재통일 하기 위한 방법을 추구하게 된 것입니다. 그 결과로 지난 2월 「남북한 사이의 화해와 불가침 및 교류협력에 관한 합의서」가 체결되었고, 이를 토대로 양측은 각분야별로 서로 거리를 좁혀가기 위한 일련의 협의를 계속해 오고있습니다.

그럼에도 불구하고 작금에 시작된 남북한간의 대화는 통일의 장정을 위한 첫걸음에 불과합니다. 침략에 의해 전복될 뻔한 잊을 수 없는 경험을 갖고 있는 국가가 타방의 침략에 대항하여 경각심을 늦출 수 없는 것은 지극히 당연한 일입니다.

그리고 남북간에 150만의 군대가 대치하고 있으며, 냉전체제가 붕괴된 오늘에도 한반도에는 평화협정 아닌 휴전협정이 존속되고 있다는 사실은 또한 주목할 만 합니다.

따라서 대한민국은 평화와 통일을 위한 진지한 대화를 적극 추진하는 한편, 북한이 여전히 조선 노동당 강령의 서문에 표명된 기본 정책으로서 "남조선 민족 해방을 위한 인민 혁명의 실현" 즉, 전 한반도의 공산화를 선언하고 있는 상태에서는 대한민국의 자유민주주의 체제를 위해하려는 체제 전복 세력을 견제하는 노력을 계속 해야만 합니다.

이러한 맥락에서 한국은 하나의 곤경에 처해 있다고 할 수 있습니다. 북한은 평화, 협력, 교류 및 통일과 같은 문제에 대한 중요한 대화 상대이어야 하는 한편, 그 실체는 대한민국을 불안에 빠뜨리려는 전략으로 인하여 남한의 안보에 명백하고 현존하는 위협이 되고 있기 때문에, 국가 안보와 체제 통합의 수단으로서 대한민국이 채택한 국가보안법은 여전히 그 존재이유가 있다고 할 수 있습니다.

국가보안법에 대해서는 최근들어 남.북간의 교류와 접촉이 확대됨에 따라 국내 일각에서 개정 내지 폐지해야 한다는 주장이 대두되고 있으나, 대부분의 대한민국 국민들은 체제 전복 행위로부터 국가를 수호하기 위해 동 법률이 존치되어야 한다고 믿고 있습니다. 그러나, 휴전 협정이 평화 협정으로 대체되고 남북 관계가 정상화 되면 국가보안법은 자연히 그 기능이 폐기될 것이라고 저는 확신하고 있습니다.

한편, 대한민국 정부는 헌법과 규약이 허용하는 한도를 넘어 동 법률의 적용으로부터 야기될 수 있는 어떠한 인권 침해의 소지를 불식시킨다는 확고한 결의를 하고 있습니다.

이러한 결정은 국가보안법의 적용범위를 한정시키는 1990년 헌법재판소의 결정사항이 1991년 5월 국가보안법 개정에 포함됨으로써 구체화되었습니다. 헌법재판소의 결정은 헌법조항을 엄격히 준수하도록 하는데 있어 "국가안보와 생존을 위태롭게 하는", "기본적 자유민주 질서를 위태롭게 하는" 등의 개념에 대한 보다 더 명백하고 엄밀한 정의를 내려준 것입니다.

[인권 신장을 위한 앞으로의 계획]

인권신장을 위한 향후 계획으로서, 정부는 「고문방지 협약」에도 가입하기로 원칙적인 방침을 정하고 관계부처간 가입을 위한 세부 사항을 협의중에 있습니다.

나아가 정부는 죄형법정주의의 원칙 강화와 영장 실질 심사제 도입등을 위해 형법과 형사소송법의 개정안을 작성하였습니다. 우리는 이 개정안이 금년말 까지는 국회를 통과할 것으로 예상하고 있습니다.

한편, 정부는 국제노동기구 가입을 계기로 동 기구산하 제협약에의 가입을 추진 중입니다. 정부는 노동관계 국내법을 합리화하고 근로자의 권리향상을 위해 근로자와 사용자 및 정부를 대표하는 동수의 위원으로 구성된 연구위원회를 수립 하였습니다. 동 연구위원회는 현행법하에 금지된 단일 작업장에서의 복수 노조 허용등 노동조합법의 개선을 위한 검토를 진행하고 있습니다.

대한민국은 헌법과 규약에 규정된 인권보장의 정신과 원칙이 국민의 일상 생활속에 올바로 구현될 수 있도록 제도와 관행을 개선하는 노력을 계속해 나갈 것입니다. 우리 정부는 또한 인권보장을 위한 국제적 및 지역적 노력에도 적극 동참해나갈 것입니다.

이러한 맥락에서 대한민국 정부는 내년 6월 비엔나에서 개최 예정인 세계인권 회의의 성공적인 결실에 큰 기대를 갖고 있습니다. 동 회의를 통해 세계적으로 인권보호의 차원을 한단계 높일 수 있는 계기가 되고, 모든 국제인권협약의 보다 효율적이고 보편적인 이행이 가능해질 것으로 믿고 있습니다. 이를 위해 대한민국 정부는 동 세계회의에도 적극 참여할 계획입니다.

끝으로, 본인의 설명이 위원 여러분들에게 한국의 인권 보장 실태를 이해 하는데 도움이 되기를 희망하면서, 우리 보고서의 심의가 인권 보장을 향상하기 위한 위원 여러분과 우리 정부간의 건설적인 대화의 과정인 만큼, 여러분들의 코멘트와 질문에 성실하게 답변드리고자 합니다. 감사합니다. 끝.

관리 번호	92-632

	분류번호	보존기간

발 신 전 보

번 호 : WGV-1028 920707 1550 DG 종별 :

수 신 : 주 제네바 대사. ~~총영사~~

발 신 : 장 관 (연이)

제 목 : 인권이사회

~~1.~~ 아국 보고서 심의 관련, 우리나라의 인권규약 가입 2주년이 되는 7.10에 별첨과 같이 언론보도할 예정임(7.9.오후 국제기구국장 기자브리핑)을 참고바람.

~~2. 외국 언론에 대한 보도는 상기 참조, 귀지에서 적의 실시바람.~~

첨부 : 보도자료(Fax). 끝.

WGVF-270

(국제기구국장 김재섭)

보안 통제	

앙 고 재	92년 7월 7일	UN2과	기안자 성명		과 장	심의관	국 장		차 관	장 관
			김종훈				정일			

외신과통제

0248

報 告 畢

長官報告事項

1992. 7. 8.
國際機構局
國際聯合2課(37)

題 目 : 第45次 人權理事會 言論對策

第45次 人權理事會에서 있을「市民的.政治的 權利에 관한 國際規約」에 따른 우리나라의 最初報告書 檢討와 관련한 言論對策을 아래 報告드립니다.

1. 記者단 브리핑

o 우리 報告書 提出經緯, 報告書의 主要內容, 代表團의 活動計劃, 報告書 檢討의 意義 等에 대해 7.9.오후 別添 內容으로 國際機構局長이 記者團 브리핑 豫定

- 同 規約加入 2주년인 7.10 言論報道 豫想

2. 理事會 檢討結果 브리핑

o 駐제네바 大使의 現地 特派員 브리핑 또는 報道資料 配布

* 同 理事會에는 民辯側人士 等 現地 參觀豫程

3. 關聯事項(A.I.보고서)

o 國內外 報道에 의하면, 7.9. 發表 豫定인 92년 國際赦免委 ~~人權~~ 年例 報告書에 우리나라에 85명 以上의 良心囚가 있다는 等 內容包含

- 北韓에는 약 1천명이 集團收容所에 收監되어 있음을 指摘

o 同 報告書 入手후 法務部에서 對應 聲明 發表토록 協議中

- 駐英大使館에 報告書 入手 旣指示

첨부 : 報道資料. 끝.

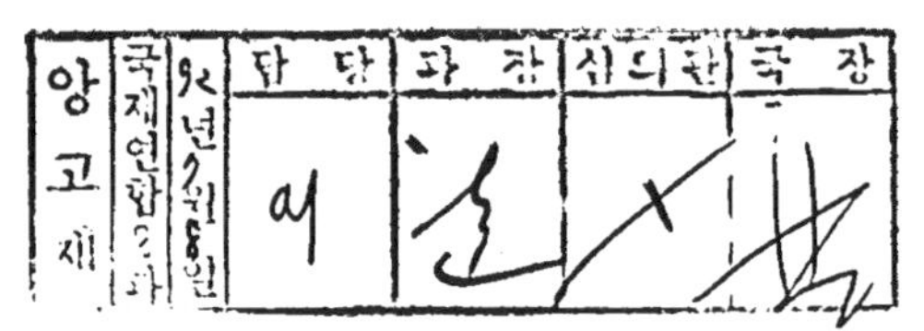

0249

報 告 畢
(서명)

1992. 7. 8.
國 際 機 構 局
國際聯合2課(37)

長 官 報 告 事 項

題 目 : 第45次 人權理事會 言論對策

第45次 人權理事會에서 있을 「市民的.政治的 權利에 관한 國際規約」에 따른 우리나라의 最初報告書 檢討와 관련한 言論對策을 아래 報告드립니다.

1. 記者단 브리핑

o 우리 報告書 提出經緯, 報告書의 主要內容, 代表團의 活動計劃, 報告書 檢討의 意義 等에 대해 7.9.오후 別添 內容으로 國際機構局長이 記者團 브리핑 豫定

- 同 規約加入 2주년인 7.10 言論報道 豫想

2. 理事會 檢討結果 브리핑

o 駐제네바 大使의 現地 特派員 브리핑 또는 報道資料 配布

* 同 理事會에는 民辯側人士 等 現地 參觀豫定

3. 關聯事項(A.I.보고서)

o 國內外 報道에 의하면, 7.9. 發表 豫定인 92년 國際赦免委 年例報告書에 우리나라에 85명 이상의 良心囚가 있다는 等 內容包含

- 北韓에는 약 1천명이 集團收容所에 收監되어 있음을 指摘

o 同 報告書 入手후 法務部에서 對應 聲明 發表토록 協議中

- 駐英大使館에 報告書 入手 旣指示

첨부 : 報道資料. 끝.

0250

보 도 자 료

외 무 부

제 92- 호 문의전화 : 720-2408~10 보도일시 : 1992 . 7 . 10 . : 시

제 목 : 시민적.정치적 권리에 관한 국제규약에 따른 우리나라의 보고서 검토

92.7.13-31간 제네바에서 개최되는 제45차 인권이사회(Human Rights Committee) 회의에서 시민적.정치적 권리에 관한 국제규약(International Covenant on Civil and Political Rights)에 따라 우리나라가 제출한 최초보고서에 대한 검토(study and comment)가 7.13-15간 있을 예정이다.

1. 우리 보고서 제출 경위

o 규약 제40조에 의하면, 각 당사국은 규약 발효후 1년 이내에 규약의 이행을 위해 취한 조치에 관하여 인권이사회에 보고서를 제출토록 되어 있음. (그 이후에는 매 5년마다 추가보고서를 제출)

o 우리나라는 90.4.10. 동 규약에 가입서를 기탁함에 따라 동 규약은 90.7.10. 우리나라에 대해 발효하였으며, 이에 따라 정부는 91.7월 최초보고서를 제출하였음.

* 우리나라는 동 규약과 함께 동 규약 선택의정서와 경제적.사회적.문화적 권리에 관한 국제규약에도 가입하였음. (규약요지 별첨)

2. 인권이사회의 보고서 검토

o 7.13-31, 제네바에서 개최되는 제45차 인권이사회에서는 우리나라를 포함, 브룬디, 몽골, 벨라루스, 페루, 아프가니스탄 등 6개국의 인권규약 보고서를 검토하며, 우리나라의 보고서에 대한 검토는 7.13-15. 기간중 있을 예정임.

o 인권이사회의 각국 보고서 검토는 그 나라의 보고서를 소개, 설명하는 수석대표의 기조발언에 이어 보고서 내용과 관련한 인권이사회 위원들의 논평과 질의가 있게되며, 수석대표가 이에 대해 답변하는 식으로 진행됨.

o 인권이사회는 인권규약 당사국 회의에서 선출되는 임기 4년의 18인의 위원으로 구성되며, 통상 위원들은 법률문제와 국제인권법 분야의 전문가들임.

* 인권이사회 위원 명단 : 별첨
* 인권이사회(Human Rights Committee)는 인권규약(시민적.정치적 권리에 관한 국제규약)에 의해 설치된 협약기구로서, 유엔 경제사회이사회 산하의 인권위원회(Commission on Human Rights)와 다름.(우리나라는 93-95간 3년 임기의 인권위원회 이사국으로 활동예정임)

o 인권이사회는 각국의 보고서를 검토한 후 종합관찰(concluding observations)을 첨부한 회의결과를 유엔 경제사회이사회와 총회에 제출함.

o 이사회의 보고서 검토는 대상국의 인권상황 자체를 논의하는 것이 아니고, 각국이 제출한 보고서의 내용과 관련하여 해당국이 규약의 이행을 위해 국내적으로 취한 조치가 규약을 이행함에 있어 충분하였는가 등에 촛점을 두고 검토하는 것임.

2

0252

3. 우리 보고서의 주요내용

o 우리 보고서는 기본적 인권보장에 관한 우리 헌법의 규정과 이에 따른 국내법령 규정 등 법제도적인 측면, 법원과 헌법재판소의 기본권 관련 판결과 결정내용 및 인권보장과 관련한 정부의 조치내용 등을 규약의 조문에 따라 자세하게 기술하고 있으며, 보고서 작성지침에 따라 우리나라의 가입일인 90.7.10. 이후의 인권보장 관련 사항을 주로 다루고 있음.

o 동 보고서에서는 인권규약에 규정된 권리는 우리의 헌법에도 거의 그대로 규정되어 있을 뿐 아니라 동 규약이 헌법에 따라 체결 공포되었기 때문에 규약의 제규정은 국내법과 동일한 효력을 갖는다는 것이 강조되었음.

o 이러한 점에서 인권규약은 헌법과 함께 우리나라 인권법 체계의 주축을 이룬다고 볼 수 있음.

o 다만, 인권규약 규정중 상소권 보장(제14조 5항), 일사부재리 또는 이중처벌금지(제14조 7항), 결사의 자유(제22조)에 관한 3개 조항은 우리 국내법과 약간의 상충이 있어, 이에 관해서는 그 적용에 있어 부분적인 유보를 표명하였다는 것을 밝히고 있음.
  - 상소권 보장 : 계엄하 군사재판에서의 부분적인 단심 적용
  - 일사부재리 : 외국에서 처벌받은 범법자도 국내에서 소추되나 감형 등 고려
  - 결사의 자유 : 공무원, 교원 등에 노조결성 불인정

* 우리 보고서(영문 유엔문서 양식으로 70페이지)는 91.11. 유엔에서 발간, 배포된 바 있음.

4. 우리 대표단의 활동계획

o 우리나라는 이번 인권이사회에 박수길 주제네바 대사를 수석대표로 하고, 외무부, 법무부 등 국제인권업무 관련부서 관계관으로 구성된 대표단을 파견함.

o 우리 대표는 기조발언을 통해 제6공화국 헌법하에서 이루어진 인권신장과 민주화의 진전 등에 관해 설명하고, 인권보호 및 인권신장 분야에서 우리나라가 앞으로 취할 조치에 대해서도 소개할 예정임.

- 인권관련 국제협약 가입 의사(ILO 관련 협약 포함)
- 형법 및 형사소송법 개정 방향
- 세계인권회의(93.6. 비엔나) 등 국제적 인권향상 노력에 적극 동참 의사

o 우리 대표는 또한, 우리나라에서 법원과 헌법재판소가 실질적 인권보장에 있어 최고의 권위를 가지고 활발히 기능하고 있음과 이러한 추세에 맞게 사회내 민간 인권단체에 의해서도 적극적인 인권신장 노력이 전개되고 있다고 지적하고, 이를 우리사회가 인권보장에 있어 바람직한 방향으로 가고 있음을 나타내는 현상으로 평가할 것임.

5. 보고서 검토의 의의

o 7.10은 우리나라가 인권규약에 가입하여 동 규약이 우리나라에 대해 발효한지 2주년이 되는 날인 만큼, 이 싯점에서 인권보장 문제에 있어 국제적으로 가장 권위있는 전문기관인 인권이사회에서 우리의 인권규약 이행 보고서에 대한 검토가 있게되어 더욱 그 의의가 크다고 하겠음.

o 금번 인권이사회의 보고서 검토를 통해, 우리의 그간 인권보호 및 인권신장을 위한 노력을 국제사회에 소개하고 이러한 노력의 과정에서 겪는 우리의 어려운 점에 대해서도 이해를 증진시킬 수 있는 기회를 갖는 한편,

우리의 인권보장 실태에 관하여 국제적인 평가를 받게 됨으로써 우리 사회가 앞으로 인권보장을 더욱 향상시켜 나가는데 있어 주요한 계기가 될 것임.

o 우리나라는 인권규약에 가입하였을 뿐 아니라, 동 규약의 선택의정서에도 가입함으로써, 우리 국민이 인권침해에 대해 국내에서 구제절차를 통해 권리구제가 이루어지지 않았다고 판단할 경우 인권이사회에 이를 직접 진정할 수 있도록 하였는 바, 이는 우리의 인권보장과 관련하여 타국이 문제를 제기할 수 있도록 동 규약 제41조에 따른 인권이사회의 권능을 수락한 것과 함께, 개인에 대한 인권보장을 국제적으로도 확보토록 하여 우리나라의 인권보장을 더욱 확고하고 효과적으로 지켜나가겠다는 의지를 표명하였다는 점에서 주목할만함.

* 규약당사국 : 104개국(단, 규약 41조 수락국가 : 33개국),
선택의정서 당사국 63개국

o 또한 우리나라는 지난 4월 유엔 경제사회이사회에서 인권이사회 위원회 (Commission on Human Rights) 이사국으로 피선됨으로써, 6공화국 이래 이룩한 민주화를 바탕으로하여 앞으로 인권이사국으로서 세계적인 시각에서 인권문제를 거론할 수 있는 위치가 되었음은 물론, 유엔 인권회의 아주 그룹내에서도 일본 등과 함께 인권 선진국으로서 주도적 입장을 취하게 되었음.

첨부 : 1. 인권이사회 위원 명단
2. 시민적.정치적 권리에 관한 국제규약 요지
3. 동 선택의정서 요지
4. 경제적.사회적.문화적 권리에 관한 국제규약 요지

[별첨 1]

인권이사회(Human Rights Committee) 위원 명단(18명)

- F.J. Aguillor Urbina(코스타리카)
- Janos Fodor(헝가리)
- Rosalyn Higgins(영국)
- Rajsoomer Lallah(모리셔스)
- Andreas Mavrommatis(사이프러스)
- Rein A. Myullerson(러시아)
- Fausto Pocar(이태리)
- A. Serrano Caldera(니카라과)
- Amos Wako(케냐)
- Nisuke Ando(일본)
- Christine Chanet(프랑스)
- Vojin Dimitrijevic(유고)
- Omran El Shafei(이집트)
- Kurt Herndle(오스트리아)
- Birame N'Diaye(세네갈)
- Waleed Sadi(요르단)
- Julio Prado Vallejo(에쿠아돌)
- Bertil Wennergren(스웨덴)

[별첨 2]

시민적.정치적 권리에 관한 국제규약 요지

(전문, 6부 53개조로 구성)

가. 실체 규정

제 1 조 자결권 및 자원처분권

제 2 조 모든 종류의 차별금지 및 기본권의 침해에 대한 효과적 구제 보장

제 3 조 남녀평등권 확보

제 4 조 비상사태하에서의 기본권 제한, 제한의 한계 및 타당사국에 대한 통보 의무

제 5 조 규약에 인정되지 아니한 이유로 인한 기본권의 경시 금지

제 6 조 생명권

- 사형은 권한있는 법원이 선고한 최종파결에 의해서만 집행가능
- 18세 미만의 연소자에 대한 사형선고 불가 및 임산부에 대한 사형집행 금지

제 7 조 고문 금지

제 8 조 노예제도 및 강제노동 금지

제 9 조 신체의 자유와 안전에 대한 권리

- 자의적인 체포 또는 억류의 금지
- 체포 또는 억류시 신속하게 사법관헌에게 회부될 권리
- 억류에 대한 법원의 합법성 심리
- 불법체포 및 억류에 대한 보상

제 10 조 인신구속자에 대한 인도적 대우

- 기결수와 미결수의 분리
- 미성년자는 격리 수감

제 11 조 계약상 의무의 이행불능을 이유로 한 구금 금지

제 12 조 거주이전 및 퇴거의 자유

제 13 조　합법적 거류외국인의 추방요건 및 구제

제 14 조　공정한 재판을 받을 권리

- 도덕, 공공질서 또는 국가보안상 필요한 경우를 제외하고는 공개재판을 받을 권리
- 형사피의자의 유죄입증시까지 무죄 추정
- 신속한 재판, 변호인의 조력을 받을 권리
- 불리한 진술 또는 유죄의 자백의 강요 금지
- 일사부재리의 원칙

제 15 조　형법불소급의 원칙

제 16 조　법률상 인격인정

제 17 조　사생활, 가정, 통신의 침해 금지

제 18 조　사상, 양심 및 종교의 자유

제 19 조　표현의 자유 및 그 제한의 한계

제 20 조　전쟁선전 금지

제 21 조　평화적 집회의 권리

제 22 조　노동조합의 결성을 포함한 결사의 자유

제 23 조　가정의 보호, 혼인의 자유와 혼인기간중 및 혼인해소시에 양배우자의 권리와 책임의 평등 확보

제 24 조　어린이의 보호

제 25 조　참정권

제 26 조　법앞의 평등 및 법의 평등한 보호를 받을 권리

제 27 조　소수민족의 보호

나. 실시규정 - 규약준수 보장 조치

제 28조 - 45조

o 인권이사회 설치(제28조 - 39조)
  - 18명의 위원으로 구성
  - 위원은 지리적 분포, 상이한 문명과 법적체계 고려, 선출

o 규약당사국이 규약에서 인정된 제권리의 준수를 실현하기 위하여 취한 조치 및 진전사항에 대한 보고서 제출 의무(제40조)

* 제41조 규약당사국은 다른 당사국의 규약 불이행 사항을 이사회에 통보할 수 있으며, 이사회는 이를 접수, 심리함. (단, 통보국 및 규약 불이행국 모두 제41조 규정에 의한 이사회의 심리권한 인정을 선언한 경우에 한함)

다. 최종 규정

제 48조 - 53조 규약의 서명, 비준, 가입, 발효, 적용범위 개정 및 인증등본

[별첨 3]

시민적.정치적 권리에 관한 국제규약에 대한 선택의정서 요지

(전문, 14개조로 구성)

가. 실체 규정

제 1조 - 5조 B규약상 인정된 제권리의 침해를 받은 개인의 통보를 접수, 조사하는 인권이사회의 권한 인정 (단, B규약의 당사국이지만 의정서 당사국이 아닌 국가에 관계되는 사항은 접수치 않음)

나. 최종 조항

제 8조 - 14조 의정서의 서명, 비준, 가입, 발효, 적용범위, 개정, 탈퇴, 인증등본

[별첨 4]

경제적, 사회적 및 문화적 권리에 관한 국제규약 요지

(전문, 5부 31개조로 구성)

가. 실체규정

제 1 조　자결권 및 자원처분권

제 2 조　모든 종류의 차별금지

제 3 조　남녀평등권 확보

제 4 조　기본권의 제한시 법률유보원칙 적용

제 5 조　규약에 규정되지 아니한 이유로 인한 기본권의 경시 금지

제 6 조　근로의 권리

제 7 조　공정하고 유리한 근로조건의 향유권

제 8 조　노동조합구성권

제 9 조　사회보장권

제 1 0조　가정, 임산부 및 어린이의 보호
- 가정의 보호 및 혼인의 자유
- 근로임산부에 대한 유급휴가
- 어린이와 연소자의 경제적, 사회적 착취로부터의 보호

제 11 조　적당한 생활수준에 대한 권리 및 기아로부터의 해방을 위한 국제협력

제 12 조　신체적, 정신적 건강의 향유권

제 13 조　교육에 대한 권리
- 초등교육의 무상의무교육
- 고등교육의 기회균등

제 14 조　초등교육의 무상의무교육을 위한 계획수립

제 15 조　문화, 과학, 예술활동의 권리 및 저작권 보호

나. 실시 규정

제 16조-25조 규약당사국이 규약에서 인정된 제권리의 준수를 실현하기 위하여 취한 조치 및 진전사항에 대한 보고서 제출의무

다. 최종 조항

제 36조-31조 규약의 서명, 비준, 가입, 발효, 적용범위, 개정 및 인증등본

보 도 자 료

외 무 부

제 92- 호 문의전화 : 720－2408～10 보도일시 : 1992. 7. 10. 00 : 00 시

제 목 : 시민적.정치적 권리에 관한 국제규약에 따른 우리나라의 보고서 검토

92.7.13-31간 제네바에서 개최되는 제45차 인권이사회(Human Rights Committee) 회의에서 시민적.정치적 권리에 관한 국제규약(International Covenant on Civil and Political Rights)에 따라 우리나라가 제출한 최초보고서에 대한 검토(study and comment)가 7.13-15간 있을 예정이다.

1. 우리 보고서 제출 경위

o 규약 제40조에 의하면, 각 당사국은 규약 발효후 1년 이내에 규약의 이행을 위해 취한 조치에 관하여 인권이사회에 보고서를 제출토록 되어 있음. (그 이후에는 매 5년마다 추가보고서를 제출)

o 우리나라는 90.4.10. 동 규약에 가입서를 기탁함에 따라 동 규약은 90.7.10. 우리나라에 대해 발효하였으며, 이에 따라 정부는 91.7월 최초보고서를 제출하였음.

* 우리나라는 동 규약과 함께 동 규약 선택의정서와 경제적.사회적.문화적 권리에 관한 국제규약에도 가입하였음. (규약요지 별첨)

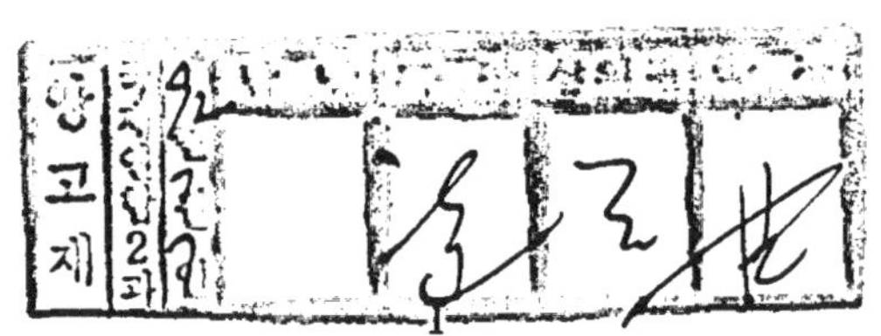

0263

2. 인권이사회의 보고서 검토

o 7.13-31, 제네바에서 개최되는 제45차 인권이사회에서는 우리나라를 포함, 브룬디, 몽골, 벨라루스, 페루, 아프가니스탄 등 6개국의 인권규약 보고서를 검토하며, 우리나라의 보고서는 7.13-15. 기간중 있을 예정임.

o 인권이사회의 각국 보고서 검토는 그 나라의 보고서를 소개, 설명하는 수석대표의 기조발언에 이어 보고서 내용과 관련한 인권이사회 위원들의 논평과 질의가 있게되며, 수석대표가 이에 대해 답변하는 식으로 진행됨.

o 인권이사회는 인권규약 당사국 회의에서 선출되는 임기 4년의 18인의 위원으로 구성되며, 통상 위원들은 법률문제와 국제인권법 분야의 전문가들임.

* 인권이사회 위원 명단 : 별첨

* 인권이사회(Human Rights Committee)는 인권규약(시민적.정치적 권리에 관한 국제규약)에 의해 설치된 협약기구로서, 유엔 경제사회이사회 산하의 인권위원회(Commission on Human Rights)와 다름.(우리나라는 93-95간 3년 임기의 인권위원회 이사국으로 활동예정임)

o 인권이사회는 각국의 보고서를 검토한 후 종합관찰(concluding observations)을 첨부한 회의결과를 유엔 경제사회이사회와 총회에 제출함.

o 이사회의 보고서 검토는 대상국의 인권상황 자체를 논의하는 것이 아니고, 각국이 제출한 보고서의 내용과 관련하여 해당국이 규약의 이행을 위해 국내적으로 취한 조치가 규약을 이행함에 있어 충분하였는가 등에 촛점을 두고 검토하는 것임.

2

0264

우리의 인권보장 실태에 관하여 국제적인 평가를 받게 됨으로써 우리 사회가 앞으로 인권보장을 더욱 향상시켜 나가는데 있어 주요한 계기가 될 것임.

o 우리나라는 인권규약에 가입하였을 뿐 아니라, 동 규약의 선택의정서에도 가입함으로써, 우리 국민이 인권침해에 대해 국내에서 구제절차를 통해 권리구제가 이루어지지 않았다고 판단할 경우 인권이사회에 이를 직접 진정할 수 있도록 하였는 바, 이는 우리의 인권보장과 관련하여 타국이 문제를 제기할 수 있도록 동 규약 제41조에 따른 인권이사회의 권능을 수락한 것과 함께, ~~우리나라의~~ 개인에 대한 인권보장을 국제적으로도 확보토록 함에 ~~한 것으로~~서, 우리나라의 인권보장을 더욱 확고하고 효과적으로 지켜나가겠다는 의지를 표명하였다는 점에서 ~~나타낸 것으로~~ 주목할만함.

* 규약당사국 : 104개국(단, 규약 41조 수락국가 : 33개국),

선택의정서 당사국 63개국

첨부 : 1. 인권이사회 위원 명단

2. 시민적.정치적 권리에 관한 국제규약 요지

3. 동 선택의정서 요지

4. 경제적.사회적.문화적 권리에 관한 국제규약 요지

유엔人權報告書 審議會 準備狀況 報告

1992. 7.9.
報告者:第1行政調整官 이희주

□ UN審議概要

ㅇ 政府 最初報告書 및 提出

- 國際人權規約(B規約) 및 選擇議政書 加入 發效('90.7.10) 및 政府 最初報告書 提出('91.7)
  . 유엔審議會 開催 : 報告書 提出後 1-2年 後
    ※ 2次 報告書부터는 매 5年 間隔 提出

ㅇ 유엔國際人權規約審議會 概要

- 審議日程 : '92.7.13~15(第45次 유엔人權理事會, 제네바)
- 審議對象 : "市民的.政治的 權利에 관한 最初報告書"
- 審議委員 : 各國 國際人權分野 專門家 18人(議長國-이태리)
- 細部日程 : 7.13(月) - 首席代表 發言, 各 委員 質疑
  7.14(火) - 休會(答辯準備)
  7.15(水) - 政府答辯, 委員論評, 委員會 Comment 發表

□ UN人權報告書 審議會 展望

ㅇ 審議會 雰圍氣

- 우리 政府報告書에 대해 KNCC.민변에서 具體的인 統計資料를 包含한 세밀한 反駁報告書를 提出(92.5.28)하였고,
- 國內外 在野團體 關係者 多數가 現地 活動하는 등 순조롭지 못한 雰圍氣에서 進行될 것으로 豫想됨

0266

o 代表團 構成

- 首席代表 : 駐제네바 大使(박수길)
- 副 代 表 : 法務部 人權課長(류국현)外 6名
  * 7.8 出國

o 審議會 對應 및 展望

- 國內의 在野團體 關係者가 現地 活動을 하더라도 傍聽만 할 뿐 質疑.應答의 權限이 없으며
  . KNCC.민변의 反駁報告書를 事前入手, 充分한 分析을 통해 對應資料를 準備하였으므로 큰 問題없이 審議에 임할 수 있으리라 展望됨

- 다만, KNCC등에서 提出한 反駁報告書에서 주로 다룬 國家保安法, 集示法上의 集會.結社의 自由 및 表現.思想의 自由등에 관한 審議時

  第6共和國 政府에서 처음으로 人權伸長을 위해 이들 問題와 關聯한 法令 改正등 可視的 措置를 취한 바 있으며,

  政治先進國 水準에는 다소 未洽할지 몰라도 UN人權規約 加入을 契機로 向後 持續的인 發展을 이루어 나가고 있는바

  . 아직도 南.北韓 敵對關係가 解消되지 않고 있는 國內狀況에 비추어 最善의 努力을 傾注하고 있다는 點을 充分히 認識되도록 說明할 計劃임

0267

우리측 첫報告書검토
13일 유엔人權이사회

오는 13일부터 31일까지 제네바에서 개최되는 제45차유엔인권이사회는 우리나라가 지난해 「시민적·정치적권리에 관한 국제규약」에 따라 제출한 최초 보고서에 대해 13, 15일 양일간 검토한다고 외무부가 10일 밝혔다.

이 인권이사회는 유엔인권규약에 의해 설치된 협약기구로 1백4개국이 가입해있으며 우리나라는 지난90년7월10일에 가입, 지난해7월 최초보고서를 제출했었다.

우리나라는 최초보고서 가입일인 지난90년7월이후 인권보장관련사항을 주로다루고있으며 기본적인권보장에 관한 우리헌법의 규정과 이에따른 국내법령규정등법제도적인 측면과 법원및헌법재판소의 기본권 관련 판결내용등을 기술했다.

한국일보 1면 92. 7.10.

0268

정부 人權이사회에 대표단 파견

한국등 인권규약 보고서 검토

(서울=聯合) 정부는 오는 13일부터 제네바에서 개최되는 제45차 인권이사회 회의에 朴銖吉駐제네바대사를 수석대표로 외무부 법무부등 국제인권업무 관련부서 관계관으로 구성된 대표단을 파견할 예정이라고 외무부가 9일 밝혔다.

이달말까지 계속되는 이번 회의에서는 우리나라를 비롯 부룬디 몽골 벨라루스 페루 아프가니스탄등 6개국이 제출한 인권규약 보고서에 대한 내용검토가 있을 예정이다.

인권이사회는 각국의 보고서를 검토한후 종합관찰 내용을 첨부한 회의결과를 유엔경제사회이사회와 총회에 제출하게 된다.

우리나라는 지난 90년 <시민적.정치적 권리에 관한 국제규약>에 가입함에 따라 이 규약의 이행을 위해 취한 국내조치등에 관한 최초보고서를 지난해 7월 인권이사회에 제출한 바 있으며, 이번 이사회는 이 보고서의 내용을 검토하게 된다.

인권규약의 당사국은 규약 발효후 1년 이내에 규약의 이행을 위해 취한 조치에 관해 최초보고서를 인권이사회에 제출토록 돼있으며 이후 매 5년마다 추가보고서를 제출해야 한다.

정부는 이번 회의에서 朴대사의 기조발언을 통해 제6공화국 헌법하에서 이뤄진 인권신장과 민주화의 진전등에 관해 설명하고 인권보호및 인권신장 분야에서 앞으로 취할 조치등을 소개할 예정이다.

우리나라는 인권규약중 공무원 고원등의 노조결성등 국내법과 상충되는 일부 조항의 적용을 유보해놓고 있다.(끝)

GLGL
o0318 ASI/AFP-AZ04-----
u i Cambodia-NKorea 07-09 0112
Cambodia's national assembly chief winds up Pyongyang trip

TOKYO, July 9 (AFP) - Chea Sim, chairman of the Cambodian National Assembly, left Pyongyang on Thursday for China after a three-day visit to North Korea, the Korean Central News Agency said in a dispatch monitored here.

Chea Sim visited the hardline communist state with a high-powered delegation from the Cambodian People's Party, which he heads.

Chea Sim met North Korea's long-ruling President Kim Il-Sung Wednesday, according to an earlier dispatch by the official news agency.

Kim has been close to Prince Norodom Sihanouk, who heads Cambodia's Supreme National Council.

sps/gh
AFP 091242 GMT JUL 92

외교문서 비밀해제: 한국 인권문제 7

한국 인권문제 시민적 · 정치적 권리 국제규약 인권보고서 2

초판인쇄 2024년 03월 15일
초판발행 2024년 03월 15일

지은이 한국학술정보(주)
펴낸이 채종준
펴낸곳 한국학술정보(주)
주 소 경기도 파주시 회동길 230(문발동)
전 화 031-908-3181(대표)
팩 스 031-908-3189
홈페이지 http://ebook.kstudy.com
E-mail 출판사업부 publish@kstudy.com
등 록 제일산-115호(2000. 6. 19)

ISBN 979-11-7217-061-5 94340
979-11-7217-054-7 94340 (set)

책에 대한 더 나은 생각, 끊임없는 고민, 독자를 생각하는 마음으로 보다 좋은 책을 만들어갑니다.